Temporary Knowledge Ecologies

For Clare and Fiona

Temporary Knowledge Ecologies

The Rise of Trade Fairs in the Asia-Pacific Region

Edited by

Harald Bathelt

Canada Research Chair in Innovation and Governance, University of Toronto, Canada

Gang Zeng

Professor of Economic Geography, East China Normal University, PR China

Edward Elgar PUBLISHING

Cheltenham, UK • Northampton, MA, USA

Published by
Edward Elgar Publishing Limited
The Lypiatts
15 Lansdown Road
Cheltenham
Glos GL50 2JA
UK

Edward Elgar Publishing, Inc.
William Pratt House
9 Dewey Court
Northampton
Massachusetts 01060
USA

A catalogue record for this book
is available from the British Library

Library of Congress Control Number: 2014957095

This book is available electronically in the **Elgar**online
Economics subject collection
DOI 10.4337/9781782548096

FSC
www.fsc.org
MIX
Paper from
responsible sources
FSC® C013056

ISBN 978 1 78254 808 9 (cased)
ISBN 978 1 78254 809 6 (eBook)

Typeset by Servis Filmsetting Ltd, Stockport, Cheshire
Printed and bound in Great Britain by T.J. International Ltd, Padstow

Contents

Contributors

Harald Bathelt, Professor and Canada Research Chair in Innovation and Governance, Departments of Political Science and Geography & Program in Planning, University of Toronto, Toronto, Canada; Zijiang Visiting Professor, Department of Urban and Regional Economy, East China Normal University, Shanghai, China.

Jung-Ying Chang, Assistant Professor, Graduate Institute of Urban Planning, National Taipei University, New Taipei City, Taiwan.

Liang-Chih Chen, Assistant Professor, Graduate Institute of Building and Planning, National Taiwan University, Taipei, Taiwan.

Tsu-Lung Chou, Professor, Graduate Institute of Urban Planning, National Taipei University, New Taipei City, Taiwan.

Ling-I Chu, Ph.D. Candidate, Graduate Institute of Building and Planning, National Taiwan University, Taipei, Taiwan.

Francesca Golfetto, Professor, Department of Marketing and CERMES, Bocconi University, Milan, Italy.

Douglas R. Gress, Associate Professor, Department of Geography Education, Seoul National University, Seoul, South Korea.

Jinn-Yuh Hsu, Professor, Department of Geography, National Taiwan University, Taipei, Taiwan.

Xin Jin, Lecturer, Department of Tourism, Sport and Hotel Management, Griffith University, Southport, Australia.

Ronald V. Kalafsky, Associate Professor, Department of Geography, University of Tennessee, Knoxville, USA.

Xiang Kong, Professor, Department of Resource and Environmental Science, East China Normal University, Shanghai, China.

Peng-Fei Li, Banting Postdoctoral Fellow, Department of Political Science, University of Toronto, Canada.

Peter Maskell, Professor, Department of Innovation and Organizational Economics, Copenhagen Business School, Copenhagen, Denmark.

Diego Rinallo, Associate Professor, Department of Marketing, Kedge Business School, Marseille, France; CERMES Affiliate, Bocconi University, Milan, Italy.

Karin Weber, Associate Professor, School of Hotel and Tourism Management, Hong Kong Polytechnic University, Hong Kong, SAR China.

Sally A. Weller, ARC Future Fellow, School of Geography and Environmental Science, Monash University, Clayton, Australia.

Yutaka Yokura, Assistant Professor, Graduate School of Arts and Sciences, University of Tokyo, Tokyo, Japan.

Gang Zeng, Professor, Department of Urban and Regional Economy, East China Normal University, Shanghai, China.

Yu-Fei Zhang, M.A., Department of Resource and Environmental Science, East China Normal University, Shanghai, China.

Yi-Wen Zhu, Ph.D. Candidate, Department of Urban and Regional Economy, East China Normal University, Shanghai, China.

Preface

The idea for this edited volume was developed in 2010 and 2011 during empirical investigations in one of our collaborative research projects in China. During our usual late-night discussions about our experiences in investigating Chinese firms and regional economies, we realized that trade fairs had received little academic attention within the context of Asian economic development, at least from the perspective of economic geography and political economy, as well as other disciplines. The consequence of our discussions was a plan to draft a targeted conference with a workshop character that brings together key individuals and members of research groups that specialize on trade fair research and can provide important insights into the rise, development and implications of trade fair activity in the Asia-Pacific region. While the focus of our enquiry was on the development in East and Southeast Asia, we also included Australia in our comparative framework due to the manifold linkages that unfold between Asian economies and Australia.

We decided to organize this event in Shanghai and scheduled a program of topics to be discussed and contributors to be invited to it. East China Normal University viewed this as an ambitious academic endeavor and was willing to sponsor the conference. With financial support in place, we approached about 15 leading researchers from different countries and invited them to participate in the event. Finally, on 25–26 May 2012, the 'Asia-Pacific Conference on Trade Fair Ecologies' took place in Shanghai at the Jin Sha Hotel in the vicinity of East China Normal University (see http://iurp.ecnu.edu.cn/APCTFE/; accessed 2 September 2014). This two-day event and the days immediately before and after the conference provided a unique opportunity to discuss the latest trends in trade fair development, learn from expert experiences and try to apply new concepts to Asia-Pacific trade fairs. Because of the shortcomings in existing research, the idea was developed to generate a consistent edited volume on the rise and development of trade fair activities in the Asia-Pacific region based on the joint experiences during the conference.

The intention of this edited book is to attract a broad readership from the fields of economic geography, economics, management/marketing, political science and sociology, as the analyses and implications presented in this book directly address contemporary debates in these disciplines about the role of trade fairs in supporting and enabling local industrial development and globalization processes. The book is directed to researchers and students, as well as to policy makers, regional planners and operating/organizing firms (operators/organizers) in the trade fair industry. The book chapters present conceptual and empirical findings that are relevant for disciplinary and trans-disciplinary debates in the social sciences about economic development, the function of the state, drivers and consequences of trade fair development, the role of the Asia-Pacific region in the globalizing knowledge economy, and the diverse development paths of political economies in the region. While we do not aim to present a complete overview of the entire region, our book fills substantial gaps in the existing literature. By arguing and demonstrating how trade shows become important building blocks for understanding globalization, innovation and national/local economic development processes, the edited volume intersects with different disciplines in the social sciences.

It is clear that such an endeavor is based on the help of and collaboration with many individuals that provided crucial support throughout all stages of this project. We would like to point out a few individuals who brought much dedication and passion to this project. In particular, we would like to thank Rachael Gibson, Michael Kunz, Li-Ang Liu, Ye Liu, Rui-Yi Mao, Tang-Wei Teng, Xiao-Rui Xin and Yi-Wen Zhu for excellent research support. The organization of the 2012 Shanghai conference would not have been possible without crucial support by Xiao-Wen Bao and Qi Tang, for which we are very grateful. We are especially indebted to Sufyan Katariwala and David Adams for thoroughly and efficiently copy-editing the book manuscript and to the anonymous Reviewers for providing manifold suggestions for improvements of the individual chapters. Furthermore, we wish to thank Alex O'Connell and Alex Pettifer from Edward Elgar Publishing for their confidence in and support of this book project. Financial support from the National Natural Science Foundation of China, East China Normal University and the Canada Research Chair in Innovation and Governance at the University of Toronto is greatly appreciated. Last, but not least, we wish to emphasize that this has become a truly joint adventure that would have not been possible without the commitment and engagement of every single contributor to this book, in generating a consistent manuscript and carrying this research agenda further. In the end, this book is also a reflection of the deep friendship and partnership between both editors that has developed over more than 25 years.

Harald Bathelt and Gang Zeng
Toronto and Shanghai, September 2014

1. Asia-Pacific trade fair dynamics: an introduction

Gang Zeng and Harald Bathelt

AGENDA

When considering the importance of political and economic changes in the Asia-Pacific region and the decisive role of trade fairs in supporting and enabling such developments, it is surprising how little research exists about the rise, nature and dynamics of such events. Trade fairs provide the basis for wider trade flows and exchanges of goods between local/regional, national and international firms and thus contribute to the economic globalization of regions and national states. Given the lack of related research, the agenda behind this book is to bridge important knowledge gaps regarding the trade fair business in the Asia-Pacific region. Specifically, the goals of this book project are as follows: First, we aim to provide an overview of trade fair developments in the Asia-Pacific region and identify which factors impact these processes. Second, we aim to show how the evolution of trade fair activities differs between the countries and sub-regions of the Asia-Pacific region and in which way political and economic changes impact these varied development trajectories. Third, we synthesize these developments to conceptualize more broadly the rise of Asia-Pacific trade fairs and discuss their implications. Although a distinction could be made between 'trade fairs' and 'trade shows' (Bathelt et al. 2014), we follow many studies in the field that use both terms more or less synonymously.

This book project is conceptualized as an edited volume focusing on understanding, investigating and theorizing the rise and development of Asia-Pacific trade fairs. The strong growth of Asia-Pacific economies since the 1990s has resulted in the manifestation of new production spaces in different countries and regions. Following the examples of Japan, South Korea, Taiwan, Hong Kong and Singapore, other economies have followed, and India and Mainland China have developed into powerful players in the world economy (World Bank 1993; Bertrand 2013). In conjunction with the rise of Asian economies, trade fairs have grown quickly from export-promoting platforms to knowledge-sharing spaces. In less-developed and developing contexts in Asia, new trade fair activities have rapidly spread and received increasing attention, while events in Europe and North America have grown at a much slower pace or even stagnated (UFI 2012; Bathelt et al. 2014). To catch up with the recent trade fair boom in many of the major urban centers of the Asia-Pacific region, especially in China (Bathelt and Zeng 2014), new large convention and exhibition centers have been built, and new venues have been established for the exchange of goods, innovations and knowledge.

These dynamic processes of trade fair development in the Asia-Pacific region will likely have a strong impact on the spatial structure of the global trade fair business and correspondingly on the development of regional and national industries. Potentially, they will also influence global knowledge transfer patterns and generate new global linkages between the Asia-Pacific region, Europe and North America. Within the landscape of Asian trade fairs, a remarkable feature is that developments of trade fairs are extremely heterogeneous and have been shaped by specific national economic conditions and respective state policies. These strong regional and national differences require a differentiated exploration of trade fairs in the Asia-Pacific region. Following this requirement, the chapters in this edited volume investigate and analyze the present structures and trends of trade fairs in specific Asia-Pacific economies and develop conceptions to understand these trends and formulate conclusions from a broad social science perspective.

This book has unique characteristics that set it apart from previous published work on related issues. First, it provides an innovative view of trade fairs by combining knowledge and trade perspectives and transferring them to the Asia-Pacific region. Second, the book presents information about recent trends in the Asia-Pacific trade fair business that have not yet been intensively studied. Third, it presents a comparative perspective in analyzing the developments of trade fairs in different countries and regions. Fourth, the book is interdisciplinary in nature as it draws on views and perspectives from economic geography, management/marketing, hospitality management and political economy. Fifth, it integrates both conceptual and empirical findings from leading international scholars in the field, who have in-depth knowledge about the local/national circumstances of trade fair developments in the Asia-Pacific region.

CONCEPTUAL FOUNDATIONS

This book draws on a number of related novel conceptualizations of trade fairs and examines these against the context of the heterogeneous landscape of Asia-Pacific economies. Trade shows have long been seen as marketing or sales events where firms from a specific industrial field showcase their products to existing and potential customers. Alternatively, they have been considered in their role as events that bring business tourists to certain trade fair cities and provide jobs and incomes to a segment of the local/national economy that has specialized in servicing these events (for an overview, see Golfetto 1991). Conventional conceptualizations of trade fairs are, however, sometimes shortsighted and neglect the significant role of such events in the circulation of new ideas and knowledge and on the formation of networks in the context of the global knowledge economy. Little research has focused on analyzing trade fairs as places where international networks are created and maintained, where inputs for innovations are discussed, and where important knowledge is circulated and acquired that feeds into strategic decision-making processes. And few studies have investigated trade fairs in the context of the Asia-Pacific region or asked whether a knowledge perspective of trade fairs is useful to understanding the diverse regional and national economies (Bathelt and Zeng 2014; Li 2014). However, it is clear from the nature of these events that the largest trade fairs, in particular, connect firms, clusters and cities that are located in different parts of the world. As such, we can expect that trade fairs play a significant role in the economic development of the Asia-Pacific region (Bathelt et al. 2014).

Based on similar considerations, a new conceptualization of trade fairs was developed during the 2000s based on the work of Maskell et al. (2006) on 'temporary clusters' and Borghini et al. (2004) and Rinallo and Golfetto (2011) on 'temporary markets'. This conceptualization investigates trade fairs from a comprehensive knowledge perspective (Bathelt et al. 2014). Accordingly, studies in economic geography, business management and other disciplines have begun to conceptualize and explore the role of trade fairs as nodes in the global learning economy that contribute to the generation and dissemination of decisive knowledge flows between agents (firms), sometimes at a global scale. In this book, we focus on the analysis of business-to-business trade fairs and discuss whether and in which ways a knowledge perspective can be applied to the Asia-Pacific region that is characterized by large disparities in economic development between highly developed, developing and less-developed countries. The chapters in this book investigate how trade fairs stimulate trade and economic development in diverse institutional contexts, how trade fair activities have changed over time, and why and under which conditions knowledge flows become drivers of trade fair development along with regional/national economic growth. In the context of rising and developing trade fair activities in the Asia-Pacific region, we wish to emphasize four perspectives that go beyond conventional conceptualizations: (i) trade fairs and the developmental state, (ii) trade fairs as temporary markets, (iii) trade fairs as temporary clusters and (iv) trade fairs as cyclical relational spaces. These perspectives are briefly discussed below.

(i) Trade Fairs and the Developmental State

When studying trade fair developments in Asian economies (leaving Australia out of our considerations for a moment), one is faced with a political context of national states, which are not only extremely diverse but also fundamentally different from their European counterparts such as Germany and England (Gerschenkron 1962), in that industrialization and economic performance have been strongly influenced by ongoing systematic state intervention or what has been called the 'developmental state' (Johnson 1982; Wade 1990). Compared to Europe and North America, Asian economies are governed by a 'hard state' that is characterized by stronger hierarchies, control, centralization, authoritarian tendencies and weaker democratic traditions. A consequence of such structures is that states are more active – and have more capacity – in directly shaping, stimulating and, in many ways, interfering with economic development.

A key study in conceptualizing such state capacity was conducted by Johnson (1982), who investigated the factors underlying Japan's tremendous economic success in the post-World War II period. This study emphasized the key role of MITI, Japan's Ministry of International Trade and Industry, in triggering new industrial structures, supporting industrial and technological change and triggering economic catch-up processes through policies that supported systematic learning from developed economies, such as the US. Underlying Japan's success were also systematic market-conforming methods of state intervention and a specific elite state bureaucracy (Johnson 1982; 1995). As Freeman (1988) demonstrated in his comparative study of Japan and the US, the role of such state activity was crucial in the development of different national innovation systems.

The concept of the developmental state was developed to describe the enlarged potential and willingness of the state to direct economic development with the goal of increasing national productivity levels and achieving high economic growth, at the expense of social and welfare policies which had a lower priority (Wade 1990; Johnson 1995; Wong 2004). While related state structures were very successful in driving economic development in East and Southeast Asian economies, such as Japan, South Korea and Taiwan (Wade 1990; Amsden 1992; Woo-Cumings 1999), the diverse trajectories of industrial development and heterogeneous institutional and political conditions, cultural influences and historical socio-economic contexts suggest that there is no single model of capitalist development in the Asia-Pacific region. East and Southeast Asian economies are characterized by a variety of institutional conditions and variations in the capitalist system and in market–state interactions (Pascha et al. 2011). In Japan and South Korea, for instance, economic development has been mostly shaped by unique state bureaucracies and their interactions with large diversified firm groups (Johnson 1982; Wade 1990).

The developmental state describes how state policies and institutional conditions for economic development have driven industrial specialization processes and trade flows in specific ways. While there is an abundance of literature about the developmental state, its diverse forms in the context of Asia, and how these have changed and been adapted over time due to internal and external pressures (Woo-Cumings 1999; Wong 2004; Bertrand 2013), contributions have generally not drawn connections between the specific role of the state, the development and specialization of trade fairs, and the path of industrialization. It can be assumed, however, that the specific form of the developmental state has a direct impact on the development of trade fairs, the nature of knowledge flows and interaction patterns during these events, the specialization processes in terms of trade fair type and industrial focus, and the impact of trade fairs on industrialization processes and regional/national developments (e.g. Bathelt et al. 2014; Gibson 2015). This will become clear in the various case studies of Asian economies presented in this edited volume.

With respect to the role of trade fairs in influencing economic development and the role of the state in shaping these events, it may be interesting to link the literature about the developmental state with recent conceptualizations of so-called field-configuring events (Meyer et al. 2005; Lampel and Meyer 2008). These are events that strongly impact their underlying organizational fields, for instance the technological development trajectory of an industry, in a targeted way. Since the capacity to exercise such wide-ranging influences depends on concerted and targeted efforts by trade fair organizations in planning and structuring the respective events, this conceptualization may be particularly relevant in the context of strong states that organize and control trade fairs as instruments of economic development to help shape and structure their industrial fields. They may, for instance, provide active support to help a country's industries access international markets and link up with global value/production chains (Dicken et al. 2001; Gereffi et al. 2005). Since knowledge flows and interactions at trade fairs are highly decentralized and strongly depend on the rationales and interests of the participating firms, it is unlikely that many trade fairs could assume the form of such a field-configuring event (Möllering 2010; Bathelt et al. 2014). If anything, it could be expected that selected events, which are targeted to broadly mobilize national and international participation, impact the respective 'local field', rather than the global industry context altogether (Gibson and Bathelt 2014; Gibson 2015).

(ii) Trade Fairs as Temporary Markets

In the Middle Ages in Europe, trade fairs prospered as places where traders, and later producers, brought their products in order to sell them to consumers or industrial users. Conversely, consumers, or later industrial users, attended these events to buy products, machines and other artifacts for their direct consumption or use (e.g. Rinallo 2011). While trade fairs were thus originally market places where sales were concluded and actual exchanges of products took place, these trade patterns changed toward the end of the 19th century with the introduction of so-called sample fairs. Sample fairs were events where exhibitors would only present samples of their products, engage in negotiations with potential buyers and take orders from them. This was possible through the development of national states that went along with the establishment of standardized and enforceable systems of institutional arrangements (for instance, regarding financial transactions), reducing the uncertainties associated with taking such orders, producing reliable products and securing deliveries of orders and payments (e.g. Bathelt et al. 2014). The respective events were still organized around their market function, focusing on present or future market exchanges of products between agents/firms that were vertically linked in the value chain as buyers and sellers or as producers and users. Based on these fundamental interaction patterns, trade fairs have been conceptualized as temporary markets (Rinallo and Golfetto 2011).

While the nature of interactions has changed over time, the focus on vertical exchanges is still the raison d'être for many trade fairs today even though direct sales, market exchanges and contract negotiations have lost in importance. In many events, so-called atypical visitors, who do not intend to buy products during trade fairs, have replaced typical visitors (potential buyers), and even typical visitors do not necessarily attend these events any longer with the intent to conclude transactions of goods (Borghini et al. 2006). The conceptualization of temporary markets has generated opportunities to analyze trade shows from a knowledge-based perspective and distinguish various types of events according to the knowledge flows between different participant groups according to their origin.

This perspective is particularly useful when analyzing the development of specific types of trade fairs in relation to their underlying regional or national industry base. Depending on the competitive strengths or needs of regional industrial agglomerations, for instance, export or import trade fairs can develop that either provide wider market access for the specialized industrial firms in a region or help secure flows of required supplies that are not produced locally. Depending on the export or import functions of events, different types of interaction patterns and learning processes can be observed (Rinallo and Golfetto 2011). This perspective further helps to explain how rivalry and competition can develop between shows, venues, cities and countries for certain trade fairs, especially in the case of export events, and how trade show organizers can apply certain knowledge strategies to strengthen the competitive position of their events and underlying industries. This perspective of temporary markets is highly relevant in the context of Asia-Pacific trade fair developments in order to better understand different specialization patterns of trade fairs across the diversified national economies.

(iii) Trade Fairs as Temporary Clusters

From the perspective of communication and interaction processes between the participants, trade fairs can be conceptualized as temporary clusters which are, like permanent clusters, characterized by various knowledge flows – across vertical, horizontal and institutional dimensions – that take place within and across the communities that get together during such events (Maskell et al. 2006). These knowledge flows are not just relevant for the immediate sales and marketing activities of firms but also have important consequences for adjustments and restructuring activities in production. The vertical knowledge flows that occur in interactions of exhibitors/producers with their suppliers/users, for instance, provide important feedback from which the firms can learn about technological opportunities and customer preferences. This stimulates new research and development activities later on and impacts the strategic focus of their production programs. The users, who visit such events, can also draw important conclusions with respect to their production settings as they receive an overview about trends in their supply and service sector.

Aside from these interactions, trade fairs establish an important horizontal dimension for knowledge exchanges as they provide opportunities for producers to observe other firms that produce similar products and to compare the products and innovations of these firms with their own (Maskell et al. 2006). This is especially important during leading international business-to-business trade fairs that bring together the most important producers in an industry, as well as many small and medium-sized firms that operate in different market and institutional environments. Together, these agents generate a 'microcosm' of the respective industrial field (Rosson and Seringhaus 1995), which enables firms to receive a broad overview of the development of products and technologies. This process generates crucial benchmarks that enable firms to evaluate their own position against their competitors and the entire evolving field. It also provides important feedback and reduces uncertainties as firms, for instance, realize that they are still at the forefront of technological development, or that others have moved into new markets that may require timely adjustment of strategies (Bathelt and Schuldt 2010).

Firms showcasing their products during the events are both exhibitors – engaging in vertical interactions through myriads of short communications with users and suppliers – and at the same time visitors – scanning technological developments through dense horizontal observations. The multiplicity of knowledge flows during trade fairs is triggered by a unique mix of learning processes that involve various forms of learning by interaction and learning by observation at the vertical and the horizontal level. Firms observing their competitors may, for instance, directly approach the respective firms and engage in dialogues about their industrial field, or they may choose to stay anonymous and walk through the exhibits, inspect new developments and observe how visitors react to their rivals' exhibits. Depending on the industrial field and common practices of interaction, it may even be possible to get together with competitors at the end of the day and share a drink while reflecting upon the trade fair and developments in the industry (Bathelt et al. 2014).

The meetings, encounters and discoveries of firms that attend these events are sometimes planned and scheduled in advance and can involve systematic scanning, but they may also be less planned, spontaneous and shaped by random encounters that 'catch ones eye', or accidental meetings when bumping into former acquaintances (Bathelt and Schuldt 2010). Collectively, the short-term intensive interactions and observations generate a unique information and knowledge ecology (e.g. Grabher 2001; Bathelt and Gibson 2013) in the sense that many different, competing and complementary knowledge components are being constantly picked up and dropped by the participants, interpreted and reinterpreted individually and collectively, through conversations, interactions and observations. We use the term 'knowledge ecology' in the context of this book in a broad sense to refer to the manifold parallel and overlapping communication and interaction processes that occur during trade fairs, which differ between different types of events in different economies in the Asia-Pacific region.

What makes trade fairs with broad national and international participation particularly important is that they generate plenty of opportunities for firms to make contact and initiate partnerships with users, suppliers and all sorts of potential partners that are located in other regions and countries. Therefore, these events play an important role for local/national industries in developing trans-local or global pipelines in production and trade (Maskell et al. 2006; Ramírez-Pasillas 2008). Altogether, these regular knowledge exchanges help stabilize regional industrial clusters and increase the competitiveness of national industries in the long term. Such network-generating processes are particularly interesting from the perspective of the developmental state that intends to establish events which strongly impact the development of the national industrial field.

(iv) Trade Fairs as Cyclical Relational Spaces

The institutional dimension of trade fairs is directly linked to the manifold face-to-face interactions that occur and their impacts on future activities of participating firms located in different regions and national states (Bathelt and Schuldt 2010). These exchanges and interactions are important in understanding the different conditions for production and trade in different national/regional contexts, interpreting new technological developments and making sense of them, and generating joint understandings, expectations and views between the participants. Trade fairs in a certain industrial field are cyclical in character, as they occur at regular intervals and related events take place sequentially in different places (Power and Jansson 2008). The cyclical nature of trade fairs constitutes a powerful institutional force that shapes the reproduction of the knowledge base underlying the industrial field. It promotes the development of complex knowing communities that consist of partly overlapping and partly specialized communities of practice, epistemic communities and virtual communities (Boland and Tenkasi 1995) based on relational contextual experiences.

These shared experiences and interactions between trade fair participants are not just characterized by price negotiations, observations of peers, speculations about market trends, assessments of new technological developments and so on; participants also enjoy having a break from regular work routines, expect to find something unexpected and to experience arts and show elements, and generally want 'to have a good time' in interacting with their community (e.g. Andreae et al. 2013). As such, trade fairs can be viewed as relational spaces (Bathelt and Spigel 2012), which provide opportunities for agents from a specific industrial field to engage with each other intensively in combinations of rational or emotional and professional or private meetings over a short time period. By focusing on the nature of interactions during such events, the functions of trade fairs in specific cultural and institutional contexts, and how these roles change over time, the chapters of this book contribute to a broader discussion about the impact of trade fair ecologies on globalization processes in the knowledge economy, and their effects, on making connections between the Asia-Pacific region and other parts of the world.

The book thus links to relational and practice conceptions of economic action which pay particular attention to the context of socio-institutional relations, practices of economic interaction and their changes over time to understand how economic structures develop in a spatial perspective (Bathelt and Glückler 2003; Faulconbridge 2007; Jones and Murphy 2010). The overall conceptualization of the book is committed to a context perspective (Storper 2009) that takes into consideration the diverse political-institutional conditions for economic action in the Asia-Pacific region. It also draws on an evolutionary understanding of economic development, characterized by cumulative, experience-based technological change (Nelson and Winter 1982; Dosi 1982) and a social division of labor that requires intensive producer–user interaction (Lundvall 1988). While an evolutionary perspective is viewed as a core component to generate an adequate understanding of economic structures and their dynamics (Bathelt and Glückler 2003; Boschma and Frenken 2006; Martin and Sunley 2006), we do not view evolutionary analysis as an end in itself.

STRUCTURE OF THE BOOK

This edited volume systematically discusses recent empirical and conceptual findings about the rise and development of trade fairs in the Asia-Pacific region. It is the first time that a systematic discussion of the characteristics and developments of trade fair ecologies across the highly diverse economies of the Asia-Pacific region is presented. This is surprising because it appears that trade fairs are not just a reflection and result of economic growth and trade; they are, as argued in Bathelt et al. (2014), also the triggers of such developments. This is discussed in 15 chapters that are organized into four parts.

Part I develops the conceptual foundations of the book and discusses ways of how experiences and concepts of trade fairs can be transferred from Europe to the Asia-Pacific region. Chapter 2 contextualizes trade fairs in a broader framework of how firms access new knowledge and competencies when they extend their reach beyond the local/national scale. Maskell (*this volume*) suggests that such knowledge acquisition can be associated with substantial uncertainties, especially regarding questions as to what kind of knowledge is required and where (from whom) to access it. The framework presented in the chapter suggests that trade fairs become especially important to access remote knowledge when uncertainty is high with respect to both the type of knowledge that is needed and where and with whom it resides. While this is particularly relevant for young single-site firms, it also applies to larger established firms, especially in combination with other means of knowledge acquisition. Chapter 3 develops a knowledge-based perspective of trade fairs by suggesting that different types of international trade fairs are needed to support economic development. Depending on the specialization, competencies and needs of the industries located in the local/national catchment basin of the events, trade shows can develop into import or export fairs that generate different types of knowledge flows and have varying consequences for economic development. Golfetto and Rinallo (*this volume*) suggest that European experiences may be quite valuable in the organization of new trade fair ecologies in the Asia-Pacific region. Chapter 4 on internationalization activities of trade fair organizations is directly linked to this knowledge-based perspective. In the chapter, Rinallo and Golfetto (*this volume*) investigate the expansion of Messe Frankfurt's activities to the Asia-Pacific region. The study uses the case of Interstoff Asia to illustrate how trade fair organizers have transferred knowledge-based strategies to the Asia-Pacific region and how this has supported upgrading processes in the local textile industry. The case also shows how organizer strategies can systematically trigger changes in the trade fair type over time. Chapter 5 transfers this perspective of trade fair ecologies to learning processes in industrial production and suggests that trade fairs in developing contexts generate the largest learning potential for local/national firms if they are characterized by broad participation of both local/national and international participants on the visitor and the exhibitor side. Li (*this volume*) suggests that, although trade fairs in the Asia-Pacific region are extremely diversified, we can generally observe a development from local/national marketplaces to learning spaces with increasing international participation.

Part II applies these foundations to the rise of trade fair ecologies in China. Chapters 6 and 7 present empirical data to investigate which regions and cities are particularly attractive for trade fair participants and support the growth of related events. Jin and Weber (*this volume*) suggest that the attractiveness of trade fair destinations varies between visitors and exhibitors. They identify what they refer to as a clustering effect which indicates that a link between local/regional industry clustering and trade fair specialization may have a positive impact on trade fair development (see Chapter 6). It is concluded that this could be relevant for policy makers when organizing trade fairs in second-tier cities. While Zhu and Zeng (*this volume*) find that city size is a crucial factor in the growth of trade fair activity in China, giving large cities an advantage over small and medium-sized cities, they also suggest that transportation infrastructure, a high level of economic development and a well-developed service economy are important influences on the development of trade fair ecologies (see Chapter 7). Chapter 8 suggests that it is necessary to exercise care to avoid underestimating or over-generalizing the state of trade fair activity in China. Bathelt and Zeng (*this volume*) argue that the existing literature does not present an up-to-date view of trade fair ecologies in China. It is illustrated that common criticisms about the nature of trade fair developments are incomplete. While some events emerge as strong temporary markets with important sales activities, others are evolving into temporary clusters with a focus on innovation and knowledge generation or on relationship building and networking, similar to events in Europe and North America. The increasing differentiation of trade fair functions seems to coincide with the economic capabilities and specialization processes in the surrounding city-regions. Chapter 9 supports this perspective with an analysis of the Shanghai International Automobile Show. While not yet comparable with leading events in Europe and North America, Kong and Zhang (*this volume*) suggest that the event is well on its way to developing into an important temporary cluster of knowledge flows in the industry.

Part III extends the analytical frame to investigate trade fair developments in industrialized Asia-Pacific economies and establishes a comparative political economy perspective that links national state policies and trade fair dynamics with economic development. In this part, developments in Japan, Australia, Taiwan and South Korea are linked to globalization processes. Chapter 10 suggests that trade fairs in Japan are characterized by a limited degree of internationalization, favoring interaction between domestic firms with a focus on forming longer-term relations. The analysis of Yokura (*this volume*) particularly shows how local trade fairs strengthen the marketing capabilities of small and medium-sized firms and thus become important tools in supporting regional economic development. Chapter 11 about experiences in Australia argues that a small 'peripheral' country in the world economy cannot easily generate knowledge-intensive international events with fundamental impacts on learning, innovation and economic development. Using the example of fashion events, Weller (*this volume*) concludes that, from a policy perspective, it may be more promising to support specific regional export shows to provide market access to the respective producers, rather than aiming to establish large flagship events targeted toward the international trade fair cycle. This may be particularly important when considering the potential of increased trade fair competition due to parallel developments in the other parts of the Asia-Pacific region. In contrast to this case, Chapter 12 presents a political context of trade fair development, in which trade fairs have been crucial in avoiding 'peripheralization' by enabling national industries to link up with global value chains. Chang et al. (*this volume*) demonstrate in the case of Taiwan how state support together with trade fair initiatives have played an active role in this process and have jointly supported industrial upgrading and place upscaling. Chapter 13 further supports this in the case of the Taiwanese machine tool industry, which illustrates how large export-oriented trade fairs have enabled national producers to integrate their activities into global value chains. Chen and Chu (*this volume*) show how international trade fair settings have also provided cluster producers with unique opportunities for technological learning and stimulated regional cluster-based collaboration and institution building. Referring to the same industry context, Chapter 14 argues in the context of South Korea that internationally oriented trade fairs have been especially important for national firms in developing export market intelligence. While national interaction patterns prevail during South Korean trade fairs, Kalafsky and Gress (*this volume*) argue that there is an increasing policy interest in utilizing such events for the promotion of export activities of small and medium-sized firms.

Finally, Part IV synthesizes the findings presented in the individual chapters and discusses policy implications. Building on the various investigations of trade shows in different regional/national contexts in the Asia-Pacific region, Chapter 15 discusses prospects of conceptualizing Asia-Pacific trade fair ecologies more broadly and presents ideas toward an integrated model of trade fair development in the region (Bathelt et al., *this volume*).

REFERENCES

Amsden, A. H. (1992) *Asia's Next Giant: South Korea and Late Industrialization*, Oxford: Oxford University Press.

Andreae, M., Hsu, J.-Y. and Norcliffe, G. (2013) 'Performing the trade show: The case of the Taipei International Cycle Show', *Geoforum*, 49: 193–201.

Bathelt, H. and Gibson, R. (2013) 'Learning in "organized anarchies": Technological search processes and knowledge flows at international trade fairs', *Regional Studies*, 47: doi: 10.1080/00343404.2013.782591.

Bathelt, H. and Glückler, J. (2003) 'Toward a relational economic geography', *Journal of Economic Geography*, 3: 117–144.
Bathelt, H., Golfetto, F. and Rinallo, D. (2014) *Trade Shows in the Globalizing Knowledge Economy*, Oxford: Oxford University Press.
Bathelt, H. and Schuldt, N. (2010) 'International trade fairs and global buzz, Part I: Ecology of global buzz', *European Planning Studies*, 18: 1957–1974.
Bathelt, H. and Spigel, B. (2012) 'The spatial economy of North American trade fairs', *The Canadian Geographer*, 56: 18–38.
Bathelt, H. and Zeng, G. (2014) 'The development of trade fair ecologies in China: Case studies from Chengdu and Shanghai', *Environment and Planning A*, 46: 511–530.
Bertrand, J. (2013) *Political Change in Southeast Asia*, Cambridge: Cambridge University Press.
Boland, R. J. and Tenkasi, R. V. (1995) 'Perspective making and perspective taking in communities of knowing', *Organization Science*, 6: 350–372.
Borghini, S., Golfetto, F. and Rinallo, D. (2004) *Using Anthropological Methods to Study Industrial Marketing and Purchasing: An Exploration of Professional Trade Shows*, paper presented at the Industrial Marketing and Purchasing Conference, Copenhagen. Online. Available HTTP: <http://www.impgroup.org/paper_view.php?viewPaper=4505> (2 December 2013).
Borghini, S., Golfetto, F. and Rinallo, D. (2006) 'Ongoing search among industrial buyers', *Journal of Business Research*, 59: 1151–1159.
Boschma, R. A. and Frenken, K. (2006) 'Why is economic geography not an evolutionary science? Towards an evolutionary economic geography', *Journal of Economic Geography*, 6: 273–302.
Dicken, P., Kelly, P. F., Olds, K. and Yeung, H. W.-C. (2001) 'Chains and networks, territories and scales: Towards a relational framework for analysing the global economy', *Global Networks*, 1: 89–112.
Dosi, G. (1982) 'Technological paradigms and technological trajectories: A suggested reinterpretation of the determinants and directions of technical change', *Research Policy*, 2: 147–162.
Faulconbridge, J. R. (2007) 'London's and New York's advertising and law clusters and their networks of learning: Relational analyses with a politics of scale?', *Urban Studies*, 44: 1635–1656.
Freeman, C. (1988) 'Japan: A new national system of innovation?', in G. Dosi, C. Freeman, R. R. Nelson, G. Silverberg and L. L. G. Soete (eds) *Technical Change and Economic Theory*, London: Pinter, 330–348.
Gereffi, G., Humphrey, J. and Sturgeon, T. (2005) 'The governance of global value chains', *Review of International Political Economy*, 12: 78–104.
Gerschenkron, A. (1962) 'Economic backwardness in historical perspective', in A. Gerschenkron (ed.) *Economic Backwardness in Historical Perspective*, Cambridge, MA: Harvard University Press, 5–30.
Gibson, R. (2015) *Dynamic Capitalisms? Understanding National Specialization Patterns through Inter-firm Interaction at International Trade Fairs*, Ph.D. thesis, Department of Political Science, University of Toronto, Toronto, forthcoming.
Gibson, R. and Bathelt, H. (2014) 'Field configuration or field reproduction? The dynamics of global trade fair cycles', *Zeitschrift für Wirtschaftsgeographie*, 58: 216–231.
Golfetto, F. (1991) *L'Impatto Economico delle Manifestazioni Fieristiche (The Economic Impact of Trade Shows)*, Milano: EGEA.

Grabher, G. (2001) 'Ecologies of creativity: The village, the group, and the heterarchic organisation of the British advertising industry', *Environment and Planning A*, 33: 351–374.

Johnson, C. (1982) *MITI and the Japanese Miracle: The Growth of Industrial Policy: 1925–1975*, Stanford, CA: Stanford University Press.

Johnson, C. (1995) *Japan, Who Governs? The Rise of the Developmental State*, New York: Norton.

Jones, A. and Murphy, J. (2010) 'Theorizing practice in economic geography: Foundations, challenges, possibilities', *Progress in Human Geography*, 35: 366–392.

Lampel, J. and Meyer, A. D. (2008) 'Field-configuring events as structuring mechanisms: How conferences, ceremonies, and trade shows constitute new technologies, industries, and markets', *Journal of Management Studies*, 45: 1025–1035.

Li, P.-F. (2014) 'Global temporary networks of clusters: Structures and dynamics of trade fairs in Asian economies', *Journal of Economic Geography*, 14: 995–1021.

Lundvall, B.-Å. (1988) 'Innovation as an interactive process: From producer–user interaction to the national system of innovation', in G. Dosi, C. Freeman, R. R. Nelson, G. Silverberg, and L. L. G. Soete (eds) *Technical Change and Economic Theory*, London: Pinter, 349–369.

Martin, R. and Sunley, P. (2006) 'Path dependence and regional economic evolution', *Journal of Economic Geography*, 6: 395–437.

Maskell, P., Bathelt, H. and Malmberg, A. (2006) 'Building global knowledge pipelines: The role of temporary clusters', *European Planning Studies*, 14: 997–1013.

Meyer, A. D., Gaba, V. and Colwell, K. A. (2005) 'Organizing far from equilibrium: Nonlinear change in organizational fields', *Organization Science*, 16: 456–473.

Möllering, G. (2010) *Collective Market-Making at an Engineering Conference*, MPIfG Discussion Paper 10/2, Cologne: Max-Planck-Institut für Gesellschaftsforschung. Online. Available HTTP: <http://www.mpifg.de/pu/mpifg_dp/dp10-2.pdf> (4 September 2014).

Nelson, R. R. and Winter, S. G. (1982) *An Evolutionary Theory of Economic Change*, Cambridge, MA: Harvard University Press.

Pascha, W., Storz, C. and Taube, M. (eds) (2011) *Institutional Variety in East Asia: Formal and Informal Patterns of Coordination*, Cheltenham, UK and Northampton, MA: Edward Elgar Publishing.

Power, D. and Jansson, J. (2008) 'Cyclical clusters in global circuits: Overlapping spaces in furniture trade fairs', *Economic Geography*, 84: 423–448.

Ramírez-Pasillas, M. (2008) 'Resituating proximity and knowledge cross-fertilization in clusters by means of international trade fairs', *European Planning Studies*, 16: 643–663.

Rinallo, D. (2011) *Event Marketing*, Milan: EGEA.

Rinallo, D. and Golfetto, F. (2011) 'Exploring the knowledge strategies of temporary cluster organizers: A longitudinal study of the EU fabric industry trade shows (1986–2006)', *Economic Geography*, 87: 453–476.

Rosson, P. J. and Seringhaus, F. H. R. (1995) 'Visitor and exhibitor interaction at industrial trade fairs', *Journal of Business Research*, 32: 81–90.

Storper, M. (2009) 'Regional context and global trade', *Economic Geography*, 85: 1–21.

UFI – The Global Association of the Exhibition Industry (2012) *The Global Exhibition Industry Statistics*, Paris: UFI. Online. Available HTTP: <http://www.ufi.org/> (15 July 2013).

Wade, R. (1990) *Governing the Market*, Princeton, NJ: Princeton University Press.

Wong, J. (2004) 'The adaptive developmental state in East Asia', *Journal of East Asian Studies*, 4: 345–362.

Woo-Cumings, M. (ed.) (1999) *The Developmental State*, Ithaca, NY: Cornell University Press.

World Bank (1993) *East Asian Miracle: Economic Growth and Public Policy*, New York: Oxford University Press.

PART I

Conceptualizing trade fair ecologies in the Asia-Pacific region

2. Accessing remote knowledge – the roles of trade fairs, pipelines, crowdsourcing and listening posts

Peter Maskell

INTRODUCTION

It is now widely recognized that the achievements of cluster studies during recent decades have inadvertently resulted in a phase of excessive inward looking and an ensuing unfortunate downplay of crucial external linkages. While proximity centered research convincingly demonstrated enhanced opportunities for knowledge-based growth and entrepreneurship in certain local economic systems (Brusco 1986; Storper 1994; Maskell 2001; Gertler 2003; Wolfe and Gertler 2004; Delgado et al. 2010), closer inspection revealed how even the most successful local clusters were unable to continue to thrive in splendid isolation. On the contrary, they were periodically invigorated by external impulses that allowed them to remain competitive when technological trajectories took unexpected turns or markets suddenly demanded new combinations of capabilities not locally available (Lawson 1999; Allen 2000; Pinch et al. 2003; Giuliani 2005; Salter and Laursen 2006). Being locally unavailable excludes situations where the required knowledge could be accessed indirectly through local buzz and so on, or stem from externally well-connected proximate firms, local universities and other knowledge gatekeepers in the neighborhood (Storper and Venables 2004).

This recognition has led to increased interest in how distant firms and individuals forge links in order to exchange knowledge and advance new ideas (McEvily and Zaheer 1999; Bunnell and Coe 2001; Obstfeld 2006). However, the growing literature on corporate global search strategies (Katila and Ahuja 2000; Katila 2002; Flemming and Sorenson 2004) says little about the initial discovery and subsequent utilization of geographically and relationally remote knowledge sources. The term 'source' thus encompasses two elements or dimensions: a spatial dimension referring to where on the globe to search and a relational element referring to with whom to contact and co-develop this knowledge.

Others have investigated how local universities or certain bigger firms become local gatekeepers of knowledge and technology transmissions across space (Tushman and Katz 1980; Saxenian 1991; Agrawal and Cockburn 2003; Fontana et al. 2006). However, the focus in this discourse has so far been mainly downstream, for example how the remote knowledge acquired spreads from the focal unit to benefit the local context while fostering innovative activities (Griliches 1979; Feldman 1994).

The upstream process of how firms initially identify remote sources of complementary competencies or how such firms subsequently instigate some sort of globally extended learning is left mainly unexplored (Faulconbridge 2006). Little attention has been paid to the types of action used in the process and even less to the circumstances that make one particular approach preferable to some other.

The present chapter tries to fill part of this research gap by investigating the conditions that guide newly established single-site firms to use particular approaches when searching upstream for valuable remote solution providers and knowledge-producing partners. The conceptual arguments are supported by references to research that provide empirical evidence. The arguments advanced combine and extend two recent directions in economic geography research. One investigates firms' deliberate investments in the construction of 'pipelines' to relevant but distant knowledge providers (Bathelt et al. 2004; Giuliani and Bell 2005; Owen-Smith and Powell 2006). The other relates to the huge numbers of individuals, not necessarily known to each other, who jointly create an environment conducive to bridging geographic and relational knowledge divides within different fields by participating in international trade fairs (Maskell et al. 2006; Bathelt and Schuldt 2010). Both research strands are interested in long-distance search processes and the ways that firms subsequently utilize potential new knowledge sources by initiating knowledge transfer and learning across space (Sorenson et al. 2007; Beugelsdijk 2007). However, none of this research directly addresses the question of why one particular type of non-local search behavior is preferred to some others, and no serious attempts have been made to specify the circumstances that are decisive for the approach chosen.

The present chapter contributes by proposing a simple explanatory framework to identify significant determinants of search strategies and to analyze their interrelations, in the context of young single-site firms attempting to locate, access and acquire geographically and relationally remote knowledge and solutions.

The inquiry is developed in three main sections. The next section investigates the basic problems related to knowledge transfer across spatial and organizational divides. Valuable knowledge does not travel easily and often becomes distorted and thus less valuable when removed from its original context. The discussion is summarized in a comprehensive framework that allows for a systematic investigation of the approaches available to firms engaged in remote search, development and transfer of knowledge. The argument highlights an important distinction between the knowledge-seeking firm's awareness of the nature of its problem (what specific knowledge is required) and its possible source (where the knowledge resides). This distinction is exploited in the second section, which considers firms' knowledge search across extended geographical space, exploring in turn the relative merits and inherent limitations of using pipelines, listening posts, crowdsourcing and trade fairs. The last section concludes with a brief summary and discussion of selected points followed by suggestions for advancing research empirically and theoretically.

ACCESSING REMOTE KNOWLEDGE

Ubiquitous knowledge – locally available almost free of charge through the web or at modest cost via social media, journals, local universities and so on – is immensely useful, and if all knowledge needs could be satisfied by local sources there would be little demand for the remote knowledge types considered in this chapter (Rosenkopf and Nerkar 2001; Eisenhardt and Santos 2002). However, despite huge changes in global knowledge procurement practices enabled by the World Wide Web and assisted by the invention and elaboration of Google-type search algorithms, there is much knowledge that is far from ubiquitous (Maskell and Malmberg 1999).

Individuals have different perceptive powers, divergent insights and dissimilar attitudes to disparate problems encountered in distinctive conditions of time and place. Consequently, they need to develop a variety of solutions within an intricate, ongoing process of global learning-by-doing (Arrow 1962; Rantisi 2002). The global knowledge landscape therefore remains fundamentally inhomogeneous and opaque as an unavoidable consequence of the way by which it is constantly reproduced.

Traditionally, firms often cope with the problem of accessing non-ubiquitous knowledge across space by employing knowledgeable individuals. Learning is enhanced through the creation of knowledge overlaps enabled by cross-organizational labor mobility including transient expatriation (Saxenian and Hsu 2001; Casper 2007; Bergenholtz and Waldstrøm 2011). However, recruiting foreign labor with the appropriate set of qualifications may not be either desirable or feasible. The costs may be prohibitive, and the legal barriers to entry and work permits combine to prevent much potentially fruitful exchange of skilled labor taking place across space. In these cases, other investments dedicated to building ‘bridging instruments’ with appropriate absorptive capacity are important prerequisites for remote knowledge transfer (Cohen and Levinthal 1990; Meusburger 2009).

Before closer examination of the approaches used by young single-site firms to access and utilize geographically and relationally remote knowledge, it is worth highlighting three archetypical challenges.

(i) Knowledge Distortion

There is a body of evidence showing that the more the incentives and cognitive frames of the knowledge receiver and the knowledge producer are misaligned (Hinds and Mortensen 2005; Tallman and Phene 2007) the greater the risk that the remote knowledge will become distorted, transformed, or truncated during transmission, allowing its initial potential to be, at best, only partially captured when applied in its new setting (Gertler 2003; Sahlin and Wedlin 2008).

But even in the most fortunate circumstances – when collaborative efforts in knowledge creation and exchange concerns knowledge with a proven record of market worth (Szulanski 2000) and its exchange is facilitated among capable individuals with common values, experiences and understandings (Grabher 2002a; Faulconbridge 2006; Mudambi and Lorenzen 2013) – the knowledge obtained from afar, or co-produced with yesterday’s strangers, can in itself be associated with ambiguity as to what it is really about and what use can be made of it (Reed and DeFillippi 1990; Alvesson 1993). Because a particular piece of knowledge was successful in one context does not guarantee its success in a different setting, even when all actors involved are aligned and sensitive to the nature and complexity of the knowledge in question (Gertler 2004; Sorenson et al. 2007). Consequently, remote knowledge often provides significantly less value than expected, although pleasant surprises also sometimes occur.

(ii) Determining the Problem

Though the problem of distortion and how to minimize its negative effects are important for an investigation of remote knowledge, distortion presupposes that transfer of remote knowledge actually occurs. Yet there is in the literature a somewhat unfortunate tendency to disregard the preceding steps in which firms need to identify a remote knowledge source and specify what they are requesting. It is frequently taken for granted that once a young single-site firm discovers some restraining inadequacy in the locally available knowledge supply it can readily initiate a remote knowledge transfer as long as it has sufficiently developed absorptive capacity. Unfortunately, this is not the case. It requires considerable skill, effort and experience to identify an appropriate knowledge source and to communicate knowledge requirements.

The ability to formulate requirements entails decomposition of the problem to make it manageable. If important constituents are not fully understood it is almost impossible to define precisely what is being requested from the distant knowledge source, which initially will be ignorant of the future context in which the knowledge will be applied. Co-located partners and close competitors are likely to be able to deduce what is requested and its context of use, based on shared experiences or intuitive understanding of the nature of the request even if underspecified. However, firms in different settings with dissimilar experiences do not see things quite the same way. Misunderstandings are therefore bound to occur and a prolonged process of trial and error typically accompanies the search for knowledge across space.

Although resolving these ambiguities and misunderstandings can be time consuming and costly, it is precisely the difference in how a problem is understood and perceived that makes some firms' tough problems easily solvable by others. Dissimilar experiences in various parts of the world, different perspectives and dissimilar heuristics for problem resolution mean that the level of difficulty in resolving a problem will differ (Newell and Simon 1972; Marengo et al. 2000; Page 2007). Alternative perspectives available from a remote source may yield effective solutions to problems that appeared difficult or were unsolvable by others.

From this perspective few problems are, in principle, ever 'difficult' as such, but only in the eye of the beholder (Jeppesen and Lakhani 2010). The challenge consists of bridging between the realms of problem holder and potential problem solver. Yet the task of specifying all relevant aspects of what is required may exceed the knowledge seeker's initial abilities in problem decomposability. Poorly understood or ill-structured problems are unlikely to be solved regardless of the remote knowledge provider's superior abilities or incentives (Simon 1973).

(iii) Locating a Source

The process of defining, decomposing and describing the problem prior to searching for a remote knowledge source can be described as problem awareness as distinct from source awareness, which refers to identifying the coordinates of a possibly useful remote upstream knowledge pool from among the myriad of potential providers or partners worldwide (Jenkins and Tallman 2010). Few firms consider it sensible to invest time and energy into constructing and maintaining updated lists of remote sources that might be useful in the future, or to keep track of potential partners for some prospective joint project. Most actors are starting from scratch in the search for geographically and relationally remote knowledge (Saxenian 1994), and having identified one or more potential sources of the knowledge required, cannot be sure that some as yet unidentified remote supplier or co-producer might be much more superior or efficient.

Problem awareness and source awareness are separate in the sense that firms might be characterized by varying degrees of one regardless of the degree of the other. At one end of each continuum are firms that are fully aware of suitable knowledge sources and firms that are aware of the relevant aspects of the problem at hand. At the other end of these continua are the firms that are fumbling to find clues as to how best to proceed. As a helpful first approximation, we will consider these extreme cases only.

The resulting four simple snapshots are of the end-points of what is defined from the outset as two continua of awareness. Highlighting only the end-points helps to demonstrate how moving from one end to the other profoundly influences firms' choice of approach to seeking geographically and relationally remote knowledge or solutions. Further research might be able to extend the crude two-by-two end-point matrix shown in Figure 2.1 to provide more subtle and sophisticated interpretations. Yet for the time being investigating the four end-points provides an ample illustration of real-life phenomena that are sufficiently significant to warrant further analysis.

The vertical axis in Figure 2.1 shows situations where solution-seeking firms have conceived the problem in ways amenable to resolution, and situations where they have not. The horizontal axis pictures the solution-seeking firms' awareness of where a source might be found. Each of the resulting four cells is labeled according to the most common contemporary approach adopted by firms with that specific combination of problem and source awareness.

First, Figure 2.1 shows the case of solution seekers aware of their needs and aware of the location of remote solution providers, moving gradually from initial inquiry to bi-lateral negotiations and, if successful, to a knowledge transfer contract or the establishment of a perceived mutually beneficial scheme for future knowledge co-development. This process has been described as building pipelines (Bathelt et al. 2004). Of course, things can go wrong – on either side. The firm approached might be unable to

		SOURCE AWARENESS How high is the firm's awareness of a suitable source that can provide (or help co-produce) the wanted knowledge?	
		High	Low
PROBLEM AWARENESS How high is the firm's awareness of what specific knowledge it requests?	High	1. Contracts, agreements ('Pipelines')	3. Distributed online problem solving ('Crowdsourcing')
	Low	2. Technology scouting units ('Listening posts')	4. Trade fairs

Figure 2.1 Approaches preferred by young single-site firms when seeking remote knowledge under different combinations of awareness

deliver what was expected; and the firm making the approach might later realize that it needed something different from what it initially anticipated. However, it is often by building a pipeline that these discrepancies are revealed, allowing adjustment to the course of action.

Second, firms are sometimes aware of the existence of knowledge in a particular source but are unable ex ante to specify exactly what they require. In some cases, fields are so dynamic that specifications and requirements might change significantly during the building of a pipeline. In both cases the preferred alternative might be investment in presence in a relevant global knowledge hot-spot by establishing a small unit or 'listening post' to facilitate access to an otherwise distant knowledge stream.

Third, firms might be aware of exactly what kind of knowledge or solution they require, but have no idea where it might reside. These firms' options have been radically improved by the emergence of web-based technologies such as crowdsourcing. Online brokers facilitate self-selection among competing non-obvious problem solvers in vast virtual communities to provide useful solutions to firms' carefully decomposed problem, in return for an ex ante announced reward.

Fourth, there can be situations where firms do not have a clear awareness of the kinds of knowledge that might be helpful or what source might best provide or develop such knowledge in full or in part. In these cases, international trade fairs play a crucial role by providing an overview of novel and potentially useful ideas, schemes and designs that can be converted into usable forms, as well as of the range of potential providers.

These four approaches available to young single-site firms seeking geographically and relationally remote knowledge cannot be seen in isolation from the particular qualities and deficits of the local knowledge contexts of these firms. In many cases, most of the knowledge needed will be available directly or indirectly through local buzz or from network partners such as customers, suppliers, service providers, or dedicated knowledge producers (e.g. local universities, knowledge intensive business services) and so on. In addition to these relation-specific local sources, the young single-site firm has access to increasing amounts of knowledge and solutions through the web or social media, which can complement or replace customary information sources such as publications and mass media. Firms will exploit local knowledge in preference to time-consuming and costly searches for remote knowledge. Only if this local knowledge is insufficient for their plans, ideas and visions will firms feel compelled to initiate a search for geographically and relationally remote knowledge using one or more of the four approaches referred to above, and considered in more detail below.

KNOWLEDGE SEARCH IN EXTENDED GEOGRAPHIC SPACE

(i) Contracts and Agreements ('Pipelines')

The metaphor of a pipeline is commonly used to describe the arrangement resulting from investments aimed at establishing a channel for the exchange of goods, services and/or knowledge. Inter-firm linkages can be accomplished through a set of procedural rules involving a sequence of transactions and interactions where initially small risks are followed by larger ones as commitments and mutual trust progressively increase (Maskell et al. 1998; Lorenz 1999). In each successive step, the absorptive capacity of both parties tends to increase, which in turn enables progress and deepens the relationship.

Firms tend to build pipelines if they believe they have a reasonably good understanding of their immediate or long-term shortcomings, and concrete – often evidence-based – expectations about a remote future partner's useful complementary skills and abilities. The product innovation literature shows that firms learn from one another through interacting, and that interaction helps them solve problems that would be beyond the abilities of each individual firm (Rosenberg 1972; Keller 2002; Fifarek and Veloso 2010; Dicken 2011).

Investing in building inter-firm upstream or downstream pipelines has arguably hitherto been the most common way to extend relations forged for the development and exchange of knowledge and solutions across geographic space (Bathelt et al. 2004). Initiating a range of dyadic relations with a stable set of partners can reduce transaction costs and overcome many other limitations including chauvinistic prejudice about foreigners' (inadequate) competence (Zaheer 1995; Maskell et al. 2007). Working together over time alleviates problems related to cognitive distance (Sampson 2007), and although it is generally difficult to transfer and re-use knowledge or solutions across space, as highlighted in the second section, the difficulty is lessened if the transfer is between parties that over time have developed a shared language, make similar judgments and hold similar values (Brown and Duguid 1998; Wenger 1998; Amin and Cohendet 2000).

The relative scarcity of vertical linkages between co-located suppliers and customers identified in empirical research suggests further that investments in building pipelines are not restricted to a particular discrete spatial level (Staber 1996; Grabher 2002b; 2002c; Scott 2002; Wolfe and Gertler 2004). On the contrary, there is growing evidence to suggest that the formation and maintenance of pipelines significantly structure the contemporary world economy and have become pivotal for the transfer, translation and application of knowledge and solutions across geographic space, in the form of global value chains (Gereffi et al. 2005). Utilizing investments in already existing relationships as channels to new partners (your-friend-is-my-friend) helps minimize the cost of establishing a new pipeline or forming multiplex relational networks (Roscher 1989; Owen-Smith and Powell 2004; Gay and Dousset 2005; Coe et al. 2008).

Empirical evidence of pipeline formation includes, among many others, Gay and Dousset's (2005) analysis of the anti-body subsector of the biotech industry; Giuliani and Bell's (2005) investigation of pipelines to remote knowledge pools built by firms in a Chilean wine cluster; and Scott's (2002) study of extra-local linkages built by firms in the Hollywood motion picture and entertainment industry.

(ii) Technology Scouting Units ('Listening Posts')

'Listening posts' (Gassmann and Gaso 2004) or 'technology scouting units' (Birkinshaw and Monteiro 2007) are metaphors commonly used to describe the end-results of certain real-world investments made by firms mostly fully aware of the valuable sources of remote knowledge but less familiar with the detailed kind of knowledge they need or prefer. In some lines of industry and commerce, the geographical distribution of actors is so uneven that there are some immediately recognizable global hot-spots of economic activity and knowledge, although it may be difficult for the firm ex ante to determine which particular source would best match its knowledge requirements (Audretsch and Feldman 1996; Breschi and Lissoni 2009). The internal dynamics and rapid development of new technologies, scientific insights and patented solutions can further complicate the picture, and knowledge-seeking firms sometimes respond to this situation by developing local observatories or 'listening posts' in what they consider to be the most relevant hot-spot (McCann and Mudambi 2005; Mudambi 2008; Jenkins and Tallman 2010). Although the cost of this approach is often significant, it can be a cheaper and more flexible solution than constructing pipelines to numerous potential sources in that location.

In general, the objective of a listening post is to identify and transmit back to the parent firm pieces of potentially relevant knowledge and formal and informal information on new promising activities in the area (Cantwell 1993; Kuemmerle 1999; Branstetter 2001; Singh 2007; Feinberg and Gupta 2004). To achieve this, the listening post must have something to offer such as locally conducted R&D (Howells 2002; Morgan 2004). In order to gain access to knowledge spillovers from the hot-spot neighbors, the parent company has to accept the risk of knowledge leakage due to its listening post's activities but also because it must reveal its perceived future knowledge needs to prevent the listening post from searching in wrong directions. However, even a clear mandate and strong local presence does not guarantee capture of all available local knowledge and much is undoubtedly lost in the transmission or knowledge processing stages in the remote parent unit (Andrews and Delahaye 2000). The success of a listening post depends on its ability, first to understand the evolving needs and priorities of the parent company, second to gather knowledge available in its current location that will be useful in satisfying the company's needs and priorities, and third to transmit the acquired knowledge in a form that is useful for the parent firm. This transmission process can occasionally turn out to be the most challenging due to a variety of possible idiosyncrasies and not-developed-here attitudes in the parent firm (Katz and Allen 1982; Birkinshaw and Monteiro 2007).

The empirical research seems to indicate that, despite these inherent shortcomings and challenges, a listening post strategy enables firms – especially in fast-moving, vibrant and highly competitive research-intensive global fields such as electronics, information and communications technology (ICT) and pharmaceuticals – to remain up to date about local trends and developments in knowledge hot-spots (Wolff 1992; Chatterji 1996; Doz et al. 2001; Gassmann and Gaso 2004; Thompson and Fox-Kean 2005; Bogers and Lhuillery 2011). The empirical evidence also extends to other cases. Almeida (1996) shows how valuable knowledge flows originate from listening posts in the US set up by foreign firms, while Frost (2001) includes knowledge flows from state-level listening posts within the US and Singh (2007) uses patent data time series to show the net gains from listening posts across 30 countries and core industries (including chemicals, computers, drugs and medicines, electronics and mechanical).

(iii) Distributed Online Problem Solving ('Crowdsourcing')

Sometimes firms struggle unsuccessfully with a particular problem, over a long period, simply because they are unable to identify where to turn for help. In this respect, the Internet has helped. This infrastructural breakthrough combined with an organizational innovation in the form of online intermediaries, has made truly global searches increasingly available and allowed multitudes of smart people, often employed by a third party, to assist young single-site firms and facilitate their search for knowledge and solutions.

One novel mechanism that has emerged is distributed online problem solving, often known as 'crowdsourcing'. Crowdsourcing is aimed at providing solutions to carefully specified problems by attempting to mobilize the smallest, remotest and most unlikely knowledge pools (Horrobin 1986; Hong and Page 2001; Howe 2006; 2008; Lakhani and Jeppesen 2007; Brabham 2008; Yang et al. 2008; Poetz and Schreier 2012; Bloodgood 2013). The crowdsourcing process works as follows: Firms facing ostensibly unsolvable problems offer credible prizes for solutions. Dedicated web-based intermediaries or brokers pass on the packages of offer and problem to the vast network of under-the-radar specialists – some retired experts, others working in their spare time – which they have signed up. Specialists in the network decide individually whether to tackle the problem or not. The interested specialists then consider, in parallel, ways to solve the problem as defined by the firm offering the prize whose identity is known only to the intermediary. The solutions provided by one or more of the specialists are scrutinized by the intermediary and, if they meet the specification, are passed on to the problem holder; the prize is split between the contributing specialists and the intermediary. Some firms crowdsource by building their own communities (Bayus 2013) or skipping the intermediaries (Yang et al. 2008; Cardoso et al. 2009).

While a firm's previous internal attempts might have been unsuccessful in terms of results, their efforts usually result in an intimate understanding of the problem at hand, with a sufficient degree of problem decomposition to initiate crowdsourcing. Without a comprehensive understanding, it is difficult, if not impossible, to communicate the detailed characteristics of the problem to distributed knowledge holders to develop successful solutions.

One of the striking empirical regularities of crowdsourcing is that the most successful solutions often apply knowledge sets that are quite different from those mastered by the prize-awarding firm (Lakhani et al. 2007). Firms' previously successful searches for knowledge and solutions sometimes simply shape their mindsets in ways that result in misguided searches. In the absence of crowdsourcing, it would therefore be unlikely that the firm would ever be able to find a solution even with heavy investment in targeted searches (Amin and Cohendet 2004; Afuah and Tucci 2012).

Management of the Canadian mining giant, Goldcorp, is an example here. In 1999, it put very sensitive and previously heavily protected geological survey data in the public domain. Based on these data and spurred by a reward of $500,000 (USD), a total of 125 responding teams identified 55 new gold deposits and increased Goldcorp's annual gold output from 53,000 to 504,000 ounces while lowering the costs from $360 (USD) an ounce to $59 (USD) an ounce of gold produced. In total eight million ounces of gold were discovered, and Goldcorp's market value skyrocketed from $100 million (USD) to $9 billion (USD) (Afuah and Tucci 2013; Diamandis 2012).

Netflix – the young web-based provider of on-demand Internet streaming media – invested countless internal working hours to establishing and constantly improving its core system algorithm before deciding to crowdsource the task and offering a reward of $1 million (USD) for any 10 percent additional system improvements (Afuah and Tucci 2012). Other empirical evidence based on recent in-depth studies of major intermediaries' portfolios of problems taken on and problems solved, supports the contention that crowdsourcing is filling a gap in the range of approaches available to young single-site knowledge-seeking firms (Jeppesen and Lakhani 2010).

(iv) Trade Fairs

Firms intuitively exploit international trade fairs to obtain information to address problems that are too broad or too complex to decompose easily. They also obtain information about sources that are radically different from their existing range of customers, partners, competitors and contacts. This supports firms to renew or extend their product range and move into new markets. They can also face multiple and seemingly equally feasible technological and commercial avenues, but, with resources to cover only a few, they need guidance in the selection process. They are assisted by the fact that trade fairs gather large numbers of professionals from different parts of the world, which cause observers to view other participants as a cohesive entity revealing valuable preferences and inclinations.

Trade fairs also generate rich information flows characterized as 'global buzz' (Bathelt and Schuldt 2010). They allow news and insights to be shared, business to be conducted, networks created, reputations advanced and plans forged. By enabling face-to-face contact among a globally distributed set of people, international trade fairs improve global transparency and mobilize initially dispersed knowledge or solutions (Obstfeld 2006; Ibert 2007). Thus, international trade fairs offer almost unbiased insights about trends in industry standards and markets for products, services and technologies that are less easily accessible from any other source or by any other mechanism (Borghini et al. 2006; Gibson and Bathelt 2010). International trade fairs stimulate reflexive practices and become spaces for collective sense-making (Bathelt and Schuldt 2008; Anard and Jones 2008).

Recent sociological research has highlighted this effect and describes international trade fairs as 'field-configuring events' that shape the development of professions, technologies, markets and industries (Entwistle and Rocamora 2006; Garud 2008; Lampel and Meyer 2008; Weller 2008). Here, industry standards are forged, market paths are set out, fashion trends decided, organizational models questioned and technological trajectories broken.

Empirical evidence on the role of trade fairs is mounting rapidly (Bello and Barczak 1990; Bello 1992; Rosson and Seringhaus 1995; Sharland and Balogh 1996; Skov 2006; Ling-Yee 2006; Power and Jansson 2008; Rinallo et al. 2010) and shows how the most significant current international trade fairs are growing in scope and attractiveness across sectors and countries despite significantly higher investments in time and money compared to more widely available and increasingly advanced virtual platforms for inter-personal interaction and exchange (Ohara et al. 1993; Florio 1994; Rinallo and Golfetto 2011). In the context of developing Asian economies, trade fairs are becoming important events for domestic as well as foreign firms to acquire knowledge about non-transparent markets, unclear production competencies and potential partners in marketing, production and research (see Bathelt and Zeng, *this volume*; Li, *this volume*).

FINAL REMARKS

Much has been written about how the creation and dissemination of valuable knowledge benefits clustered firms. Local rivalry helps to accelerate the pace of new combinations (Schumpeter 1912) and geographical proximity enhances knowledge transfer through the sharing of norms and interpretive frameworks (Bathelt et al. 2004). However, the local knowledge landscape is never complete and it is being increasingly recognized that even young single-site enterprises sometimes need access to non-local knowledge to remain competitive.

The present chapter has argued that distinct combinations of awareness shape the approach chosen to access geographically and relationally remote knowledge. By focusing on the upstream process of how firms initially identify remote sources of complementary competencies and subsequently instigate some sort of globally extended learning, this chapter has tried to close a widening gap to the growing literature on the downstream process of how remote knowledge – once acquired – is disseminated and absorbed locally.

The analysis contributes to several literatures and suggests directions for further investigation: First, the issues investigated provide an additional linkage between economic geography and international business research (Beugelsdijk et al. 2010; McCann 2011), traditionally mostly concerned with offshore activities.

Second, it highlights an often-disregarded aspect about the initial stages of network formation. As young firms grow and develop, complexity increases and several approaches to accessing remote knowledge can operate simultaneously. The broader set of activities conducted by large firms may include some with full awareness of what is needed and where it can be sourced, resulting in the construction of pipelines. It may also include activities with lesser degrees of awareness where listening posts, crowdsourcing and participating in trade fairs will consequentially dominate the firms' search for useful remote knowledge.

However, growth also enables firms to acquire experience in assessing the main strengths and weaknesses of each entity on an expanding list of potential remote knowledge sources identified through the means described above. Interacting with some of these sources can be mutually beneficial and allow relation-specific investments that result in strong pipelines. While crowdsourcing might consist of a series of one-off events to access remote knowledge sources, trade fairs and listening posts serve an additional role in the longer run of providing stepping-stones to the building of novel pipelines, just as they offer options for finding a replacement when existing pipelines are discontinued for some reason.

Third, the present chapter adds a new twist to the governance literature by emphasizing the linkage between the search for remote knowledge and the subsequent formation of multinational corporations. Pipelines over time can become so vital for the long-term competitiveness and survival of the firms involved that joint ownership can become an attractive option. Regardless of which firm is the acquirer and which the acquired, the shared ambition is to enhance aggregate knowledge creation and exchange by positioning formerly independent but complementary units within a common organizational structure, under a single united managerial discretion. This ability to move beyond local knowledge sourcing and unite geographically widely separated knowledge bases has previously been identified as the main raison d'être for the emergence of the modern multinational enterprise (Kogut and Zander 1993; Zaheer 1995; Bartlett and Ghoshal 1997). So a journey that started out as a means for a young single-site firm to compensate for deficits in the local knowledge landscape might ultimately end with the formation of a multinational enterprise. However, the way that awareness – as conceived in the present chapter – shapes the path of young firms toward or away from this outcome has not yet been thoroughly investigated.

Fourth, the inherent dynamics of accessing remote knowledge by young single-site firms might constitute a particular promising line of future research. Is there a dominant sequence in the use of the labeled approaches or do firms have periods of relative stability in their knowledge portfolio, sometimes interrupted by distinctive internal or external events? The answers to this question might have significance for policy-makers concerned with improving clusters', cities', or regions' abilities to access valuable remote knowledge – and especially perhaps for young single-site firms located in areas characterized by a rather meager or one-sided local knowledge environment where policies should aim at lowering the barriers to accessing relationally and geographically remote knowledge. Further work is needed to determine how such policies could best be designed.

Fifth, the present chapter posits that there are internal reasons in firms for choosing a particular approach to seeking remote knowledge sources, which might contribute to the rapidly expanding literature on 'temporary clusters', international trade fairs, conventions, congresses and so on. Not all firms can thus be expected ever to participate in such events because their levels of problem and source awareness directs their focus toward other approaches. Firms that do participate will benefit depending on how much their particular combination of problem and source awareness opens or closes other approaches to accessing remote knowledge, but very little is known about these relationships.

Sixth, the chapter admittedly engages only briefly with the often imperative competitive aspects of property rights or with the broader aspects of protecting remote knowledge identified or developed and subsequently used. One of the main reasons for conducting knowledge generation and reproduction mainly within the firm's boundaries is to keep it secret and allow legal property rights protection to be applied. Pipelines and especially crowdsourcing limit the possibilities of concealment. More research is needed into how young single-site firms manage the trade-off between obtaining access to valuable remote knowledge and protecting their existing knowledge base.

ACKNOWLEDGMENTS

I am greatly indebted to Harald Bathelt for numerous helpful comments and assistance in finalizing the research reported in this chapter. The kind permission granted by Oxford University Press to reproduce the following materials is gratefully acknowledged: Maskell, P. (2014) 'Accessing remote knowledge: The complementary roles of trade fairs, pipelines, crowdsourcing and listening posts', *Journal of Economic Geography*, 14: 883–902.

REFERENCES

Afuah, A. and Tucci, C. (2012) 'Crowdsourcing as a solution to distant search', *Academy of Management Review*, 37 (3): 355–375.

Afuah, A. and Tucci, C. (2013) 'Value capture and crowdsourcing', *Academy of Management Review*, 38 (3): 457–460.

Agrawal, A. and Cockburn, I. (2003) 'The anchor tenant hypothesis: Exploring the role of large, local, R&D-intensive firms in regional innovation systems', *International Journal of Industrial Organisation*, 21 (9): 1227–1253.

Allen, J. (2000) 'Power/economic knowledge: Symbolic and spatial formations', in J. Bryson, P. W. Daniels, N. Henry and J. S. Pollard (eds) *Knowledge, Space, Economy*, London: Routledge, 15–33.

Almeida, P. (1996) 'Knowledge sourcing by foreign multinationals: Patent citation analysis in the US semiconductor industry', *Strategic Management Journal*, 17: 155–165.

Alvesson, M. (1993) 'Organizations as rhetoric: Knowledge-intensive firms and the struggle with ambiguity', *Journal of Management Studies*, 30 (6): 997–1015.

Amin, A. and Cohendet, P. (2000) 'Organisational learning and governance through embedded practices', *Journal of Management and Governance*, 4: 93–116.

Amin, A. and Cohendet, P. (2004) *Architectures of Knowledge: Firms, Capabilities and Communities*, Oxford: Oxford University Press.

Anand, N. and Jones, B. C. (2008) 'Tournament rituals, category dynamics and field configuration: The case of the Booker Prize', *Journal of Management Studies*, 45: 1036–1060.

Andrews, K. M. and Delahaye, B. L. (2000) 'Influences of knowledge process in organizational learning: The psychosocial filter', *Journal of Management Studies*, 37 (6): 797–810.

Arrow, K. J. (1962) 'Economic welfare and the allocation of resources for invention', in National Bureau of Economic Research (ed.) *The Rate and Direction of Inventive Activity*, Princeton, NJ: Princeton University Press, 609–626.

Audretsch, D. B. and Feldman, M. P. (1996) 'Innovative clusters and the industry life cycle', *Review of Industrial Organization*, 11: 253–273.

Bartlett, C. A. and Ghoshal, S. (1997) 'The evolution of the transnational', in I. Islam and W. Shepherd (eds) *Current Issues in International Business*, Cheltenham, UK and Lyme, NH: Edward Elgar, 108–131.

Bathelt, H., Malmberg, A. and Maskell, P. (2004) 'Clusters and knowledge: Local buzz, global pipelines and the process of knowledge creation', *Progress in Human Geography*, 28 (1): 31–56.

Bathelt, H. and Schuldt, N. (2008) 'Between luminaires and meat grinders: International trade fairs as temporary clusters', *Regional Studies*, 42 (6): 853–868.

Bathelt, H. and Schuldt, N. (2010) 'International trade fairs and global buzz, Part I: Ecology of global buzz', *European Planning Studies*, 18 (12): 1957–1974.

Bayus, B. L. (2013) 'Crowdsourcing new product ideas over time: An analysis of the Dell IdeaStorm community', *Management Science*, 59 (1): 226–244.

Bello, D. C. (1992) 'Industrial buyer behaviour at trade shows', *Journal of Business Research*, 25: 59–80.

Bello, D. C. and Barczak, G. J. (1990) 'Using industrial trade shows to improve new product development', *Journal of Business Industrial Marketing*, 5: 43–56.

Bergenholtz, C. and Waldstrøm, C. (2011) 'Inter-organizational network studies – A literature review', *Industry and Innovation*, 18 (6): 539–562.

Beugelsdijk, S. (2007) 'The regional environment and the firm's innovative performance: A plea for a multilevel interactionist approach', *Economic Geography*, 83: 181–199.

Beugelsdijk, S., McCann, P. and Mudambi, R. (2010) 'Place, space and organization – Economic geography and the multinational enterprise', *Journal of Economic Geography*, 10 (4): 485–493.

Birkinshaw, J. M. and Monteiro, F. (2007) *Centers of Excellence in Multinational Corporations*, AIM Research Working Paper Series No. 60, Coventry: Advanced Institute of Management Research.

Bloodgood, J. (2013) 'Crowdsourcing: Useful for problem solving, but what about value capture?', *Academy of Management Review*, 38 (3): 455–457.

Bogers, M. and Lhuillery, S. (2011) 'A functional perspective on learning and innovation: Investigating the organization of absorptive capacity', *Industry and Innovation*, 18 (6): 561–610.

Borghini, S., Golfetto, F. and Rinallo, D. (2006) 'Ongoing search among industrial buyers', *Journal of Business Research*, 59: 1151–1159.

Brabham, D. C. (2008) 'Crowdsourcing as a model for problem solving: An introduction and cases', *Convergence: The International Journal of Research into New Media Technologies*, 14 (1): 75–90.

Branstetter, L. (2001) 'Are knowledge spillovers international or intranational in scope?', *Journal of International Economics*, 53: 53–79.

Breschi, S. and Lissoni, F. (2009) 'Mobility of skilled workers and co-invention networks: An anatomy of localized knowledge flows', *Journal of Economic Geography*, 9 (44): 439–468.

Brown, J. S. and Duguid, P. (1998) 'Organizational learning and communities

of practice: Towards a unified view of working, learning and innovation', *Organization Science*, 2 (1): 40–57.
Brusco, S. (1986) 'Small firms and industrial districts: The experience of Italy', in D. Keeble and E. Wever (eds) *New Firms and Regional Development in Europe*, London: Croom Helm, 184–202.
Bunnell, T. G. and Coe, N. M. (2001) 'Spaces and scales of innovation', *Progress in Human Geography*, 25 (4): 569–589.
Cantwell, J. (1993) 'Corporate technological specialization in international industries', in M. C. Casson and J. Creedy (eds) *Industrial Concentration and Economic Inequality: Essays in Honour of Peter Hart*, Aldershot, UK and Brookfield, VT: Edward Elgar, 216–232.
Cardoso, M., Carvalho, J. V. and Ramos, I. (2009) *Open Innovation Communities . . . or Should it be 'Networks'?*, Working Paper, Braga: University of Minho, Portugal.
Casper, S. (2007) 'How do technology clusters emerge and become sustainable? Social network formation and inter-firm mobility within the San Diego biotechnology cluster', *Research Policy*, 36 (4): 438–455.
Chatterji, D. (1996) 'Accessing external sources of technology', *Research Technology Management*, 39 (2): 49–56.
Coe, N. M., Dicken, P. and Hess, M. (2008) 'Global production networks: Realizing the potential', *Journal of Economic Geography*, 8: 271–295.
Cohen, W. M. and Levinthal, D. A. (1990) 'Absorptive capacity: A new perspective on learning and innovation', *Administrative Science Quarterly*, 35: 128–152.
Delgado, M., Porter, M. E. and Stern, S. (2010) 'Clusters and entrepreneurship', *Journal of Economic Geography*, 10: 495–518.
Diamandis, P. H. (2012) *Abundance: The Future Is Better Than You Think*, New York: The Free Press.
Dicken, P. (2011) *Global Shift: Mapping the Changing Contours of the World Economy*, New York: Guilford Press.
Doz, Y. L., Santos, J. and Williamson, P. (2001) *From Global to Metanational: How Companies Win in the Knowledge Economy*, Cambridge, MA: Harvard Business School Press.
Eisenhardt, K. M. and Santos, F. M. (2002) 'Knowledge-based view: A new theory of strategy?', in A. Pettigrew, H. Thomas and R. Whittington (eds) *Handbook of Strategy and Management*, London: Sage, 139–164.
Entwistle, J. and Rocamora, A. (2006) 'The field of fashion materialized: A study of London Fashion Week', *Sociology*, 40 (4): 735–751.
Faulconbridge, J. R. (2006) 'Stretching tacit knowledge beyond a local fix? Global spaces of learning in advertising professional service firms', *Journal of Economic Geography*, 6 (4): 517–540.
Feinberg, S. and Gupta, A. (2004) 'Knowledge spillovers and the assignment of R&D responsibilities to foreign subsidiaries', *Strategic Management Journal*, 25: 823–845.
Feldman, M. P. (1994) *The Geography of Innovation*, Dordrecht: Kluwer.
Fifarek, B. J. and Veloso, F. M. (2010) 'Offshoring and the global geography of innovation', *Journal of Economic Geography*, 10: 559–578.
Flemming, L. and Sorenson, O. (2004) 'Science as a map in technological search', *Strategic Management Journal*, 25: 909–928.
Florio, M. (1994) 'Fair trades by trade fairs: Information providing institutions under monopolistic competition', *Small Business Economics*, 6 (4): 267–281.

Fontana, R., Genua, A. and Matt, M. (2006) 'Factors affecting university–industry R&D projects: The importance of searching, screening and signalling', *Research Policy*, 35: 309–323.

Frost, T. S. (2001) 'The geographic sources of foreign subsidiaries' innovations', *Strategic Management Journal*, 22 (2): 101–123.

Garud, R. (2008) 'Conferences as venues for the configuration of emerging organizational fields: The case of cochlear implants', *Journal of Management Studies*, 45 (629): 1061–1088.

Gassmann, O. and Gaso, B. (2004) 'Insourcing creativity with listening posts in decentralized firms', *Creativity and Innovation Management*, 13 (1): 3–14.

Gay, B. and Dousset, B. (2005) 'Innovation and network structural dynamics: Study of the alliance network of a major sector of the biotechnology industry', *Research Policy*, 34 (10): 1457–1475.

Gereffi, G., Humphrey, J. and Sturgeon, T. J. (2005) 'The governance of global value chains', *Review of International Political Economy*, 12 (1): 78–104.

Gertler, M. S. (2003) 'Tacit knowledge and the economic geography of context, or The undefinable tacitness of being (there)', *Journal of Economic Geography*, 3 (1): 75–99.

Gertler, M. S. (2004) *Manufacturing Culture: The Institutional Geography of Industrial Practice*, Oxford: Oxford University Press.

Gibson, R. and Bathelt, H. (2010) *Understanding the Dynamics of Specialization and Diffusion Processes across Capitalist Varieties: A Conceptual Intervention Regarding the Role of International Trade Fairs*, SPACES online 8 (4), Toronto and Heidelberg: www.spaces-online.com.

Giuliani, E. (2005) 'Cluster absorptive capacity: Why do some clusters forge ahead and others lag behind?', *European Urban and Regional Studies*, 12 (3): 269–288.

Giuliani, E. and Bell, M. R. (2005) 'The micro-determinants of meso-level learning and innovation: Evidence from a Chilean wine cluster', *Research Policy*, 34 (1): 47–68.

Grabher, G. (2002a) 'Cool projects, boring institutions: Temporary collaboration in social context', *Regional Studies*, 36 (3): 205–214.

Grabher, G. (2002b) 'Fragile sector, robust practice: Project ecologies in new media', *Environment and Planning A*, 34 (11): 1911–1926.

Grabher, G. (2002c) 'The project ecology of advertising: Tasks, talents and teams', *Regional Studies*, 36 (3): 245–262.

Griliches, Z. (1979) 'Issues in assessing the contribution of research and development to productivity growth', *Bell Journal of Economics*, 10: 92–116.

Hinds, P. J. and Mortensen, M. (2005) 'Understanding conflict in geographically distributed teams: The moderating effect of shared identity, shared context, and spontaneous communication', *Organization Science*, 16 (3): 290–307.

Hong, L. and Page, S. E. (2001) 'Problem solving by heterogeneous agents', *Journal of Economic Theory*, 97 (1): 123–163.

Horrobin, D. F. (1986) 'Glittering prizes for research support', *Nature*, 324 (6094): 221.

Howe, J. (2006) 'The rise of crowdsourcing', *Wired Magazine*, 14 (6): 1–4.

Howe, J. (2008) *Crowdsourcing: Why the Power of the Crowd is Driving the Future of Business*, New York: Crown Business, Random House.

Howells, J. R. L. (2002) 'Tacit knowledge, innovation and economic geography', *Urban Studies*, 39 (5–6): 871–884.

Ibert, O. (2007) 'Towards a geography of knowledge creation: The ambivalences between "knowledge as an object" and "knowing in practice"', *Regional Studies*, 41 (1): 103–114.

Jenkins, M. and Tallman, S. (2010) 'The shifting geography of competitive advantage: Clusters, networks and firms', *Journal of Economic Geography*, 10: 599–618.

Jeppesen, L. B. and Lakhani, K. R. (2010) 'Marginality and problem-solving effectiveness in broadcast search', *Organization Science*, 21 (5): 1016–1033.

Katila, R. (2002) 'New product search over time: Past ideas in their prime?', *Academy of Management Journal*, 45 (6): 995–1010.

Katila, R. and Ahuja, G. (2000) 'Something old, something new: A longitudinal study of search behavior and new product development', *Academy of Management Journal*, 45 (6): 1183–1194.

Katz, R. and Allen, T. J. (1982) 'Investigating the not invented here (NIH) syndrome: A look at the performance, tenure, and communication patterns of 50 R & D project groups', *R & D Management*, 12 (1): 7–20.

Keller, W. (2002) 'Geographical localization of international technology diffusion', *American Economic Review*, 92: 120–142.

Kogut, B. and Zander, U. (1993) 'Knowledge of the firm and the evolutionary theory of the multinational corporation', *Journal of International Business Studies*, 24: 625–645.

Kuemmerle, W. (1999) 'The drivers of foreign direct investment into research and development: An empirical investigation', *Journal of International Business Studies*, 30: 1–24.

Lakhani, K. R. and Jeppesen, L. B. (2007) 'Getting unusual suspects to solve R&D puzzles. Forethought', *Harvard Business Review*, 85 (5): 1–2.

Lakhani, K. R., Jeppesen, L. B., Lohse, P. A. and Panetta, J. A. (2007) *The Value of Openness in Scientific Problem Solving*, Harvard Business School Working Paper No. 07-050, Boston Harvard University. Online. Available HTTP: <http://www.hbs.edu/research/pdf/07-050.pdf> (3 May 2014).

Lampel, J. and Meyer, A. D. (2008) 'Field-configuring events as structuring mechanisms: How conferences, ceremonies, and trade shows constitute new technologies, industries and markets', *Journal of Management Studies*, 45 (629): 1026–1035.

Lawson, C. (1999) 'Towards a competence theory of the region', *Cambridge Journal of Economics*, 23: 151–166.

Ling-Yee, L. (2006) 'Relationship learning at trade shows: Its antecedents and consequences', *Industrial Marketing Management*, 35: 166–177.

Lorenz, E. H. (1999) 'Trust, contract and economic cooperation', *Cambridge Journal of Economics*, 23 (3): 301–315.

Marengo, L., Dosi, G., Legrenzi, P. and Pasqualli, C. (2000) 'The structure of problem-solving knowledge and the structure of organizations', *Industrial and Corporate Change*, 9 (4): 757–788.

Maskell, P. (2001) 'Towards a knowledge-based theory of the geographical cluster', *Industrial and Corporate Change*, 10 (4): 919–941.

Maskell, P., Bathelt, H. and Malmberg, A. (2006) 'Building global knowledge pipelines: The role of temporary clusters', *European Planning Studies*, 14 (8): 997–1013.

Maskell, P., Dick-Nielsen, J., Pedersen, T. and Petersen, B. (2007) 'Learning paths to global offshore outsourcing: From cost reduction to knowledge seeking', *Industry and Innovation*, 14 (3): 239–257.

Maskell, P., Eskelinen, H., Hannibalsson, I., Malmberg, A. and Vatne, E. (1998) *Competitiveness, Localised Learning and Regional Development: Specialisation and Prosperity in Small Open Economies*, London: Routledge.
Maskell, P. and Malmberg, A. (1999) 'The competitiveness of firms and regions: "Ubiquitification" and the importance of localized learning', *European Urban and Regional Studies*, 6 (1): 9–25.
McCann, D. (2011) 'International business and economic geography: Knowledge, time and transactions costs', *Journal of Economic Geography*, 11: 309–317.
McCann, P. and Mudambi, R. (2005) 'Analytical differences in the economics of geography: The case of the multinational firm', *Environment and Planning A*, 37 (10): 1857–1876.
McEvily, B. and Zaheer, A. (1999) 'Bridging ties: A source of firm heterogeneity in competitive capabilities', *Strategic Management Journal*, 20: 1133–1156.
Meusburger, P. (2009) 'Spatial mobility of knowledge: A proposal for a more realistic communication model', *disP – The Planning Review*, 177 (2): 29–39.
Morgan, K. (2004) 'The exaggerated death of geography: Learning, proximity and territorial innovation systems', *Journal of Economic Geography*, 4: 3–21.
Mudambi, R. (2008) 'Location, control and innovation in knowledge-intensive industries', *Journal of Economic Geography*, 8: 699–725.
Mudambi, R. and Lorenzen, M. (2013) 'Clusters, connectivity and catch-up: Bollywood and Bangalore in the global economy', *Journal of Economic Geography*, 13: 501–534.
Newell, A. and Simon, H. A. (1972) *Human Problem Solving*, Englewood Cliffs, NJ: Prentice-Hall.
Obstfeld, D. (2006) *Creative Projects and Combinatorial Search: Toward a Less-Routine Theory of Organizing*, Working Paper, Irvine: University of California, Irvine, Paul Merage School of Business.
Ohara, B., Palumbo, F. and Herbig, P. (1993) 'Industrial trade shows abroad', *Industrial Marketing Management*, 22: 233–237.
Owen-Smith, J. and Powell, W. W. (2004) 'Knowledge networks as channels and conduits: The effects of formal structure in the Boston biotechnology community', *Organization Science*, 15 (1): 5–21.
Owen-Smith, J. and Powell, W. W. (2006) 'Accounting for emergence and novelty in Boston and Bay Area biotechnology', in P. Braunerhjelm and M. P. Feldman (eds) *Cluster Genesis: Technology-Based Industrial Development*, Oxford: Oxford University Press, 61–85.
Page, S. E. (2007) 'Making the difference: Applying a logic of diversity', *Academy of Management Perspective*, 21 (4): 6–20.
Pinch, S., Henry, N., Jenkins, M. and Tallman, S. (2003) 'From "industrial districts" to "knowledge clusters": A model of knowledge dissemination and competitive advantage in industrial agglomerations', *Journal of Economic Geography*, 3 (4): 373–388.
Poetz, M. and Schreier, M. (2012) 'The value of crowdsourcing: Can users really compete with professionals in generating new product ideas?', *Journal of Product Innovation Management*, 29 (2): 245–256.
Power, D. and Jansson, J. (2008) 'Cyclical clusters in global circuits: Overlapping spaces in furniture trade fairs', *Economic Geography*, 84 (4): 423–448.
Rantisi, N. M. (2002) 'The local innovation system as a source of "variety": Openness and adaptability in New York City's garment district', *Regional Studies*, 36 (6): 587–602.

Reed, R. and DeFillippi, R. J. (1990) 'Causal ambiguity, barriers to imitation and sustainable competitive advantage', *Academy of Management Review*, 15 (1): 88–102.

Rinallo, D., Borghini, S. and Golfetto, F. (2010) 'Exploring visitor experiences at trade shows', *Journal of Business and Industrial Marketing*, 25: 249–258.

Rinallo, D. and Golfetto, F. (2011) 'Exploring the knowledge strategies of temporary cluster organizers: A longitudinal study of the EU fabric industry trade shows (1986–2006)', *Economic Geography*, 87 (4): 453–476.

Roscher, N. (1989) *Cognitive Economy: The Economic Dimension of the Theory of Knowledge*, Pittsburgh, PA: University of Pittsburgh Press.

Rosenberg, N. (1972) *Technology and American Economic Growth*, White Plains, NY: Sharpe.

Rosenkopf, L. and Nerkar, A. (2001) 'Beyond local search: Boundary-spanning, exploration and impact of the optical disk industry', *Strategic Management Journal*, 22: 287–306.

Rosson, P. J. and Seringhaus, F. H. R. (1995) 'Visitors and exhibitor interaction at industrial trade fairs', *Journal of Business Research*, 32: 81–90.

Sahlin, K. and Wedlin, L. (2008) 'Circulating ideas: Imitation, translation and editing', in R. Greenwood, K. Sahlin and R. Suddaby (eds) *The Sage Handbook of Organizational Institutionalism*, Los Angeles: Sage, 218–242.

Salter, A. and Laursen, K. (2006) 'Open for innovation: The role of openness in explaining performance among UK manufacturing firms', *Strategic Management Journal*, 27 (2): 131–150.

Sampson, E. C. (2007) 'R&D alliances and firm performance: The impact of technological diversity and alliance organization on innovation', *Academy of Management Journal*, 50 (2): 364–386.

Saxenian, A. (1991) 'The origins and dynamics of production networks in Silicon Valley', *Research Policy*, 20 (1991): 423–437.

Saxenian, A. (1994) *Regional Advantage: Culture and Competition in Silicon Valley and Route 128*, Cambridge, MA: Harvard University Press.

Saxenian, A. and Hsu, J.-Y. (2001) '"Bay-to-bay" strategic alliances: The network linkages between Taiwan and the U.S. venture capital industries', *International Journal of Technology Management*, 25 (1): 136–150.

Schumpeter, J. A. (1912) *Theorie der wirtschaftlichen Entwicklung (The Theory of Economic Development: An Inquiry into Profits, Capital, Credit, Interest and the Business Cycle)*, Berlin (Oxford): Duncker & Humblot (Oxford University Press).

Scott, A. J. (2002) 'A new map of Hollywood: The production and distribution of American motion pictures', *Regional Studies*, 36: 957–975.

Sharland, A. and Balogh, P. (1996) 'The value of nonselling activities at international trade shows', *Industrial Marketing Management*, 25: 59–66.

Simon, H. A. (1973) 'The structure of ill structured problems', *Artificial Intelligence*, 4 (1): 181–201.

Singh, J. (2007) 'Asymmetry of knowledge spillovers between MNCs and host country firms', *Journal of International Business Studies*, 38: 764–766.

Skov, L. (2006) 'The role of trade fairs in the global fashion business', *Current Sociology*, 54 (5): 764–783.

Sorenson, O., Rivkin, J. W. and Flemming, L. (2007) 'Informational complexity and the flow of knowledge across social boundaries', in K. Frenken (ed.) *Applied Evolutionary Economics and Economic Geography*, Cheltenham, UK and Northampton, MA: Edward Elgar, 147–159.

Staber, U. (1996) 'Accounting for variations in the performance of industrial districts: The case of Baden-Württemberg', *International Journal of Urban and Regional Research*, 20: 299–316.
Storper, M. (1994) *Institutions in a Learning Economy*, Paper presented at the OECD Conference on 'Employment and Growth in a Knowledge-based Economy', Copenhagen, 7–8 November.
Storper, M. and Venables, A. J. (2004) 'Buzz: Face-to-face contact and the urban economy', *Journal of Economic Geography*, 4 (4): 351–370.
Szulanski, G. (2000) 'The process of knowledge transfer', *Organizational Behavior and Human Decision Processes*, 82 (1): 9–27.
Tallman, S. and Phene, A. (2007) 'Leveraging knowledge across geographic boundaries', *Organization Science*, 18 (2): 252–260.
Thompson, P. and Fox-Kean, M. (2005) 'Patent citation and the geography of knowledge spillovers: A reassessment', *American Economic Review*, 95: 450–460.
Tushman, M. L. and Katz, R. (1980) 'External communication and project performance: An investigation into the role of gatekeepers', *Management Science*, 26 (11): 1071–1085.
Weller, S. (2008) 'Beyond "global production networks": Australian Fashion Week's trans-sectoral synergies', *Growth and Change*, 39 (1): 104–122.
Wenger, E. (1998) *Communities of Practice: Learning, Meaning, and Identity*, Cambridge: Cambridge University Press.
Wolfe, D. A. and Gertler, M. S. (2004) 'Clusters from the inside and out: Local dynamics and global linkages', *Urban Studies*, 41 (5/6): 1071–1093.
Wolff, M. F. (1992) 'Scouting for technology', *Research Technology Management*, 35 (2): 10–12.
Yang, J., Adamic, L. A. and Ackerman, M. S. (2008) *Crowdsourcing and Knowledge Sharing: Strategic User Behavior on Taskcn*, Proceedings of the 9th ACM Conference on Electronic Commerce, Chicago, 8–12 July.
Zaheer, S. (1995) 'Overcoming the liability of foreignness', *Academy of Management Journal*, 38 (2): 341–363.

3. The evolution of trade show systems: lessons from Europe

Francesca Golfetto and Diego Rinallo

INTRODUCTION

International trade shows have played a central role in the development of local economies in Europe since the end of World War II. As collective marketing instruments, regularly scheduled each year, European events were able to support the visibility of many local clusters and national manufacturing industries, enabling local firms to establish international pipelines and wider market ties. In Europe, trade shows also have been important drivers of business tourism, generating economic impact on the hosting cities because of visitors' and exhibitors' expenditures in the local area.

Trade fairs are present throughout all European countries, but events devoted to industrial buyers (business-to-business shows) have been especially focused in industrialized areas and, inside these, in the most accessible cities. The two key benefits of trade shows (promotion of local clusters/national industries and local economic impacts) have legitimized two different event models: export shows (local/national supply shows), with exhibitors mainly represented by local producers and visitors-buyers mainly coming from abroad; and import shows (local/national demand shows), with exhibitors-producers mainly coming from abroad and visitors-buyers mainly representing the local market. These two models have been promoted by different actors with specific interests: industrial associations, with protectionist attitudes in the former case; and local governments, interested in building a large exhibitor base (and achieving substantial local economic impacts) in the latter (Golfetto 2004; Rinallo and Golfetto 2011; Bathelt et al. 2014).

Different trade shows also contribute in a different way to knowledge circulation. As shown below, knowledge exchange depends on trade show specialization and the internationalization model (i.e. import versus export orientation). Additionally, trade show organizing firms (or organizers) can adopt specific knowledge-based strategies that help increase the learning potential at the respective events for exhibitors and visitors alike.

In Europe, a system of different events has developed over time. Such events, while competing with each other for exhibitors and visitors, have mostly co-existed peacefully as each found a market niche responding to its specialization and scheduling. Within this context, however, we observed the development of manifold so-called 'trade show wars' (Rinallo and Golfetto 2011; Bathelt et al. 2014). First, 'wars' between different local industrial clusters within the same country have developed, which sometimes generate a situation of fragmentation, with many small local supply shows not being able to join forces to create a strong export trade show representing the entire national industry. As in the case of some Italian shows, this has resulted in reduced visibility for all exhibitors-suppliers involved. Second, other 'wars' have developed between supply shows and demand shows, illustrating how well-orchestrated collective marketing events can sometimes enable smaller trade shows to overcome the visibility of larger ones. Third, we observed 'wars' between trade show organizers and locations, with the goal of establishing these shows as 'hub events', that is, the most important international European event in the respective industry.

Parallel to these trends, we also observed a general long-term weakening of export-oriented trade shows due to the increasingly polycentric structure of manufacturing industries and their respective events at a worldwide level. Today, European producers tend to follow international markets by exhibiting at local demand trade shows (in newly developing countries), reducing at the same time their investments at European export events. This, in turn, reduces incentives for buyers from overseas to visit European trade shows or, at least, requires concentrating visits only to the most representative events.

This chapter analyzes the characteristics and evolution of European trade shows with the objective to present a reference for trade show development in emerging countries, especially those in the Asia-Pacific region. Next, we analyze the transformation of European trade shows as a result of the underlying changes in the structure and geographical distribution of manufacturing industries, which caused a geographical redistribution of trade show activities. We continue with two sections that analyze the varying import–export functions of international trade shows and their different contribution to knowledge circulation. The two sections that follow are devoted to competition for trade shows between industries and cities, at the European and global level. We conclude by summarizing key lessons learned and their implications for the development of the Asian trade show system.

TRADE SHOW DEVELOPMENT IN EUROPE

Western Europe is the most highly developed trade show region with the longest tradition of trade shows in the world. This important trade show activity is linked to the specifics of industrial organization in the leading European countries (Germany, France, Italy, Spain), particularly the structure of traditional manufacturing industries, which are predominantly made up of small and medium-sized enterprises with a high export orientation (Golfetto 1988; 2004; CERMES 2013b). The relatively small firm size and relatively large distance to final markets make it very hard and costly for firms to individually reach potential customers in other markets. Additionally, European firms, due to their limited size, tend to specialize in single production phases, and thus particularly target intermediate markets, or sell to wholesalers and international distributors (European Commission 2008; 2009). Compared to large integrated US firms with complete in-house production cycles, the production of similar quantities in Europe often involves a larger number of small, specialized, disintegrated firms. Finally, many European industries (mainly in Germany, Italy and France) reach a level of exports that exceeds 50 percent of their production. As a result, the coordination between different firms and between firms and markets in Europe is highly complex. Under these conditions, collective organizations and means of communication – involving industrial clusters, consortiums, trade associations and trade shows – become decisive tools in organizing adjustments in production, trade and related knowledge flows (Pyke et al. 1990; Becattini and Rullani 1996; Golfetto 2000; Zerbini et al. 2007; Golfetto and Rinallo 2013).

Since the late-1950s, trade show activity in Europe has been marked by a continual and intense growth due to the rise of production and export capacities in its main manufacturing countries. These collective events initially emerged as generic trade fairs, with exhibitors belonging to different industries and visitors belonging to different target groups, putting together consumers and business visitors. Later, the specialization of manufacturing industries and of trade channels led to the transformation of generic fairs into specialized sector shows, attracting more international visitors.

Furthermore, many local shows that were initially held in industrial clusters moved location and gradually concentrated in more accessible cities, putting together producers from different areas to form larger trade shows. This process occurred initially at the national level and later extended internationally. In Italy, textile trade shows initially located in Prato moved to Florence and later to Milan, merging with others initially located in Como. Other textile shows moved to Paris, eventually attracting producers from different clusters in France and, later, Italy, Spain and other European countries (Rinallo and Golfetto 2006; 2011; Golfetto and Rinallo 2012). A significant boost to the internationalization of trade shows was provided by the construction and on-going expansion of specialized exhibition venues, dominated, in particular, by about a dozen very large facilities, almost all of which built on the initiative of local government bodies in the different countries.

Over the years, the European trade show system has concentrated its activity in the centers of the most industrialized regions. A corresponding reduction in trade fair activity has been observed in other regions that were characterized by a decrease in manufacturing activities – leading in some cases to the disappearance of once-established events. This happened, for example, in the case of textile and ceramics trade shows in Great Britain (CERMES 2012; Bathelt et al. 2014).

At the same time, consumer fairs have slowly declined because of the development of communication media and mass retailing. Only in later stages, some of these events have been able to renew themselves thanks to the spread of experiential marketing formulas (Pine and Gilmore 1998; Schmitt 1999; Rinallo 2011; Golfetto and Rinallo 2013). Experiential marketing has transformed many consumer events into places where firms have an opportunity to get closer to their consumers, allowing for sensory and relational experiences that emphasize the specificity of the promoted brands. Other minor trade fairs, which celebrate local traditions or religious festivities and agriculture, continue to exist, serving functions similar to those of retail markets. Although knowledge exchange and dissemination at consumer shows is limited, these events may still constitute a source of inspiration for industrial innovations as they provide manufacturers with a platform for the observation of consumer behavior (Golfetto 2004). Consumer shows are, however, not included in the schedules and cycles of the purchasing process of manufacturing industries. Instead, they often take place during time periods of good weather or are associated with agricultural and religious traditions. Overall, we have witnessed an increase in specialized trade shows and a stagnation/decline of multi-sector events (see Figure 3.1).

European trade shows also have transformed from isolated events into specialized systems of events staged at regular intervals (Power and Jansson 2008), becoming the ‘periodical rites’, during which the entire sector comes together (Borghini et al. 2006). In this cycle, the timing and frequency of events becomes an important decision for trade show organizers trying to attract relevant exhibitors and visitors. The timing of events is industry-specific and depends on industrial buyers and distribution channels. Trade show frequency also takes into account the typical pace

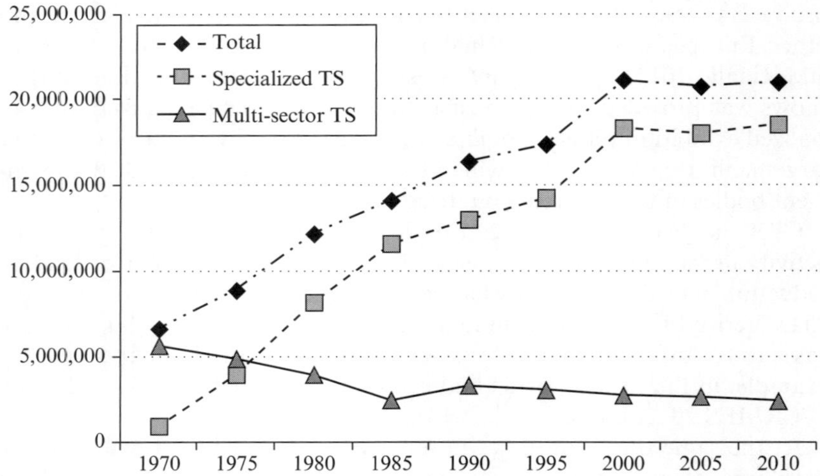

Source: CERMES (2013a).

Figure 3.1 The development of specialized trade shows in Europe, 1970–2010 (net square meters sold in Germany, Italy, France and Spain)

of innovations, leading, for instance, to semi-annual events in fashion and clothing, annual events in high-technology industries and bi-/tri-annual events in technology for traditional manufacturing industries (Golfetto 2004).

Importantly, the scheduling of individual exhibitions needs to take into account the dates of other trade shows in the same industry held around the world. This sometimes leads to a sophisticated system of balance and competition between global, international and national trade shows. In the scheduling of events, trade show organizers aim to give international buyers the opportunity to visit leading trade shows in their specific industry (Borghini et al. 2006; Power and Jansson 2008; Bathelt and Gibson 2013). At the same time, they want to enable exhibitors to contact different national and international markets, by exhibiting at respective different events.

Trade show dates are, however, sometimes also employed as a competitive tool by trade show organizers. Typically, the most important events, those at the top of an industry's hierarchy, pick their dates first. Minor events have to adapt and choose the 'second best' dates that remain available, based on customer preferences, or decide to cover slightly different products and market segments, which opens up different options for scheduling. In some cases, organizers pick dates that are partially overlapping with or that are immediately before those dates of rival events. The goal in such cases is to force exhibitors and visitors to make choices between events or to anticipate the presentation of innovations and devalue rival events and their specific knowledge ecologies.

IMPORT–EXPORT FUNCTIONS AND STAKEHOLDERS OF INTERNATIONAL TRADE SHOWS

Approximately 900 out a total of 6,900 events in Europe are international trade shows, but they are much more important both for trade and knowledge exchange than the majority of regional/national events (see Figure 3.2). International events are on average the largest ones, often involving thousands of exhibitors and sometimes hundreds of thousands of professional visitors. At the same time, they are specialized events where producers, distributors and professionals from the same industry meet. They account for approximately 40 percent of the total number of exhibitors and the total stand space at trade shows, and 35 percent of the total number of visitors. International events in Europe take place in the main manufacturing countries and within these in highly accessible cities that are often centered in traditional production areas. About 85 to 90 percent of these events are business-to-business shows, devoted to professional buyers. In comparison, national and regional events are quite widely distributed throughout Europe, with over 90 percent being business-to-consumer or mixed trade shows.

International business-to-business trade shows are events with substantial international participation, during which a large part of international trade linkages between European and non-European countries are initiated (Rosson and Seringhaus 1995; Golfetto 2004) and knowledge about production processes, trade channels, buyers' behaviors and so on are disseminated. However, these are not homogenous events. Large differences exist between different trade shows, depending on characteristics such as proximity to production areas or to consumption markets, involvement of leading firms, activity of the organizers and so on (Rinallo and Golfetto 2011; Bathelt et al. 2014). One of the main differentiating factors of trade shows is based on the geographic origin of exhibitors and visitors. This criterion highlights both the different orientation (import or export) and reach (from local to international)

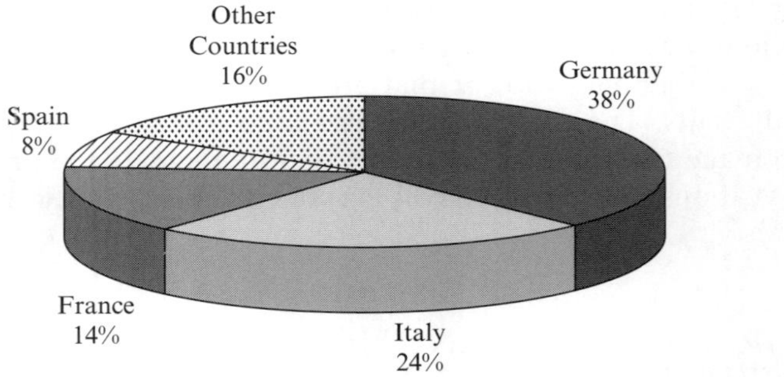

(a) International trade shows (900 events, 16.5 million square meters)

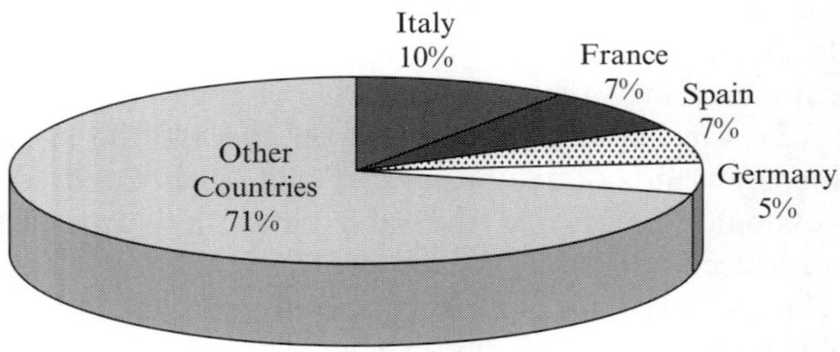

(b) National/regional trade shows (6,000 events, 25.5 million square meters)

Source: CERMES (2013a).

Figure 3.2 International and national/regional trade shows in Europe, 2012

of trade shows associated with different combinations of global–local exhibitors versus visitors. Four types of trade shows can be identified (see Figure 3.3):

1. *Local exchange trade shows* are attended by exhibitors and visitors from the same nation or region. These trade shows are now not very common in Europe, at least in business-to-business events, since local trade is carried out through commercial networks or routine interactions associated with permanent clusters or other forms of industrial networks. The large number of local trade shows that existed in Europe in the early stages of industrialization and even until the mid-to-late-20th century made sense when domestic markets were geographically fragmented.

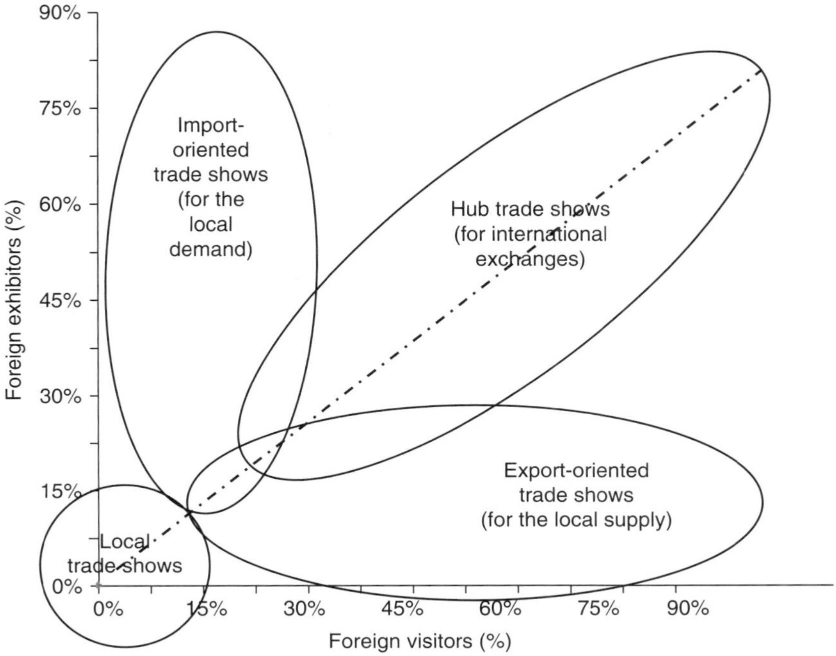

Source: Golfetto (2004).

Figure 3.3 A typology of trade shows based on exhibitor/visitor origin

2. *Export-oriented trade shows* are characterized by suppliers from the hosting area as exhibitors and the predominance of non-local buyers as visitors. These events support export activities of local manufacturers and have typically emerged as collective marketing projects for local production cores within fragmented industries such as furniture, textile, food and so on (CERMES 2012; Golfetto and Rinallo 2012; Bathelt et al. 2014). Such events can be viewed as 'for-the-local-supply' trade shows. Export-oriented trade shows operate at various geographical scales. At the regional level, most exhibitors originate from the immediate vicinity of the host region (e.g. a nearby industrial cluster), with only a minority from other regions or from abroad. At the national level, export-oriented trade shows draw most of their exhibitors from within the same country. This is usually the result of initiatives by national manufacturers associations that attract producers from different industrial clusters to a single national exhibition.

3. *Import-oriented trade shows* attract a large proportion of non-local producers as exhibitors, while most buyers originate from surrounding areas as visitors. These events are referred to as 'for-the-local-demand' trade shows. Typically, consumer shows belong to this category. Moreover, these trade shows – when devoted to professional buyers – represent the ones that are initially quite important in emerging economies, before national manufacturing industries are sufficiently developed (see Li, *this volume*). Import-oriented trade shows are frequently organized by organizations that also run exhibition centers. They are also supported by local governments which regard these exhibition centers as territorial marketing instruments that generate economic benefits in the local area related to the expenditures of exhibitors and visitors. With the increased adoption of neoliberal policies and the opening of the trade show business to international competition, many for-profit event organizers also organize import-oriented trade shows in Europe. Unlike export-oriented trade shows, import-oriented events welcome exhibitors regardless of their geographic origin: the larger the trade show, the greater its local economic impact. Similar to export-oriented trade shows, they operate at various geographic levels with regard to visitors: from regional (with most of the visitors originating from the region hosting the event) to national (with visitors from different regions within the same country).
4. *Hub trade shows* are events where most of the attendees, both exhibitors and visitors, originate from other countries. Events of this kind represent an advanced stage of trade show development and take place in cities with high international or intercontinental accessibility that are located centrally to a large group of manufacturers. This is the case, for example, for many German cities. At hub events, export and import functions take place simultaneously. Some European shows of this type may be considered as export-oriented events at the supranational level as they mainly attract exhibitors from the European Union, while simultaneously attracting visitors-buyers from other continents. Hub trade shows that are import-oriented at the supranational level allow suppliers from other continents to gain a commercial foothold in another continental market context. Many events in Europe have, at different times, acted as gateways to the western European market for manufacturers from across the world, especially from Asia (Rinallo and Golfetto 2011).

At present, the market space for true supranational hub trade shows is becoming tighter across many industrial fields. National hub trade shows have competed in the past to become mainstay events within the European Union. Very few have been able to become supranational events, forcing others to abandon any hopes for further expansion. With the emergence of newly industrialized countries and their trade shows, the global trade show business is developing a novel polycentric structure with several continental platforms (Bathelt et al. 2014). This involves each continental region developing their own import-based supranational trade shows related to the needs of the respective continental markets. As a consequence, European trade shows are likely to have less appeal for buyers from other continental areas in the future.

Within Europe, differences exist between countries and industry groups with respect to the dominant trade show type. Table 3.1 illustrates this for the four main trade show countries. It shows that the hub function of international shows is mainly concentrated in Germany – the largest European trade shows market – with international exhibitors mostly exceeding 50 percent and international visitors ranging from 20 to 45 percent. In the case of Italy – the second largest trade show market – we find both international shows with a primary import function (e.g. in the industry groups communications – office supplies, construction, industry – technology and health – environment) as well as shows that are mainly export-oriented (e.g. in the furniture industry group). In France, some industry groups focus on local demand shows (such as agricultural, sport and general fairs), while others are characterized by hub events (e.g. communications – office supplies and clothing – fashion). In Spain, the emphasis is mostly on import fairs.

These different structures and functions of international trade shows in the main European countries can partially be explained by the different types of dominant trade show stakeholders. In some cases, these are more oriented toward the support of national/regional industries (and are therefore more protectionist), while, in other cases, they are more focused on maximizing trade show revenues/service employment in the host area (and are thus more open to foreign exhibitors) (see Table 3.2). While investments in German venues, for example, have mainly been driven by the prospects of growth in the associated business tourism industry and the development of a regional trade show service economy, exhibition centers and events in Italy have focused on supporting local/regional (and later also national) manufacturing industries. Varying goals of trade show development and the diverse composition of stakeholders have generated different trade show configurations. In some cases, events have been oriented toward the needs of European demand and import activities, while, in others, the focus has been on supporting national production and export activities (Bathelt et al. 2014).

Table 3.1 Internationalization of trade shows in leading European countries by industry, 2009/2010

Industry group	GERMANY		ITALY		FRANCE		SPAIN	
	Share of foreign participants							
	Exhibitors	Visitors	Exhibitors	Visitors	Exhibitors	Visitors	Exhibitors	Visitors
Clothing – fashion	52.7%	34.5%	36.6%	36.3%	66.2%	48.0%	25.0%	3.8%
Agriculture	53.1%	15.3%	19.7%	10.1%	22.8%	3.7%	25.7%	8.1%
Food – catering	61.5%	33.1%	9.2%	7.7%	41.8%	19.6%	24.7%	11.7%
Furniture	74.6%	46.3%	23.6%	44.1%	43.6%	24.4%	32.4%	9.6%
Art – antiques	23.9%	1.6%	25.2%	0.6%	56.3%	0.0%	56.5%	0.7%
Commerce – services	28.2%	26.1%	17.4%	16.8%	58.6%	31.8%	14.6%	1.0%
Communications – office supplies	49.6%	9.4%	35.6%	6.3%	84.8%	71.3%	55.7%	0.9%
Construction	43.1%	25.8%	31.0%	17.4%	37.7%	17.3%	34.4%	9.0%
General (mixed industries)	57.2%	29.5%	11.3%	0.0%	17.9%	0.3%	52.3%	0.0%
Industry – technology	43.5%	26.5%	31.8%	15.7%	34.4%	13.6%	45.9%	8.6%
Gifts – toys	68.2%	37.9%	25.6%	13.2%	38.8%	41.4%	32.8%	2.2%
Health – environment	51.9%	21.7%	40.4%	19.4%	42.5%	28.2%	51.0%	2.9%
Sport – leisure	67.0%	21.8%	37.8%	3.7%	31.9%	1.0%	27.1%	3.6%
Transport	53.8%	17.9%	28.9%	7.9%	44.1%	6.1%	28.9%	0.3%
Total	53.7%	21.6%	28.2%	7.7%	41.3%	9.5%	33.4%	3.7%

Note: Only international events are included.

Source: CERMES (2013a)

Table 3.2 Trade show configurations and organizer stakes

Variable	Characteristics of trade shows	
	Export (for-the-local-supply) trade shows	Import (for-the-local-demand) trade shows
Exhibitors	Mostly local or domestic	Mostly foreign, from major supply countries
Visitors	Mostly foreign, from major demand countries	Mostly local or domestic
Locations	Close to production areas	Close to demand areas, in accessible cities
Typical organizers	Industry associations	Exhibition centers (supported by local governments) Private organizers
Organizer stake/approach	Protectionist Promotion of the local/national industry	Neutral Maximization of business tourism or organizer revenue

EVOLUTION OF TRADE SHOWS AND DIFFERENCES IN KNOWLEDGE EXCHANGE PRACTICES

One of the main functions of trade shows, which has recently received much attention, regards the circulation of knowledge about technology, customer behavior and marketing approaches (Bathelt and Schuldt 2008; Bathelt and Gibson 2013; Bathelt et al. 2014). At the heart of such knowledge exchanges have always been – and will continue to be – the presence of products, innovations and other artifacts shown by the exhibitors to the visitors of the events, along with the interaction between exhibitors-suppliers and visitors-buyers (and their respective technical staff). This has given rise to specific business and work communities (Wenger 1998; Rinallo et al. 2012) and led to the formation of important material practices. Trade show participants are able to inspect, touch or smell the products that are being presented, notice who is buying, engage in discussions with technicians and so on. These material practices reinforce cognitive processes and encourage dialogue between firms. Since these exchanges take place in a material context, where hundreds and sometimes thousands of exchanges take place simultaneously, an opportunity for collective sense-making is created. This enables participants to sharpen their view of the state of the industry and its trends and also encourages convergent interpretations regarding the future direction of the industry (Borghini et al. 2006; Rinallo et al. 2010; Rinallo and Golfetto 2011; Golfetto and Rinallo 2012).

Knowledge exchanges at trade shows are made possible in the first place by the exhibitors, who cover most of the cost of trade show organization by renting exhibition space. They need to achieve a return on their investments to satisfy their promotional or sales goals (Rinallo and Golfetto 2011). Exhibitors treat trade shows as a communication instrument, whereas the acquisition of knowledge is often considered as a by-product of the exhibition process. Organizers often pay attention to this aspect by encouraging vertical exchanges of knowledge between exhibitors-suppliers and visitors-buyers and by restricting the presence of atypical visitors (non-buyers) (Rinallo and Golfetto 2011). Nevertheless, in Europe the knowledge-exchange function has obtained an increasing recognition, both in academic conceptions (Bathelt and Schuldt 2008; Bathelt and Gibson 2013; Bathelt et al. 2014) and in trade show organizers' practices (Golfetto and Rinallo 2013), as an important consequence of the evolution of trade shows. First, by becoming more specialized and attracting more homogenous audiences, trade shows have become valuable meeting places for business and professional communities, beyond their mere commercial functions (Borghini et al. 2006). Second, the development of modern information technologies and especially the Internet has released trade shows from their prior function of providing basic pre-purchase information.

This has created space for more elaborate knowledge exchanges in the interests of both visitors and exhibitors. On the visitors' side, trade show participation is now more oriented toward the comprehension of market trends and the generation of new ideas, rather than making immediate purchases. These ideas are generated through intellectual and sensory stimulation, perceptions of the market climate, by contacts with extreme trends and from interaction with and perceptions of the behavior of others. In short, ideas flow from this vast sensory immersion that opens a window to understanding the future. In essence, visitors expose themselves to exhibitors' promotional activities to obtain professional knowledge. On the exhibitors' side, particularly in the context of the leading and most internationalized trade shows, many firms have adapted to the new demands of visitors by setting up stands that are geared toward the presentation of their skills and their ability to be a partner, instead of merely promoting product sales (Golfetto and Mazursky 2004; Golfetto and Gibbert 2006; Zerbini et al. 2007; Golfetto and Rinallo 2013; Zerbini and Borghini 2014).

As discussed below, the role of trade shows in knowledge circulation varies depending on the origin of their exhibitors and visitors and the reach of associated knowledge pipelines (i.e. local, national or international). Horizontal exhibitor–exhibitor and visitor–visitor interactions also come into play here, as knowledge exchanges are not restricted to vertical exchanges and are not solely for sale purposes (Bathelt et al. 2014; see Maskell, *this volume*; Li, *this volume*).

At the vertical level, *export-oriented trade shows* allow manufacturers to build pipelines with buyers from other territories, both nationally and internationally. At the horizontal level, the reach of these trade shows varies significantly. At one extreme, we find regional trade shows, which are often commercial offshoots of permanent industrial clusters. These trade shows are small and represent pivotal moments in the development of permanent clusters as the direct comparison with neighboring firms results in local producers making greater efforts to 'show off' their competencies and innovations to both their rivals and non-local buyers. Horizontal interactions and comparisons with local rivals occur in a more intensified form than in everyday exchanges, during which new products cannot be examined. Yet, fear of letting the 'enemy' (non-local suppliers) into such events may inhibit learning processes and limit innovation incentives, which normally arise from observing and comparing oneself to non-local competitors with different technological, organizational and market cultures.

When interacting with non-local visitors, exhibitors at these events benefit from developing more in-depth and long-term contacts. The manufacturers' operations may be located near the trade show center, thus generating opportunities for exchanges to continue at these sites. While this generates learning opportunities for exhibitors and visitors alike, it restricts opportunities for visitors to inspect product varieties that may be quite different and available in other markets. To receive a complete overview of international product offerings in an industry, visitors thus need to attend numerous other regional export trade shows. While the absence of non-local competitors protects exhibitors from undesired comparisons, it also reduces the overall information value for visitors.

National-level supply trade shows provide visitors and exhibitors with greater learning opportunities due to greater product variety than the more homogeneous local events. More specifically, this type of trade show reduces visitor knowledge acquisition costs and enables exhibitors to observe and compare their products with those of their national competitors from different industrial clusters. The establishment of horizontal and vertical knowledge pipelines at a global level, however, only occurs at trade shows that are able to attract exhibitors from many different countries. Such export-oriented hub events create a knowledge environment that is much richer than that in normal export-oriented shows. Exhibitors can observe and compare themselves with other participating firms adopting similar strategies based on the quality, creativity and innovation of their respective production contexts, thereby ensuring robust processes of horizontal learning. Furthermore, by aggregating a large number of manufacturers, these shows attract visitors from across the world – beyond what could be achieved by a national- or district-level supply trade show.

Import-oriented trade shows allow exhibiting firms to build knowledge pipelines with customers from a specific geographical market (local or national). At the horizontal level, these events allow exhibitors to observe and compare themselves with competitors from various countries that are interested in serving the same regional/national market. The reach of this trade show type can vary. Over time, there has been a notable increase in the number of trade shows with a regional/national focus. Exhibitors use these events when they have reached an advanced stage in international development and attend import-oriented trade shows in larger or developing geographical markets. Due to the large number of different national markets, firms that attend such national/regional events rationalize their participation by investing less in individual shows (e.g. having smaller booths, fewer products and less technical personnel) or by attending such events only indirectly through agents or distributors (i.e. wholesalers or importers). Consequently, the promotional knowledge exhibitors release at these events mainly involves commercial information regarding product range, prices, delivery dates and so on. As a result, knowledge flows are more limited than at large hub trade shows where manufacturers participate directly, present their latest innovations, send research and development experts and discuss future programs (see Li, *this volume*). From the visitors' perspective, import events enable local buyers to learn about product and alternative solutions from a selection of international suppliers interested in interacting with them. While the resulting knowledge exchanges are more limited than at international events, the reduced costs of participating in regional/national events partially compensate for this.

Import-oriented supranational trade shows enable exhibitors to observe and compare themselves with a broad set of foreign competitors. The main difference between these exhibitions and export-oriented hub events lies in the fact that the exhibiting firms are more heterogeneous. The exhibitor selection process carried out by the organizers is less rigid because they prefer large events that maximize revenues and local/regional economic impacts. Horizontally, exhibitors find themselves dealing with competitors that have both similar and dissimilar strategies in terms of their market focus, manufacturing processes, technological/raw material basis, product quality, innovation and/or price level. Vertically, visitors can access information about a broad range of products, solutions and suppliers, as well as select the best purchase options. For both exhibitors and visitors, there is generally great potential for knowledge cross-fertilization at these trade shows.

On the negative, the large attendance and limited amount of time spent visiting these shows sometimes generates a sense of discomfort among participants. This pertains to the superficial nature of some of the contacts made, as well as a general sense of lost opportunities. The physical fatigue and sensory and information overload seen at smaller trade shows (Borghini et al. 2006; Rinallo et al. 2010) occur here at a higher and more intensified level. This is especially true when comparing these events to niche trade shows, which focus on specific technology fields or market segments.

All of these aspects need to be seen in combination with the important role trade show organizers sometimes have in the knowledge circulation processes during events. In addition to determining the scale, reach and variety of products and markets at trade shows, organizers use a large number of strategies to increase or control knowledge release and acquisition among trade show participants (see Table 3.3). These strategies include, for example, involving leaders, organizing special exhibits that focus on innovation themes, holding technical or socializing events, building knowledge of the sector or mobilizing broader processes for the affirmation of product styles and technologies. All of these activities increase knowledge circulation, both in terms of individual and collective interactions. This makes trade shows more appealing for participants and stronger in the competition among similar industry events organized by different organizers with different territorial interests. Organizers can, however, adopt strategies that limit knowledge access to typical visitors (buyers), for example by admitting only those visitors who are able to demonstrate that they made purchases in preceding years or by accepting that exhibitors set up closed stand designs accessible through invitation only (Rinallo and Golfetto 2011).

COMPETITION BETWEEN INDUSTRIES AND CITIES

In Europe, the development of specialized trade shows and the availability of new, modern exhibition centers have brought together producers belonging to different clusters and production regions to single venues. Due to the great number and variety of products presented and the concentrated promotional expenses, the attendance at trade shows has offered national industries higher visibility and has attracted more visitors from abroad, especially from non-European markets. In some cases, trade shows have even been able to facilitate collaboration between national

Table 3.3 Knowledge-based strategies of trade show organizers

Strategy	Associated activities
Marking the boundaries of the temporary cluster	• Selection of the actors allowed to participate in the temporary cluster according to ○ Geographic origin (import/export trade shows with a local to global reach) ○ Product assortment and visitor segment (general/niche trade shows)
Improving knowledge release and acquisition	• Active search for, and visibility of, market leaders and innovative leader producers • Organizing market-sensitive exhibition layout solutions • Highlighting key innovations through innovation areas • Organizing technical seminars • Organizing social events
Hindering undesired knowledge spillovers	• Offering incentives to buyers and restrictions for non-buyers • Photo ban • Intellectual property protection measures
Investing in new market or technological knowledge development	• Investing in research and development activities • Mobilizing actors to generate new relevant knowledge and to support specific achievements • Supporting the affirmation of specific styles and technologies
Building culture of the industry	• Presenting the historical roots of the sector • Educating the market about differences in the functional and symbolic quality of products

Source: Adapted from Rinallo and Golfetto (2011).

industries that were traditionally fragmented and in competition with each other, thanks to the mediation of trade associations (Golfetto and Rinallo 2012).

However, competition between European leading manufacturing countries and between local clusters within national environments has never stopped. Rivalry has been particularly prevalent in countries where trade shows were viewed as tools for the promotion of the local/national industry (i.e. as export events) and where industry associations have preferred to hold separate events for each country, instead of joining forces and organizing pan-European events (Golfetto and Rinallo 2012). Indeed, national-level trade shows offer various advantages to local firms, including greater visibility, reduced exhibition costs and possibilities to interact with buyers inside their premises (Bathelt et al. 2014). Additional benefits include the support of local governments, better control of the events and the possibility to establish protectionist policies.

As a consequence, the large number of international and national events that still exist in each industry is only partially a reflection of trade show specialization. To some extent, it is also the result of competition between different national industries and local industrial clusters in search of separate visibility and preferential contacts with non-local partners. While internal competition may sometimes be advantageous, it can also harm the national industry. This is, for example, the case in Italian clothing textile trade shows, which found it hard to overcome rivalry between local clusters and therefore has long remained separate in different locations. As a whole, it appears that the separation of Italian events has weakened the Italian clothing textile industry, leading to a loss of visitors to competing French events (Golfetto and Rinallo 2012). In a few other industries, national trade associations have been able to overcome rivalry and support a single European-level event, thus contrasting the development of competing trade shows (e.g. Première Vision in France and Salone del Mobile in Italy; see Bathelt et al. 2014).

In addition to the rivalry between local/national industries, competition also exists between the numerous exhibition complexes in major European countries (Rubalcaba-Bermejo and Cuadrado-Roura 1995), especially after a major building boom of large exhibition centers since the 1980s and 1990s. This boom was largely driven by a desire to generate local/urban revenues from related business tourism and strengthen the production image of the host region (Golfetto 1991; Golfetto and Rinallo 2000; Fondazione Fiera Milano 2001; 2006; AUMA 2012a; CCI Paris Ile-de-France 2012). As a consequence, exhibition capacity in Europe has continued to grow significantly in the 2000s (UFI 2011; 2012a; 2012b), despite the fact that demand appears basically saturated (AUMA 2012b; CERMES 2013a; 2013b). This has generated pressure for the creation of new shows and the replication of existing ones in other exhibition centers – to a point where this development goes against the interests of the producers, who feel forced to take part in a larger number of events than necessary. The proliferation of venues has also resulted in a waste of public resources as in many cases the venue-building investments were not economically sustainable and the local catchment basin too small. As a consequence, some exhibition complexes have had to close down across

Europe, with tremendous losses after having hosted only few events for many years.

FROM LOCAL TO GLOBAL COMPETITION BETWEEN TRADE SHOWS

More recently, the challenges facing European manufacturing, together with increased intercontinental competition, have stimulated an inversion of the trend toward trade show fragmentation and led to a fast reorganization of the entire industry. On the one hand, the economic recession has led to a drop in the number of exhibitors at trade shows (up to 20–25 percent over the period 2008–2012), particularly in regions with restricted intercontinental accessibility such as some smaller cities in Italy, Spain and France. This tendency has been less visible, however, in central European countries like Germany, and in major trade show cities such as Paris and Milan, which continue to appeal strongly to intercontinental visitors (AUMA 2012a; CERMES 2013a).

On the other hand, the growth of manufacturing in other parts of the world has led to the development of 3–4 continental trade show platforms in many industries, with major events in Europe, North and South America, China and Southeast Asia and/or India and the Middle East. This has resulted in a decrease in the number of non-European visitors at many European shows, as well as in budget cut-backs by European exhibitors that now need to devote parts of their overall trade show budget to non-European shows. At the same time, the multiplication of trade show platforms makes it increasingly difficult for international visitors to attend more than one or two trade shows in each continent. The consequence of these trends is that a geographical concentration of European international-level events may be emerging, potentially generating more aggressive competition between venues and events in the future (AUMA 2012a; Golfetto and Rinallo 2013).

The development of a new world trade show system also marks a departure from the past, when the leading trade shows (those that revealed the trends of the entire industry) were mainly concentrated in Europe and, to a smaller extent, in the US. The emerging new global trade show system reflects the shifts in global industrial demand. Accordingly, exhibitors now regularly go to present their products and innovations in new and growing trade shows located in new demand areas (such as in the BRIC countries). Parallel to these trends, European international trade shows may be partially losing in importance as main forums of innovation for many manufacturing industries. Additionally, export-oriented trade shows may be losing appeal for European exhibitors. In the past, these events (especially in Italy) were conceived as collective commercial platforms, where local firms that were unable to approach extra-European markets on their own presented their products to attract visitor-buyers from the rest of the world. Today, as a consequence of the restructuring of global supply chains, the trade show system is becoming increasingly polycentric and the different continental regions create their own shows (Golfetto and Rinallo 2013).

Deprived of their export-oriented shows, many small-sized European firms may suffer a lack of visibility in the future. This future world order of trade shows will force European events to define their rhythm and timing according to the main events in other continents. In terms of long-term trends, it appears that manufacturing industries in Europe will be concentrating their trade show activity to one or two intercontinental events that are able to attract non-European visitors to inspect the entire European product offering. Other trade shows will necessarily have to serve new functions and may be left to serve local/national markets as import shows. Faced with these changes, many European trade show organizers have intensified their activities and investments in non-European markets (AUMA 2012a). This serves the interests of national exhibition centers and organizers and provides the conditions for exhibitors to shift or swap activities between different world regions.

The pioneers in this internationalization trend were German trade show organizing firms, which launched their first events outside of Europe during the 1980s (see Rinallo and Golfetto, *this volume*). In recent years, many organizers from other countries have adopted similar strategies. While such multinational activities originally covered a limited share of the organizers' total turnover (about 5 to 15 percent), this share has increased, especially due to the strong involvement in Asian markets (sometimes up to 20 to 35 percent of total turnover of European organizers; see AUMA 2012a; 2012b). Unlike German organizers, which enjoyed first-mover advantages and invested directly in the creation of new trade shows, other organizers investing in emerging economies today face a crowded event market. New investments by European organizers (particularly smaller ones) often aim to create joint ventures with local organizers, acquire exhibition areas, and rent them out to European exhibitors.

A threat of such practices may be the resulting 'fragmented' competitive behavior, which may create 'battles' among non-European trade shows driven by European organizers. The drive for separate visibility of some of the organizers produces multiple joint ventures and participation in non-European shows, with the outcome being that groups of European producers take part in different shows in the same sector and country, under the banner of different exhibition organizer groups. This feeds the 'battle of the venues' originally started in Europe and now exported to the new trade show countries.

CONCLUSION

This chapter has aimed to trace the evolution of trade shows in Europe, paying particular attention to their collective marketing and knowledge dissemination functions, and to highlight key developments over the past half century. As history may sometimes repeat itself, we conclude by highlighting key lessons that can be learned from this European experience and that could be of interest to trade show organizers, venues and local and national governments in the Asia-Pacific region.

Today, the trade fair ecologies of many Asian countries, in particular – but not only – China, are characterized by fast growth processes that are in stark contrast with stage maturity, stagnation or decline faced by many European trade shows. Growth, however, may not last forever. The adoption of a life-cycle approach that recognizes that phases of maturity and possibly stagnation may follow the initial growth phase of trade show activity can help to exploit opportunities in the short- and medium-term, while, at the same time, plan for challenges in the future. Had European players adopted a similar approach, some of the current difficulties could have been dealt with long before and in a better way.

In this chapter, we have emphasized that trade shows differ based on the geographic origin of exhibitors and visitors (i.e. import-oriented versus export-oriented) and by reach (from local to international). The typology of trade shows suggested (see Figure 3.3) can also be applied to Asia-Pacific trade shows to provide a fine-grained view of their structure and role in the global knowledge economy (Bathelt et al. 2014; Li, *this volume*). At the macro-level, the analysis of economic specialization tendencies of trade shows in specific countries can help policy makers and local governments to manage the complex relationships between trade shows and their underlying industries. As shown elsewhere (Bathelt et al. 2014), trade show specialization both reflects and impacts territorial specialization. By developing virtuous relationships between local clusters and national industries, on the one hand, and national trade show systems, on the other hand, trade shows can impact local economic development, export promotion, and technological and market knowledge circulation.

As examples of European shows demonstrate, however, the proliferation of multiple trade shows serving the same industry in a country can become dysfunctional and potentially damage that country's position in the global trade show system. Data from Asia shows a 'building boom' in terms of venues and an increasing number of trade fairs (see Bathelt and Zeng, *this volume*; Jin and Weber, *this volume*) referring to the same industries and product groups, which in some cases may not have a clear market or only replicate existing events. Under these circumstances, the early success of some of these events and venues will not necessarily continue in the future. Economic sustainability and longer-term strategies should be key concerns of the trade show organizers, organizations running exhibition complexes and their stakeholders.

Inside every industry, a hierarchy of trade shows exists ranging from the top events unanimously recognized as the most important in the field to lower-ranking events of more limited scope and relevance. The case of Europe illustrates that trade show hierarchies can be quite dynamic and once-leading events can lose much of their importance when challenged by more aggressive and innovative competitors. Periods of stability are thus followed by periods of discontinuity and the development of 'trade show wars' surrounding exhibitors, rented surfaces and visitors. Some of these wars can be domestic (e.g. between Madrid and Barcelona), while others are international (e.g. between Milan and Paris and between Paris and Frankfurt). There is no doubt that the Asia-Pacific region will also experience such 'trade fair wars' in the future, which can be more or less dysfunctional for the underlying national industries.

Finally, this analysis also highlights the role of trade show organizers. As the functions of trade shows evolve, some organizers have adopted strategies to distinctly develop knowledge-rich places where firms and professionals have a multitude of learning opportunities during business-to-business events (see Table 3.3). In Europe, organizers have typically underinvested in such aspects. We thus still find a situation in which the 'container' (i.e. general trade show layout) often receives more attention than the 'content', typically taken care of by exhibitors (e.g. showcase of innovation, involvement of technical staff). The adoption of knowledge-based strategies for trade shows, which can support the development of a competitive advantage over rival events, requires financial and human resources to develop useful knowledge contents for participating actors. This is another aspect that organizers in the Asia-Pacific region may want to pay attention to.

REFERENCES

AUMA – Association of the German Trade Fair Industry (2012a) *German Trade Fair Industry: Key Figures 2012*, Berlin: AUMA.

AUMA (2012b) *German Trade Fair Industry: Review 2012*, Berlin: AUMA.

Bathelt, H. and Gibson, R. (2013) 'Learning in "organized anarchies": Technological search processes and knowledge flows at international trade fairs', *Regional Studies*, 47: doi: 10.1080/00343404.2013.782591.

Bathelt, H., Golfetto, F. and Rinallo, D. (2014) *Trade Shows in the Globalizing Knowledge Economy*, Oxford: Oxford University Press.

Bathelt, H. and Schuldt, N. (2008) 'Between luminaires and meat grinders: International trade fairs as temporary clusters', *Regional Studies*, 42: 853–868.

Becattini, G. and Rullani, E. (1996) 'Local systems and global connections: The role of knowledge', in International Institute for Labour Studies (eds) *Research Series, 103*, Geneva: International Institute for Labour Studies, 159–174.

Borghini, S., Golfetto, F. and Rinallo, D. (2006) 'Ongoing search among industrial buyers', *Journal of Business Research*, 59: 1151–1159.

CCI Paris Ile-de-France (2012) *Tourisme d'affaire a Paris-Ile-de France*, Paris: CCI Paris Ile-de-France. Online. Available HTTP: <http://www.etudes.cci-paris-idf.fr/telecharger?lien=sites%2Fwww.etudes.cci-paris-idf.fr%2Ffiles%2Fupload%2Fpublications%2Fetudes-salons-1303.pdf> (5 October 2013).

CERMES – Research Centre on Markets and Industrial Sectors (2012) *Fiere e Marketing Collettivo. Mezzo Secolo di Storie Tra Distretti Industriali e Distretti Commerciali (Trade Shows and Collective Marketing. Half a Century of Histories about Industrial and Commercial Clusters)*, unpublished research report, Milan: Bocconi University.

CERMES (2013a) *Trade Show Observatory*, Database of European trade show activity, Milan: Bocconi University.

CERMES (2013b) *Annual Report on the Italian Trade Shows Industry, 1990–2010*, unpublished research report, Milan: Bocconi University.

European Commission (2008) *Small Business Act for Europe (SBA)*, Brussels: European Commission. Online. Available HTTP: <http://ec.europa.eu/enterprise/policies/sme/documents/sba/index_en.htm#h2-1> (5 October 2013).

European Commission (2009) *European Business: Facts and Figures, 2009*, Brussels: European Commission. Online. Available HTTP: <http://epp.eurostat.ec.europa.eu/cache/ITY_OFFPUB/KS-BW-09-001-01/EN/KS-BW-09-001-01-EN.PDF> (5 October 2013).

Fondazione Fiera Milano (2001) *Le Ricadute Economiche dell'Attività di Fiera Milano sul Territorio (The Economic Benefits of Fiera Milano in the Territory)*, Milan: Guerini.

Fondazione Fiera Milano (2006) *Impatto Fiera. Imprese e Professioni Intorno al Polo Espositivo di Rho-Pero (The Fair Impact. Firms and Professions around the Exhibition Centre of Rho-Pero)*, Milan: Fiera Milano Edizioni.

Golfetto, F. (1988) *Il Sistema Fieristico Internazionale (The International Trade Fair Industry)*, Milan: Angeli.

Golfetto F. (1991) *L'Impatto Economico delle Manifestazioni Fieristiche (The Economic Impact of Trade Shows)*, Milan: EGEA.

Golfetto F. (2000) 'Reti di imprese e meta-organizzatori: Il ruolo delle fiere (Firm networks and meta-organizers: The trade shows role)', *Sinergie*, 18: 189–211.

Golfetto, F. (2004) *Fiere e Comunicazione. Strumenti per le Imprese e il Territorio (Trade Fairs and Communication. Tools for Business, Venues and Host Areas)*, Milan: EGEA.

Golfetto, F. and Gibbert, M. (2006) 'Marketing competencies and the sources of

customer value in business markets', *Industrial Marketing Management*, 35 (8): 904–912.
Golfetto, F. and Mazursky, D. (2004) 'Competence-based marketing', *Harvard Business Review*, 51 (November): 26.
Golfetto, F. and Rinallo, D. (2000) 'L'immagine del territorio e le manifestazioni fieristiche: Una verifica empirica (Trade fairs and host areas' image: An empirical test)', in E. Valdani and F. Ancarani (eds) *Strategie di Marketing del Territorio (Place Marketing Strategies)*, Milan: EGEA, 311–321.
Golfetto, F. and Rinallo, D. (2012) 'Competition and collective marketing: A history of the European textile industry trade shows', in S. Borghini, A. Carù, F. Golfetto, S. Pace, D. Rinallo, L. Visconti and F. Zerbini (eds) *Prodotto, Consumatore e Politiche di Mercato Quarant'Anni Dopo. Scritti in Onore di Stefano Podestà (Product, Consumer and Market Policies Forty Years Later. Writings in Honor of Stefano Podestà)*, Milan: EGEA, 369–394.
Golfetto, F. and Rinallo, D. (2013) 'Trade show events, from live to digital: Towards the development of new competencies', in Fondazione Fiera Milano (ed.) *Exhibitions in Years 2.0: Between Internalization and Local Development*, Milan: EGEA, 119–153.
Pine, B. J. II and Gilmore, J. H. (1998) 'Welcome to the experience economy', *Harvard Business Review*, 76: 87–105.
Power, D. and Jansson, J. (2008) 'Cyclical clusters in global circuits: Overlapping spaces in furniture trade fairs', *Economic Geography*, 84: 423–448.
Pyke, F., Becattini, G. and Sengenberger, W. (eds) (1990) *Industrial Districts and Inter-firm Co-operation in Italy*, Geneva: International Institute for Labour Studies.
Rinallo, D. (2011) *Event Marketing*, Milan: EGEA.
Rinallo, D., Borghini, S. and Golfetto, F. (2010) 'Exploring visitor experiences at trade shows', *Journal of Business and Industrial Marketing*, 25: 249–258.
Rinallo, D., Borghini, S. and Golfetto, F. (2012) 'The influence of occupational communities on buying behavior', in S. Borghini, A. Carù, F. Golfetto, S. Pace, D. Rinallo, L. Visconti and F. Zerbini (eds) *Prodotto, Consumatore e Politiche di Mercato Quarant'Anni Dopo. Scritti in Onore di Stefano Podestà (Product, Consumer and Market Policies Forty Years Later. Writings in Honor of Stefano Podestà)*, Milan: EGEA, 369–394.
Rinallo, D. and Golfetto, F. (2006) 'Representing markets: The shaping of fashion trends by French and Italian fabric companies', *Industrial Marketing Management*, 35: 856–869.
Rinallo, D. and Golfetto, F. (2011) 'Exploring the knowledge strategies of temporary cluster organizers: A longitudinal study of the EU fabric industry trade shows (1986–2006)', *Economic Geography*, 87: 453–476.
Rosson, P. J. and Seringhaus, F. H. R. (1995) 'Visitor and exhibitor interaction at industrial trade fairs', *Journal of Business Research*, 32: 81–90.
Rubalcaba-Bermejo, L. and Cuadrado-Roura, J. R. (1995) 'Urban hierarchies and territorial competition in Europe: Exploring the role of fairs and exhibitions', *Urban Studies*, 32: 379–400.
Schmitt, B. H. (1999) *Experiential Marketing: How to Get Customers to SENSE, FEEL, THINK, ACT, RELATE to Your Company and Brands*, New York: The Free Press.
UFI – The Global Association of the Exhibition Industry (2011) *The World Map*

of Exhibitions Venues 2011, Paris: UFI. Online. Available HTTP: <http://www.ufi.org/> (15 July 2013).

UFI (2012a) *The Global Exhibition Industry Statistics*, Paris: UFI. Online. Available HTTP: <http://www.ufi.org/> (15 July 2013).

UFI (2012b) *Eurofair Statistics 2012*, Paris: UFI. Online. Available HTTP: <http://www.ufi.org/> (15 July 2013).

Wenger, E. (1998) *Communities of Practice: Learning, Meaning, and Identity*, Cambridge: Cambridge University Press.

Zerbini, F. and Borghini, S. (2014) 'Release capacity in the vendor selection process', *Journal of Business Research*, 67: doi: 10.1016/jbusres.2014.06.008.

Zerbini, F., Golfetto, F. and Gibbert, M. (2007) 'Marketing of competence: Exploring the resource-based content of value-for-customers through a case study analysis', *Industrial Marketing Management*, 36: 784–798.

4. Internationalization and knowledge-based strategies of European trade show organizers in Asia: the case of Messe Frankfurt

Diego Rinallo and Francesca Golfetto

INTRODUCTION

Various observers have highlighted the state of maturity (and, possibly, decline) faced by the European trade show industry and the heightened growth of trade shows in China and elsewhere in Asia (Bathelt et al. 2014; Golfetto and Rinallo, *this volume*; Jin and Weber, *this volume*, Bathelt et al., *this volume*). These two phenomena are interdependent for a variety of reasons. First, with the decline of manufacturing in Europe and the accelerated growth in Asia, the number of potential exhibitors in the catchment basins of European trade shows decreases, whereas the market potential of Asian events increases. Second, to exploit the commercial opportunities in high-growth Asian markets, European producers need to exhibit at Asian trade shows. This causes a reduction in the promotional budgets allocated to trade show participation in Europe, where commercial presence is more established and other promotional instruments can be employed to maintain relationships with buyers (e.g. individual events and existing sales force). In contrast, the budget for Asian events increases. Third, Asian buyers have more limited incentives to travel to European trade shows as a result, since they can see much of the European offering at local events.

As a consequence, the outlook of European trade shows for the future is not optimistic. There are, however, at least two strategies trade show organizations (organizers) can implement to resist decline and escape local economic dependence (Cox and Mair 1988) from European firms' trade show expenditures. The first entails the attraction of non-European exhibitors (from Asia and elsewhere), who can at least partially compensate for the losses in rented exhibition surfaces from European firms. The second (and more radical) strategy for trade show organizers is the exploration of overseas market opportunities through foreign direct investments that create new events. From the perspective of organizers, the trade show industry is not geographically bound as in the case of venues. Many trade show organizers, in fact, manage their activities as multinational firms.

The goal of this chapter is to analyze the international expansion of the German trade show organizer 'Messe Frankfurt GmbH', which is today one of the top ten trade show organizers in Asia (UFI 2011). Messe Frankfurt has a global portfolio of more than 100 events, most of which are outside of Germany, in various industry groups, including consumer goods, textiles and textile technology, mechanical engineering and entertainment. This chapter focuses on textile events and particularly investigates the evolution of Interstoff Asia in Hong Kong between 1987 and 2013, which was the first trade show organized by Messe Frankfurt outside of Germany. As shown below, Messe Frankfurt built its competitive advantage by exporting some of its knowledge-based strategies that were successfully developed in Europe to Asia. From a political economy perspective, this chapter helps to identify potentials and challenges when transferring trade show concepts from Europe to developing contexts in the Asia-Pacific region.

The structure of this chapter is as follows. First, recent literature on the knowledge-based view of trade shows is reviewed, which constitutes the theoretical basis of our study. This literature conceives trade shows as central places in the global knowledge economy and provides a starting point for the analysis of the relationships between trade shows and their host areas, the knowledge geographies constituted by these events, and the strategies available to organizers in shaping exhibitor and visitor learning. We continue with a methodological note regarding the data sources used and analytical procedures conducted. The main part presents our research findings about Messe Frankfurt and its international expansion, with a specific focus on the clothing textile industry and Interstoff Asia. We conclude by critically discussing our findings and, more generally, their contribution to scholarship on trade shows in the Asia-Pacific region.

MARKET AND KNOWLEDGE EXCHANGES AT INTERNATIONAL TRADE SHOWS

Trade shows are traditionally conceived as temporary markets where suppliers (i.e. exhibitors) meet buyers. In economic terms, these events are transaction-cost-reducing 'institutions' (Florio 1994) that lubricate the economic system by facilitating the meeting of supply and demand. By bringing together, in the same place and at the same time, a large number of exhibitors (suppliers/producers), trade shows provide a cost-efficient way for buyers (users) to identify and locate potential suppliers. Industrial buyers consider trade shows as important sources of information, particularly in the central phases of the purchase process (Gopalakrishna and Lilien 1995; Rosson and Seringhaus 1995). Conventional marketing studies provide industrial marketers – preoccupied with the 'exorbitant cost of exhibiting' – with suggestions on how to make the most of these promotional tools and maximize returns on investments (for a review, see Borghini et al. 2006).

Despite this emphasis on market exchanges and promotional goals, marketing studies also show that exhibitors and visitors learn from each other at trade shows (Ling-Yee 2006; Bettis-Outland et al. 2010) – sometimes through 'ongoing search' processes not associated with short-term purchases (Borghini et al. 2006; Rinallo et al. 2010). It is especially through recent work in economic geography that, building on a knowledge-based view of the firm and the industrial cluster, learning processes at trade shows have been put in the spotlight. From this perspective, these events are conceived as relational spaces that provide participants with opportunities for observing and interacting with geographically distant actors (Maskell et al. 2006; Bathelt and Schuldt 2008; 2010; Bathelt and Gibson 2009; Maskell 2014). These events can therefore be seen as temporary clusters, because they enable 'knowledge-exchanging mechanisms similar to those found in permanent clusters, albeit in a short-lived and intensified form' (Maskell et al. 2006, p. 999).

Since many visitors attend trade shows to satisfy broader learning needs, and not (or not only) for making purchases from exhibitors (Borghini et al. 2006), temporary clusters and temporary markets need to be viewed as two sides of the same coin (Bathelt et al. 2014). Trade show operations are enabled by the promotional expenditures sustained by exhibitors to contact customers and potential buyers (Rinallo and Golfetto 2011). They are thus designed to facilitate vertical interactions between suppliers/producers (exhibitors) and buyers/users (typical visitors). While other interactions are clearly important, they sometimes occur as side-effects when they are not actively blocked by exhibitors, who can, for example, adopt a 'closed' stand design with limited controlled access to protect themselves from imitation and counterfeiting. Along the same lines, organizers may adopt photo bans and other measures to protect exhibitors' intellectual property rights (Rinallo and Golfetto 2011).

When analyzing vertical buyer–seller interactions, a useful way to make sense of differences in the knowledge environments constituted by trade shows is by jointly taking into consideration exhibitor and visitor origin (Golfetto and Rinallo, *this volume*; see also Golfetto 2004; Rinallo and

Golfetto 2011; for a perspective that also focuses on production-related learning, see Bathelt et al. 2014 and Li 2014). According to this conception, events attracting only exhibitors and visitors from nearby areas (i.e. local exchanges trade shows) do not enable the establishment of knowledge pipelines with geographically distant actors. Export-oriented trade shows enable the establishment of relationships between local suppliers and foreign customers; whereas import-oriented trade shows facilitate interaction between local customers and foreign manufacturers. Finally, hub trade shows are cosmopolitan places where actors from around the world convene, resulting in the establishment of truly global knowledge pipelines.

In prior research, we have intensively investigated the knowledge-based practices that organizers can employ to 'enrich' the knowledge opportunities provided by trade shows, as our study of leading European trade shows in the clothing fabric industry illustrates (Rinallo and Golfetto 2011). Recently, thanks to empirical material from an extended sample of industries, we have proposed in Bathelt et al. (2014) that trade show organizers can enrich exhibitor and visitor learning in many ways: (i) by carefully selecting participants in their temporary clusters; (ii) by improving knowledge release and acquisition (e.g. by attracting market leaders and innovative producers, organizing market-sensitive exhibition layout solutions, staging innovation or trend areas, and organizing seminars and other special events); (iii) by hindering undesired knowledge spillovers (e.g. by restricting access to non-buyers, banning photos and taking intellectual property protection measures); (iv) by investing in the development of new knowledge (e.g. by investing in research and development activities, mobilizing actors to generate new relevant knowledge and supporting the affirmation of specific product designs); and (v) by 'building culture' with respect to the industry (e.g. by emphasizing the historical roots of the sector and educating the market about differences in the functional and symbolic quality of products).

Some trade show organizers today are multinational corporations that organize events worldwide. They benefit from the fact, as studies have shown, that the leveraging of knowledge from geographically disparate subsidiaries can be an important source of competitive advantage (e.g. Kogut and Zander 1993; Yang et al. 2008). In our study, we focus on analyzing a German trade show organizer that acquired industry-specific competences and developed knowledge-based practices in the context of the more advanced European trade show market. When leveraging such competences in Asia, Messe Frankfurt had a competitive advantage compared with local organizers. By following the deployment of knowledge-based practices from mature to developing markets, our study shows how multinational trade show organizers such as Messe Frankfurt have contributed to the development of trade shows in Asia and, as a consequence, have exerted a positive influence on the development of Asian industries. In this chapter, we aim to contribute to a better understanding of trade show organizers and their little-studied international expansion strategies which provide important insights into the role trade shows play in the global knowledge economy.

METHODOLOGY

The data used in our study originates from a variety of sources, which we integrated in our attempt to reconstruct a narrative of Messe Frankfurt's international expansion process. This includes: (i) news articles from trade publications covering the textile industry in the period from 1987 to 2013 based on a systematic search of the electronic database Factiva using 'Interstoff Asia' as the keyword (overall, we retrieved 542 English articles); (ii) Messe Frankfurt's annual reports from 2002 to 2013, which contain trade show statistics and general information about the firm's history, internationalization strategies and branding practices; and (iii) press releases, brochures and other promotional documents regarding Interstoff Asia, available online, for the period from 2008 to 2013.

Our data gathering efforts resulted in a rich collection of stories and figures about Messe Frankfurt, the firm's events and their exhibitors and visitors, which we analyzed in a number of stages. First, we employed the data found to make sense of the firm's internationalization strategy with reference to the Asian market and analyzed Messe Frankfurt's textile trade show portfolio and its evolution over time. Next, we used Rinallo and Golfetto's (2011) categorization of trade shows to identify the import/export functions of the events. Based on news articles and promotional material, we then reconstructed a time line of key developments related to the events and the knowledge-based strategies adopted by Messe Frankfurt. We also took note of external threats and opportunities in the economic and political context that affected the development of the respective events. In this stage of the analysis, we employed a narrative strategy involving the reconstruction of a detailed story from raw data (Langley 1999).

Before presenting the findings of this research, the next section provides a summary of prior research on Interstoff Frankfurt (Golfetto 2000; 2004; Rinallo et al. 2006; Rinallo and Golfetto 2006; 2011; Golfetto and Rinallo 2008; 2012; Bathelt et al. 2014), with background information about

Messe Frankfurt and the trade show – which no longer exists – that gave Interstoff Asia its name.

INTERSTOFF FRANKFURT: BIRTH AND DEATH OF A FLAGSHIP FAIR

Messe Frankfurt GmbH was established in 1907 to manage the newly built Frankfurt exhibition venue, the 'Festhalle' (today, hall number 2 in Frankfurt's exhibition complex; see Messe Frankfurt 2014a). Frankfurt has been an important trade fair city since at least the 12th century (Holtfrerich 1999) and, at the end of the 19th century, it hosted various agricultural and industrial exhibitions scattered across various venues. These venues were, however, too small to host very large events. After the First World War, the city financially supported the construction of additional exhibition halls around Festhalle and, in 1919, the first Frankfurt International Trade Fair (named 'Internationale Einfuhrmesse' or International Import Fair) was held and attracted more than 3,000 exhibitors on a surface of 16,500 square meters (Messe Frankfurt 2014b). Trade fair activities in Frankfurt were severely affected by the economic crisis starting in 1929 and, subsequently, the Second World War, when much of Festhalle and the surrounding exhibition grounds were destroyed. In 1946, the reconstruction of Frankfurt's trade fair infrastructure became a priority for the city. The government of Frankfurt believed that trade fair activities could help the local economy's recovery from war damages. In 1949, the first post-Second World War international sample fair attracted 1,771 exhibitors from 32 different industries in an exhibition area of 60,000 square meters (Messe Frankfurt 2014c). In subsequent years, Messe Frankfurt became a pioneer in the creation of industry-specific events, often for trade/business people only (i.e. not the general public).

Today, Messe Frankfurt GmbH is a holding company, owned by the City of Frankfurt/Main (60 percent) and the German state of Hessen (40 percent), which controls two independent subsidiaries: Messe Frankfurt Venue GmbH & Co. KG (responsible for the management of the technical and service side of events, the marketing of the exhibition center to guest organizers, and the maintenance and further expansion of the Frankfurt exhibition grounds) and Messe Frankfurt Exhibition GmbH (responsible for organizing trade shows directly or indirectly through domestic or foreign subsidiaries, for the management of Messe Frankfurt's trade show brands and for the development of new exhibition themes) (Messe Frankfurt 2014d). With group sales of approximately €545 million (EUR), 1,999 employees and 113 events organized in Germany and elsewhere (Messe Frankfurt 2014e), Messe Frankfurt GmbH is one of the largest and most strongly internationalized trade show organizations worldwide.

Messe Frankfurt organized its first trade show dedicated to clothing fabrics in 1959. The inaugural edition of 'Interstoff' (the term 'stoff' means fabric in German) attracted 60 exhibitors and 2,600 visitors. Being the first specialized event in the industry, and thanks to Frankfurt's central geographical position and international accessibility, Interstoff soon became a large event and meeting place also for non-German exhibitors. The resulting variety in fabrics in turn attracted a growing number of visitors, European and non-European alike (Rinallo and Golfetto 2011). In the early 1990s, at the height of its success, Interstoff had almost 1,200 exhibitors on a surface of more 40,000 square meters, and approximately 24,000 visitors (CERMES 2013; Golfetto and Rinallo 2012). Almost 80 percent of the exhibitors and over 60 percent of the visitors came from outside of Germany. Attendance of non-European exhibitors accounted for 20 to 25 percent of all exhibitors, while non-European visitors represented approximately 15 to 18 percent of all visitors. Interstoff thus became a 'hub event' where trade people would meet and establish commercial relationships and knowledge exchanges with geographically and culturally distant partners.

For more than 20 years, Interstoff remained the leading trade show in the industry (CERMES 1994). Other trade shows dedicated to clothing fabrics existed in Europe, but none was as large and internationalized as the Frankfurt event. During the 1990s, however, the show's supremacy was challenged by the much younger and smaller French trade show 'Première Vision' in Paris, which provided an attractive alternative to dissatisfied exhibitors and visitors (CERMES 1994; Golfetto and Rinallo 2008; 2012). The ensuing rivalry between the two events became more fierce and developed into a 'competitive war' (Rindova et al. 2004), that is, a period of intensified competitive activities with both contenders attempting to mobilize the support of key constituencies (i.e. exhibitors, visitors and the media) in their favor, highlighting their own strengths and each other's weaknesses.

Interstoff, the incumbent trade show, had on its side its legitimacy as the oldest and largest trade show in the industry and the wider range of products on display. Première Vision, the new entrant, differentiated itself by adopting specific knowledge-based strategies that would transform the show into a hotspot of knowledge about fashion trends and innovative fabrics (Rinallo and Golfetto 2006; 2011; Bathelt et al. 2014). The image of Paris as a fashion capital further strengthened Première Vision's attractiveness. Interstoff's countermoves were manifold. First, the German show imitated some of its French contender's knowledge-based strategies.

However, the long-held association between Paris and fashion provided Première Vision with an advantage that Interstoff could not match. As a result, Première Vision was considered to be the more influential source of fashion information in the industry. Second, Messe Frankfurt aggressively marketed Interstoff to American and Asian fabric producers as a point of entry into the European Union market, pointing to the fact that all other European trade shows would not admit non-European producers (Golfetto and Rinallo 2012).

In 1999, however, a new trade fair, Texworld, was launched in Paris by a private organizer, putting an end to Interstoff's monopoly on extra-European exhibitors (Gledhill 2001). Reduced to a fragment of what it once was, Interstoff gave up direct competition with Première Vision and re-focused on sportswear fabrics. These measures were not enough, however, to compensate for the prior exhibitor and visitor drain. The autumn/winter 1999 edition of Interstoff only attracted 2,600 visitors, leading Messe Frankfurt to put an end to one of its oldest trade shows (Golfetto and Rinallo 2012).

MESSE FRANKFURT'S INTERNATIONALIZATION: 'IF THEY WOULD NOT COME TO THE FAIR, THE FAIR WOULD HAVE TO COME TO THEM'

In 1987, Messe Frankfurt organized its first trade show outside of Germany with an Asian version of Interstoff. For an organizer running an exhibition venue owned by local stakeholders (whose support was motivated by the local economic benefits generated by exhibitor and visitor expenditures), the idea of launching an event abroad was counter-intuitive, and even revolutionary. As Messe Frankfurt itself explained in its 2012 annual report, which marked the 25th anniversary of its activities in China:

> The rationale behind this step was the reasoning that – although Messe Frankfurt is a highly international trade fair venue – only a small proportion of potential exhibitors and visitors from outside Germany would make the trip to Frankfurt. So if they would not come to the fair, the fair would have to come to them. This not only pushed the door wide open for the German companies traditionally represented at the flagship fairs in Frankfurt for globalization of their business. After becoming acquainted with the different event brands abroad more and more foreign exhibitors and visitors have in the intervening years also found their way to the leading trade fairs in Frankfurt – so it's a win-win situation. (Messe Frankfurt 2013, p. 16)

Interstoff Asia was the first experiment in what became later a standard geographical expansion strategy for Messe Frankfurt (Messe

Frankfurt 2007): the creation of new events in high-growth geographical markets that replicate the formula and adopt the brand names of existing 'flagship' fairs in Frankfurt. However, Messe Frankfurt also developed independent brands (i.e. events with no corresponding flagship fair in Frankfurt) to exploit business opportunities linked to the needs of regional markets or as a result of the acquisition of existing events from other organizers. Since 1987, Messe Frankfurt's foreign activities have increased exponentially. In 2012, 69 of the 109 total trade shows and exhibitions took place outside of Germany, attracting 34,431 exhibitors (about 44 percent of total exhibitors) over a net exhibition surface of 791,785 square meters (around 35 percent of total net areas rented) and had 1,173,757 visitors (almost 42 percent of total visitors) (Messe Frankfurt 2013). Key markets outside of Germany (in terms of volume of activity and growth potential) are China, Russia, India, Dubai and Turkey. Foreign operations are managed through a network of subsidiaries – fully owned or in partnership with local organizers – in Italy, France, Russia, Turkey, the US, Mexico, Brazil, Argentina and Hong Kong (Messe Frankfurt 2013).

Textile fairs represent one of Messe Frankfurt's core areas of competence, with 26 events, 12,509 exhibitors over a net exhibition area of 377,794 square meters and 339,227 visitors in 2012 (see Table 4.1). Clothing textile events, the focus of this study, represented 49 percent of total exhibitors, 44 percent of total visitors and 36 percent of rented areas in 2012. Home textile events were another major sector of activity (39 percent of overall exhibitors, 45 percent of visitors and 58 percent of rented areas). Messe Frankfurt also organized niche shows in technical textiles and, more recently, in apparel.

The current textile event portfolio reflects a complex and dynamic history of business expansion into different geographical areas and product groups. Interstoff Asia still exists in Hong Kong, despite being now focused on functional fabrics and eco-textiles under the new brand name of Interstoff Asia Essential. Interstoff Rossija, another Interstoff event, was launched in Moscow in 2005 but only survived for four editions before being terminated in 2007. Messe Frankfurt also operates with other brand names in the clothing fabric industry. Texworld Paris, whose acquisition from a private organizer in 2002 was one of the first reactions to the lost battle over Interstoff Frankfurt, constitutes a sort of 'flagship' fair outside Germany. Its formula was successfully replicated in the US (since 2006) and, albeit for only three editions, in India (2006–2008). Intertextile, founded in 1995 in Shanghai in cooperation with CCPIT TEX (the Sub-Council of Textile Industry of the China Council for the Promotion of International Trade) and originally covering both home and clothing textiles, tripled in number over the years with one edition in Beijing and two

Table 4.1 Textile fairs portfolio of Messe Frankfurt, 2012

Trade show	Number of events	Number of exhibitors (% foreign)	Net exhibition area (sq.m.)	Number of visitors (% foreign)
		CLOTHING TEXTILES		
Interstoff Asia Essential – Autumn		178 (82%)	1,458	6,527 (25%)
Interstoff Asia Essential – Spring		245 (88%)	2,939	7,625 (29%)
Intertextile Beijing Apparel Fabrics		1,018 (22%)	24,179	26,279 (17%)
Intertextile Shanghai Apparel Fabrics		2,522 (25%)	72,373	65,778 (24%)
Texworld (Paris) – Autumn		808 (100%)	14,625	14,370 (85%)
Texworld (Paris) – Spring		638 (99%)	12,403	13,436 (85%)
Texworld USA – Autumn		328 (92%)	3,693	3,297 (12%)
Texworld USA – Spring		162 (86%)	1,911	3,357 (9%)
Yarn Expo Autumn (Shanghai)		100 (51%)	1,221	4,812 (10%)
Yarn Expo Spring (Shanghai)		153 (27%)	2,187	4,502 (14%)
Total clothing textiles	10	6,152	136,989	149,983
		HOME TEXTILES		
Heimtextil (Frankfurt)		2,601 (87%)	119,960	67,451 (65%)
Heimtextil Russia (Moscow)		284 (54%)	8,005	14,652 (2%)
Home Textiles Sourcing Expo (New York)		146 (97%)	1,707	749 (11%)
Intertextile Guangzhou Home Textiles		202 (3%)	7,833	21,142 (21%)
Intertextile Shanghai Home Textiles – Autumn		1,331 (2%)	65,310	39,035 (12%)
Intertextile Shanghai Home Textiles – Spring		279 (2%)	14,465	10,304 (6%)
Total home textiles	6	4,843	217,280	153,333

Table 4.1 (continued)

Trade show	Number of events	Number of exhibitors (% foreign)	Net exhibition area (sq.m.)	Number of visitors (% foreign)
		TECHNICAL TEXTILES[1]		
Cinte Techtextil China		437 (28%)	10,198	19,066 (10%)
Techtextil North America (Atlanta)		314 (47%)	4,534	4,275 (19%)
Techtextil Russia		192 (80%)	2,260	4,510 (22%)
Total technical textiles	3	943	16,992	27,851
		APPAREL		
Apparel Sourcing Paris (Autumn)		162	1,860	–[2]
Apparel Sourcing Paris (Spring)		64	771	–[2]
Green Showroom and Ethical Fashion Show (Berlin) – Autumn		82 (50%)	1,038	1,970 (20%)
Green Showroom and Ethical Fashion Show (Berlin) – Spring		62 (39%)	906	1,865 (15%)
Ethical Fashion Show (Paris) – Autumn		42	341	1,811
Ethical Fashion Show (Paris) – Spring		25	144	1,173
International Apparel Sourcing Show (New York)		134	1,473	1,241
Total apparel	7	571	6,533	8,060
Overall total	26	12,509	377,794	339,227

Notes: sq.m. = square meters.

1 The flagship fair Techtextil (Frankfurt) occurs bi-annually and did not take place in 2012. Data for 2011 are: 1,226 exhibitors (64 percent foreign); 27,072 sq.m. net exhibition area; 24,915 visitors (55 percent foreign) (based on Messe Frankfurt's 2011 annual report).

2 Visitor data for Apparel Sourcing Paris are not reported, as the show took place together with Texworld.

Source: Based on data reported in Messe Frankfurt (2013).

in Shanghai, each portraying different product specializations (clothing fabrics and accessories versus home textiles). Yarn Expo is a smaller event dedicated to yarns and fibers (since 2004), taking place at the same time as Intertextile Shanghai Apparel Fabrics.

The vast majority of Messe Frankfurt's textile trade show activity is concentrated in Asia: Interstoff Asia is a relatively small event compared to its Mainland Chinese counterparts and can be considered an import trade fair serving the needs of Hong Kong clothing producers. The two Intertextile Apparel Fabric trade shows in Shanghai and Beijing dominate the other events in terms of exhibitors, visitors and rented areas. As Figures 4.1 and 4.2 demonstrate, these events have grown significantly, reflecting the accelerated development of the underlying Chinese market. Initially marketed by Messe Frankfurt to European fabric producers, these shows predominantly attract Chinese exhibitors and can therefore be considered domestic exchange trade shows. Texworld Paris is the largest clothing fabric event organized by Messe Frankfurt outside of Asia, and is also the most internationalized event. With 100 percent foreign exhibitors and 85 percent foreign visitors, it is a hub trade show dedicated to international exchanges. When considering that the exhibitors are predominantly from Asia and the visitors from Europe, however, this event is better characterized as a continental import trade fair, for Europe as a whole. Finally, the relatively small Texworld USA, with 92 percent foreign exhibitors and 12 percent foreign visitors in 2002, is an import trade show that serves the procurement needs of the US clothing industry.

INTERSTOFF ASIA AND ITS MANY INCARNATIONS

During its inaugural edition in October 1987, Interstoff Asia attracted approximately 5,400 visitors (mostly from Hong Kong and other Asian countries) and 169 exhibitors (approximately 75 percent of which were European) (South China Morning Post 1991a). Hong Kong, which until 1997 was a British Dependent Territory, was the best location for an Asian Interstoff spin-off at the time due to the large number of potential exhibitors and visitors in the area's catchment basin. At the time, Mainland China was not a viable alternative as a location because of trade restrictions, barriers to foreign investments and the fact that the local textile and clothing industry was still underdeveloped. In Hong Kong, however, these industries employed more than 40 percent of the manufacturing workforce and accounted for 37 percent of exports (Chan 1990). Also, Hong Kong's international accessibility with respect to Mainland China and other Asian countries made Hong Kong an ideal location for an Asian Interstoff event.

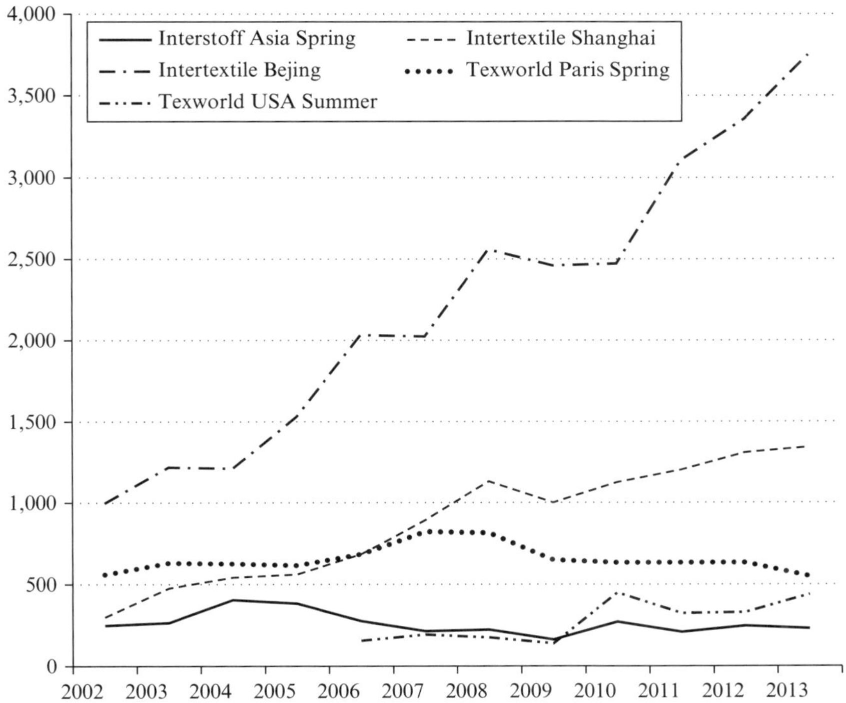

Notes: Only clothing textile trade shows still existing in 2013 are reported. In the case of events with two editions per year, only the spring or summer edition is included. In 2012, Texworld USA Summer was renamed Texworld USA Autumn.

Source: Based on data reported in Messe Frankfurt's annual reports (2002–2013).

Figure 4.1 Exhibitors at selected clothing fabric trade shows of Messe Frankfurt, 2002–2013

After 1987, the show grew steadily. In 1994, with a record number of 340 exhibitors, all available show space had been taken up and accommodating further requests was not possible (Kerr 1994b). This upward trend continued and, in an effort to satisfy exhibitor demand in 1995, Messe Frankfurt decided to split the show and create a bi-annual event (South China Morning Post 1995), analogously to European textile shows that followed the fashion cycle (i.e. spring/summer and fall/winter collections). As a result, the October event (now renamed Interstoff Asia Autumn) specialized in winter fabrics and accessories, whereas in the new April edition Interstoff Asia Spring showcased lighter fabrics for spring and summer.

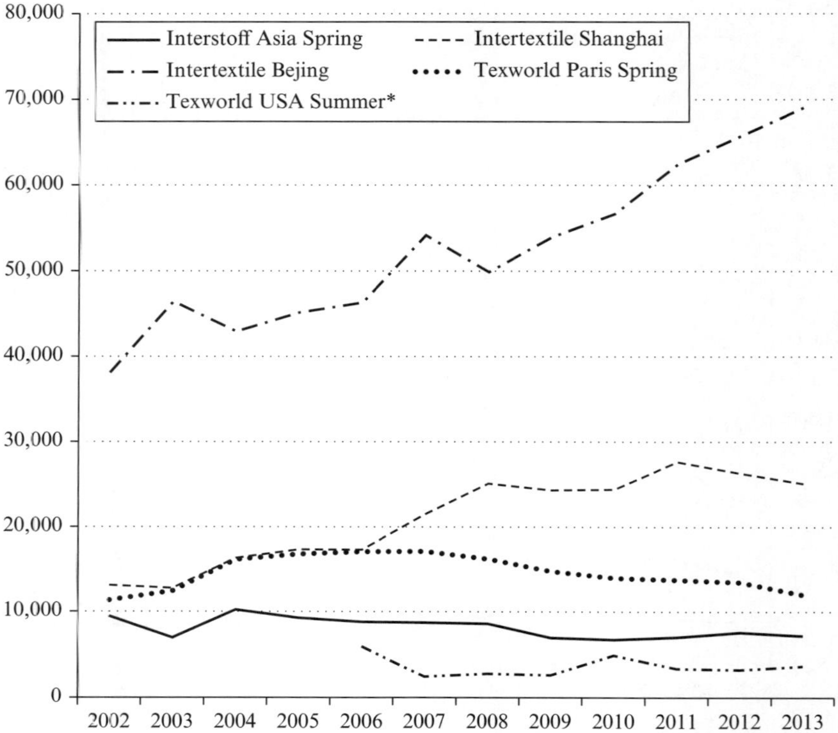

Notes: Only clothing textile trade shows still existing in 2013 are reported. In the case of events with two editions per year, only the spring or summer edition is included. In 2012, Texworld USA Summer was renamed Texworld USA Autumn.

Source: Based on data reported in Messe Frankfurt's annual reports (2002–2013).

Figure 4.2 Visitors at selected clothing fabric trade shows of Messe Frankfurt, 2002–2013

The spring event, with 200 exhibitors in its 1996 inaugural edition (South China Morning Post 1996a), remained slightly smaller (typically in the range of 250–350 exhibitors during the 1990s) than its autumn counterpart (typically 300–400 exhibitors, with a peak of 497 during its tenth-year anniversary in 1997). The shows grew also in terms of attendance, with about 10,000 to 13,000 visitors for most of the 1990s.

With most visitors coming from Hong Kong and nearby countries and a predominance of European exhibitors (mostly from Italy, Germany, France, the UK; see Serjeant 1990a), Interstoff Asia was initially an import-oriented trade show, which became a commercial platform for European fabric producers to explore and establish relationships with Asian clothing manufacturers. In the early 1990s, European firms benefitted from the increasing demand for higher quality fabrics in Hong Kong, as local clothing manufacturers were trying to upgrade the quality of their products (Chan 1990). By incorporating better fabrics and accessories, these manufacturers were able to sell their products at higher prices to their export markets. European exhibitors were later joined by US textile producers that were virtually absent during the first four editions of Interstoff Asia. These producers were less export-oriented than their European counterparts related to the size and vitality of their domestic market (Serjeant 1990a). By exhibiting at Interstoff Asia, western producers were able to learn at an accelerated pace how to adapt their fabric design and production competencies to the needs of the emerging Asian markets. Hong Kong clothing manufacturers, on the other hand, were able to buy high quality fabrics and accessories and get the latest information about new production techniques and design ideas. According to observers, the show also provided 'the chance to compare standards between Hong Kong's designers and manufacturers and their international counterparts' (Serjeant 1990b). This was essential to improve product quality in order to meet the rising standards of European and North American clothing importers.

Already in 1991, however, Messe Frankfurt officials declared that Interstoff Asia was 'no longer a trade fair for import from Europe' (Furlong 1991, p. 4). During the 1990s, the show established itself as the Asian hub for the clothing fabric industry (Markau 1993). In terms of exhibitors, the number of Hong Kong producers (which initially represented the largest national contingent) declined over time as increasing labor costs led manufacturers to move production to Mainland China and elsewhere. Across Asia, thanks to an influx of European and US textile technology, production facilities were modernized and firms that previously acted as subcontractors became independent clothing producers. Additionally, in many Asian countries, growing consumer incomes stimulated the emergence of distinct market segments, leading local producers to offer broader product ranges in smaller batches (Markau 1993). At Interstoff Asia, textile producers from Asian countries were able to get international exposure and expand their foreign markets. Among them, one of the largest national contingents was represented by India, whose producers initially offered cheap, unrefined fabrics in direct competition with Chinese rivals but soon learned to give their products a higher finish or blended the fabric with new yarns to sell them at higher prices as value-added products (South China Morning Post 1994a). The number of

Taiwanese exhibitors also increased steadily during the 1990s. At the end of the decade, they were the dominating exhibitors at Interstoff Asia. The show also attracted many fabric producers from Mainland China, Japan, Pakistan, South Korea, Thailand and Australia. While always maintaining a significant presence, the number of European exhibitors was subject to ups and downs for a variety of reasons (Furlong 1991; South China Morning Post 1991b), related to economic difficulties in their home countries, the need to be present at other shows (in Europe and elsewhere) and the perception that Interstoff Asia increasingly attracted buyers interested in the lower-price Asian textiles. Still, Messe Frankfurt continued marketing the show to European producers, as their presence contributed to Interstoff Asia's positioning as a wellspring of knowledge for the Asian textile and clothing industry (South China Morning Post 1994b).

To this end, the show adopted many of the knowledge-based practices first developed in the context of European shows (Rinallo and Golfetto 2011; Bathelt et al. 2014). In 1991, Messe Frankfurt established a 'trend table' with leading experts that were to develop fashion and fabric trend predictions, which were later showcased in special 'trend areas' during Interstoff Asia (Serjeant 1990a). These trend areas enabled visitors to 'touch and feel' fabric samples and identify their producers. According to a survey conducted in 2001, 88 percent of the visitors used such trend areas as a fashion guide for the upcoming season (Pawlyna 2002). An official trend guide with detailed descriptions of fashion predictions in terms of colors, textures, looks, materials and accessories was made available and distributed starting in 1993 (Frank-Keyes 1993). In the same year, Hong Kong designers were asked to create fashion collections that integrated Interstoff Asia's trend predictions with fabrics provided by selected exhibitors (Kerr 1994a). This initiative was established in cooperation with the Hong Kong Trade Development Council, which saw this as an opportunity to demonstrate that the local fashion industry was in a process of upgrading its design capabilities (South China Morning Post 1994c). Similar goals led to the creation of the Designers' Gallery later on, a competition for young textile designers which aimed to stimulate the show's exhibitors to develop original fabric designs (Tomlinson 2001). Also, a program of well-attended seminars on fashion trends and technological and market developments was added to the show in 1995 (South China Morning Post 1996b).

Interstoff Asia also experimented with market-sensitive exhibition layouts. For a long time, trade shows in Europe and elsewhere had arranged the exhibitor layout according to nationalities. One of the reasons behind such practices was related to the fact that national pavilions were often organized and financially backed by national export promotion policies (Seringhaus and Rosson 1998), which rented larger exhibition areas from trade fair organizers and offered them to national firms at a subsidized price. Exhibitors at these collective stands were typically small and medium-sized firms in the early phases of their internationalization processes, lacking the marketing competencies and financial resources necessary to take part in international trade fairs on their own. During the 1990s, Interstoff Asia organized the exhibitor layout according to product groups in order to help buyers find the product groups they were looking for more easily, but national pavilions still remained an important feature of the show. As reported by Haisma-Kwok (2001, p. 10), buyers often complained about this: 'I just wish they'd organize by fabric and not by country . . . It doesn't matter where it's from, we just want to see what we need', said a US buyer of fabric; 'I also prefer to categorize by fabric', replied Interstoff Asia's project manager. 'However, this show is also supported by government association, like Korea's and Taiwan's. The companies cannot support themselves, they come in a group and ask to adhere to a group.'

Additionally, Interstoff Asia started attracting exhibitors from new product groups to reflect underlying technological and market trends. In 1999, a new computer-aided design/computer-aided manufacturing (CAD/CAM) pavilion was added, where leading high-tech firms from Europe, Asia and the East Coast of North America exhibited computer-aided solutions in the design and manufacturing of fabrics. During an interview, the managing director of Messe Frankfurt Hong Kong disclosed that attracting such firms was not an easy task, 'because the textile industry forms only a minor share of the market for this technology' (Parkinson 1999, p. 12). In the same year, a separate exhibition area dedicated to functional fabrics with specific properties, such as thermal balance, lightweight strength, greater resistance or built-in scent was added (Parkinson 1999). Initially employed for work wear or sportswear, these fabrics were increasingly in demand for fashion-related applications.

Similarly, in 2002 a new Feature Pavilion for the first time introduced exhibitors specializing in lingerie, underwear, swimwear and nightwear fabrics (South China Morning Post 2002), and, in 2005, the show divided itself into three sections 'creation', 'function' and 'fashion' (Rothrock 2005). In 2006, Interstoff Asia began promoting itself as a fair for sourcing eco-friendly fabrics by identifying 'green' exhibitors with especially designed eco-labels (i.e. a green leaf for environmentally friendly components or for eco-friendly manufacturing processes, and a silver leaf logo identified firms whose entire manufacturing system was certified to be environmentally friendly by an independent watchdog organization) (South China Morning Post 2006).

Despite its continuing relevance as a source of knowledge about fashion trends and textiles, Interstoff Asia was impacted by major changes in the global textile and clothing industry. During its first years, the show had operated under the influence of the General Agreement on Tariffs and Trade's (GATT's) Multifibre Arrangement (1974–1994), which allowed developed countries to set quotas to imports of textile and clothing products – outside of the normal World Trade Organization (WTO) rules. Over the period 1995–2005, these artificial limits were progressively removed and, as a result, Asia's (particularly China's) share of clothing exports skyrocketed during the 2000s (Brambilla et al. 2010; Nordås 2004). Due to increased labor costs, Hong Kong did not benefit from these developments to the same extent as other Asian countries (Drapers Record 1998). With the establishment of Intertextile in 1995, Messe Frankfurt reacted to this shift in the textile and clothing industry. Initially, Intertextile was established in Shanghai to serve the country's largest catchment basin of clothing producers in the South and Southeast, in Fujian, Jiangsu, Jiangxi, Shandong, Guangxi and Zhejiang (Drapers Record 2003). After eight years, Intertextile was duplicated in Beijing in close proximity to firms in the North and Northeast, in Tianjin, Shanxi, Hebei and Heilongjiang, which represented China's second largest concentration of clothing producers (Drapers Record 2003).

The success of Intertextile (see Figures 4.1 and 4.2) contributed to a reduced market potential for Interstoff Asia, which was now competing with 'cousin' shows in other cities. European and Asian fabric producers now had different quality events that could help to penetrate the Chinese market. Similarly, Chinese clothing producers now saw limited use for a Hong Kong-based trade show; and European, North American and Asian fabric buyers found a greater variety of cheaper products in Shanghai and Beijing. As a result, Messe Frankfurt rationalized its Asian event portfolio and repositioned Interstoff Asia. Building on previous developments, the show was renamed to 'Interstoff Asia Essential' in 2007 to focus on multifunctional fabrics and eco-textiles. As explained by a Messe Frankfurt spokesperson:

> By rebranding the fair we want buyers to think of Interstoff Asia Essential as the place they go for something new, something pioneering . . . We wanted to look beyond basic textiles that most trade fairs offer to special and new fabrics that have added value and unique characteristics. The change is really to cope with what buyers are wanting from the market. (Li 2007)

The move was an attempt to differentiate the show in reaction to the, in part self-inflicted, competition from Mainland China or India.

In the years that followed, the new positioning was strengthened in various ways, with seminars, display forums and trend areas. In particular, initiatives aimed at 'building culture' on eco-textiles were introduced. As part of this, exhibitors were educated about the market potential for green fabrics, for example through market research on ethical fashion consumption trends and seminars on the impact of green policies on procurement activities. In the spring 2008 edition, Interstoff Asia Essential introduced a new eco-labeling system that identified exhibitors' fabrics based on the use of environmentally friendly raw materials, manufacturing processes, finishing processes or a combination of these characteristics (Haisma-Kwok 2008). And in the fall 2012 edition, a special Research and Education Zone was set up in cooperation with non-governmental organizations (NGOs), such as Greenpeace, with the goal of educating visitors and business leaders on environmental impacts in the textile supply chain (Pakistan Textile Journal 2012).

With this repositioning, Interstoff Asia Essential had successfully differentiated itself from Intertextile as a niche fair with a smaller size, where clothing producers could find fabrics 'with a cutting edge'. Exhibitors now predominantly originated from Mainland China, with a significant presence still from Hong Kong, Taiwan, South Korea and Japan. Meanwhile, the presence of European fabric producers is weaker than in the past. In 2012, the leading countries according to visitors were Hong Kong (71 percent), Mainland China, Australia, India, Indonesia, Japan, Korea, Taiwan, Thailand and the US. About 2 percent were buyers from department and chain stores, including representatives of major fashion brands and high-street retailers such as Adidas, Benetton, Burberry, H&M, Marks & Spencer, Puma, Tommy Hilfiger, Victoria Secret and Zara (Messe Frankfurt 2012a; 2012b). As a whole, the show now predominantly serves as a platform for Chinese fabric producers to network and make business with clothing producers and buying offices of overseas brands and retailers based in Hong Kong.

CONCLUSION AND IMPLICATIONS

In this chapter, we have investigated the internationalization strategy of Messe Frankfurt, with a focus on clothing textile fairs and, specifically, Interstoff Asia. First, the study presented is one of the first studies of an organizer's international expansion. As anticipated, it shows that such organizations can be footloose and manage their activities as multinational corporations. Consistent with a competence-based view of the firm (Prahalad and Hamel 1990; Barney 1991), Messe Frankfurt expanded its activities by originally accumulating industry-specific competences in central places, which were subsequently exploited in emerging peripheral geographical areas. Here, these competences were rare and difficult to imitate or substitute by local competitors. Additionally, Messe Frankfurt employed a brand extension strategy, based on the replication of successful flagship fairs in large, high-growth geographical markets. New events were localized in areas characterized by high international accessibility and large local catchment basins (e.g. Hong Kong, Shanghai and Beijing). The German organizer adopted a portfolio logic in the management of its events (e.g. Cooper et al. 2001), aimed at balancing established events and new initiatives. Several new trade shows were launched during our study period. While some failed after a few editions (i.e. Interstoff Rossija and Interstoff India), others such as Intertextile Shanghai and Beijing developed fairly well. Existing events were also continually monitored and corrective actions were taken to avoid decline as market conditions changed. This illustrates that trade shows are dynamic events that serve the evolving needs of underlying exhibitor and visitor markets. Some of these changes that affected Interstoff Asia were deliberately planned (e.g. the decision to attract producers from new product groups), whereas others were the result of underlying industry trends. The case study also supports that strategies in the trade fair business are at times deliberate and at other times emergent, as managerial intentions collide with and adjust to a changing reality (Mintzberg 1978).

Second, the study shows that Messe Frankfurt built its competitive advantage by exporting to Asia some of the knowledge-based strategies that were successfully developed in Europe (Rinallo and Golfetto 2011; Bathelt et al. 2014). Interstoff Asia was thus from the very beginning designed to be a 'knowledge-rich' place where visitors could easily find the suppliers and products they were looking for and, at the same time, learn about key trends affecting the industry. To reach this goal, Interstoff Asia implemented various knowledge practices, including the attraction of innovative producers, the organization of trend tables and trend areas and so on. After repositioning the event, Interstoff Asia Essential developed various initiatives to 'build culture' around eco-textiles and functional fabrics. Through this, Interstoff Asia established a distinct market position as a central source for knowledge in the textile and fashion industries.

Conceptually, the study links to the literature on field-configuring events (Lampel and Meyer 2008), which suggests that trade shows can deeply affect the development of markets, industries and technologies. While some empirical research, including our own (e.g. Rinallo and Golfetto 2006), supports such a 'strong effect' view of field configuration, other investigations have instead concluded that most trade shows affect markets and technology fields in a less direct and more subtle manner and should therefore be considered as field-reproducing or field-maintaining events (Schüessler et al. 2014; Bathelt et al. 2014; Gibson and Bathelt 2014). This study shows how Interstoff Asia contributed to and supported the upgrading of the Hong Kong clothing industry by providing knowledge about and easy access to fabrics, fashion trends and, in a later phase, eco-textiles and functional fabrics. With the rebranding, exhibitors were encouraged to showcase products consistent with the new positioning and – since buyers were interested in such products – fabric producers had commercial incentives to do so. Ultimately, whether events can configure or just reproduce fields is an empirical question. Based on our findings, we suggest that much depends upon the organizers' industry-specific competences, which can put them in a position to adopt knowledge-based strategies that result in some degree of influence over the underlying industries. Organizers lacking such competences can only manage the 'container' and, as a result, their influence on field evolution is much weaker, as it depends upon the uncoordinated interactions between the actors taking part in their events (Golfetto and Mazursky 2004; Golfetto and Rinallo 2013; Borghini and Zerbini 2014).

Another recently emphasized issue in the trade show literature addresses the relationship between trade shows and their underlying industries (Bathelt et al. 2014). Depending on the disciplinary background, research question and methodology, studies (e.g. on field-configuring events) sometimes imply that trade shows strongly influence their underlying industries or suggest that the evolution of events merely reflects macro-economic trends (as, for example, in Weber's (1961) classical analysis on the rise and fall of medieval fairs). The research presented here is based on a paradigmatic position of interdependence (i.e. two-way influences) between trade shows and their underlying industries, as developed in Bathelt et al. (2014). This perspective appreciates the role of economic structures on agency but, at the same time, recognizes the agency of key actors and their effects on structures. Accordingly, we have analyzed trade show evolution in the context of concurrent developments in the global textile and clothing industry but, at the same time, are not 'theoretically blind' to the ways in which trade show organizers and other key actors actively react to or anticipate economic trends and institutional changes in the global organizational field.

Finally, recent research in economic geography sees trade shows as temporary clusters that reproduce – for a short duration, but in a more intense form – the learning and interaction dynamics typical of permanent clusters (Maskell et al. 2006; Bathelt and Schuldt 2008). Some of these studies, building on the local buzz and global pipelines approach (Bathelt et al. 2004; Bathelt 2007), conceive trade shows as relational spaces that can enable local firms to establish knowledge pipelines with distant actors (Bathelt and Gibson 2009; Bathelt and Schuldt 2010; Maskell 2014). Related to these conceptualizations, recent work has highlighted how different types of trade fairs contribute in different ways to local–global knowledge flows (Rinallo and Golfetto 2011; Bathelt et al. 2014; Li 2014). In our study, we have adopted Rinallo and Golfetto's (2011) four-fold typology of trade shows (i.e. local exchange, import-oriented, export-oriented and hub or international events), using the geographical origin of exhibitors and visitors to investigate the trade and knowledge pipelines facilitated by Messe Frankfurt's trade shows in Asia. Using such a perspective helps us identify and understand the way in which the relational nature of trade shows can shift over time. The case of Interstoff Asia shows, in fact, how an event can evolve from one trade show type to another.

Interstoff Asia, for instance, started off as an import trade show, serving the evolving needs of the Hong Kong clothing industry. While comparisons of Asian trade shows have suggested that events where import or export functions are very dominant tend to be more trade-oriented than learning-based from a perspective of industrial producers (Li 2014; *this volume*; see also Bathelt et al., *this volume*), our analysis emphasizes instead that knowledge-acquisition practices can also play an important role at events of this kind. The distinction between trade and learning at trade shows may therefore be more of a rhetorical construction than an accurate description of the practices taking place at these events, especially as trade show development enters a more advanced stage. At trade shows, learning occurs because of trade. From a marketing perspective, the intertwining of trade and learning is evident at various levels of our analysis: especially in the knowledge-based strategies adopted by trade show organizers, and in the behaviors of exhibitors and visitors (Borghini et al. 2006). Visitors still use trade shows to access market-related knowledge that, ultimately, is a much-needed resource to survive in the hyper-competitive business world.

REFERENCES

Barney, J. B. (1991) 'Firm resources and sustained competitive advantage', *Journal of Management*, 17: 99–120.

Bathelt, H. (2007) 'Buzz-and-pipeline dynamics: Toward a knowledge-based multiplier model of clusters', *Geography Compass*, 1: 1282–1298.

Bathelt, H. and Gibson, R. (2009) 'Global buzz and global pipelines: International fairs as the glue of the global political economy', *Discourse*, 18 (3): 6–7.

Bathelt, H., Golfetto, F. and Rinallo, D. (2014) *Trade Shows in the Globalizing Knowledge Economy*, Oxford: Oxford University Press.

Bathelt, H., Malmberg, A. and Maskell, P. (2004) 'Clusters and knowledge: Local buzz, global pipelines and the process of knowledge creation', *Progress in Human Geography*, 28: 31–56.
Bathelt, H. and Schuldt, N. (2008) 'Between luminaries and meat grinders: International trade fairs as temporary clusters', *Regional Studies*, 42: 853–868.
Bathelt, H. and Schuldt, N. (2010) 'International trade fairs and global buzz, Part I: Ecology of global buzz', *European Planning Studies*, 18: 1957–1974.
Bettis-Outland, H., Cromartie, J. S., Johnston, W. J. and Borders, A. L. (2010) 'The return on trade show information (RTSI): A conceptual analysis', *Journal of Business and Industrial Marketing*, 25: 268–271.
Borghini, S., Golfetto, F. and Rinallo, D. (2006) 'Ongoing search among industrial buyers', *Journal of Business Research*, 59: 1151–1159.
Borghini, S. and Zerbini, F. (2014) 'Release capacity in the vendor selection process', *Journal of Business Research*, 67: doi: 10.1016/j.jbusres.2014.06.008.
Brambilla, I., Khandelwal, A. K. and Schott, P. K. (2010) 'China's experience under the Multi-fiber Arrangement (MFA) and the Agreement on Textiles and Clothing (ATC)', in R. C. Feenstra and S.-J. Wei (eds) *China's Growing Role in World Trade*, Chicago: University of Chicago Press, 345–387.
CERMES – Research Centre on Markets and Industrial Sectors (1994) *Tendenze della Domanda di Servizi Fieristici: Rapporto Moda-Persona (Trends in the Demand of Trade Fair Services: Report on the Fashion Industry)*, unpublished research report, Milan: Bocconi University.
CERMES (2013) *Trade Show Observatory*, Database of European trade show activity, Milan: Bocconi University.
Chan, S. K. (1990) 'Upgrading key to maintaining fashion sector's growth', *South China Morning Post*, 12 November: 12.
Cooper, R. G., Edgett, S. J. and Kleinschmidt, E. J. (2001) *Portfolio Management for New Products*, Cambridge: Perseus.
Cox, K. R. and Mair, A. (1988) 'Locality and community in the politics of local economic development', *Annals of the Association of American Geographers*, 78: 307–325.
Drapers Record (1998) 'Hong Kong squares up to labour crisis', *Drapers Record*, 31 October: 8.
Drapers Record (2003) 'Trading with China', *Drapers Record*, 12 April: 24.
Florio, M. (1994) 'Fair trades by trade fairs: Information providing institutions under monopolistic competition', *Small Business Economics*, 6: 267–281.
Frank-Keyes, J. (1993) 'Trade fair points way to future of fashion', *South China Morning Post*, 4 November: 1.
Furlong, S. (1991) 'Interstoff – Asia show comes of age as designers go it alone', *South China Morning Post*, 1 November: 4.
Gibson, R. and Bathelt, H. (2014) 'Field configuration or field reproduction? The dynamics of global trade fair cycles', *Zeitschrift für Wirtschaftsgeographie*, 58: 216–231.
Gledhill, G. (2001) 'Buyers praise Texworld', *Drapers Record*, 10 March: 4.
Golfetto, F. (2000) 'Reti di imprese e meta-organizzatori: il ruolo delle fiere (Firm networks and meta-organizers: The role of trade shows)', *Sinergie*, 18: 189–211.
Golfetto, F. (2004) *Fiere e Comunicazione: Strumenti per le Imprese e il Territorio (Trade Fairs and Communication: Tools for Firms and the Territory)*, Milan: EGEA.

Golfetto, F. and Mazursky, D. (2004) 'Competence-based marketing', *Harvard Business Review*, 51 (November): 26.
Golfetto, F. and Rinallo, D. (2008) 'Reshaping markets through collective marketing strategies: Lessons from the textile industry', in K. Tollin and A. Carù (eds) *Strategic Market Creation: Realizing Radical Innovation from a Marketing Perspective*, Chichester: Wiley, 97–123.
Golfetto, F. and Rinallo, D. (2012) 'Competition and collective marketing: A history of the European textile industry trade shows', in S. Borghini, A. Carù, F. Golfetto, S. Pace, D. Rinallo, L. M. Visconti and F. Zerbini (eds), *Prodotto, Consumatore e Politiche di Mercato Quarant'Anni Dopo. Scritti in Onore di Stefano Podestà (Product, Consumer and Market Policies Forty Years Later. Writings in Honor of Stefano Podestà)*, Milan: EGEA Online: 369–394.
Golfetto, F. and Rinallo, D. (2013) 'Trade show events, from live to digital: Towards the development of new competencies', in Fondazione Fiera Milano (ed.), *Exhibitions in years 2.0: Between Internalization and Local Development*, Milan: EGEA, 119–153.
Gopalakrishna, S. and Lilien, G. L. (1995) 'A three stage model of industrial trade show performance', *Marketing Science*, 14 (Winter): 22–42.
Haisma-Kwok, C. (2001) 'Anxieties aired at Interstoff', *Women's Wear Daily*, 3 April: 10.
Haisma-Kwok, C. (2008) 'Clearing the air: Interstoff Asia wades through the confusing world of eco-textiles', *DNR*, 31 March: 19.
Holtfrerich, C.-L. (1999), *Frankfurt as a Financial Centre: From Medieval Trade Fair to European Banking Centre*, Munich: Oscar Beck.
Kerr, J. (1994a) 'Designers launch trends with theme', *South China Morning Post*, 11 October: 2.
Kerr, J. (1994b) 'The biggest fabric and textile show in Asia – Interstoff', *South China Morning Post*, 11 October: 2.
Kogut, B. and Zander, U. (1993) 'Knowledge of the firm and the evolutionary theory of the multinational corporation', *Journal of International Business Studies*, 24: 625–645.
Lampel, J. and Meyer, A. D. (2008) 'Field-configuring events as structuring mechanisms: How conferences, ceremonies, and trade shows constitute new technologies, industries, and markets', *Journal of Management Studies*, 45: 1025–1035.
Langley, A. (1999) 'Strategies for theorizing from process data', *Academy of Management Review*, 24: 691–710.
Li, A. (2007) 'Rebranded event focuses on latest trends in industry: Trade fair will showcase cutting-edge fabrics and environmentally friendly materials, rather than ordinary textiles', *South China Morning Post*, 7 March: 4.
Li, P.-F. (2014) 'Global temporary networks of clusters: Trade fair dynamics in Asian economies', *Journal of Economic Geography*, 14: 995–1021.
Ling-Yee, L. (2006) 'Relationship learning at trade shows: Its antecedents and consequences', *Industrial Marketing Management*, 35: 166–177.
Markau, E. (1993) 'Regional challenges lie ahead – Textiles', *South China Morning Post*, 4 November: 1.
Maskell, P. (2014) 'Accessing remote knowledge: The roles of trade fairs, pipelines, crowdsourcing and listening posts', *Journal of Economic Geography*, 14: 883–890.
Maskell, P., Bathelt, H. and Malmberg, A. (2006) 'Building global knowledge

pipelines: The role of temporary clusters', *European Planning Studies*, 14: 997–1013.

Messe Frankfurt (2007) *2006 Annual Report*, Frankfurt: Messe Frankfurt.

Messe Frankfurt (2012a) *Interstoff Asia Essential Spring: Show Review Report*, Brochure, Frankfurt: Messe Frankfurt. Online. Available HTTP: <http://messe-frankfurt.kenti-creative.com/expo/IAES11/IAS10%20SHOW%20Review-ENG.pdf> (15 September 2014).

Messe Frankfurt (2012b) *Final Report: Interstoff Asia Essential Spring*, Press release, March 20, Frankfurt: Messe Frankfurt. Online. Available HTTP: <http://messefrankfurt.kenti-creative.com/expo/IAES11/IAS10%20SHOW%20Review-ENG.pdf> (15 September 2014).

Messe Frankfurt (2013) *2012 Annual Report*, Frankfurt: Messe Frankfurt.

Messe Frankfurt (2014a) *Our History*, Frankfurt: Messe Frankfurt. Online. Available HTTP: <https://www.messefrankfurt.com/frankfurt/en/messe/messe_leitbild/geschichte.html> (15 September 2014).

Messe Frankfurt (2014b) *Start of the Modern Era*, Frankfurt: Messe Frankfurt. Online. Available HTTP: <https://www.messefrankfurt.com/frankfurt/en/messe/messe_leitbild/geschichte/messen_neuzeit.html> (25 September 2014).

Messe Frankfurt (2014c) *Reconstruction and the 'Frankfurt Principle'*, Frankfurt: Messe Frankfurt. Online. Available HTTP: <https://www.messefrankfurt.com/frankfurt/en/messe/messe_leitbild/geschichte/frankfurter_prinzip.html> (25 September 2014).

Messe Frankfurt (2014d) *Group Structure*, Frankfurt: Messe Frankfurt. Online. Available HTTP: <https://www.messefrankfurt.com/frankfurt/en/messe/unternehmensprofil/konzernstruktur.html> (25 September).

Messe Frankfurt (2014e) *2013 Annual Report*, Frankfurt: Messe Frankfurt.

Mintzberg, H. (1978) 'Patterns in strategy formation', *Management Science*, 24: 934–948.

Nordås, H. K. (2004) *The Global Textile and Clothing Industry Post the Agreement on Textile and Clothing*, Discussion Paper, 5, Geneva: World Trade Organization.

Pakistan Textile Journal (2012) 'Interstoff Asia Essential Autumn opens 3rd to 5th October 2012', *Pakistan Textile Journal*, 31 October: 61.

Parkinson, L. (1999) 'Fair focuses on hi-tech', *South China Morning Post*, 20 October: 12.

Pawlyna, A. (2002) 'Spotting the trends before they happen', *South China Morning Post*, 19 March: 9.

Prahalad, C. K. and Hamel, G. (1990) 'The core competence of the corporation', *Harvard Business Review*, May–June: 79–91.

Rinallo, D., Borghini, S. and Golfetto, F. (2010) 'Exploring visitor experiences at trade shows', *Journal of Business and Industrial Marketing*, 25: 249–258.

Rinallo, D. and Golfetto, F. (2006) 'Representing markets: The shaping of fashion trends by French and Italian fabric companies', *Industrial Marketing Management*, 35: 856–869.

Rinallo, D. and Golfetto, F. (2011) 'Exploring the knowledge strategies of temporary cluster organizers: A longitudinal study of the EU fabric industry trade shows (1986–2006)', *Economic Geography*, 87: 453–476.

Rinallo, D., Golfetto, F. and Gibbert, M. (2006) 'Consocia et impera: How the French and Italian fabric producers cooperate in order to affirm the "dominant design" in the fashion industry', in M. Gibbert and T. Durand (eds), *Strategic Networks*, Oxford: Blackwell, 88–106.

Rindova, V. P., Becerra, M. and Contardo, I. (2004) 'Enacting competitive wars: Competitive activity, language games, and market consequences', *Academy of Management Review*, 29: 670–686.
Rosson, P. J. and Seringhaus, F. H. R. (1995) 'Visitor and exhibitor interaction at industrial trade fairs', *Journal of Business Research*, 32: 81–90.
Rothrock, V. (2005) 'Interstoff Asia evolves with the times', *Women's Wear Daily*, 27 September: 18b.
Schüessler, E., Rüling, C. and Wittneben, B. (2014) 'On melting summits: The limitations of field-configuring events as catalysts of change in transnational climate policy', *Academy of Management Journal*, 57: 140–171.
Seringhaus, F. H. R. and Rosson, P. J. (1998) 'Management and performance of international trade fair exhibitors: Government stands vs. independent stands', *International Marketing Review*, 15: 398–412.
Serjeant, J. (1990a) 'Spotlight shines as Interstoff Asia '90, the fabric trade fair, takes off', *South China Morning Post*, 12 November: 11.
Serjeant, J. (1990b) 'Interstoff '90 offers designers a chance to catch up on the latest trends', *South China Morning Post*, 12 November: 11.
South China Morning Post (1991a) 'Mirror on trends in the world's textile markets', *South China Morning Post*, 1 November: 2.
South China Morning Post (1991b) 'Interstoff fashion showcase', *South China Morning Post*, 1 November: 2.
South China Morning Post (1994a) 'Jeans giant looks to India for their denim – Interstoff Asia', *South China Morning Post*, 11 October: 3.
South China Morning Post (1994b) 'Show needs to attract more Europeans in order to grow – Interstoff Asia', *South China Morning Post*, 11 October: 3.
South China Morning Post (1994c) 'Collection brings out creativity – Interstoff Asia', *South China Morning Post*, 11 October: 3.
South China Morning Post (1995) 'Rag trade heads for HK at the double', *South China Morning Post*, 18 August: 4.
South China Morning Post (1996a) 'Show in spring offers platform for all seasons', *South China Morning Post*, 16 April: 3.
South China Morning Post (1996b) 'Top team presents seminars', *South China Morning Post*, 16 April: 3.
South China Morning Post (2002) 'Textile buyers in the mood', *South China Morning Post*, 19 March: 8.
South China Morning Post (2006) 'Green fabrics make fashion statement in garment trade', *South China Morning Post*, 15 March: 8.
Tomlinson, P. (2001) 'Hi-tech gallery shaped for global exchange', *South China Morning Post*, 9 October: 9.
UFI – The Global Association of the Exhibition Industry (2011) *The Trade Fair Industry in Asia*, 7th edition, Paris: UFI.
Weber, M. (1961) *General Economic History*, Translated by F. H. Knight, from the original German edition of 1923, New York: Collier Books.
Yang, Q., Mudambi, R. and Meyer, K. E. (2008) 'Conventional and reverse knowledge flows in multinational corporations', *Journal of Management*, 34: 882–902.

5. Temporary clustering in developing economies: trade fairs in South and Southeast Asia

Peng-Fei Li

INTRODUCTION

In the past several years, a knowledge-based theory of temporary gatherings has fundamentally changed our understanding and interpretation of trade fairs (Maskell 2001; Bathelt et al. 2014). As events that can be traced back to traditional societies, trade fairs have long been regarded as market places where transactions are made (Allix 1922; Milgrom et al. 1990). They are viewed as configurations that solved the fundamental problem of creating market arrangements for the exchange of goods in early stages of capitalism before the modern trading system had existed (Epstein 1994). In geography, traditional trade fairs were explained as underdeveloped central places in areas where there was not sufficient demand to support the development of permanent commercial centers (Berry and Parr 1988).

Although such market-based understandings of trade fairs still describe some important features of current events, the transformation of trade fairs in the knowledge economy brings about new dimensions of these events that go beyond traditional explanations. In many industries and fields, leading trade fairs have become learning places where new products and solutions can be found. They are also social spaces where social relations can be sustained and extended. Even in less innovative events, participants focusing on trading activities can acquire important market information and product feedback. It becomes clear under these conditions that learning and knowledge sharing gain increasing significance for the success of these temporary events (Borghini et al. 2006; Power and Jansson 2008; Ramirez-Pasillas 2008).

From a knowledge perspective, trade fairs connect with both the global economy and local communities. On a broader scale, business practices and technological advances of different countries can quickly diffuse based on such global temporary gatherings. Because of this, some international fairs have become landmark events for specific fields, thereby reinforcing industrial competitive advantages of host cities, regions and countries (Bathelt et al. 2014). In the global knowledge landscape of industries, leading trade fairs become temporary hubs that connect knowledge pools from different regions. As a consequence, trade fairs provide an opportunity to learn in external settings for firms that operate in local contexts. By developing knowledge pipelines through trade fairs and transnational investment, local economies become aware of discontinuous or radical changes that occur at a distance and thus reduce their risk of becoming locked into certain technological paradigms that may be dominant within their regional contexts.

Significant as the knowledge-based understanding of trade fairs is, it still requires more empirical analysis. As the argument of trade fairs as temporary clusters has been developed within the context of developed economies, it is important to explore how trade fairs develop and transform in dynamic developing backgrounds. Questions about how trade fairs grow under weak infrastructure conditions and how they evolve with the upgrading of local/national economies are best explored in developing economies. Based on such considerations, this chapter investigates these questions by focusing on trade fairs in South and Southeast Asian economies. Two explanations help in understanding the choice of this research area: First, South and Southeast Asian economies have grown remarkably in the past decades and recovered quickly after the global financial crisis in 2008 (OECD 2012). In the past several years, countries in South and Southeast Asia, especially India and Singapore, have shown an exceptional growth of exhibition activities compared to other economies in the world (UFI 2014). Furthermore, the respective economies are quite heterogeneous and differ substantially in terms of economic development stages and the growth of trade fairs. These diverse economies provide interesting cases to compare trade fairs in different developing contexts. Second, although South and Southeast Asia plays an important role in the global geography of exhibition activities, systematic research of trade fairs in these countries is still largely underdeveloped.

This chapter is structured as follows: The next section proposes a dynamic framework of trade fairs in developing contexts in terms of how they are linked with the development of regional industries. After a brief introduction of the data used, the section that follows analyzes uneven geographical, industrial, and structural development patterns of trade fairs in South and Southeast Asia in relation to the characteristics of these corresponding national economies. At the end, conclusions are drawn.

TRADE FAIRS IN DEVELOPING CONTEXTS: A DYNAMIC FRAMEWORK

To extend the knowledge-based theory of trade fairs to developing contexts, different types of temporary gatherings have to be distinguished (Rinallo and Golfetto 2011). When held in a developing context, trade fairs are usually attended by firms with varied capabilities in terms of learning and innovation. As a result, in a developing context with participating firms that are characterized by weak absorptive capabilities, trade fairs may not operate as temporary clusters where firms can learn efficiently through horizontal and vertical interactions. Due to the absence of global producers or buyers, horizontal or vertical learning may, in contrast, sometimes be quite weak in developing economies.

Consistent with different learning capabilities of local and global fairgoers, trade fairs can be systematically classified into five types of settings (Li 2014), each with different configurations of participants and different knowledge ecologies (see Figure 5.1). In the lower-left corner of Figure 5.1,

Source: Li (2014).

Figure 5.1 A knowledge-based framework for analyzing trade fairs

local gatherings are mainly composed of exhibitors and visitors from local and nearby regions. Since they come from the same context, participating firms in such gatherings are likely to know many of the other participants and can easily be connected to others through some common friends or business partners. In other words, geographical proximity of firms in local communities brings about relational proximity of participants at local gatherings. For small and medium-sized firms, one advantage of attending local trade fairs is to get familiar with industrial communities within the country and extend business networks beyond local territories. On the negative side, however, being familiar with other participants generates redundancy and relatively homogenous knowledge ecologies at these local events. Little can be expected in terms of new ideas from local visitors or fundamentally different technologies from exhibiting local firms.

Import and export platforms are two other types of events that are trade-intensive. Import fairs are characterized by the dominance of global exhibitors and local visitors. On the contrary, export fairs are mainly configured by global buyers and local producers. Usually, these two trade-oriented fair types develop in different contexts. Import events often develop when a weak manufacturing base exists in local economies. Export fairs tend to develop in relation to the presence of strong industries in the regions/national states where they are held. Although most local firms attend trade-oriented events with the clear goal to obtain business orders, knowledge may also be shared through intensive interaction between local and global participants. From global exhibitors or global visitors, local firms can better understand market developments and industrial trends in other countries. In export events, it is very helpful for small local producers to get direct feedback from global buyers on their products. This provides direction for the firms to improve design capabilities. As a result, these trade-oriented events can constitute an interactive space that is helpful for product improvement and market expansion. Asian economies, including South and Southeast Asian countries, have been successful in using export fairs as an effective tool to boost the development of local industries (Wilkinson and Brouthers 2006; Evers and Knight 2008).

Despite these impacts, export and import fairs are less helpful in Asia's developing contexts in building innovative regional economies. Compared to permanent clusters, temporary trade-oriented events involve primarily vertical learning channels. Horizontal learning opportunities are rare in these settings because global and local producers are functionally excluded in export and import fairs, respectively. In this sense, these events are only partial gatherings of global business communities that limit technological learning opportunities. Without comparisons and interactions between local and global competitors, technological knowledge, which is crucial for upgrading of local industries in developing economies, is less likely to be found in these settings.

Dominated by global visitors and exhibitors, international hub fairs involve both vertical and horizontal learning channels. On a global scale, these events may work as knowledge hubs where different ideas from distant regions and countries can be shared. However, since local firms are not well represented in international hub fairs, the role of these events for regional economies is also limited. In the context of South and Southeast Asia, some small city-states with high international accessibility, such as Singapore, are prime candidates for international hub fairs (Skov 2006).

The most appropriate temporary settings that support and enable knowledge circulation and exchange processes between local and global communities are events with a mixed configuration of participating firms from different contexts, involving equally local and global firms. Such events can be interpreted as local–global clustering spaces for firms in specific fields. Working in the same or related industries but coming from diverse contexts, participants in these events share different but overlapping knowledge bases. By being in the same specific field, they know the technical language for effective communication and are sensitive to even some small changes of products and solutions presented by their competitors. By originating from different contexts, local and global firms often have dissimilar understandings on the dynamics of technologies and industries, which may stimulate reflections on existing structures and help create new ideas. On this account, local–global clustering events generate a temporary milieu that encourages learning and knowledge creation processes. The variety and amount of knowledge that is accessible in local–global clustering fairs distinguishes these events from other kinds of temporary settings. Compared to permanent clusters, these local–global events generate similar knowledge ecologies with various mechanisms for learning, but combine different knowledge sources beyond the local context. From this, local–global clustering events can work most effectively to facilitate knowledge flows between local and global communities (Li 2014).

Although temporary gatherings of a mixed configuration of local and global participants are especially beneficial for knowledge sharing, they cannot easily be established in developing economies. In the proposed typology of trade fairs, different types of temporary gatherings are associated with regional economies in different development stages. This framework can be best interpreted in a dynamic way by examining how trade fairs evolve in relation to the growth of regional economies.

Before industrialization, an economy does not have a strong manufacturing base to support the development of export fairs or local–global clustering events. It is also unlikely that international hub fairs would or could be held in an underdeveloped economy, because the required infrastructure for global accessibility does not exist and global firms are not attracted to an economy that is insignificant in their fields. From this it can be expected that only local events or import fairs would be found in an early developing economy. With the growth of manufacturing activities in regional economies, more fairs can be organized naturally within the local context. Since industries in this stage are still weak, participation of global firms is low. The events would often remain local fairs. To learn internationally from the outside, local firms would have to attend more developed trade fairs in other countries at this stage. As local economies grow further, global firms may be increasingly attracted to participate in trade fairs in these areas in order to better understand local industrial development. Local events in developing economies can thus undergo an internationalization process by attracting more global visitors or more global exhibitors. It can be expected that trade fairs in fast-growing developing economies will be configured by a higher proportion of global firms than those in the events in early developing economies. In Figure 5.1, this implies a developmental path of trade fairs from the lower-left corner to either the upper-left or the lower-right corner.

As learning opportunities increase in internationalizing events, local industries may further develop with improved learning capabilities. At later stages, if a local economy turns from a knowledge-absorbing into a knowledge-creating economy, the intensity of learning and knowledge exchange processes between local and global communities can substantially increase. As local economies may have grown up to become interesting hotspots in specific industries or markets, global firms may recognize that it is worth visiting these areas regularly during trade fairs to catch up with the dynamics of local communities. It is at such later stages of development that local–global clustering events are able to develop in these contexts.

This dynamic knowledge-based typology describes a dynamic process through which local economies and trade fairs co-evolve in interrelated ways. If local economies, for instance, develop unevenly across industries, it can be expected that trade fairs also grow unevenly in different industries. As a mechanism for trans-local learning, trade fairs will first develop in those industries in which local economies have a strong base and where more knowledge exchange is required. In sum, based on this dynamic framework, uneven development patterns of temporary gatherings in developing economies should be observable.

DATA AND METHODS

To illustrate the above conceptual framework on trade fair dynamics in developing economies, empirical studies would need to focus on specific countries and explore how trade fairs evolve and interact with local industries over longer periods of time. Such a research strategy is hard to pursue, however, because most countries (not even highly developed economies – e.g. Bathelt and Spigel 2012) do not record detailed time series data on trade fairs. An alternative path, pursued here, to empirically support the dynamic framework developed in this chapter is to take trade fair snapshots of countries at different stages of economic development and compare the trade fair structure between these countries from the perspective of the knowledge-based typology. Such a research design requires selecting countries and regions with large disparities in economic development. Following this requirement, the countries in South and Southeast Asia were selected to explore national patterns of trade fair development.

In general, reliable data on trade fairs is difficult to find in South and Southeast Asia. Various sources were synthesized here and triangulated to provide a reliable picture of trade fairs in this region. Data on 962 fairs between 2009 and 2011 in South and Southeast Asia were retrieved from the database of the Association of the German Trade Fair Industry (AUMA 2012). This is the most detailed and comprehensive source of trade fair activity available for South and Southeast Asian economies. For most trade fairs, the database includes the events' names, the cities where they are held and numbers of domestic and foreign exhibitors and professional visitors. To inspect the representativeness of AUMA data for South and Southeast Asian countries, several trade fair reports of the Asian consulting firm Business Strategies Group (BSG), which is recognized by the Global Association of the Exhibition Industry (UFI), have been used for comparisons (BSG 2009–2011) (see Table 5.1).

At the national level, both databases portray a similar map of trade fair activities in South and Southeast Asia. As such, India, Vietnam, Thailand, Singapore, Malaysia and Indonesia are key players of the trade fair industry in South and Southeast Asia. The two databases are consistent with respect to India and Vietnam, but AUMA records only about half of the trade fairs in the other countries, compared to BSG. A reason for these differences could be that AUMA, being a German association, observed more international exhibitions, while many small local events were not covered in their database but were accounted for by the Asian firm BSG. Assuming that this may be a valid explanation, these unrecorded small events do not have a substantial effect on the following structural analysis of trade fairs in different Asian economies. Since no other information on

Table 5.1 Number of trade fairs in South and Southeast Asia by country, around 2010

Country	Number of trade fairs from 2009–2011 (AUMA 2012)	Number of trade fairs from 2008–2010 (BSG 2009–2011)	AUMA/BSG (%)
India	367	370	99
Vietnam	132	121	109
Thailand	105	217	48
Singapore	105	223	47
Malaysia	69	139	50
Indonesia	65	127	51
Philippines	57	132	43
Pakistan	43	78	55
Bangladesh	17	0	–
Cambodia	2	0	–
Total	962	1,407	68

Sources: Based on AUMA (2012) and BSG (2009–2011).

trade fairs was available, only six countries with more than 60 trade fairs in the AUMA database – India, Vietnam, Thailand, Singapore, Malaysia and Indonesia – were analyzed in this study.

UNEVEN TRADE FAIR DEVELOPMENT IN SOUTH AND SOUTHEAST ASIA

(i) Geographical Development Patterns

At a global scale, trade fairs in South and Southeast Asia are less developed than those in North America and Europe. Many industries, such as automobiles and engineering, have very specific requirements regarding exhibition facilities and require very large venues. If exhibition spaces can be regarded as an indicator of trade fair development, it should be noted that only two of the world's largest 66 venues in 2011 were located in South and Southeast Asia: one in Bangkok and one in Singapore (UFI 2011). Figure 5.2 shows the spatial patterns of trade fairs in South and Southeast Asia. At the city scale, Singapore, New Delhi, Mumbai, Bangkok and Ho Chi Minh City are centers of trade fair activity in South and Southeast Asia. Although these five cities host a similar number of events, Singapore outperforms the other cities with respect to the quality and influence of

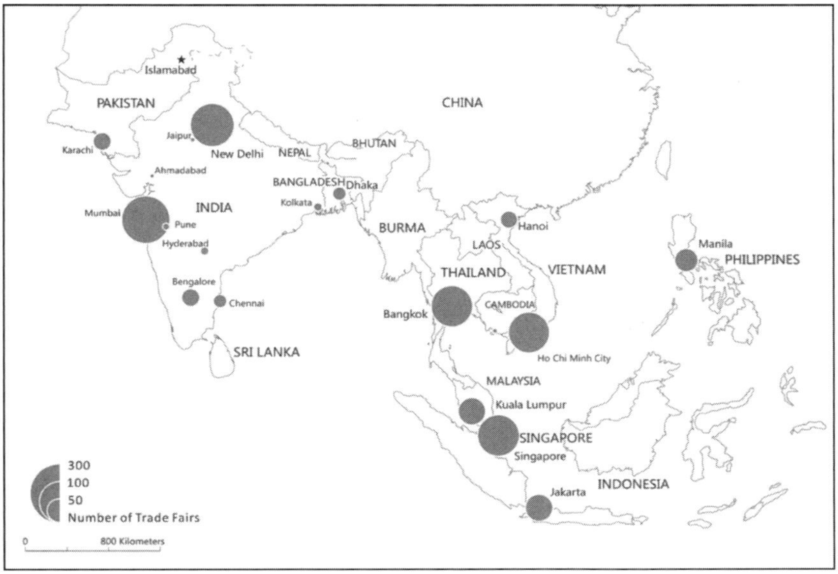

Source: Based on AUMA (2012).

Figure 5.2 Geography of trade fairs in South and Southeast Asia, 2009–2011

fairs and organizes a significant proportion of international trade fairs (as discussed below). In all these economies (except Singapore), trade fairs are highly concentrated in the capital city or the largest city. The reason for this spatial concentration of trade fairs is that these are the only cities that can provide large exhibition venues and surrounding infrastructure that meet the requirements of high accessibility for professional gatherings. For this reason, trade fairs in South and Southeast Asian economies show a similar geographical pattern at the national and the city levels.

In developing economies, the development of trade fair activities is influenced by many factors, such as economic growth, geographical location and government support. The reason that there are more than 100 fairs in Mumbai and New Delhi is clearly based on the background that India is the second-largest developing economy globally. However, although India takes the lion's share of trade fairs in the region, the exhibition industry in the country is still not well developed. As a comparable economy, China holds twice as many trade fairs as India (AUMA 2012) (see, also, Bathelt and Zeng, *this volume*; Golfetto and Rinallo, *this volume*). The main constraint for the growth of trade fairs in India is the lack of sufficient exhibition space, resulting from a lack of government investment initiatives (Gandhi 2010). This shortage of trade fair venues not only restricts the development of exhibition events, but can also be regarded as one of the reasons for India's weakness in import and export activities (Chopra 2010).

In Singapore, a large number of trade fairs can be attributed to the city-state's economic development, its global linkages and its traditional gateway function in Southeast Asia. However, the same argument, that is economic development, does not explain why more trade fairs are organized in Thailand and Vietnam compared to Malaysia, a more developed economy, or Indonesia, a much larger economy (see Table 5.1). In 2011, Indonesia's GDP was $847 billion (USD), while that of Vietnam and Thailand was only $124 (USD) and $346 billion (USD), respectively. The GDP per capita in Malaysia was $9,656 (USD), while that in Vietnam and Thailand was only $1,411 (USD) and $4,972 (USD), respectively (WTO 2012).

Trade fairs in Thailand partly owe their growth to strong government support and large venue investments. In 2002, the Thai government created the Thailand Convention and Exhibition Bureau to provide consulting and financing services to promote and facilitate trade fair development. IMPACT Exhibition and Convention Center in Bangkok, which was built in 1998 and expanded in 2005, is the largest venue in South and Southeast Asia. Vietnam, despite being a much smaller economy, is highly integrated in the global economy through exports and imports compared to other developing countries in the region (WTO 2012). In this case, the openness of the national economy supports the development of trade fairs in Ho Chi Minh City. For Malaysia and Indonesia, the underdevelopment of trade fairs may be related to their proximity to the global city of Singapore.

In an era of increasing globalization, trade fairs in South and Southeast Asian economies are, of course, similar to other world regions affected by the turbulences in the global economy. Figure 5.3 shows the development of the number of trade fairs in Thailand since the recent global financial crisis. Before 2009, Thailand held about 100 trade fairs annually. As the global economy entered into recession in 2009 and 2010, 30 trade fairs, or nearly one-third of former exhibitions, especially international events, were discontinued in Thailand (Thailand Convention and Exhibition Bureau 2007–2013). In the internationalizing South and Southeast Asian countries, the recession in the developed world had a strong impact on their regional economies, including the exhibition industry. However, in Thailand, as illustrated in Figure 5.3, as well as in some other South and

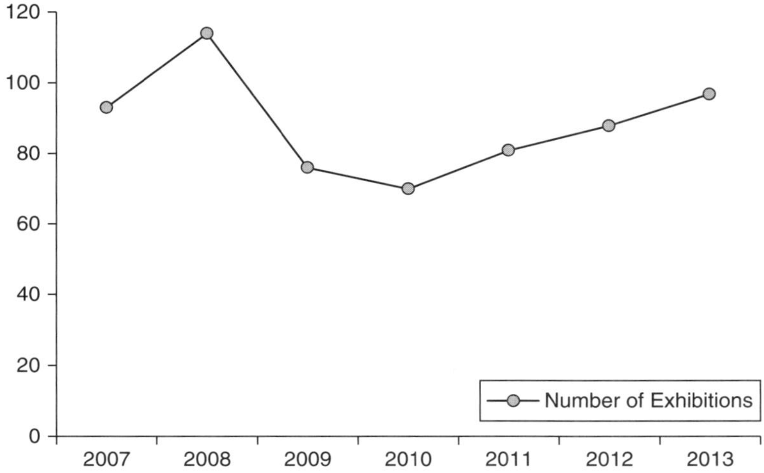

Source: Based on Thailand Convention and Exhibition Bureau (2007–2013).

Figure 5.3 Number of exhibitions in Thailand, 2007–2013

Southeast Asian countries, trade fair activity recovered relatively quickly after 2010 (UFI 2014).

(ii) Industrial Development Patterns

Trade fairs in South and Southeast Asian economies develop unevenly not only in a geographical perspective but also across industries. As suggested in the theoretical framework, exhibitions are more likely to develop in the industries where regional economies have strong bases and are competitive. In developing economies, it is expected that trade fairs develop in a sectoral pattern that is consistent with regional economic structure. Figure 5.4 shows the sectoral patterns of trade fairs in four South and Southeast Asian economies with a critical mass of at least 100 trade fairs in the AUMA database (see Table 5.1). In Figure 5.4, dotted lines indicate the share of employment in different industries in each economy, while solid lines represent the share of trade fair events in the respective industries of the total of trade fairs in a country. In general, the sectoral specialization patterns of trade fairs in the four largest South and Southeast Asian countries of trade fair activity show a remarkable consistency with the underlying sectoral specialization patterns. As a rule, in industries that are highly developed in regional economies, more exhibition events are organized.

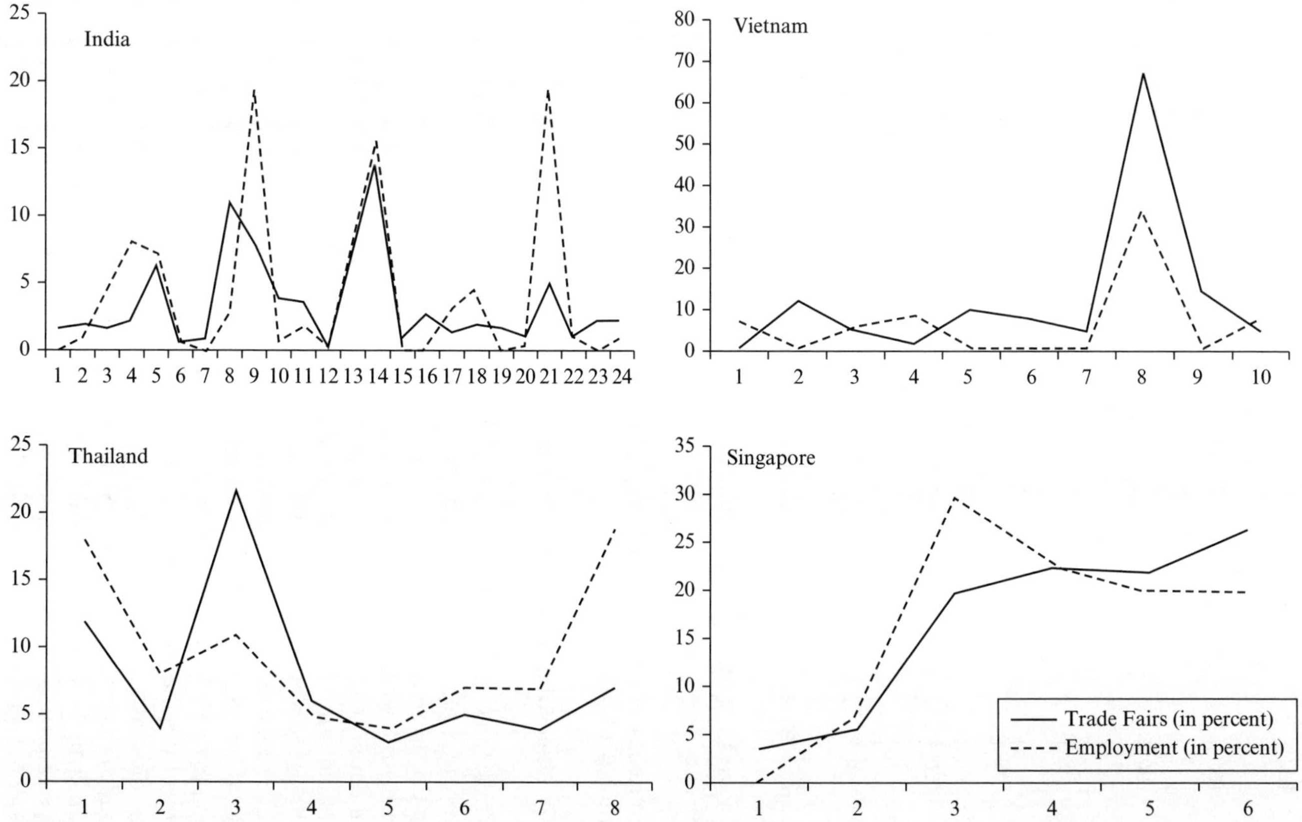
India
Vietnam
Thailand
Singapore
Trade Fairs (in percent)
Employment (in percent)

Notes: The y-axes represent the shares of trade fairs in an industry of all fairs or the shares of employment in that industry of overall employment in the respective economies, while the numbers on the x-axes correspond to different industries, arranged alphabetically from left to right. For India, the 24 industries shown are aerospace, agriculture, auto and motorcycle, chemicals, construction, cosmetics, defense, electronics, food, jewelry and watches, leather and shoes, lighting, medical, metal and machinery, mining, movies, plastics and rubber, publishing, safety, shipbuilding, textile and clothing, transportation, waste recycling, and wood and furniture. For Vietnam, the following 10 industries are displayed: accommodation, agriculture, construction, education, energy, finance, information, manufacturing, professional services, and public services. For Thailand, the eight industries included are food, furniture, metal and machinery, non-metal mining, motor, plastics and rubber, telecommunications, and apparel. For Singapore, six industries are listed: biochemical manufacturing, chemicals, electronics, general manufacturing, precision engineering, and transport engineering.

Sources: Trade fair data based on AUMA (2012); employment data based on Ministry of Statistics and Programme Implementation of India (2011), General Statistics Office of Vietnam (2007), National Statistical Office of Thailand (2007), and Ministry of Trade and Industry of Singapore (2011).

Figure 5.4 Sectoral concentration patterns in employment and trade show activity in India, Vietnam, Thailand and Singapore, early 2000s

For example, as an early developing economy, India developed large textile and clothing, food, metal and machinery industries, each employing more than 15 percent of total employment (the three peaks of the dotted line in the India quadrant in Figure 5.4). Nearly 30 percent of all trade fairs in India are events organized in these three sectors (AUMA 2012; Ministry of Statistics and Programme Implementation of India 2011). There is, however, one industry which only employs 3 percent of the labor force and yet is responsible for 11 percent of trade fairs in India. This is the electronics industry, in which India builds on strong competitive advantages at a global scale, primarily related to the Bangalore region (Saxenian 2006).

In similar ways, general manufacturing activities in Vietnam account for 34 percent of the total labor force and also represent 67 percent of all trade fairs organized (AUMA 2012; General Statistics Office of Vietnam 2007). Similarly in Thailand, the three largest industries of food, metal and machinery, and clothing are also the industries with the largest numbers of trade fairs. In Singapore, the country's employment is especially concentrated in the electronics, precision engineering and transport engineering industries, which also account for the most trade fairs.

(iii) Trade Fair Structure

Regional economies do not only influence the size of trade fairs, but also, as conceptualized above, affect their structure with respect to the event type. Table 5.2 shows the average participant structure of trade fairs in six major South and Southeast Asian economies. By measuring different configurations of foreign and domestic exhibitors and visitors at trade fairs, fairs can be assigned to a certain type of event and interpreted in relation to the respective level of regional economic development. Doing this on a country-by-country basis enables us to draw conclusions about the co-development of trade fairs and their regional economies.

Vietnam is an early developing economy, driven mainly by the exploitation of national resources. As a small economy, the country is well integrated in the global economy through export and import activities. In 2011, the proportion of export value in GDP in Vietnam was 78 percent. Most of the exports are related to agriculture and resource processing industries, such as wood and furniture. The ratio of merchandise imports to GDP was 86 percent, most of which were manufacturing products (WTO 2012). Corresponding to the latter numbers, trade fairs in Vietnam are mostly import-oriented events, except for one export fair in the furniture industry.

In relation to the small and open economy of Vietnam, the Indian

Table 5.2 Average participant structure of trade fairs in South and Southeast Asian economies, 2011/2012

Country	GDP/capita	Exhibitors		Visitors		No. of fairs	Type of fairs
		Domestic	Foreign	Domestic	Foreign		
Vietnam	1,411	35%	65%	83%	17%	36	Import
India	1,488	67%	33%	91%	9%	70	Local
Indonesia	3,494	48%	52%	94%	6%	36	Import
Thailand	4,972	52%	48%	92%	8%	25	Internationalizing
Malaysia	9,656	46%	54%	89%	11%	20	Internationalizing
Singapore	46,238	27%	73%	56%	43%	44	Hub

Note: GDP/capita = gross domestic product per capita in 2011.

Sources: GDP data based on WTO (2012); trade fair data based on AUMA (2012).

economy is much larger and more closed. The industrialization process in the country is still underway, although some competitive industries, such as information technology and software, are emerging. In 2011, the ratio of exports to GDP was only 17 percent, much lower than those of other developing countries in Asia (WTO 2012). Generally, the Indian economy is relatively strongly inward-oriented, and as a result, most fairs are local events with mostly domestic exhibitors and visitors.

Indonesia is another large developing economy that relies on national resources. Compared to India, the Indonesian economy is more open, but less industrialized. 40 percent of Indonesia's exports are related to oil and mining products, while 60 percent of the country's imports are manufacturing products (WTO 2012). In line with this economic structure, most trade fairs are import events with a dominance of domestic visitors/buyers and a substantial share of foreign exhibitors.

Vietnam, India and Indonesia have in common that they are developing economies with a relatively weak industrial base. In the contexts of these countries, many trade fairs are therefore dominated by foreign producers as exhibitors and local/national buyers. Consequently, learning opportunities at the events are limited. As discussed above, however, trade fairs become more internationalized with the continuous upgrading of regional economies. This can be seen for trade fairs in Thailand and Malaysia, two rapidly growing developing economies in Southeast Asia, where trade fairs are quickly internationalizing.

Thailand has already reached the take-off stage in its industrialization process. As a consequence, the Thai economy has strong global connections, with a 66 percent ratio of both export and import values to GDP. Overall, 24 percent of Thailand's imports were in fuels and mining resources, and 70 percent of exports in manufacturing products (WTO 2012). In an upgrading economy like Thailand, local professional knowledge accumulates quickly and frequent external interaction is required to stimulate fast learning processes. In this context, it is understandable why trade fairs in Thailand attract a large number of foreign exhibitors and visitors, although they have at the same time many local/national participants.

Malaysia is more industrialized than Thailand with only 20 percent of the labor force working in agriculture (WTO 2012). The Malaysian economy is also characterized by strong exports of industrial products. This economic pattern is reflected in the structure of trade fairs. Exhibitors and visitors are more diversified in terms of their domestic/foreign origin than those in other South and Southeast Asian countries.

Singapore is the only developed economy in South and Southeast Asia. The city-state overwhelmingly depends on economic linkages with the global economy. Singapore's exports and imports are equivalent to 171 percent and 153 percent of the GDP, respectively (WTO 2012). In accordance with this developed economic structure, most trade fairs in Singapore can be classified as international hub events. Since the country acts as a gateway to the South and Southeast Asian economies, many trade fairs in Singapore are composed of participants from surrounding countries, but these events also attract many European and North American firms. With the establishment of new convention centers in other countries in South and Southeast Asia, especially in Thailand, some relocation and decentralization tendencies of trade fair activity from Singapore can be expected in the future (Bathelt et al. 2014).

Overall, the above comparisons illustrate a strong relationship between trade fair development and regional economic development in South and Southeast Asian countries. When viewing these regional economies sequentially from early developing to fast-developing and finally developed countries, the types of trade fairs that dominate seem to evolve from local and import events with unbalanced configurations of participants to internationalizing exhibitions with more foreign firms, and finally toward international events with more diverse origins of participants. This international comparative analysis of trade fairs in South and Southeast Asian economies provides initial and tentative evidence supporting the dynamic framework proposed in this chapter.

CONCLUSION

In recent years, a knowledge-based perspective has developed that views trade fairs as temporary gatherings for trans-local knowledge exchanges and associated learning processes (Bathelt et al. 2014). This conceptualization has been developed to understand the nature of international trade fairs in developed contexts. Little research has investigated such temporary gatherings in the context of developing countries and how these events are being shaped by and are actively shaping their corresponding regional economies. Many trade fairs in developing economies, however, cannot be classified as international knowledge-intensive events. Related to different configurations of visitors and exhibitors according to their domestic/foreign origin, following the work of Rinallo and Golfetto (2011), a typology of trade fairs has been developed in this chapter (see Figure 5.1) that allows us to relate trade fair development with different developmental stages of the countries' respective economies.

Generally, most trade fairs in early developing economies start as local gatherings or import events because the local contexts are at this stage characterized by a weak manufacturing base. Export fairs with predominantly international visitors and local exhibitors can only develop with the support of strong local industries. In the case of both export and import fairs, vertical interaction about product and market information is especially intensive, while horizontal observations regarding technological innovations play a minor role. The limitations of such knowledge acquisition at temporary gatherings are due to partial exclusion, instead of broad inclusion, of global industrial communities. Knowledge circulation and creation are most likely in trade fairs with a mix of diverse participants that include domestic as well as foreign firms.

Trade fairs in South and Southeast Asia provide strong support for this dynamic understanding of trade fairs versus their regional economies. First, the prior analysis shows that trade fairs are more developed in industries in which local economies have a strong basis. In the economies of India, Vietnam and Thailand, for instance, food, textile and clothing, as well as some light industries, have developed first. As a result, in all three countries more trade fairs focus on these industries. India is an exception in the electronics and software industries where it has developed international linkages. This has been accompanied by a remarkable rise in the number of trade fairs in this field, particularly held in Bangalore, New Delhi, and Mumbai. Similarly, Singapore has developed strong electronics and engineering clusters, and consequently has a substantial share of its exhibitions in these fields.

Second, when comparing structures of trade fairs in early developing, fast-developing and developed economies in South and Southeast Asian countries, there seems to be a specific evolutionary pattern. This seems to indicate that temporary events become more international with the development of embedded economies. As an inward-oriented, early developing economy, typical Indian fairs are local events. As open economies relying on natural resources, Vietnam and Indonesia host more import fairs. In the industrializing Thai and Malaysian economies, trade fairs attract more foreign exhibitors and visitors. And, finally, trade fairs in Singapore are highly internationalized with some having continental hub character.

Although the evidence from South and Southeast Asia presented in this chapter is still tentative, it does illustrate how a dynamic knowledge-based theory of fairs can cast new light on the understanding of regional development in the global knowledge economy. Trade fairs matter when knowledge becomes a crucial input for regional and global production systems. At the regional level, trade fairs have different functions and characteristics and may evolve in different ways in interaction with local industries (see Xin and Weber, *this volume*; Bathelt and Zeng, *this volume*). Although trade fairs in South and Southeast Asia seem to develop along a path from import and local events to international gatherings, it is still unclear which might be the best evolutionary path of trade fairs under the specific conditions of developing economies. Substantial research is required before trade fairs can be used as an effective tool to promote industrial upgrading and technological learning in regional economies.

At the global scale, the growth of international trade fairs in developing economies reflects the changing landscape of global exhibition activity (see Golfetto and Rinallo, *this volume*). By viewing trade fairs as temporary clusters for knowledge exchange, this suggests an emerging new architecture for global knowledge flows, which may, in turn, impact the global knowledge economy. It would be interesting to further explore how new knowledge that is generated in local communities can be quickly broadcast to other territories through trade fairs and other pipelines and how these temporary spaces of learning may affect the global knowledge economy.

REFERENCES

Allix, A. (1922) 'The geography of fairs: Illustrated by old-world example', *Geographical Review*, 12: 532–569.

AUMA – Association of the German Trade Fair Industry (2012) *Trade Fair Data Worldwide*, Berlin: AUMA. Online. Available HTTP: <http://www.auma.de/_pages/MessenWeltweit/MessenWeltweit.aspx?sprache=e> (5 June 2012).

Bathelt, H., Golfetto, F. and Rinallo, D. (2014) *Trade Shows in the Globalizing Knowledge Economy*, Oxford and New York: Oxford University Press.
Bathelt, H. and Spigel, B. (2012) 'The spatial economy of North American trade fairs', *Canadian Geography*, 56: 18–38.
Berry, B. J. L. and Parr, J. B. (1988) *Market Centers and Retail Location: Theory and Applications*, Englewood Cliffs, NJ: Prentice Hall.
Borghini, S., Golfetto, F. and Rinallo, D. (2006) 'Ongoing search among industrial buyers', *Journal of Business Research*, 59: 1151–1159.
BSG – Business Strategies Group (2009–2011) *The Trade Fair Industry in Asia: An UFI Report*, 5th–7th editions, Hong Kong [drawn from Thailand Convention and Exhibition Bureau (ed.) (2011) *The International Exhibition Market in Asia Report*, Bangkok (in Thai). Online. Available HTTP: <http://www.tceb.or.th/about-us/tceb-intelligence-center/mice-publications.html> (15 September 2012)].
Chopra, J. (2010) 'India's expo venues: The long march', *Exhibition World*, 1 April: 16–18.
Epstein, S. R. (1994) 'Regional fairs, institutional innovation, and economic growth in late Medieval Europe', *Economic History Review*, 47: 459–482.
Evers, N. and Knight, J. (2008) 'Role of international trade shows in small firm internationalization: A network perspective', *International Marketing Review*, 25: 544–562.
Gandhi, M. (2010) 'The Indian dilemma', *Exhibition World*, 1 April: 12–14.
General Statistics Office of Vietnam (2007) *Establishment Census of Vietnam 2007*, Hanoi. Online. Available HTTP: <http://www.gso.gov.vn/default_en.aspx?tabid=481&idmid=4&ItemID=8385> (4 November 2012).
Li, P.-F. (2014) 'Global temporary networks of clusters: Structures and dynamics of trade fairs in Asian economies', *Journal of Economic Geography*, 14: 995–1021.
Maskell, P. (2001) 'Towards a knowledge-based theory of the geographical cluster', *Industrial and Corporate Change*, 10: 921–943.
Milgrom, P., North, D. C. and Weingast, B. R. (1990) 'The role of institutions in the revival of trade: The law merchant, private judges, and the Champagne fairs', *Economics and Politics*, 2: 1–23.
Ministry of Statistics and Programme Implementation of India (2011) *Statistical Year Book India*, Delhi. Online. Available HTTP: <http://mospi.nic.in/Mospi_New/upload/statistical_year_book_2011.htm> (1 November 2012).
Ministry of Trade and Industry of Singapore (2011) *Economic Survey of Singapore 2010*, Singapore. Online. Available HTTP: <http://www.mti.gov.sg/ResearchRoom/Pages/Economic%20Survey%20of%20Singapore%202010.aspx> (12 March 2013).
National Statistical Office of Thailand (2007) *The 2007 Industrial Census*, Bangkok. Online. Available HTTP: <http://web.nso.go.th/en/census/indus07.htm> (2 March 2013).
OECD – Organisation for Economic Co-operation and Development (2012) *Southeast Asian Economic Outlook 2013*, Paris: OECD.
Power, D. and Jansson, J. (2008) 'Cyclical clusters in global circuits: Overlapping spaces in furniture trade fairs', *Economic Geography*, 84: 423–448.
Ramirez-Pasillas, M. (2008) 'Resituating proximity and knowledge cross-fertilization in clusters by means of international trade fairs', *European Planning Studies*, 16: 643–663.

Rinallo, D. and Golfetto, F. (2011) 'Exploring the knowledge strategies of temporary cluster organizers: A longitudinal study of the EU fabric industry trade shows (1986–2006)', *Economic Geography*, 87: 453–476.

Saxenian, A. (2006) *The New Argonauts: Regional Advantage in a Global Economy*, Cambridge, MA: Harvard University Press.

Skov, L. (2006) 'The role of trade fairs in the global fashion business', *Current Sociology*, 54: 764–782.

Thailand Convention and Exhibition Bureau (2007–2013) *Meetings, Incentives, Conventions and Exhibitions Statistics*, Bangkok. Online. Available HTTP: <http://www.businesseventsthailand.com/why-thailand/resources/mice-statistics/> (26 March 2014).

UFI – The Global Association of the Exhibition Industry (2011) *The 2011 World Map of Exhibition Venues*, Paris. Online. Available HTTP: <http://www.ufi.org/Public/Default.aspx?Clef_SITESMAPS=142&Clef_SITESMAPS=144#worldmap> (30 October 2012).

UFI (2014) *The Global Exhibition Industry Statistics 2014*, Paris. Online. Available HTTP: <http://www.ufi.org/Public/Default.aspx?Clef_SITESMAPS=142&Clef_SITESMAPS=144#survey> (26 March 2014).

Wilkinson, T. and Brouthers, L. E. (2006) 'Trade promotion and SME export performance', *International Business Review*, 15: 233–252.

WTO – World Trade Organization (2012) *Trade Profiles Statistics Database*, Geneva. Online. Available HTTP: <http://stat.wto.org/CountryProfile/WSDBCountryPFHome.aspx?Language=E> (November 2012).

PART II

The rise of Chinese trade fair ecologies

6. Exhibition destination attractiveness: dimensions and perceptual differences between exhibitors and visitors of China's exhibitions

Xin Jin and Karin Weber

INTRODUCTION

The exhibition industry has experienced substantial growth rates over the past few decades on a global scale. The continued growth can be credited to ever-increasing trade and commerce across national boundaries, increased corporate travel budgets and the value marketers put on face-to-face contact with customers and leads (UFI 2012). The development of the exhibition industry in a region is also closely related to the state of its economic attributes, such as market leadership, industry sector characteristics and economic and spatial concentration (industry agglomeration). Furthermore, factors such as global economic environment, competition of the exhibition industry at the regional level and internal management challenges impact exhibition development (UFI 2012).

CHINA'S EXHIBITION INDUSTRY

Owing to the continent's thriving economy, Asia has become one of foci of global exhibition industry development (see, also, Golfetto and Rinallo, *this volume*). This has created a supportive environment for the growth of China's exhibition business. The country has been a leading player in the Asia-Pacific exhibition market, with its exhibition sector being regarded as a valuable platform to promote internal and external trade and commerce, as well as functioning as a revenue generator for host cities (Guo 2012). Its exhibitions have played a significant role in the breakthrough of Chinese brands and Chinese-made products into international markets. In

2010, China had a total of 4.7 million square meters of indoor exhibition space, accounting for 15 percent of the world's total. This put the country in second place, following the U.S. and preceding Germany, in terms of domestic venue capacity (UFI 2011). In 2011, there were 153 convention and exhibition centers in 36 cities, with 28 of them having more than 80,000 square meters of indoor exhibition space (CCES 2012).

The 2008 global financial crisis and its repercussions have significantly affected the exhibition industry at a global level. Despite decreases in net exhibition space rented in Europe and North America, net exhibition space rented in China reached a new peak with 13 million square meters in 2010, a 6 percent increase over the previous year (UFI 2011). This demonstrates that China remains a strong growth market for exhibitions, consistent with practitioners' positive outlook towards China's exhibition industry. They attribute the expansion of the industry to a number of factors (UFI 2007), namely: (i) the need to enlarge facilities to keep growing exhibitions from moving to other locations; (ii) the growing awareness by local authorities of the benefits of the industry, in terms of direct, indirect and induced economic impacts; and (iii) the coexistence of various economic models and financial expectations.

China hosted approximately 7,000 exhibitions of a diverse nature and scale in 2011, with machinery, building materials, food, textile, fashion and leather being the most actively and frequently exhibited industrial sectors (CCES 2012). Despite the rapid growth in exhibition activity, performance indicators show relatively low results for China. For instance, the average rental utilization rate (equivalent to the share of exhibition space rented out over the entire year) has been lingering around 15 to 20 percent over the past decade (Kay 2005; Guo 2012). Compared with international utilization rates of approximately 40 percent, space in purpose-built centers in China has been under-utilized. This has especially been the case compared to facilities located in globally successful exhibition destinations. For example, the Hong Kong Convention and Exhibition Centre (HKCEC) had a high utilization rate of more than 70 percent (Cheung 2011). Occupancy rates of convention and exhibition space in Las Vegas varied from 40 to 72 percent in the period from 1997 to 2008, and this even triggered concerns regarding potential over-capacity (Yang and Gu 2012). The exhibition industry is becoming more and more mature and competitive, and, as a result, an exhibition center's performance is increasingly connected to a destination's competitive advantages, mainly market conditions, facilities, destination appeal, infrastructure, amenities, technology and management (Detlefsen and Vetter 2008). Thus, it is important to evaluate destination and venue attractiveness that can lead to potential demand.

Based on city size, prestige, economic strength, tradition and history in hosting exhibitions, and the number of exhibitions held on an annual basis, Shanghai, Beijing and Guangzhou are typically classified as first-tier exhibition cities, whereas provincial capital cities or economically developed cities striving to build the exhibition industry are classified as second-tier cities (e.g. Chan 2007; Guo 2007). While first-tier cities have largely dominated the exhibition market over the past two decades, and consequently enjoy high occupancy rates of their exhibition venues, many state-of-the-art exhibition facilities constructed in second-tier cities across the country are under-utilized (see, for some exceptions, Bathelt and Zeng, *this issue*). As abundant exhibition space surpasses demand in most cities, it is critical to understand destination attributes that attract exhibitions to a city and fill exhibition space. Thus, it is of value to study factors that affect both exhibitors' and visitors' decisions to travel to a particular destination to attend a specific exhibition. A poor understanding of their behavior may ultimately result in a waste of scarce resources.

This chapter reports key findings of a series of studies that focused on an assessment of exhibition destination attractiveness attributes (see, also, Zhu and Zeng, *this volume*) from the perspective of two primary stakeholders in the exhibition context, namely exhibitors and visitors. The objectives of this chapter are: (i) to identify dimensions of exhibition destination attractiveness from the perspectives of both stakeholders; (ii) to investigate the importance of these dimensions; and (iii) to compare perceptions of the stakeholders, with respect to first-tier and second-tier cities. We introduce the methodology for our various studies next, before reporting key findings and detailing study implications.

METHODOLOGY

To investigate this, a series of empirical studies focusing on exhibition destination attractiveness have been conducted since 2008. In particular, an extensive survey program was administered to investigate factors influencing exhibition destination attractiveness and the subsequent impact of these factors. Surveys were conducted in five cities across China at ten exhibitions of varied nature. Both exhibitors and visitors were interviewed.

Table 6.1 reports the host city, venue, exhibition scale (in terms of the number of exhibitors), exhibitor and visitor samples obtained and organizer characteristics of these exhibitions. When choosing survey exhibitions and locations, consideration was given to sample international and national exhibitions of diverse ownership, staged in venues in both

Table 6.1 Sampled exhibitions

Survey no.	Exhibitors (number)	Exhibitor sample (number)	Visitor sample (number)	Location	Venue	Organizer characteristics
1	≈1,000	217	–	Guangzhou	China Import and Export Fair Pazhou Complex (CIEF)	A well-known international exhibition company
2	1,158	107	173	Shanghai	Shanghai New International Exhibition Center (SNIEC)	A well-known international exhibition company
3	227	94	30	Shanghai	Shanghai International Exhibition Center (INTEX)	A national quasi-governmental division
4	≈100	49	23	Wuhan	Wuhan International Convention and Exhibition Center (WHCEC)	A local private exhibition company
5	1,982	79	78	Shanghai	Shanghai New International Exhibition Center (SNIEC)	A well-known international exhibition company
6	≈200	58	59	Shanghai	Shanghai Ever-Bright Convention and Exhibition Center (EVER-BRIGHT)	A local private exhibition company

7	≈200	75	41	Nanjing	Nanjing International Exhibition Center (NJIEC)	Joint cooperation between a local industrial association and an external exhibition company
8	≈100	42	24	Nanjing	Nanjing International Exhibition Center (NJIEC)	Local government divisions
9	≈300	81	89	Hangzhou	Hangzhou Peace International Convention and Exhibition Center (PEACE)	An external exhibition company
10	155	58	30	Shanghai	Shanghai International Exhibition Center (INTEX)	Joint cooperation between a national industrial association and an overseas exhibition company

Notes: Survey 1 = pilot study; surveys 2–10 = main survey. Total number of exhibitors was obtained from the event organizers.

first-tier and second-tier cities and covering varied industry sectors. The pilot test obtained 217 valid exhibitor responses from an exhibition hosted in Guangzhou. The main survey covered nine further exhibitions in four cities in China's Yangtze River and Pearl River Deltas and collected 643 responses from exhibitors and 547 responses from visitors. Prior to analysis, data was screened for entry errors and missing values that may impair the data analyses. This resulted in 215 valid responses for the pilot test, 616 valid responses from exhibitors and 535 valid responses from visitors for the main survey. Although this excluded exhibitions in other second-tier or third-tier destinations, given the leading position of the two regions in China's exhibition industry, the sampled exhibitions and destinations can be considered crucial to the overall population.

The statistical analysis was conducted using SPSS 12.0/18.0 and AMOS Graphics 17 0/19.0. The exhibitor and visitor data were analyzed separately, applying the same methodology. Exploratory factor analysis (EFA) was first utilized to explore the dimensionality of the destination attractiveness factors. Varimax rotation was employed for each EFA analysis. The dimensionality was then tested and verified by conducting confirmatory factor analysis (CFA). Two steps were taken in CFA to validate the EFA factor solutions. Initially, first-order CFA was conducted to verify the dimensionality. Then second-order CFA was conducted to confirm that exhibition destination attractiveness consists of the proposed sub-dimensions. The models were solved using maximum-likelihood. The standard factor loadings, t-values, squared multiple correlations (SMC), composite reliability (CR) and average variance extracted (AVE) were used to indicate the reliability and validity of the CFA models. In the following analysis, only CFA results are reported. Differences in perceptions of destination attractiveness variables were assessed between exhibitors/visitors in exhibitions hosted in one first-tier city (Shanghai) versus exhibitors/visitors in exhibitions hosted in three second-tier cities (Hangzhou, Wuhan and Nanjing). Thus, independent sample t-tests were conducted at the factor level, based on the CFA results.

FINDINGS

This section reports the findings of both exhibitor and visitor analysis of destination attractiveness. It is organized according to the steps of the data analysis (i.e. first-order CFA results, second-order CFA results and t-test results). Differences between the exhibitor and visitor data are discussed in each sub-section.

(i) Factors of Exhibition Destination Attractiveness

Several measures for exhibition destination attractiveness were identified in the context of China's exhibition industry, drawing on first-order CFA. From the perspective of exhibitors, and with the details reported in Table 6.2, destination attractiveness attributes fall into six distinct dimensions:

1. destination leisure environment
2. cluster effect 1 (host city leadership in the industry)
3. venue facilities
4. accessibility
5. cluster effect 2 (host city/region as a source of exhibitors)
6. destination economic environment.

Of particular interest are the two dimensions that can be related to clustering effects: (i) host city leadership in the industry; and (ii) host city/region as a source of exhibitors. These effects refer to the perceived impact of the clustering of industries and/or manufacturing firms in the host region on the respective industries' exhibition activities from the perspective of exhibitors (and visitors). The factor host city leadership in the industry was characterized by high factor loadings (which represent correlations between the factors and items) for items such as the host city being an important distribution hub of a specific industry sector, having support from related industries and possessing a strong professional industry association. The factor host city/region as a source of exhibitors had high loadings for items related to the proximity of the host city to the manufacturing base of the exhibited sector, as represented by suppliers and distributors located in the respective city or nearby regions.

In contrast, from the perspective of exhibition visitors, and with details reported in Table 6.3, destination attractiveness attributes fall into five distinct dimensions:

1. cluster effect 2 (host city/region as a source of exhibitors)
2. destination leisure environment
3. destination economic environment
4. venue facilities
5. accessibility.

The main difference between exhibitors' and visitors' perceptions is that the clustering effect 1 (leadership of the host city in the industrial sector for exhibition) is the most important factor for exhibitors in evaluating

Table 6.2 Factors/items of exhibition destination attractiveness for exhibitors – First order confirmatory factor analysis

Factor/item	Standard loading	t-value	SMC	CR
Destination leisure environment				*0.80*
I feel safe in this city.	0.740	10.375	0.558	
The weather in this city is pleasant.	0.661	n/a	0.437	
The local people of this host city are friendly.	0.705	9.531	0.467	
This city has many tourist attractions.	0.610	8.697	0.351	
This city is clean.	0.651	9.234	0.417	
I have no language barriers in this city.	0.505	7.591	0.255	
Cluster effect I (Leadership of the host city in the industry)				*0.64*
There is a strong professional association of our industrial sector in this city.	0.614	9.695	0.405	
This city is an important distribution hub of our industrial sector in China.	0.596	n/a	0.355	
This city has support from industries related to this exhibition.	0.773	9.477	0.598	
This city is a leading city of an industrial belt where most products/equipment in this exhibition are manufactured.	0.633	8.472	0.401	
Venue facilities				*0.80*
The exhibition center layout is easy for people to find their way.	0.748	11.294	0.559	
Transportation to this exhibition center is convenient.	0.645	9.998	0.416	
The location of this exhibition center is excellent.	0.535	8.316	0.286	
This exhibition center has sufficient space to accommodate this exhibition.	0.721	n/a	0.520	
The facilities of the exhibition center are excellent.	0.699	10.441	0.483	
Accessibility				*0.75*
It is easy to get information about this host city.	0.765	9.237	0.587	
It is easy to get to the city.	0.705	9.095	0.491	
The geographical location of this host city is convenient.	0.662	n/a	0.442	

Table 6.2 (continued)

Factor/item	Standard loading	t-value	SMC	CR
Cluster effect 2 (Host city/region as sources of exhibitors)				*0.74*
China's manufacturing firms in our industry are especially located in this city or nearby regions.	0.595	8.23	0.361	
Most suppliers in this exhibition are located in this city or nearby regions.	0.714	n/a	0.517	
Most distributors of the products/ equipment exhibited come from this city or nearby regions.	0.781	10.617	0.593	
Destination economic environment				*0.75*
The overall economic condition of this city is among the top five in China.	0.657	8.627	0.441	
This city has a large number of international firms.	0.881	n/a	0.747	

Notes: χ^2 = 435.279, df = 211, $p<0.001$; χ^2/df = 2.063; Goodness-of-Fit Index = 0.886; CFI = 0.914; RMSEA = 0.060, n = 293. CR = Composite Reliability; SMC = Squared Multiple Correlations; CFI = Comparative Fit Index; RMSEA = Root Mean Square Error of Approximation.

exhibition destination attractiveness, whereas it is not identified as an important factor by visitors. Only clustering effect 2 (host city/region as sources of exhibitors) is recognized as an important factor by visitors.

(ii) Importance of Destination Attractiveness Attributes

In the next step of our analysis, the importance of destination attractiveness factors was measured, drawing on second-order CFA of both exhibitor and visitor data (see Table 6.4). From the perspective of exhibitors, clustering effect 1 (host city leadership in the industry) had the greatest impact on exhibition destination attractiveness, followed by venue facilities and clustering effect 2 (host city/region being a source for exhibitors). Results show that exhibitors were aware of and preferred host city destinations in which clustering effects exist that developed over time. This supports arguments that the maturity of an industry in a destination is important to the development of exhibitions for that specific industry sector (Chan 2005; Butler et al. 2007), and that exhibitions mirror local/

Table 6.3 Factors/items of exhibition destination attractiveness for visitors – First-order confirmatory factor analysis

Factor/item	Standard loading	SMC	t-value	CR
Cluster effect 2 (Host city/region as sources of exhibitors)				*0.71*
China's manufacturing firms in our industry are especially located in this city or nearby regions.	0.650	0.422	n/a	
Most distributors of the products/equipment exhibited come from this city or nearby regions.	0.702	0.492	11.449	
Most suppliers in this exhibition are located in this city or nearby regions.	0.663	0.439	11.175	
Destination leisure environment				*0.82*
The local people of this host city are friendly.	0.714	0.509	n/a	
The environment of this city is clean.	0.709	0.503	14.628	
This city has many tourist attractions.	0.700	0.490	14.460	
The weather in this city is pleasant.	0.795	0.632	16.060	
Destination economic environment				*0.83*
Compared with other cities in China, the cost of exhibiting in this city (excluding booth rental fees) is low.	0.584	0.341	n/a	
The business environment of this city is excellent.	0.773	0.598	12.967	
This city has support from industries related to this exhibition.	0.784	0.614	13.062	
This city has a large number of international firms.	0.795	0.632	13.154	
Venue facilities				*0.77*
This exhibition center has sufficient space to accommodate this exhibition.	0.582	0.339	n/a	
The exhibition center layout is easy for people to find their way.	0.810	0.656	12.627	
The facilities of the exhibition center are excellent.	0.777	0.604	12.464	
Accessibility				*0.71*
It is easy to get to the city.	0.637	0.406	n/a	
It is easy to get information about this host city.	0.556	0.309	10.380	

Table 6.3 (continued)

Factor/item	Standard loading	SMC	t-value	CR
The geographical location of this host city is convenient.	0.597	0.356	11.001	
Transportation to this exhibition center is convenient.	0.674	0.454	11.982	

Notes: $\chi^2 = 436.438$, df = 123, $p < 0.001$; $\chi^2/df = 3.548$; Goodness-of-Fit Index = 0.921; CFI = 0.914; RMSEA = 0.069 (Lo90 = 0.062, Hi90 = 0.076), n = 535. CR = Composite Reliability; SMC = Squared Multiple Correlations; Hi and Lo indicates the range of RMSEA values.

regional economic and industry development (Kirchgeorg 2005; see, also, Li, *this volume*; Rinallo and Golfetto, *this volume*). From the standpoint of exhibitors, accessibility and a destination's economic and leisure environments also had a significant impact on exhibition destination attractiveness (as SMC values of the three constructs are all above 0.4), albeit to a lesser extent compared to the clustering factors. The economic environment was measured by strong economic conditions and the presence of a large number of international firms. This is in line with previous studies that stress the importance of the economic standing of an exhibition destination (e.g. Fuchslocher 2005; Rubalcaba-Bermejo and Cuadrado-Roura 1995).

From the perspective of visitors, although all factors had a significant impact on destination attractiveness, accessibility had the greatest impact, followed by venue facilities and leisure environment, whereas economic environment and clustering effects were less important compared to the other factors. The main difference between exhibitors' and visitors' perceptions is that clustering effect 1 (leadership of the host city in the industrial sector for exhibition) was the most important factor for exhibitors in evaluating exhibition destination attractiveness, but was much less important for visitors. By contrast, accessibility was less important for exhibitors but represented the most important factor for visitors.

All of this indicates that successful large-scale trade shows may have potential to expand to second-tier cities. This finding is well aligned with an earlier study (Jin et al. 2010) that reported findings of a survey conducted in Guangzhou in 2008. Duplicate shows are frequently held in second-tier cities with the aim to attract similar groups of exhibitors and visitors as the original events. Our earlier study explored respondents' preferences of China's second-tier cities as potential host destinations for

Table 6.4 Factors/items of exhibition destination attractiveness for (i) exhibitors and (ii) visitors – Second-order confirmatory factor analysis

(i) Exhibitors

Factor/item	Standard loading	t-value	SMC	AVE	CR
Destination attractiveness				*0.59*	*0.90*
Cluster effect 1 (Host city leadership in the industry)	0.969	10.647	0.939	0.41	0.73
Venue facilities	0.804	10.467	0.647	0.44	0.80
Cluster 2 (Host city/region as a source of exhibitors)	0.737	n/a	0.543	0.48	0.73
Destination leisure environment	0.712	9.941	0.506	0.43	0.82
Destination economic environment	0.702	10.401	0.492	0.58	0.82
Accessibility	0.665	9.155	0.442	0.51	0.75

Notes: $\chi^2 = 712.831$, df = 220, $p < 0.001$; $\chi^2/df = 3.240$; Goodness-of-Fit Index = 0.905; CFI = 0.909; RMSEA = 0.060, n = 616. SMC = Squared Multiple Correlations; CFI = Comparative Fit Index; AVE = Average Variances Extracted; RMSEA = Root Mean Square Error of Approximation.

(ii) Visitors

Factor/item	Standard loading	t-value	SMC	AVE	CR
Destination attractiveness				*0.59*	*0.88*
Accessibility	0.893	13.207	0.797	0.45	0.71
Venue facilities	0.778	11.241	0.605	0.53	0.82
Destination leisure environment	0.771	13.542	0.594	0.49	0.74
Destination economic environment	0.715	9.996	0.511	0.53	0.77
Cluster effect	0.672	10.541	0.452	0.38	0.71

Notes: $\chi^2 = 391.075$, df = 112, $p < 0.001$; $\chi^2/df = 3.492$; Goodness-of-Fit Index = 0.923; CFI = 0.914; RMSEA = 0.068 (Lo90 = 0.061, Hi90 = 0.076), n = 535. SMC = Squared Multiple Correlations; CFI = Comparative Fit Index; AVE = Average Variances Extracted; RMSEA = Root Mean Square Error of Approximation; Hi and Lo indicates the range of RMSEA values.

a large-scale international beauty and cosmetic trade show that was held at the time in Guangzhou (Jin et al. 2010). Findings indicated that visitors rated a destination's leisure environment attributes very highly, whereas exhibitors rated a destination's business environment higher, when considering what may influence their exhibition attendance decision-making. This difference indicates that, while exhibitors may go anywhere that there is potential for successful business, visitors prefer exhibition destinations with good accessibility to minimize travel time and with an attractive leisure environment that offers some degree of enjoyment in addition to taking care of business.

(iii) Perceptual Differences of Exhibition Destination Attractiveness between Exhibitors and Visitors, with Respect to First-Tier and Second-Tier Cities

Potential differences in the attractiveness of first-tier and second-tier cities as exhibition destinations were separately explored for exhibitors and visitors, utilizing independent sample t-tests. Table 6.5 reports differences in perceptions of both exhibitors and visitors, comparing those who attended exhibitions in a first-tier city with those attending exhibitions in second-tier cities.

Our study results provide interesting additional insights. From the exhibitors' perspective, the first-tier city Shanghai attracted higher ratings for the factors economic environment, clustering effect 1 and clustering effect 2, but had slightly lower ratings in accessibility and leisure environment than the three second-tier cities Nanjing, Hangzhou and Wuhan. Independent sample t-tests showed that there was a significant difference in terms of cluster 1 (leadership of host city in the industry), economic standing of the destination and leisure environment, indicating that exhibitors regard a first-tier city's economic standing and leadership quite highly, but valued the leisure environment higher in second-tier cities. There was no significant difference between first-tier and second-tier cities in terms of venue facilities, destination as a source of exhibitors, and accessibility. This suggests that second-tier cities were perceived as having venue facilities and accessibility at least on par with the first-tier city Shanghai.

Comparing perceptions of visitors who attended exhibitions in the first-tier city with those who attended exhibitions in second-tier cities, the former gave higher ratings in only two dimensions: economic environment and venue facilities. However, only the difference in ratings for economic environment was significant and there was no significant difference in the ratings of venue facilities between visitors in the first-tier city and the second-tier cities, resonating with exhibitors' perceptions

Table 6.5 Factors of exhibition destination attractiveness for (i) exhibitors and (ii) visitors – First-tier versus second-tier cities

(i) Exhibitors

Factor	First tier (n = 379)		Second tier (n = 236)		Mean difference	t-value	Significance
	Mean	Rank	Mean	Rank			
Economic environment	5.97	1	4.28	6	1.70	16.193	0.000*
Accessibility	5.52	2	5.59	1	−0.06	−0.649	0.512
Leisure environment	5.16	3	5.40	2	−0.24	−2.699	0.007*
Cluster effect 1	5.14	4	4.68	4	0.46	4.976	0.000*
Venue facilities	5.00	5	5.03	3	−0.030	−0.304	0.761
Cluster effect 2	4.80	6	4.67	5	0.13	1.227	0.220

Note: * = significant at $\chi \leq 0.05$

(ii) Visitors

Factor	First tier (n = 324)		Second tier (n = 166)		Mean difference	t-value	Significance
	Mean	Rank	Mean	Rank			
Economic environment	5.415	1	5.054	4	0.362	−7.151	0.000*
Venue facilities	5.317	2	5.292	3	0.025	0.741	0.459
Accessibility	5.234	3	5.744	2	−0.511	−2.772	0.006*
Leisure environment	5.211	4	5.964	1	−0.752	−7.922	0.000*
Cluster effect 2	4.831	5	5.000	5	−0.169	2.341	0.020*

Note: * = significant at $\chi \leq 0.05$

that differences in exhibition venues were insignificant. Interestingly, visitors rated Shanghai significantly lower in terms of accessibility, leisure environment and clustering effect than visitors of the second-tier cities. Overall, visitors' perceptions resonated with those of exhibitors that second-tier cities have better accessibility and leisure environments. This may be due to the vast expansion of Shanghai as an urban center, with inner city transportation having consequently become more difficult and time-consuming. Conversely, the three second-tier cities possess excellent transportation networks that offer easy access to exhibition venues. Nanjing and Hangzhou are also well known as pleasant and atmospheric tourist destinations.

DISCUSSION AND CONCLUSION

This chapter summarizes findings of two studies (Jin et al. 2012; Jin and Weber 2013) on factors influencing exhibition destination attractiveness, from the perspective of (i) exhibitors and (ii) visitors who attend exhibitions in China. Findings indicate that exhibitors and visitors have different views on clustering effects (i.e. the localization of exhibitions in close proximity to corresponding agglomerations of respective industries and/or exhibitors) as one of the most important factors that comprise exhibition destination attractiveness. Findings also indicate that exhibitors and visitors rate first-tier and second-tier cities similarly in terms of attractiveness, suggesting that there may be good prospects for second-tier cities to develop as exhibition destinations.

The findings confirm prior propositions by several researchers (e.g. Chan 2005; Rubalcaba-Bermejo and Cuadrado-Roura 1995) about the link between industry agglomerations and exhibition destination development. This link is also observed in exhibitors' responses. A two-dimensional scale was developed to measure clustering effects in the exhibition industry, related to: (i) host city leadership in the industry; and (ii) host city as a source of exhibitors. The impact of these two clustering effects on exhibition destination attractiveness appears to be different. First, the two dimensions bear different weights of importance on perceived destination attractiveness. Second, the two dimensions indicate a different impact of agglomeration patterns between first-tier and second-tier cities on exhibition development. A first-tier exhibition city has a strong leadership status and is typically a major city, defined in terms of population and economic output. Its pattern of industrial clustering encompasses a larger variety of industry sectors, whereas in second-tier or third-tier cities a more specialized pattern of industrial concentration develops. This resonates with Rubalcaba-Bermejo and Cuadrado-Roura's (1995) argument that larger cities have a higher level of industry diversification and a larger number of exhibitions. Clustering effect 1 explains the leadership of a few gateway cities in exhibition development. Thus, the three first-tier cities in China's exhibition industry – Shanghai, Beijing and Guangzhou as the leading cities of the three largest industrial belts (i.e. the Yangtze River Delta, Beijing-Tianjin and Pearl River Delta Industrial

Belts) – could strengthen their leadership further in the future. Gateway cities have more of a competitive edge as they may gain support from several clusters in their surrounding region. Clustering effect 2 provides support for the development of exhibitions in such second-tier or third-tier cities where manufacturing facilities/factories are concentrated. It also explains why some specialized exhibitions hosted in smaller cities are well recognized by exhibitors. However, second-tier or third-tier cities with more specialized industrial agglomerations may have to bear in mind that it may be difficult for them to develop exhibitions for which they do not possess a clustering effect advantage. It is also noted in our analysis that exhibitors and visitors have different perceptions of clustering effects and assign varying weights to these effects in relation to overall exhibition destination attractiveness. Generally speaking, the clustering effects on exhibition destination attractiveness are more important to exhibitors than they are to visitors.

China's exhibition industry development shows some similarities with the patterns observed in Germany and Italy, where exhibitions gained strength due to clustering effects and economic development of the host regions, resulting from both the legacy of past industrial developments and current rapid advances (Brenner and Gildner 2006). Given the perceived importance of clustering effects from the exhibitors' perspective, it is likely difficult to start an exhibition in a city in China without respective clustering advantages. This is different compared to exhibitions that developed, for example, in Las Vegas, where exhibition development is based on available space, professional operation and touristic value (e.g. Yang and Gu 2012) rather than clustering effects. For successful exhibition destinations in China, cities with a favorable leisure environment in terms of tourist facilities, safety and cleanliness may also be competitive in developing exhibitions. Accessibility as measured by location, ease of access to the city and ease of acquiring information about the city was perceived as important in our study, lending support to similar findings in previous studies on convention site selection and exhibition center success factors (e.g. Hiller 1995; Rubalcaba-Bermejo and Cuadrado-Roura 1995; Crouch and Louviere 2004). Since second-tier cities were rated favorably in terms of accessibility, leisure environment and venue facilities, these cities could be successful when developing larger exhibitions to attract both exhibitors and visitors.

Finally, it must be pointed out that exhibition destination attractiveness factors constitute a necessary, but not sufficient condition for destinations to successfully attract and retain exhibitions. Exhibition-related factors were found to be more important to establish and retain an exhibition in a locality, with organizer performance and key show features being essential factors in exhibitors' and visitors' attendance decision-making, compared to a destination's macro and business environment (Jin et al. 2010). Specifically, the relationship between organizers and exhibitors, as manifested in trust, commitment, organizer service quality and relationship satisfaction, is a determining factor for exhibition brand preference from the exhibitors' perspective (Jin and Weber 2013). Thus, the success of an exhibition and the establishment of exhibition brands depend on exhibitions meeting both exhibitors' needs and objectives, in addition to the organizers' ability to build trust and commitment with exhibitors. Destination attractiveness factors play an important role, as services provided by organizers are inseparable from the quality of venue facilities and services.

REFERENCES

Brenner, T. and Gildner, A. (2006) 'The long-term implications of local industrial clusters', *European Planning Studies*, 14 (9): 1315–1328.

Butler, C., Bassiouni, Y., El-Adly, M. and Widjaja, A. (2007) 'Revamping the value chain in exhibition facilities: The case of the Dubai exhibition industry', *Facilities*, 25 (11/12): 419–436.

CCES – China Convention and Exhibition Society (2012) *Statistics and Analysis Report of China's Exhibition Industry 2011*, Beijing: CCES. Online. Available HTTP: <http://www.cces2006.org/report/> (20 March 2013).

Chan, C. (2005) *Exhibition Theory and Practice*, Shenzhen: Haitian Publications.

Chan, C. (2007) *On Spatial Distribution of China's Exhibitions*, Beijing. Online. Available HTTP: <http://www.cnki.net> (4 October 2009).

Cheung, W. (2011) *Hong Kong Trade Exhibition – An Industry Review (Phase 2)*, Hong Kong: The Chinese University of Hong Kong, BMT Asia Pacific. Online. Available HTTP: <http://www.legco.gov.hk/yr11-12/english/panels/ci/papers/ci1115cb1-661-1-e.pdf> (12 April 2014).

Crouch, G. I. and Louviere, J. J. (2004) 'The determinants of convention site selection: A logistic choice model from experimental data', *Journal of Travel Research*, 43 (2): 118–130.

Detlefsen, H. and Vetter, N. (2008) *Convention Centers: Is the Industry Overbuilt? 2008 Update*, HVS. Online. Available HTTP: <http://www.hvs.com/article/3180/convention-centers-is-the-industry-overbuilt-2008/> (12 November 2013).

Fuchslocher, H. (2005) 'Analysis of exhibitors – An instrument of fair controlling', in M. Kirchgeorg, W. Giese and W. Dornscheidt (eds) *Trade Show Management: Planning, Implementing and Controlling of Trade Shows, Conventions and Events*, Wiesbaden: Gabler, 287–303.

Guo, J. (2007) *The Report on Development of China's Convention and Exhibition Economy 2006–2007*, Beijing: Social Sciences Academic Press.

Guo, J. (2012) *Annual Report on China's Convention and Exhibition Economy 2012*, Beijing: Social Sciences Academic Press.

Hiller, H. (1995) 'Conventions as mega-events: A new model for convention–host city relationships', *Tourism Management*, 16 (5): 375–379.

Jin, X., Bauer, T. and Weber, K. (2010) 'China's second-tier cities as exhibition destinations', *International Journal of Contemporary Hospitality Management*, 22 (4): 552–571.

Jin, X. and Weber, K. (2013) 'Developing and testing a model of exhibition brand preference: The exhibitors' perspective', *Tourism Management*, 38: 94–104.

Jin, X., Weber, K. and Bauer, T. (2012) 'Impact of clusters on exhibition destination attractiveness: Evidence from Mainland China', *Tourism Management*, 33 (6): 1429–1439.

Kay, A. (2005) 'China's convention and exhibition center boom', *Journal of Convention and Event Tourism*, 7 (1): 5–22.

Kirchgeorg, M. (2005) 'Characteristics and forms of trade shows', in M. Kirchgeorg, W. Giese and W. Dornscheidt (eds) *Trade Show Management: Planning, Implementing and Controlling of Trade Shows, Conventions and Events*, Wiesbaden: Gabler, 33–56.

Rubalcaba-Bermejo, L. and Cuadrado-Roura, J. R. (1995) 'Urban hierarchies and territorial competition in Europe: Exploring the role of fairs and exhibitions', *Urban Studies*, 32 (2): 379–400.

UFI – The Global Association of the Exhibition Industry (2007) *The World Map of Exhibition Venues and Future Trends*, Paris: UFI. Online. Available HTTP: <http://www.ufinet.org/media/publicationspress/2007_ufi_world_map_of_exhibition_venues.pdf> (10 February 2008).

UFI (2011) *Global Exhibition Industry Statistics, 2011*, Paris: UFI. Online. Available HTTP: <http://www.ufi.org/Medias/pdf/thetradefairsector/2011_exhibiton_industry_statistics.pdf> (9 November 2012).

UFI (2012) *The Global Exhibition Barometer – Survey of the Exhibition Industry*, Paris: UFI. Online. Available HTTP: <http://www.ufi.org/Medias/pdf/thetradefairsector/surveys/ufi_global_exhibition_barometer_july_2012.pdf> (20 March 2013).

Yang, L.-T. and Gu, Z. (2012) 'Capacity optimization analysis for the MICE industry in Las Vegas', *International Journal of Contemporary Hospitality Management*, 24 (2): 335–349.

7. The spatial distribution of China's exhibition industry

Yi-Wen Zhu and Gang Zeng

INTRODUCTION

In recent years, China's exhibition industry has developed quite rapidly (see Golfetto and Rinallo, *this volume*; Jin and Weber, *this volume*). In 1997, China hosted approximately 1,000 exhibitions overall. By 2011, the number had increased to approximately 7,300 exhibitions (Wang 2004; Guo 2013). Accordingly, China's direct revenues from exhibitions increased from approximately $490 million (USD) in 2001 to $2.65 billion (USD) in 2008 (Guo 2011). As a result of this growth, the exhibition industry has become more important as an economic factor in many urban areas. And along with this, scholars have begun to study trade fairs and related activities in China more intensively (see Bathelt and Zeng, *this volume*; Kong and Zhang, *this volume*). From the perspective of economic geography, the spatial distribution of the trade fair industry and its dynamics in Mainland China are, however, not yet fully understood (see, also, Jin and Weber, *this volume*). Key questions with respect to the spatial distribution of trade fairs in Mainland China are the following: Where are trade fairs located and where does most of the trade fair activity take place? Which are the factors (variables) that influence trade fair activity and development? In other words: what are the characteristics of cities that have large trade fair activity? If we are able to answer these questions, we may be able to draw important lessons regarding urban economic policy.

With respect to the spatial distribution of the centers of China's exhibition industry, there are different views among Chinese researchers. Some argue that there are five main centers of China's exhibition industry (Tian 2006): Beijing, Shanghai, Guangzhou, Dalian and Chengdu. Others only view Beijing, Shanghai and Guangzhou as the key centers of trade fair activity in the country (Ju et al. 2006). Furthermore, existing Chinese research investigates the domestic exhibition industry at different geographical scales, adding to the confusion. Some explore trade fairs at the urban level (Hu 2004; Ye 2004); while others focus on the provincial level (Wang 2003; Hu 2008). And they often use different indicators to investigate trade fair activity. All of this makes it difficult to compare the results of related studies.

In attempting to explain the spatial distribution of the exhibition industry, many influential factors (variables) have been proposed in the literature as having a potential impact on trade fair activity. Some studies mentioned general variables, such as the city size and the economic development status (Jin et al. 2010), while others highlight specific variables, such as the gross domestic product (GDP) share of service industries (Hu 2004; Wang 2004).

Using this as a starting point, this chapter is structured as follows: The next section analyzes the spatial distribution of the Chinese exhibition industry at the urban level. Then, possible variables are selected from a systematic investigation of the literature that have a potential impact on the location of trade fair activity. This is followed by a quantitative analysis at the urban level of the variables that influence the number of exhibitions. Finally, the significance of these variables is evaluated and compared with findings in the literature on China's exhibition industry.

SPATIAL DISTRIBUTION OF CHINA'S EXHIBITION INDUSTRY

(i) Scale and Measurement of Trade Fairs in China

In the literature, the exhibition industry in China has been analyzed at both the urban scale (e.g. Hu 2004) and the provincial scale (e.g. Wang 2003). Such varying scales have contributed to obscuring the true spatial pattern of trade fairs. In this analysis, we analyze trade fairs at the urban level for two reasons: First, although the urban centers/municipalities of Beijing, Shanghai, Tianjin and Chongqing are political units with equal status as provinces in China, it would be confusing to compare trade fairs in these four urban centers with those in entire provinces that include many different cities. For example, it would not make much sense to compare the number of exhibitions in Beijing with those in Guangdong province, which consists of Guangzhou, Shenzhen and many other cities. Second, the intra-provincial distribution of trade fairs differs substantially between the Chinese provinces. In some provinces, the exhibition industry is almost completely concentrated in its capital city (e.g. in Sichuan), while in other provinces it is more dispersed over several different cities (e.g. Guangdong). As a result, an analysis of trade fairs at the provincial scale obscures these differences while an investigation at the urban scale (city level) will likely draw a clearer picture of the true spatial distribution.

Aside from the scale of the analysis, there is another source that sometimes creates confusion when conducting a comparative study, as the exhibition activity can be measured according to different variables. These include the number of exhibitions, the number of UFI (The Global Association of the Exhibition Industry) events, the number of exhibition halls or the total exhibition area (Chen and Lu 2003; Hu 2004; Xu and Zhu 2004). Of these four variables, we first excluded the number of exhibition halls and the total exhibition area as target variables for our quantitative analysis. Exhibition halls are, of course, important because they provide the spatial context that allows exhibitions to take place. In China, the number and size of exhibition halls is, however, not truly representative of the status of exhibition activities. Chinese local governments are willing to build large and luxurious exhibition halls without necessarily attracting many exhibitions in the short or medium term (Kay 2005). Often the goal is to strengthen the cities' images or to trigger local GDP growth through state spending. However, once new exhibition halls are completed, some are rarely used (Wang 2005), or are under-utilized (see Jin and Weber, *this volume*).

As for the number of UFI events, which would be a potential indicator of well-organized, internationally acknowledged trade fairs, there were only nine cities in Mainland China in 2011 that had events certified by UFI. Of the 58 events certified by UFI overall, 34 were concentrated in Shanghai and Beijing (UFI 2011b). And of the nine cities with UFI events, five had only three or less events (see the lower part of Figure 7.1). Because of the small numbers of cases, this indicator does not describe the spatial distribution of the entire exhibition industry very well. As a consequence, we use the number of exhibitions per city in the following analysis of the exhibition industry in Mainland China as our dependent variable. Compared to the number of exhibition halls or the total exhibition area, this variable provides a better characterization of the status of exhibition activities. Compared to the number of UFI events, it is better suited for a quantitative analysis because it allows us to include a larger number of cases and thus generates a more robust analysis. Indeed, many cities in China already have a considerable number of exhibitions. Twenty-nine of these cities were included in our analysis as explained below.

(ii) Spatial Distribution of Trade Fairs in China

The upper part of Figure 7.1 shows the spatial distribution of trade fairs in Mainland China as measured by the number of exhibitions in 2010 – our

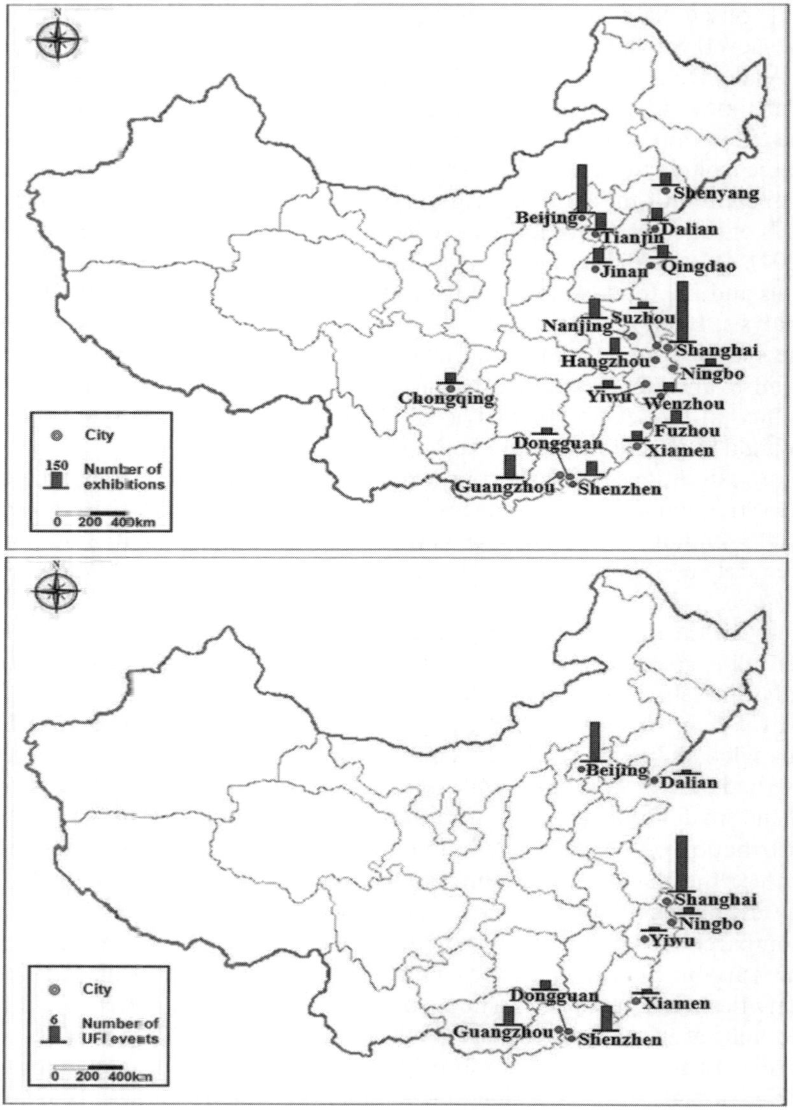

Note: The upper part of the figure only lists cities with at least 50 exhibitions.

Sources: Wang and Guo (2010) and UFI (2011b).

Figure 7.1 Number of exhibitions, 2010, and number of UFI events, 2011, by city in Mainland China

dependent variable. On the whole, this graph shows that exhibitions are concentrated in eastern coastal areas of the country. Among all cities with exhibitions, Shanghai takes the lion's share of trade fairs in China, with a total of 557 events in 2010. Besides Shanghai, Beijing (440 exhibitions) and Guangzhou (207 exhibitions) in the North and South, respectively, are also major centers of the exhibition industry. Several cities near Shanghai also hold exhibitions, particularly Nanjing (180 exhibitions) and Hangzhou (131 exhibitions). Among the cities close to Beijing, Tianjin (153 exhibitions) also hosts a larger number of trade fairs. In the area around Guangzhou, Shenzhen (118 exhibitions) is home to more than 100 exhibition events. In addition, the inland city of Chongqing (87 exhibitions) also holds a notable number of exhibitions (see, also, Jin and Weber, *this volume*; Bathelt and Zeng, *this volume*).

The lower part of Figure 7.1 illustrates the spatial distribution of UFI certified events in 2011, which are usually larger international exhibitions. Compared to the spatial distribution of trade fairs overall, these certified exhibitions are much more concentrated in the largest urban centers, particularly in the global cities Beijing and Shanghai, which host 24 and 20 UFI events, respectively.

The upper part of Figure 7.2 illustrates the number of exhibition halls (with an indoor exhibition capacity greater than 5,000 square meters) across Chinese cities in 2011; and the lower part shows the total exhibition area in these cities in the same year. The spatial distribution of overall exhibition space clearly indicates the historically important role of Guangzhou which was the location of the famous Canton Fair – an important site for international trade in Mainland China since the late 1950s (see Bathelt and Zeng, *this volume*). Adjacent to Guangzhou, which has 12 exhibition halls and 856,995 square meters of exhibition space, Dongguan (three exhibition halls and 132,500 square meters of exhibition space) and Shenzhen (five exhibition halls and 142,910 square meters of exhibition space) are also important trade fair cities in the South. Similarly, around Shanghai, which has 13 exhibition halls and 418,805 square meters of exhibition space, Hangzhou (nine exhibition halls and 291,589 square meters of exhibition space), Ningbo (four exhibition halls and 135,730 square meters of exhibition space) and Yiwu (three exhibition halls and 105,200 square meters of exhibition space) also show up as centers of exhibition activity. Near Beijing, which has 16 exhibition halls and 382,146 square meters of exhibition space, Tianjin (four exhibition halls and 133,380 square meters of exhibition space) and Dalian (three exhibition halls and 98,800 square meters of exhibition space) also have many large exhibition facilities.

In sum, the exhibition industry is mainly distributed along the eastern coastal area of the country with three prominent centers of exhibition

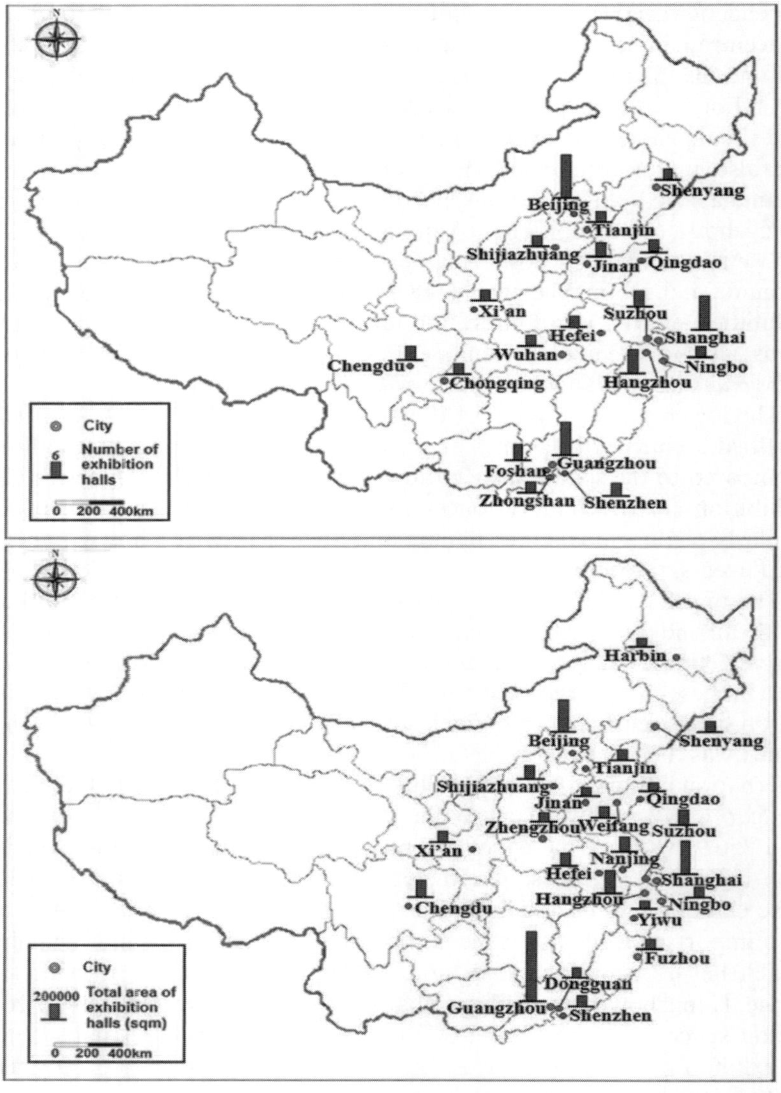

Notes: The upper part of the figure only lists cities with at least four exhibition halls; the lower part only lists cities with an exhibition area of at least 100,000 square meters.

Source: Guo (2011).

Figure 7.2 Number of exhibition halls and total exhibition area by city in Mainland China, 2011

activity. No matter which measure is adopted, we generally find a similar spatial pattern of Mainland China's exhibition industry around these three centers. These are, interestingly, wider regional agglomerations that extend beyond the urban scale. A major characteristic of these figures is that Shanghai, Beijing and Guangzhou are the centers of trade fairs in terms of the number of exhibition events, the number of exhibition halls and total exhibition space.

EXPLAINING THE GEOGRAPHY OF TRADE FAIRS IN CHINA

(i) Independent and Control Variables

As mentioned above, existing research on trade fair activity in China discusses many possible factors influencing the spatial distribution of the exhibition industry. From this literature, we can identify seven groups of factors and one crucial control variable (city size) that may substantially influence the location of exhibition activity:

1. *Infrastructure conditions*: As temporary gatherings of individuals and firms from many different regions, trade fairs require excellent infrastructure conditions such as highways and airport connectivity. For exhibitions with a high proportion of international participants, what is required is not only an efficient transportation system within the host city, but also high international accessibility via direct flight connections. Infrastructure conditions, both internally and externally, are an important factor for the growth of trade fairs that has been emphasized in many studies (Zheng 2000; Chen et al. 2003; Wei 2003; Xu et al. 2003; Hu et al. 2004; Wang 2004; Zhu 2004; Dong 2005; Fu 2006; Zhao 2006; Li 2007; Zhang 2008). To consider different transportation modes for internal and external movements of people, we selected three variables: length of highway network (in kilometers) per square kilometer, number of flight passengers going through the city's airport per capita and length of the subway network (in kilometers) per square kilometer. In order to avoid scale effects that are simply due to city size, all variables were normed in terms of per capita or per area unit measures. The indicators cover various transportation methods for fair-goers, including cars, aircraft and city subways as discussed in the literature.
2. *Economic development status*: The state of economic development, as measured by the GDP, is regarded in many studies as another

important factor that stimulates the development of trade fairs. The rationale behind this variable is that it is assumed that exhibition activity increases with economic strength. In China as well as other countries, large exhibition revenues are realized in cities with high economic development status. Cities with strong economies have a larger number of firms that could potentially exhibit their products, for instance in export-oriented events, but also need a larger number of supplies from other firms that they may inspect during trade fairs. Such economically strong centers form important markets and are attractive for firms from other regions and countries that participate in import-oriented events. Getting feedback from customers in major urban markets becomes an important reason for firms to attend trade fairs in these centers (Ying 2001; Huang 2002; Gao 2003; Liu 2003; Tao 2003; Hu 2004; Wang 2004; Dong 2005; Tian 2006; Zhao 2006; Qiao and Hu 2010; Jin et al. 2010). In order to avoid scale effects, we selected GDP per capita as an independent variable in our analysis to represent the economic development status of a city.

3. *Hospitality infrastructure*: Studies have argued that the hospitality infrastructure, including hotels, restaurants and supporting facilities, is also important for the success of trade fairs in some cities (Zheng 2000; Ying 2001; Huang 2002; Chen et al. 2003; Gao 2003; Tao 2003; Wei 2003; Hu 2004; Zhu 2004; Dong 2005; Fu 2006; Zhao 2006; Li 2007; Zhang 2008). Trade fairs are not just business as usual but provide a special experience for business travelers that includes getting away from home and staying elsewhere overnight. Therefore, trade fair participants do not only require services offered by the event organizers, but also complementary amenities, including comfortable hotels, which they can enjoy with their business partners and clients during a short-term stay. It can be expected that cities with good hospitality infrastructure will attract more and larger exhibitions. Star hotels that are certified by the National Tourism Administration of China are often suggested as an indicator that measures the influence of the hospitality infrastructure on trade fairs activity in cities (Zhao 2006; Zheng 2000). In this analysis, we used the number of star hotels per 10,000 people as an independent variable.
4. *Support/service infrastructure*: Studies about trade fairs also discuss the impact of the local/regional industrial structure on trade fair activities, especially related to specific service industries. Indicators used include modern service activities or the proportion of service activities in GDP, although these indicators are quite unspecific (Huang 2002; Tao 2003; Hu 2004; Wang 2004; Zhu 2004; Dong 2005; Fu 2006; Li 2007; Zhang 2008). Trade fairs can be described as services provided

by organizers to exhibiting firms. A large number of individuals and firms being together at trade fairs also generates opportunities for an entire set of service industries in the host city that specialize in serving needs related to trade fair activity. Therefore, cities with more exhibitions likely stimulate the development of a related service economy. At the same time, it can be expected that cities with a large service/support sector will stimulate the growth of exhibition activities. In order to avoid scale effects, we selected the proportion of service industries in GDP as an independent variable in our analysis.

5. *Governmental support/private organization capacity*: In the context of developing countries, the government also plays an important role for the development of the exhibition industry, as demonstrated in many chapters in this edited book (see Chang et al., *this volume*; Chen and Chu, *this volume*; Kalafsky and Gress, *this volume*; Li, *this volume*). In analyzing trade fair development, existing research discusses factors such as policy support, political status, regulatory agencies, industry associations and the number of professional event organizers as potential influences on the extent of trade fair activity. In urban areas, local governments are crucial decision-makers for the construction of exhibition venues and supporting infrastructure. Correspondingly, trade fairs in Mainland China are relatively regulated and controlled by local governments or the central government (Wang 2005). In general, this is not necessarily a negative factor as the organization of large trade fairs can benefit from and may even require strong government support. Furthermore, various urban policies regarding exhibition activities can also promote the development of trade fairs (Zheng 2000; Ying 2001; Chen et al. 2003; Gao 2003; Tao 2003; Zhu 2004; Fu 2006; Tian 2006; Zhao 2006; Zhang 2008; Qiao and Hu 2010). To measure this government impact, we used a dummy variable that indicates whether a city is the capital city of the respective province, as government support in Mainland China is usually strongest in capital cities. Additionally, we chose a dummy variable that indicates whether a city has professional exhibition enterprises certificated by UFI to measure the capabilities to organize trade fairs.
6. *Openness*: Some studies argue that an open economy helps the growth of trade fairs and suggest using indicators, such as export and foreign direct investment (FDI), to measure the influence of city openness on trade fair activity (Tao 2003; Hu et al. 2004; Zhu 2004; Dong 2005; Fu 2006). The hypothesis behind this is that an open economy has a positive impact on the development of trade fairs. In order to avoid scale effects, we used the share of exports and FDI in GDP, respectively, to measure the openness of urban economies in two different ways.

7. *Environmental conditions*: Additionally, studies on exhibition activity also mention the natural environment and environmental conditions as an influence on trade fair activities, as business travelers may prefer an attractive clean environment and opportunities for sightseeing to combine their work at the exhibition center with recreational activities in the region (Zhu 2004; Tian 2006; Li 2007; Qiao and Hu 2010). Given the serious air pollution problems that currently exist in many large Chinese cities, this may indeed be a concern for participating firms. In our analysis, we selected two indicators to measure the impact of environmental conditions on trade fair activity: green areas as a percentage of the overall city area and the proportion of days per year with acceptable air-quality levels, during which the air quality is classified as being 'level 1' or 'level 2' according to the Air Quality Index defined by the Ministry of Environmental Protection of China (this index is divided into five levels, where 'level 1' and 'level 2' represent 'excellent' or 'good' air quality, respectively).
8. *Control variable*: Any such analysis, of course, has to be aware that city size may play a major role on trade fair activity in that a large city with a large urban economy may provide more business opportunities for trade with partners from other regions and countries. Large cities may also have larger markets and attract a larger number of exhibitors to trade fairs looking for market access. In this case, trade fair activity to some extent may simply be a function of city size. However, this is a trivial relationship that is not of interest in our analysis. We therefore chose to use the permanent population (in 10,000 people) as a control variable in our quantitative analysis. We expect this control variable to be highly significant and are interested to see which independent variables also have a significant influence on trade fair activity in urban areas in Mainland China. This way, we measure the impact of all variables discussed in this section beyond scale effects.

(ii) Data and Methodology

The objective of this study is to measure the importance of different independent variables on trade fair activity in Chinese cities and to compare these influences in a quantitative manner. This was investigated through a series of ordinary least square (OLS) multiple regression analyses. The goal was to analyze the relationship between the dependent variable and the joint group of independent and control variables to identify those variables that have a significant impact – a method commonly used in the literature (Costa-i-Font and Rodriguez-Oreggia 2005; Hervas-Oliver and Albors-Garrigos 2008; Fritsch and Schindele 2011). As discussed before, the number of exhibitions per city was to be used as the dependent variable and the population as the control variable. In total, 12 factors were included as independent variables. The original model is as follows:

$$\begin{aligned} Exhibitions_i = {} & Const. + \beta_1 POPL_i + \beta_2 \mathrm{HIGH}_i + \beta_3 \mathrm{AIRL}_i + \beta_4 \mathrm{SUBW}_i \\ & + \beta_5 \mathrm{GDP}_i + \beta_6 \mathrm{HOTL}_i + \beta_7 \mathrm{SERV}_i + \beta_8 \mathrm{CAPT}_i + \beta_9 \mathrm{ENTP}_i \\ & + \beta_{10} EXPO_i + \beta_{11} FDI_i + \beta_{12} GREN_i + \beta_{13} AIRQ_i \end{aligned}$$

In our model, index i refers to city I; the following abbreviations were used for the dependent, independent and control variables:

DEPENDENT VARIABLE:
Exhibitions: number of exhibitions

CONTROL VARIABLE:
POPL: permanent population (in 10,000 people)

INDEPENDENT VARIABLES:
HIGH: length of highway network (in kilometers) per square kilometer
AIRL: flight passengers going through the city's airport per capita
SUBW: city subway network (in kilometers) per square kilometer
GDP: GDP per capita
HOTL: number of star hotels per 10,000 people
SERV: proportion of service industries in GDP
CAPT: provincial capital dummy
ENTP: organizational capacity dummy (existence of professional UFI member exhibition enterprises)
EXPO: share of exports in GDP
FDI: share of FDI in GDP
GREN: percentage of green area of overall area
AIRQ: proportion of days per year with acceptable air-quality levels

Before conducting the statistical analysis, we selected those cities in Mainland China which had the largest numbers of exhibitions. During the data collection process, we found that most sources were available at the provincial level, while there was a lack of comparable data at the urban scale. Our goal was to generate a reliable database that contained the most important exhibition cities in Mainland China. In the end, this database included 29 cities with exhibition activities. Overall, these cities held 3,111 exhibitions in 2010, which accounted for over 76 percent of the overall exhibition industry in China (Wang and Guo 2010). We have to keep in mind, however, that the sample size is relatively low with n = 29, especially considering that we have 12 variables as independents and one as a control. Therefore, we have to exercise care in our interpretation of results.

For most independent variables and the control variable, data for the 29 cities in the year 2010 was extracted or calculated from the respective local Statistical Yearbooks. The Statistical Yearbooks of each Chinese city are official reports released by the respective local Bureaus of Statistics each year. We used an online database of these local Statistical Yearbooks, that is the Chinese Socioeconomic Development Statistical Database, which generates data access to all different cities/urban areas (CSDSD 2014). The provincial dummy variable was established according to the current administrative division of China; and the organizational capacity dummy (existence of professional UFI member exhibition enterprises) was defined according to UFI (2011a).

The next section reports our analysis. First, we conducted a correlation analysis between all variables to check for indications of multicolinearity. Second, we entered the control variable into the regressions model, and then tested a series of tri-variate models that contain the control variable and one independent variable. This step identified those variables that have significant influences on trade fair activity regardless of scale effects and regardless of the other independent variables. Third, we entered all significant independent variables into a single multivariate regression model, tested the model and explained the outcome.

(iii) Analysis and Results

Table 7.1 shows the correlation coefficients between all variables included in the model and the corresponding 2-tailed significance tests of these correlation coefficients. The correlation coefficients used were simple Pearson correlation coefficients.

The correlation table shows that our dependent variable has numerous significant correlations with the independent and control variable, which is what our model eventually aimed to quantify further. Of all variables, the control variable POPL had the strongest correlation with the number of exhibitions – our dependent variable. The correlations between the dependent variable and the independent variables HIGH, SUBW, SERV and ENTP are also significant at the 10 percent, 5 percent or 1 percent level.

In addition, there are also high correlations between some of the independent variables. These have to be watched carefully as they could create problems in our analysis. High significant correlations were found between AIRL & SERV, GDP & HOTL, GDP & EXPO, HOTL & EXPO and CAPT & EXPO. While there are clearly numerous worrisome

Table 7.1 Correlation matrix of the variables

	Exhibitions	HIGH	AIRL	SUBW	GDP	HOTL	SERV	CAPT	ENTP	EXPO	FDI	GREN	AIRQ	POPL
Exhibitions	1	.484***	.087	.528***	.114	−.002	.463**	.193	.334*	.066	.103	.275	−.251	.659***
HIGH		1	−.363*	.248	.223	.017	−.125	−.045	.222	.375**	.094	.123	−.021	.406**
AIRL			1	.118	.434**	.342*	.575***	−.014	.095	.220	.051	.305	.324*	−.241
SUBW				1	.254	−.002	.189	.217	.383**	.142	.228	.261	−.089	.565***
GDP					1	.695***	.127	−.276	.279	.713***	.084	.279	.290	−.193
HOTL						1	.381**	−.084	.131	.544***	.085	.310	.054	−.322*
SERV							1	.376**	−.125	−.079	−.027	.342*	−.136	.009
CAPT								1	−.396**	−.588***	.048	.036	−.367**	.205
ENTP									1	.385**	.217	.281	.102	.343*
EXPO										1	.065	.253	.459**	−.143
FDI											1	.374**	.283	.193
GREN												1	.247	.079
AIRQ													1	−.344*
POPL														1

Notes: * significant at the 10 percent level; ** significant at the 5 percent level; *** significant at the 1 percent level (2-tailed tests).

correlations, we decided not to eliminate variables at this stage, but used a different strategy to reduce the number of variables for the multiple regression models as described below.

In the next stage of our analysis, we entered the control variable POPL into the regression model, and then tested a sequence of different tri-variate regressions with each independent variable and the control variable. The regression results are shown in Table 7.2.

The results indicated that our control variable POPL, the population of the city, was highly significant and had a strong positive impact on exhibition activity. The control variable POPL was significant in every model at the 1 percent level. This suggested that the number of trade fairs in a city grew with city size, but was also an indicator of the overall economic strength both in terms of the number of producers (industrial firms) and the size of the market (consumers and users). When entering the independent variables successively to test their additional explanatory value, only four of the 12 variables turned out to have a significant impact on the dependent variable. These were the length of the highway network (HIGH), the extent of air traffic (AIRL), the per-capita economic product (GDP) and the size of service economy (SERV). The independent variable SERV was significant at the 1 percent level, and the other three variables were significant at the 10 percent level. It seemed surprising at first that only a few of the independent variables were significant in these tri-variate regressions, but upon closer examination, this was clearly related to two effects: First, city size as measured by population was clearly the dominant factor influencing the exhibition activity in Mainland China overall. Second, that many independent variables were significantly correlated with the control variable (see Table 7.1), despite the fact that they were normed to a per-unit base, suggested that they did not have much explanatory power beyond the effects of city size. Aside from city size, the proportion of service industries in a city's economy had the strongest impact on the number of exhibitions.

In the following step of our analysis, we entered the control variable POPL and the four significant independent variables HIGH, AIRL, GDP and SERV into a single multiple regression model. The regression results are shown in Table 7.3.

In this final multivariate model, we found that the control variable POPL and two of the independent variables HIGH and SERV were significant at the 5 percent or 1 percent level. The independent variables AIRL and GDP were not significant, which was related to their correlations with other independent variables (see Table 7.1). More specifically, the correlations between AIRL & HIGH, AIRL & SERV and GDP & AIRL were all very high and significant at the 10 percent, 5 percent or 1 percent level.

Table 7.2 OLS regression coefficients for the number of exhibitions per city: Individual variable influences with control

	(1) POPL	(2) POPL & HIGH	(3) POPL & AIRL	(4) POPL & SUBW	(5) POPL & GDP	(6) POPL & HOTL	(7) POPL & SERV	(8) POPL & CAPT	(9) POPL & ENTP	(10) POPL & EXPO	(11) POPL & FDI	(12) POPL & GREN	(13) POPL & AIRQ
Const.	11.85	−37.84	−21.69	9.34	−29.35	−39.76	−289.46***	2.89	3.90	−11.18	15.81	−194.02	58.03
	(0.43)	(−0.96)	(−0.68)	(0.34)	(−0.83)	(−0.94)	(−3.60)	(0.08)	(0.13)	(−0.33)	(0.43)	(−1.46)	(0.22)
POPL	0.12***	0.10***	0.13***	0.10***	0.13***	0.13***	0.12***	0.12***	0.11***	0.12***	0.12***	0.12***	0.12***
	(4.55)	(3.61)	(5.04)	(3.06)	(4.98)	(4.93)	(5.59)	(4.30)	(3.97)	(4.69)	(4.42)	(4.54)	(4.13)
HIGH		67.79*											
		(1.69)											
AIRL			12.77*										
			(1.82)										
SUBW				55.99									
				(1.32)									
GDP					30.54*								
					(1.76)								
HOTL						168.58							
						(1.57)							
SERV							6.16***						
							(3.90)						
CAPT								15.60					
								(0.40)					
ENTP									29.03				
									(0.78)				
EXPO										47.33			
										(1.12)			
FDI											−133.61		
											(−0.16)		
GREN												5.26	
												(1.58)	
AIRQ													−0.49
													(−0.17)
Adj. R^2	0.414	0.451	0.460	0.430	0.456	0.444	0.616	0.395	0.405	0.419	0.392	0.445	0.392

Notes: DV: number of exhibitions per city; * significant at the 10 percent level; ** significant at the 5 percent level; *** significant at the 1 percent level; T-values in brackets.

Table 7.3 OLS regression coefficients for the number of exhibitions per city: Two possible multivariate models

	(1) POPL & HIGH & AIRL & GDP & SERV	(2) POPL & HIGH & SERV
Const.	−375.32***	−382.51***
	(−4.42)	(−4.95)
POPL	0.10***	0.09***
	(4.47)	(4.59)
HIGH	81.48**	88.03***
	(2.15)	(2.95)
AIRL	1.29	
	(0.15)	
GDP	9.74	
	(0.56)	
SERV	6.35***	6.74***
	(3.50)	(4.81)
Adj. R- squared	0.687	0.704

Notes: DV: number of exhibitions per city; * significant at the 10 percent level; ** significant at the 5 percent level; *** significant at the 1 percent level; T-values in brackets.

Due to the interrelations between independent variables, some variables were insignificant when used simultaneously in the model. Because of this, we removed the insignificant variables AIRL and GDP from our model in the final stage of our analysis.

The regression results are shown in the last column in Table 7.3. The adjusted R-square of the final model was quite high at 0.704, which indicated that about 70 percent of the variation of the number of trade fairs across the 29 largest Chinese centers of such activity can be explained by the two independent variables and the one control variable. All variables in this model were significant at the 1 percent level. The final model suggested that urban exhibition activity as measured by the number of trade fairs was strongly impacted by city size (POPL), the density of the transportation network (HIGH) and the development of the service economy (SERV). Other variables were not significant, as some information represented by these variables was already contained in the other variables. The final model can be summarized as follows:

$$\text{Exhibitions} = -382.51 + 0.09\ \text{POPL} + 88.03\ \text{HIGH} + 6.74\ \text{SERV}$$

CONCLUSION

Our analysis of the spatial distribution of the exhibition industry in Mainland China showed that trade fair activity is mainly concentrated in three larger regions, each of which consists of several urban regions. The centers of these main exhibition regions are Shanghai, Beijing and Guangzhou. Based on our analysis of trade fairs at the urban level in China, we identified numerous influencing factors on the spatial distribution of exhibitions. First, and most importantly, trade fair activity was a function of city size. As cities grow into mega-urban regions, they develop huge markets for intermediate and final products and develop agglomerations of industries. This provides an ideal combination of factors supporting the growth of the exhibition activity. Second, additional factors identified in our analysis were transportation infrastructure, economic development status and the service sector, all of which have an additional positive impact on the trade fair industry (see, also, Jin and Weber, *this volume*).

The transportation infrastructure becomes an important factor that supports the growth of exhibition activity in Chinese cities. The transportation infrastructure influences trade fairs in two important ways: First, large transportation nodes are important because they connect urban centers with other cities/regions in the country, as well as overseas. These are important in bringing in trade fair participants, especially exhibitors, from outside. Second, a high-quality intra-metropolitan transportation network is also important to provide quick access to the exhibition venues as traffic congestion becomes an increasing problem in many large urban centers in China.

The importance of the economic development stage for trade fair activity was also supported by this research. A high economic development status as measured by per-capita GDP indicates that there are more highly developed production, research and marketing activities, high value-added production stages and so on. All of this provides a favorable setting for the establishment of trade fairs that support knowledge flows between local exhibitors/visitors and other domestic and foreign participants. In particular, the development of the service sector of a city appears to be strongly related to trade fair activity. Although this indicator is rather general and necessarily not strongly linked to trade fair activity on a substantive basis, it may indicate the development state of the knowledge economy and as such emphasize the sophistication of industry development as an influence for trade fair development. It should also be mentioned that the effect of the service sector may be a reactive one rather than a trigger for trade fair activity, as the growth of the number of trade fairs may stimulate the growth of related local services (Zhen and Ouyang 2001; Bathelt et al. 2014).

The results of this research suggest that although provincial capitals still exercise control over important resources for trade fair development (Yu and Lu 2005), and although a large proportion of trade fairs are still at least partially organized by state authorities (Wang 2005), their impact on exhibition activity may be limited overall. In our research, the spatial distribution of trade fair activity in Mainland China depended on the size of the urban centers, their economic strength and the development of sophisticated service functions, but not so much on direct state influence and support. This is an important finding that suggests that the impact of central/provincial state authorities on trade fair development is not as strong as is sometimes assumed (e.g. Kay 2005). Equally, professional exhibition enterprises may be important for the organization of trade fairs, yet their local presence does not appear to be decisive for the growth of overall exhibition activity.

The influence of openness of the urban economy, represented by the degree of export and FDI flows, did not show up as a significant factor in our models. Three explanations may help understand this: First, we can assume that a high degree of openness and export activities are generally crucial factors for the development of urban economies. However, the level of export activity is highly correlated with other variables of economic strength and thus does not show up as an independent factor. Second, it should be emphasized that the enormous size of the Chinese economy suggests that trade fairs are in the first place national events that provide tremendous opportunities for domestic firms from different cities and regions to link with new markets in Mainland China (see Bathelt and Zeng, *this volume*). It appears therefore that domestic interactions are the driving forces of trade fair development, although this may change in the future. Third, openness may also not show up because of the present structure of China's exhibition industry, which has been described as lacking professionally organized events that could attract foreign exhibitors (Huang and Xu 2005; Wang and Tian 2008). Some cities may indeed not have realized the importance of attracting exhibitors from abroad, although this appears to be changing quickly (see Bathelt and Zeng, *this volume*).

Altogether, the findings of this chapter support some arguments in the literature about the Chinese trade fair industry but also emphasize different dimensions. For future research, it would be important to increase the sample size of studies, include more trade-fair-specific variables and complement the results with qualitative case studies.

ACKNOWLEDGMENTS

Earlier versions of this chapter were presented at the 'Academic Salon of Human Geography and Regional Economy, East China Normal University' and the 'Asia-Pacific Conference on Trade Fair Ecologies' in Shanghai in April and May 2012, respectively. We would like to thank all participants of these meetings, especially Xiang Kong, Diego Rinallo and Tang-Wei Teng. Finally, we would like to thank Harald Bathelt, Michael Kunz and Peng-Fei Li for reviewing this chapter carefully and providing comments in several rounds of revisions, especially regarding the methodological approach.

REFERENCES

Bathelt, H., Golfetto, F. and Rinallo, D. (2014) *Trade Shows in the Globalizing Knowledge Economy*, Oxford: Oxford University Press.

Chen, C., Xie, C. and Wang, Y. (2003) 'Dalian convention and exhibition industry development trend and countermeasures', *Research on Financial and Economic Issues*, 9: 78–80 (in Chinese).

Chen, H. and Lu, H. (2003) 'How to develop the trade fairs in China: An international review', *China Business and Market*, 3: 29–32 (in Chinese).

Costa-i-Font, J. and Rodriguez-Oreggia, E. (2005) 'Is the impact of public investment neutral across the regional income distribution? Evidence from Mexico', *Economic Geography*, 81: 305–322.

CSDSD – Chinese Socioeconomic Development Statistical Database (2014) *Chinese Socioeconomic Development Statistical Database*, Shanghai. Online. Available HTTP: <http://tongji.cnki.net/kns55/Dig/dig.aspx> (15 June 2014).

Dong, S. (2005) *A Study on Industry Cluster and Industry's Competitiveness of Chinese Convention and Exhibition Industry*, Master's thesis, Beijing: Beijing University of Technology (in Chinese).

Fritsch, M. and Schindele, Y. (2011) 'The contribution of new businesses to regional employment – An empirical analysis', *Economic Geography*, 87: 153–180.

Fu, H. (2006) *Study on the MICE Industry's Space Pattern in Yangtze River Region*, Master's thesis, Shanghai: East China Normal University (in Chinese).

Gao, J. (2003) 'A preliminary study into the development conditions and driving force system of MICE industry', *Tourism Science*, 1: 24–27 (in Chinese).

Guo, J. (2011) *Annual Report on China's Convention and Exhibition Economy 2011*, Beijing: Social Science Academic Press (in Chinese).

Guo, J. (2013) *Annual Report on China's Convention and Exhibition Economy 2013*, Beijing: Social Science Academic Press (in Chinese).

Hervas-Oliver, J.-L. and Albors-Garrigos, J. (2008) 'The role of the firm's internal and relational capabilities in clusters: When distance and embeddedness are not enough to explain innovation', *Journal of Economic Geography*, 9: 263–283.

Hu, B. (2004) *Research on the Development Impetus System of Cities' Convention*

Exhibition Industry in China, Master’s thesis, Shanghai: Shanghai Normal University (in Chinese).

Hu, B., Wang, C. and Hu, B. (2004) ‘Analysis of Shanghai convention and exhibition industry and studying on its developing goals and countermeasures’, *Human Geography*, 19: 33–21 (in Chinese).

Hu, P. (2008) ‘An analysis of regional differences of the MICE competition in China: From an exhibition halls perspective’, *Journal of Business Economics*, 197: 64–74 (in Chinese).

Huang, K. and Xu, Y. (2005) ‘The research on German exhibition industry and its reference for China’s exhibition industry after WTO accession’, *World Trade Organization Focus*, 7: 19–25 (in Chinese).

Huang, X. (2002) ‘On the development of our country’s economy of conference and exhibition’, *Commercial Research*, 237: 117–119 (in Chinese).

Jin, X., Bauer, T. and Weber, K. (2010) ‘China’s second-tier cities as exhibition destinations’, *International Journal of Contemporary Hospitality Management*, 22: 552–571

Ju, S., Lu, L., Yang, X. and Zhu, T. (2006) ‘Research on the spatial structure of China’s exhibition economy based on urban system’, *Urban Planning Forum*, 161: 93–97 (in Chinese).

Kay, A. L. K. (2005) ‘China’s convention and exhibition center boom’, *Journal of Convention and Event Tourism*, 7: 5–22.

Li, Y. (2007) ‘On the construction of Guangzhou as the center of the regional MICE urban system’, *Economic Research Guide*, 6: 151–153 (in Chinese).

Liu, X. (2003) ‘Convention and exhibition economic development positioning and strategy selection of Nanjing’, *Social Science in Nanjing*, 3: 86–90 (in Chinese).

Qiao, X. and Hu, P. (2010) ‘The comparative analysis of the exhibition center between China and Germany: With Shanghai, Munich and Frankfurt as examples’, *Shanghai Economic Research*, 10: 91–97 (in Chinese).

Tao, T. (2003) ‘Conference and exhibition economy: The propeller for the new round of development of Shanghai – An analysis and countermeasures study on the status quo of conference and exhibition industry in Shanghai’, *Journal of Finance and Economics*, 29: 43–51 (in Chinese).

Tian, T. (2006) *Analysis on the Space Layout of Modern C&E Industry*, Master’s thesis, Chengdu: Sichuan University (in Chinese).

UFI – The Global Association of the Exhibition Industry (2011a) *Member Search*, Paris. Online. Available HTTP: <http://www.ufi.org/Public/ufimembers/memberorganisations.aspx?Clef_SITESMAPS=81&Clef_SITESMAPS=82> (10 December 2011).

UFI (2011b) *UFI Approved Events*, Paris. Online. Available HTTP: <http://www.ufi.org/Public/ufimembers/UFIApprovedEvents.aspx?Clef_SITESMAPS=52&Clef_SITESMAPS=87> (10 December 2011).

Wang, D. and Tian, S. (2008) ‘A discussion on the reflection and trend of the development of China’s MICE industry’, *Future and Development*, 3: 47–51 (in Chinese).

Wang, F. and Guo, J. (2010) *Annual Report on China’s Convention and Exhibition Economy 2010*, Beijing: Social Science Academic Press (in Chinese).

Wang, H. (2003) ‘Analysis on the regional economic conditions of the exhibition industry’, *Journal of Beijing International Studies University*, 5: 32–37 (in Chinese).

Wang, X. (2004) *Studies on Exhibition Economy of China*, Doctoral thesis, Changchun: Jilin University (in Chinese).
Wang, Y. (2005) *Study on the Chinese Government's Roles in the Development of Conference and Exhibition Industry*, Master's thesis, Shanghai: East China Normal University (in Chinese).
Wei, X. (2003) 'The strategy of MICE industry success in Singapore', *Journal of Guilin Institute of Tourism*, 14: 85–88 (in Chinese).
Xu, F. and Zhu, J. (2004) 'The contemporary trends of international exhibition economic development and the measures to promote China's exhibition industry', *Productivity Research*, 2: 117–126 (in Chinese).
Xu, M., Zhang, Y. and Wang, X. (2003) 'The mode of site selection and facility planning for exhibition centers in Germany', *City Planning Review*, 27: 32–48 (in Chinese).
Ye, H. (2004) *Study on the Development of China's Convention and Exhibition Industry*, Master's thesis, Wuhan: Wuhan University (in Chinese).
Ying, L. (2001) 'Analysis on the status quo of exhibition industry in Chongqing', *Journal of Chongqing Institute of Technology*, 15: 43–58 (in Chinese).
Yu, Y. and Lu, Y. (2005) 'Studies on centrality of provincial capitals', *Jing-Ji-Di-Li (Economic Geography)*, 25: 352–357 (in Chinese).
Zhang, N. (2008) *A Study on Evolution Laws and Mechanism of Exhibition Spatial Distribution in Guangzhou*, Master's thesis, Guangzhou: Guangzhou University (in Chinese).
Zhao, L. (2006) *The Appraisal Index System Study on the Competitiveness of City Meeting and Exhibition Industry*, Master's thesis, Shanghai: East China Normal University (in Chinese).
Zhen, M. and Ouyang, B. (2001) 'Exhibition economy, the booster of urban economy', *The Southern Economy*, 7: 42–44 (in Chinese).
Zheng, J. (2000) 'An analysis of the present state and developing trend of Shanghai's industry of large conference and exhibition', *Tourism Tribune Bimonthly*, 6: 40–44 (in Chinese).
Zhu, H. (2004) 'Study and inspiration on the spatial distribution of overseas MICE industry: Taking Germany and Hong Kong as examples', *Human Geography*, 19: 93–96 (in Chinese).

8. Trade, knowledge circulation and diverse trade fair ecologies in China

Harald Bathelt and Gang Zeng

INTRODUCTION

According to many indicators, China is among the largest and fastest growing economies in the world and leader of the development processes in Asia. Related to this growth, the country has witnessed fast growth of trade fair activity in recent years (see Golfetto and Rinallo, *this volume*). At present, however, our knowledge about the structure and trends of the developing trade fair business in China is limited and has been under-researched in academic work.

The development of trade fairs and the construction boom surrounding their infrastructure has been unique over the past 20 years (AUMA 2008; UFI 2011; Guo 2011; 2012). By 2009, there were a total of 31 large convention centers (with an indoor exhibition space of at least 50,000 square meters) in Chinese cities, offering a total indoor exhibition space of almost 2.5 million square meters. Within just two years, this infrastructure was extended by almost another 1 million to a total of 3.4 million square meters (+ 38 percent). The overall number of large convention centers increased from 31 to 38 (Bathelt and Zeng 2014; Bathelt et al. 2014). Shanghai, Beijing and Guangzhou were leading this development, each hosting several hundred trade fairs on an annual basis (see Table 8.1). Even less well known and much smaller Yiwu in Zhejiang province, one of the case studies in this chapter, had 65 trade shows in 2009.

The driving forces behind this trade fair and convention center growth in China were: (i) ongoing strong economic growth that led to a sharp increase in demand from both the public and private sectors; (ii) state investments and tax incentives available for convention center expansion; (iii) global mega events in China, such as the 2008 Beijing Olympic Games and the 2010 Shanghai World Expo, directing additional state funds to the trade fair business; and (iv) globalization and relocation processes of industries and trade fairs from Europe to China (Kay 2005; Jin et al. 2010b). In this context of growth, this chapter explores the emerging trade fair ecologies

Table 8.1 Number of trade fairs in Chinese cities, 2009

City/province	Trade fairs (number)
Shanghai	557
Beijing	440
Guangzhou/Guangdong	207
Nanjing/Jiangsu	180
Tianjin	153
Hangzhou/Zhejiang	131
Jinan/Shandong	128
Shenzhen/Guangdong	118
Fuzhou/Fujian	113
Dalian/Liaoning	107
Qingdao/Shandong	105
Shenyang/Liaoning	99
Chongqing	87
Xiamen/Fujian	70
Wenzhou/Zhejiang	68
Yiwu/Zhejiang	65
Ningbo/Zhejiang	62
Suzhou/Jiangsu	50
Total	2,740

Source: Wang and Guo (2010).

in China. More specifically, our aim is to show that a highly differentiated and complex field of trade fair activity which performs diverse functions is developing in the country: from temporary marketplaces where business is made and contracts are signed (Rinallo and Golfetto 2011) to temporary clusters of knowledge circulation, relationship-building and networking (Maskell et al. 2006; Bathelt and Schuldt 2010).

The discussions in this chapter are as follows: In the next section, a brief summary is provided of the historical development of trade fairs in China since the 1950s and existing literature is analyzed to describe the state of the Chinese trade fair business since the early 2000s. From this, the analytical focus of this study is derived. We argue that existing literature does not sufficiently acknowledge the development of complex trade fair ecologies in China as is demonstrated in four case studies in the remainder of the chapter: (i) the former Canton Fair in Guangzhou that provided international market access to an otherwise isolated economy since the late 1950s; (ii) the China International Industry Fair in Shanghai that connects the domestic metal/machinery industry to international knowledge flows and innovation; (iii) the China International Exhibition on Gases Technology, Equipment and Application which provides a temporary meeting place for relationship-building and networking; and (iv) the China Yiwu International Commodities Fair in Yiwu which establishes a high-buzz periodic marketplace. At the end, the most important findings are summarized and conclusions are drawn.

DEVELOPMENT OF CHINESE TRADE FAIR ACTIVITIES SINCE THE 1950s

From the limited research that exists, we know that trade fairs in China became increasingly important in the late 1970s, supported through the opening policy of the country. Initially, this development was state-directed (Schellkes 2003). Prior to China's opening policy, the establishment of trade fairs was politically driven with the goal to present the country favorably to the world and stimulate international trade (Kay 2005). In this time period, relatively small trade fair centers with about 10,000 square meters of indoor exhibition space were established according to Russian conceptions and architecture. Such complexes were opened in Shanghai and Beijing, as well as in other large Chinese cities. Already in 1956, Guangzhou became the location of the now famous Canton Fair (today: the China Import and Export Fair). With the opening policy in the 1980s under Deng Xiaoping, the Chinese trade fair business expanded. Many trade fairs were organized jointly with trade fair organizers from Hong Kong or the US, while larger fairs were still under government control. In this period, the number of foreign firms participating in these events grew quickly. They attended trade fairs to market their products in the Chinese market. It was not until Jiang Zemin's regime in the early 1990s, however, that new convention centers were systematically built on a larger scale. At that point, trade fair centers were primarily concentrated in the Coastal Special Economic Zones. In this period, Shanghai became an important center of trade fair activity in China while the convention center building boom continued (Kay 2005). This boom is still visible today as illustrated by ongoing plans in Shanghai to build another large convention center complex with an exhibition space of 400,000 square meters around the facilities of the former Hongqiao airport (Shi 2012). At the present time, experienced foreign trade fair organizers are involved in running the new trade fair centers or organizing new trade fairs that resemble the formats of well-established events in developed economies (see Rinallo and Golfetto, *this volume*).

In terms of an evaluation of this growth, the literature offers substantial criticism although the number of investigations is limited. Studies indicate that the state-planned character of Chinese trade fairs has introduced inefficiencies and that their organization is often shaped by political goals (e.g. Kay 2005; Jin et al. 2010b), leaving behind unsatisfied participants. Along with this, it has been criticized that political motives rather than demand considerations drive the development of convention center construction – with the effect that many such centers would be underutilized (e.g. Jin et al. 2010a; Jin and Weber, *this volume*), facing the challenge to survive as other cities and venues establish competing events. Furthermore, it has been argued that Chinese trade fairs focus on direct sales and sales promotion activities rather than knowledge exchange, as indicated by practices of exhibitors primarily showing established technologies rather than leading-edge innovations (e.g. Young 2004).

However, this critique does only seem to capture part of the developing Chinese trade fair activity. While it is probably true that less successful and unprofessional trade fairs can be found in underutilized venues, this should not come as a surprise. It appears to be a typical process to be found in a developing context, in which state and industry associations try to establish events to support broader regional and national industrial development and trade flows, especially imports and exports. In fact, we came across two such early-stage events during the China International Industry Fair in Shanghai in 2010 (Bathelt and Zeng 2014): the Information and Communication Technology Show (ICTS) and Scientific and Technological Innovation Show (STIS). The events occupied one exhibition hall with about 11,500 square meters of exhibition space each and did not have the character of true trade fairs. They were established by the government in order to create a multi-sector trade show similar to Hannover Messe. For this purpose, state-owned firms, research organizations and universities had been requested to attend and present exhibits. As these events were not well organized, did not match customer expectations and were too diversified, they left behind frustrated exhibitors and did not attract many potential user industries. However, as will be shown below, these were exceptions in our study.

The Shanghai New International Expo Centre (SNIEC), for instance, can be characterized as a top venue with modern technology and superb access to international and national transportation networks (Geduhn 2012), rather than a mismanaged trade fair center. After several stages of expansion, the facilities had an overall exhibition space of over 150,000 square meters and hosted 94 trade fairs in 2011 with over 80,000 exhibitors and about 4 million visitors (see Table 8.2). The professional organization of the venue and careful planning of events led to a constant increase in the rate of utilization of the venue. This is illustrated by the turnover rate,

Table 8.2 Development of trade fair activity at the Shanghai New International Expo Centre (SNIEC), 2002–2011

Year	Trade fairs (number)	Exhibitors (number)	Visitors (number, millions)	Available exhibition space (sq.m.)	Turnover rate
2002	43	17,750	1.5	57,500	16
2003	45	22,350	1.6	57,500	18
2004	66	35,950	2.4	80,500	24
2005	67	46,400	2.5	80,500	29
2006	72	52,000	2.7	103,500	27
2007	78	58,750	3.1	103,500	30
2008	80	67,600	2.7	126,500	30
2009	78	61,750	2.8	126,500	28
2010	80	70,000	3.1	150,340	31
2011	94	81,700	4.0	150,340	32

Notes: sq.m. = square meters (1 square meter = 10.76 square feet); the turnover rate measures the number of times the entire exhibition space is rented out per year.

Source: Geduhn (2012).

which doubled in the 2000s from 16 to 32, suggesting that the entire exhibition space was rented out 32 times in 2011. Such a high turnover rate is hardly ever achieved by other convention centers, even in highly developed economies.

Considering many of the venues and the new trade fairs have been organized with the support and involvement of experienced trade fair organizers from Western Europe and North America, we can expect the development of a complex trade fair landscape with modern events that provide the basis for temporary clusters of knowledge exchange and interaction within the focused communities of the respective industries (Maskell et al. 2006; Borghini et al. 2014; Bathelt et al. 2014). The fact that such developments would prioritize knowledge-intensive exchanges and push back sales-related events, of course, leads us to ask where actual transactions take place if they are no longer focused on such events. As will be argued in this chapter, this is not a simple question of 'either/or'. We can witness the development of a diverse, highly differentiated trade fair environment with trade-oriented fairs attracting many buyers in some venues and knowledge-creation events in others that are characterized by non-buying, a-typical visitors (Sharland and Balogh 1996; Borghini et al. 2006). In short, what we found are different configurations of temporary

Table 8.3 Comparison of selected trade fairs in Chengdu, Guangzhou, Shanghai and Yiwu, 2010/2011/2012

Trade fair city	Event selected	Length (days)	Exhibition space (sq.m.)	Exhibitors (number)	Visitors (number)	Business turnover ($ billion (USD))
Chengdu	IG China (2010)	3	12,000	220	10,000	n.a.
Guangzhou	Canton Fair (Autumn 2012)	20	1,160,000	24,840	188,150	32.8
Shanghai	CIIF (2011)	5	140,000	1,650	105,700	0.2
Yiwu	Yiwu Fair (2012)	5	180,000	3,050	193,550	2.6

Notes: IG China = China International Exhibition on Gases Technology, Equipment and Application; Canton Fair = China Import and Export Fair; CIIF = China International Industry Fair; Yiwu Fair = China Yiwu International Commodities Fair; sq.m. = square meters (1 square meter = 10.76 square feet); n.a. = not available.

Sources: China Import and Export Fair (2012), China International Exhibition on Gases Technology, Equipment and Application (2010), China International Industry Fair (2012) and China Yiwu International Commodities Fair (2012).

markets and temporary clusters (Bathelt et al. 2014) that develop parallel to each other, yet have little in common with the types of inefficient events that have been described in the literature.

To illustrate this, we investigate four events in different Chinese cities in this chapter: the China Import and Export Fair (Canton Fair) in Guangzhou, the China International Industry Fair (CIIF) in Shanghai, the China International Exhibition on Gases Technology, Equipment and Application (IG China) in Chengdu and the China Yiwu International Commodities Fair (Yiwu Fair) in Yiwu (see Table 8.3). Although these are events of different size in different parts of China, they all take place in modern convention/exhibition centers. The four trade fairs range from 200 exhibitors and 10,000 visitors (IG China) to almost 25,000 exhibitors and 190,000 visitors (Canton Fair) and have a length of three to 20 days, respectively. Following the classification of Jin et al. (2010a), they include two first-tier trade fair cities (i.e. Shanghai and Guangzhou) as well as one second-tier and one even smaller third-tier trade fair city (i.e. Chengdu, Sichuan province and Yiwu, Zhejiang province, respectively).

The research presented in this chapter is largely qualitative and draws on mixed methodology. On the one hand, existing studies, trade fair reports and data from trade fair organizers were analyzed. On the other hand, we conducted a total of 102 semi-structured interviews among exhibitors at CIIF in Shanghai and IG China in Chengdu in 2010 (Bathelt and Zeng 2014; Bathelt et al. 2014). This was coupled with systematic observations conducted at these events, including visits to the Yiwu trade fair facilities and several visits to CIIF editions in consecutive years. From this extensive experience, we are able to triangulate the information acquired from multiple sources and are confident that this enables us to identify some fundamental structures of the emerging Chinese trade fair ecologies. The following sections discuss the nature of trade show activity for each of the four trade fairs.

CANTON FAIR IN GUANGZHOU – GATEWAY TO THE GLOBAL MARKET

The China Import and Export Fair (here referred to by its former name the Canton Fair) in Guangzhou is one of the world's largest trade fairs with an exhibition space of over 1 million square meters, about 190,000–210,000 visitors and 25,000–40,000 exhibitors per edition (see Table 8.3 and Table 8.4). The Canton Fair is also unusually long as it goes over three weeks. It consists of two editions, one in the spring and one in fall of each year, taking place in an exhibition center that was particularly built to host the event. An edition of the fair is organized in three consecutive phases which each last one week and are characterized by a different industry focus (China Import and Export Fair 2012). The Canton Fair, originally established in 1956 at a time when China was largely isolated

Table 8.4 Buyers and revenues at China Import and Export Fair (Canton Fair) in Guangzhou, 2008–2012

Year	Buyers (number)		Business turnover ($ billion (USD))	
	Spring edition	Autumn edition	Spring edition	Autumn edition
2008	192,000	174,500	38.2	31.6
2009	165,500	188,000	26.2	30.5
2010	204,000	200,500	34.3	n.a.
2011	207,000	209,000	36.9	37.9
2012	210,000	188,000	36.0	32.7

Note: n.a. = not available.

Source: China Import and Export Fair (2012).

from world trade, quickly became China's gateway to the global market. It provided opportunities for Hong Kong traders to organize production in close-by Guangdong province and provided opportunities, especially for low-cost small and medium-sized Chinese producers, to engage with global buyers from a range of different industries, particularly from Europe and North America (Powell 2007; Jin and Weber 2008; Bathelt and Zeng 2014). The Canton Fair developed into a place where global buyers from a variety of industries would go to inspect Chinese producers, make choices of which firms to collaborate with and place orders for larger batches of products, ranging from toys and textiles to plastics and metal products – and more recently electronics products. US buyers were especially attractive partners for Chinese producers because they would pay a substantial amount of the overall order up front, thus reducing the risks for the domestic, often regional, producers. It has been suggested that the Canton Fair was the place where a substantial share (possibly even the majority) of the overall Chinese export activities were negotiated (Fu et al. 2007) – although it is not completely clear how credible this information is.

While the Canton Fair is still an important place for small and medium-sized Chinese producers to make direct contact with international buyers and users (Fu et al. 2007), and while it is an important global sales event for many domestic industries, its purpose has become broader and now involves systematic knowledge exchanges with respect to production and innovation activities. The fair is a unique event that generates a 'microcosm of global trade' (Powell 2007; see, also, Rosson and Seringhaus 1995) and provides a crucial benchmark function for Chinese producers vis-à-vis their domestic counterparts and global buyer preferences, both in terms of price and quality. The Canton Fair also reduces the risks for international buyers as it provides a near-complete overview of Chinese production developments and, by means of comparison, enables buyers to acquire commodities with sufficient quality at the lowest price.

CHINA INTERNATIONAL INDUSTRY FAIR IN SHANGHAI – INTERNATIONAL KNOWLEDGE CIRCUITS

Although the China International Industry Fair in Shanghai is also an annual event that builds on a multi-sectoral design and involves a total of eight specialized industry fairs (see Table 8.5), it is characterized by a different communication and knowledge ecology than the Canton Fair (Bathelt et al. 2014). It is organized by different levels of government and

Table 8.5 Exhibitors at the China International Industry Fair (CIIF) in Shanghai by individual show, 2012

Individual shows at CIIF	Domestic exhibitors (number)	Domestic exhibitors (share)	Foreign exhibitors (number)	Foreign exhibitors (share)	Total
Metalworking and CNC Machine Tool (MWCS)	380	77.7%	109	22.3%	489
Industrial Automation (IAS)	260	56.2%	203	43.8%	463
Environmental Protection Technology (EPTES)	165	45.8%	195	54.2%	360
Information and Communication Technology (ICTS)	166	87.4%	24	12.6%	190
Energy (ES)	69	98.6%	1	1.4%	70
Scientific and Technological Innovation (STIS)	123	88.5%	16	11.5%	139
New Energy Auto (NEAS)	80	87.0%	12	13.0%	92
China Aerospace and Aviation (CAATS)	56	84.9%	10	15.1%	66
Total	1,299	69.5%	570	30.5%	1,869

Source: China International Industry Fair (2013).

receives strong support from several national ministries and academies. The trade fair was set up to mirror the global hub show Hannover Messe in Germany that has a similar structure of individual events. In 2011, the China International Industry Fair had over 1,600 exhibitors (and almost 1,900 in 2012) and attracted more than 105,000 visitors (see Table 8.3). The fair is the largest such event in China and one of the largest in Asia. It is well linked to the global cycle of similar industry fairs (Power and Jansson 2008) and matches events in Korea, Taiwan, the US and Germany (see Kalafsky and Gress, *this volume*; Chen and Chu, *this volume*). It is not surprising that over 30 percent of the exhibitors in 2012 were of foreign origin (see Table 8.5). The China International Industry Fair includes numerous industries from metalworking/machine tools and industrial automation through aerospace and aviation. The core individual events

Table 8.6 Domestic and international exhibitors at the China International Industry Fair (CIIF) in Shanghai, 2012

Region/country of exhibitor origin	Exhibitors (number)	Exhibitors (share)
A. Domestic exhibitors	1,299	100.0%
Shanghai region	838	64.5%
Rest of China	461	35.5%
B. International exhibitors	570	100.0%
Japan	232	40.7%
Germany	118	20.7%
Taiwan	73	12.8%
USA	35	6.1%
Italy	29	5.1%
Other countries	83	14.6%

Source: China International Industry Fair (2013).

are the Metalworking and CNC Machine Tool Show (MWCS) and the Industrial Automation Show (IAS) which occupied the largest part of the exhibition space in 2012 and accounted for about half of the exhibitors (Metalworking and CNC Machine Tool Show 2011).

In terms of the participants, almost two thirds of the domestic exhibitors in 2012 originated from the greater Shanghai region, which is characterized by a large concentration of respective industries (see Table 8.6). As such, the China International Industry Fair mirrors the economic strength in the catchment basin of the fair in a similar way as trade fairs in Germany or Italy (see Jin and Weber, *this volume*; Bathelt et al. 2014). International exhibitors came primarily from industrialized Asian economies, such as Japan and Taiwan, which accounted for over 50 percent of the foreign exhibitors, but also included numerous firms from other highly developed manufacturing countries, such as Germany, Italy and the US.

In terms of the reasons for participating in the event, the China International Industry Fair was very different from the Canton Fair. It was clearly not a sales event. The majority of visitors attended in order to gather general market and product information, look for innovative products, interact with existing suppliers and customers/buyers and/or search for specific technical solutions (see Table 8.7). In contrast, less than 15 percent of the firms attended for the purpose of placing purchasing orders. Although the China International Industry Fair was still in a state of formation when we conducted interviews at MWCS in 2010

Table 8.7 Reasons for visitor attendance at the China International Industry Fair (CIIF) in Shanghai, 2010 and 2011

Reasons for visitor attendance	Visitors (share)	
	2010	2011
Gather general market/product information	22.9%	20.6%
Find innovation	18.5%	15.0%
Contact existing suppliers and buyers	14.1%	19.4%
Place purchasing orders	14.0%	11.8%
Seek for special solutions	11.9%	15.9%
Identify new distributors/partners	9.8%	9.9%
Attending forum/conference	6.6%	4.6%
Others	2.3%	3.0%

Sources: China International Industry Fair (2011; 2012).

(with hidden exhibitors screening the hallways and pulling suitcases with product samples), the communication processes observed and the interview responses clearly demonstrated that this was a knowledge-based event about a specific industry/technology field and was not focused on sales activities. In fact, not one of the 45 firms interviewed at MWCS mentioned that sales, contract negotiations or taking orders were main reasons for attending the trade fair. In contrast, between 20 and 40 percent explained that they would try to establish initial customer contact, promote their brand in the country and establish their firm's image, and/or present new products and technologies to the market (Bathelt and Zeng 2014).

As a consequence, the communication and interaction processes of the exhibitors had a technology, production and/or application focus and were less about marketing and advertising. Exchanges with potential customers at the exhibits were focused on the characteristics of the products on display, specific solutions required and trends in innovations – while price aspects were less important. Firms would also use the opportunity to get an overview of their competition and compare their own products and innovations with those of others. Some interviewees mentioned how this provided both an incentive and pressure to make changes to their own production program to remain competitive. Overall, the communication processes at MWCS were similar to those at knowledge-intensive fairs in highly developed countries although leading-edge innovation did not play the same central role. Still, two thirds of the firms interviewed explained that they would receive ideas for innovation during the event and that they would actively look for potential new partners in production and marketing (Bathelt and Zeng 2014).

IG CHINA IN CHENGDU – RELATIONSHIP-BUILDING AND NETWORKING

Similar to the China International Industry Fair, IG China in Chengdu is a professionally managed event in the gas technology and equipment industry, with a location that shifts from year to year. The event is organized by the respective industry association (China International Exhibition on Gases Technology, Equipment and Application 2010). Since Chengdu has sometimes been considered to be a second-tier trade fair city (Jin et al. 2010a) located outside of China's coastal area (see Table 8.1), we expected a venue that was in a process of formation, being underutilized and less busy than, for instance, SNIEC in Shanghai. What we found in 2010, however, was quite different. The newly established Chengdu New International Exhibition and Convention Center had over 50,000 square meters of indoor exhibition space with nine exhibition halls and modern infrastructure (Chengdu Municipal Government 2008). A check of the venue's advertising material showed that the utilization rate of the exhibition complex appeared quite high and, during our visit, all exhibition halls were booked with several different parallel trade fairs and conventions (Bathelt and Zeng 2014). Throughout 2010, the exhibition complex hosted numerous primarily medium-sized events, although eight events had at least 10,000 visitors with a maximum of 170,000 participants at the Chengdu International Furniture Exhibition. Although most events were regional and national in character, some, such as Western China International Fair, had a foreign exhibitor share up to one third (see Table 8.8). Considering the fast economic growth in the Chengdu region, it can be expected that the city will become an even larger center of trade activity with more events in the future.

In 2010, IG China occupied one exhibition hall and hosted 220 exhibitors (9 percent of which were foreign exhibitors) and about 10,000 visitors (see Table 8.3 and Table 8.8). While most trade fairs in Chengdu had the character of regional or national exchange or import fairs, IG China had a mixed national/international character and was not focused on sales activities (Bathelt et al. 2014). IG China was similar in this respect to the China International Industry Fair, although knowledge exchanges were more limited and innovations rare. Even though some exhibitors of a new addition to the trade fair were disappointed because they participated with the goal of making contact with new customers, most of the

Table 8.8 Top trade fairs in Chengdu, 2010

Top trade fairs in Chengdu	Exhibitors (number)	International exhibitors (share)	Visitors (number)	International visitors (share)
– China International Exhibition on Gases Technology, Equipment and Application	220	9.1%	10,000	3.0%
– China National Pharmaceutical Machinery Exposition	800	n.a.	60,000	n.a.
– Western China International Fair	3,150	32.6%	70,000	6.6%
– China Electronics Fair	400	5.0%	10,750	0.9%
– Chengdu Home, Leisure Products and Gift Fair	500	n.a.	30,000	n.a.
– Chengdu International Building Decoration Materials and Housing Department Exhibition	160	n.a.	30,000	n.a.
– Western China International Equipment Manufacturing Expot	700	n.a.	50,000	n.a.
– Chengdu International Furniture Exhibition	600	n.a.	170,000	n.a.
– Autumn China Midwest Medical Equipment Exhibition	204	n.a.	7,850	n.a.

Sources: Information provided by the New International Exhibition and Convention Center in Chengdu.

participants knew this was not the nature of the event. In a mature industry field with gradual innovation and highly specialized producers, many of the firms were only partial competitors. A firm's rivals in one product segment were often important suppliers or customers in other segments. They were at the same time competitors and transaction partners (Bathelt and Zeng 2014). At the core of the participation at IG China were interactions with existing partner-competitors, building firm/product image and showing market presence. In line with the work of Prüser (2003), many interviewees pointed at the relationship-maintaining and network-generation activities during the event. Interviewees emphasized the closely knit networks that had developed over time as everybody basically knew everybody else in this mature industry context. IG China offered opportunities to discuss problems in existing inter-firm relationships and, overall, contributed to the field-reproducing processes in the industry (Gibson and Bathelt 2014) – much different from the interaction patterns at the Yiwu Fair.

YIWU FAIR IN YIWU – HIGH-BUZZ MARKET EXCHANGE

As an increasing number of trade fairs in China's modern convention centers have become temporary clusters for intensive knowledge exchange and network generation, this has generated 'windows of locational opportunity' (Storper and Walker 1989) for new venues and events in other places to establish alternative platforms for market transactions, placing orders and making deals – that is, for activities that were originally concentrated in the older venues of trade fair activity in large metropolitan centers. Yiwu is a prime example south of Shanghai, which exemplifies these countertendencies (China Yiwu International Commodities Fair 2012). Held in modern facilities, the Yiwu Fair was started in 1995 and has since developed into one of the largest export-oriented commodity fairs in China (Zhang and Zhang 2006), with almost 200,000 visitors/buyers and 3,000 exhibitors in 2012 (see Table 8.3). As pressure has grown in large metropolitan centers to provide appropriate settings for temporary clusters of knowledge generation and exchange, developments such as those in Yiwu could be interpreted as a trend towards the establishment of new temporary markets in more peripheral regions.

In 2012, three quarters of the exhibitors at the Yiwu Fair were of domestic origin (see Table 8.9). Of the Chinese exhibitors, about 70 percent were from the larger Yiwu region; and of the international exhibitors, 60 percent came from other Asian countries. While the visitor/buyer base was also primarily from Asia, it also included buyers from other countries around the world.

Table 8.10 and Table 8.11 clearly indicate from the perspectives of attending buyers and exhibitors that the Yiwu Fair is characterized by an overwhelming orientation on trade and sales activities. On the side of the visitors/buyers, 75 to 80 percent had a primary orientation towards acquiring products, searching for collaborators/partners (for instance, with respect to extending value-chain relationships), ordering new products or acquiring customers. Both domestic and international buyers had

Table 8.9 Domestic and international exhibitors at the China Yiwu International Commodities Fair (Yiwu Fair) in Yiwu, 2012

Region of exhibitor origin	Exhibitors (number)	Exhibitors (share)
A. Overall exhibitors	3,050	100.0%
Domestic exhibitors	2,281	74.8%
International exhibitors	769	25.2%
B. Domestic exhibitors	2,281	100.0%
Yiwu region	1,622	71.1%
Rest of China	659	28.9%
C. International exhibitors	769	100.0%
Asia (without China)	467	60.7%
Africa	98	12.8%
Europe	94	12.2%
Latin America	62	8.1%
North America	37	4.8%
Oceania	11	1.4%

Source: China Yiwu International Commodities Fair (2012).

Table 8.10 Reasons for buyer attendance at the China Yiwu International Commodities Fair (Yiwu Fair) in Yiwu by domestic and international buyers, 2012

Reasons for buyer attendance	Domestic buyers (share)	International buyers (share)
Acquisition of products	41.6%	36.2%
Search for collaborators/partners	19.8%	7.4%
Ordering new products	14.6%	32.9%
Understanding the industry's development	14.0%	15.1%
Customer acquisition	5.7%	2.0%
Preparation for next trade fair	4.3%	4.3%
Others	0.0%	2.2%

Source: China Yiwu International Commodities Fair (2012).

a similar trade-related focus. This was also matched by the expectations of exhibitors, with over half being primarily interested in sales activities or the search for collaborators (see Table 8.11). As such, the Yiwu Fair can be characterized as a temporary, periodic market (Rinallo and Golfetto

Table 8.11 Reasons for exhibitor attendance at the China Yiwu International Commodities Fair (Yiwu Fair) in Yiwu, 2012

Reasons for exhibitor attendance	Exhibitors (number)	Exhibitors (share)
Increase of sales activities	1,224	34.8%
Search for collaborators/partners	715	20.3%
Strengthen corporate image	680	19.3%
Collect market information	486	13.8%
Investment plans	246	7.0%
Transfer of technology	125	3.5%
Retail sales	11	0.3%
Others	35	1.0%
Total	3,522	100.0%

Source: China Yiwu International Commodities Fair (2012).

2011) that focuses on transactions across a wide variety of industries from traditional crafts to electronics products.

An indication for the high priority given to the development of such specialized places for national and international trade is the strong support by the Chinese Ministry of Commerce (Zhang and Zhang 2006). The success of the Yiwu Fair is not only related to the changing trade fair landscape in China but also its local origins. With China's opening policy, Zhejiang province quickly developed into a low-cost region for industrial production based on family enterprise structures, guanxi relations and an entrepreneurial spirit that is famous in China (Wei et al. 2007). The central location and high accessibility for firms in economic centers in China's coastal region, as well as proximity to Hangzhou's international airport were important preconditions for the rise of the fair. The growth of the Yiwu Fair was also related to the Shanghai government's aim to move traditional industries out of the city in order to create space for the expansion of the city and for the development of new modern industries (Zeng 2001). In the end, one could say that the upgrading process of Shanghai's trade fair business and its increasing focus on technology- and design-intensive knowledge-based events has created favorable conditions for the growth of temporary markets in Yiwu. What we may be witnessing is therefore a division of functions between trade fairs consistent with the development of their underlying different regional economies.

CONCLUSION

From the structures and developments of the four trade shows illustrated in this chapter, it is an arduous task to identify typical trade fair activities in China because what we find is a diverse mix of events. It is clear that simplistic stereotypes of places for local exchanges or inefficient events in underutilized venues are not the rule. What our research suggests instead is that the picture of Chinese trade fairs needs to be redrawn, as temporary clusters with complex communication and knowledge ecologies emerge (Bathelt and Zeng 2014), triggered by the continuous growth of the Chinese economy. Many trade fairs in large metropolitan areas are highly developed and characterized by knowledge exchanges, and some focus on innovation processes, intensive customer and supplier interaction, relationship-building and/or networking (as in the cases of the China International Industry Fair in Shanghai and IG China in Chengdu). At the same time, however, important sales activities, contract negotiations and deal-making are concentrated in other specialized cities and their venues (as in the cases of the Canton Fair in Guangzhou and the Yiwu Fair in Yiwu), which have become temporary exchange markets (Bathelt et al. 2014) that enable transactions of goods within and beyond the national borders.

The development of trade fair activity since the 1980s and its acceleration in the 2000s is an indication for both the enormous economic success and the rise of a large trade fair business in China. In a period when trade fair activities in the established cities and venues in Western Europe and North America are growing at a slow pace and are characterized by increasing competition (Rinallo and Golfetto 2011), the growth in China points at a new center of attention in the industry. Certainly, trade fairs and their venues in China are important places where foreign producers exhibit their products to get access to the market (e.g. Lee 2008), look for potential partners and receive strategic feedback on their production program. This is especially important as there is a great degree of uncertainty as to what kind of knowledge is required or useful to enter the Chinese market and who to approach for such contextualized knowledge (Maskell 2014). Trade fairs provide a unique opportunity to find solutions to these questions at a low risk. However, trade fairs also still have an important function as temporary markets (see Rinallo and Golfetto, *this volume*). While these could be interpreted as remnants of the role of trade fairs in early stages of development, we view these temporary marketplaces as efficient platforms for trade. It could be argued that beyond a certain threshold size of an economy, it becomes difficult to generate a representative overview of such a large market. This situation may well describe the Chinese case, where transparency is difficult to achieve due to the large size and constant change of the transitioning economy (see Maskell, *this volume*). Trade fairs, such as those in Yiwu and Guangzhou, solve this coordination problem by providing a broad market overview in the 'neighborhood context' of the exhibition venue. Through face-to-face observation and interaction, firms are able to successfully find producers with complementary manufacturing capabilities and/or place orders while controlling quality and price at the same time.

Although we are not witnessing the rise of global flagship fairs in China at the present time, many of the fairs that have been established in the first-tier and second-tier trade fair cities in the country (Jin et al. 2010a) have become temporary microcosms of their industries (Rosson and Seringhaus 1995) and have achieved national and (some) international importance. Selected events are now part of the cyclical knowledge-creation and field-reproduction processes at a global scale (Power and Jansson 2008; Gibson and Bathelt 2014), as part of the development of continental trade fair platforms (Golfetto and Rinallo 2014; Li 2014) that span the globe and adjust to specific continental demand conditions and institutional settings. Furthermore, we observe trends towards an increasing differentiation of trade fair functions – a division of functions between events in line with the proposed interrelationship between territorial specialization and trade fair specialization (Bathelt et al. 2014). It appears that the growth of knowledge-intensive manufacturing and service industries in the Shanghai region has not only sparked the development of knowledge-based trade show formats with increasing focus on knowledge exchanges and innovation, but also supported the development of temporary marketplaces in nearby Yiwu – a region that has historically been a leader in China in terms of trade functions.

ACKNOWLEDGMENTS

We wish to thank Sufyan Katariwala, Xiao-Rui Xin and Yi-Wen Zhu for their research support and one Reviewer for providing helpful comments. This chapter has also benefited from manifold discussions with the participants of the 2012 Conference on 'The Rise of Trade Fair Ecologies in the Asia-Pacific: Economic and Geographical Challenges' in Shanghai.

REFERENCES

AUMA – Ausstellungs- und Messeausschuss der deutschen Wirtschaft (2008) *Messemarkt China (Trade Fair Market China)*, Berlin: AUMA. Online. Available

HTTP: <http://www.auma.de/_pages/d/04_MessemaerkteAusland/0402_Laensderprofile/040208_China/download/Messemarkt_China.pdf> (10 June 2012).

Bathelt, H., Golfetto, F. and Rinallo, D. (2014) *Trade Shows in the Globalizing Knowledge Economy*, Oxford: Oxford University Press.

Bathelt, H. and Schuldt, N. (2010) 'International trade fairs and global buzz, Part I: Ecology of global buzz', *European Planning Studies*, 18 (12): 1957–1974.

Bathelt, H. and Zeng, G. (2014) 'The development of trade fair ecologies in China: Case studies from Chengdu and Shanghai', *Environment and Planning A*, 46: 511–530.

Borghini, S., Golfetto, F. and Rinallo, D. (2006) 'Ongoing search among industrial buyers', *Journal of Business Research*, 59: 1151–1159.

Borghini, S., Golfetto, F. and Rinallo, D. (2014) *Using Anthropological Methods to Study Industrial Marketing and Purchasing: An Exploration of Professional Trade Shows*, SPACES 2014-02, Toronto and Heidelberg. Online. Available HTTP: <http://www.spaces-online.com> (15 April 2014).

Chengdu Municipal Government (2008) *Exhibition and Convention Industries*, Chengdu. Online. Available HTTP: <http://www.chengdu.gov.cn/echengdu/news/detail.jsp?id=274977> (6 January 2012).

China Import and Export Fair (2012) *Canton Fair Online – Statistics*, Guangzhou. Online. Available HTTP: < http://www.cantonfair.org.cn/html/cantonfair/cn/about/.shtml> (5 December 2012).

China International Exhibition on Gases Technology, Equipment and Application (2010) *IG China 2010*, Chengdu. Online. Available HTTP: <http://www.igchina-expo.com/home.php?> (7 November 2010).

China International Industry Fair (2011) *After Show Report 2010*, Shanghai. Online. Available HTTP: <http://www.ciif-expo.com/uploadfile/article/uploadfile/201012/20101231092500457.pdf> (5 January 2012).

China International Industry Fair (2012) *After Show Report 2011*, Shanghai. Online. Available HTTP: <http://www.ciif-expo.com/article/show.php?itemid=1321> (3 October 2011) (in Chinese).

China International Industry Fair (2013) *After Show Report 2012*, Shanghai. Online. Available HTTP: <http://www.ciif-expo.com/uploadfile/article/uploadfile/201306/20130605015638873.pdf> (26 March 2014).

China Yiwu International Commodities Fair (2012) *China Yiwu International Commodities Fair*, Yiwu. Online. Available HTTP: <http://www.yiwufair.com/> (2 December 2012).

Fu, H., Yang, G. and Qi, Y. (2007) 'Factors affecting trade show effectiveness for Chinese small and medium-sized exporters', *International Management Review*, 3 (3): 84–96.

Geduhn, H.-J. (2012) *Shanghai New International Expo Centre*, presentation at the Shanghai New International Expo Centre, Shanghai (25 May 2012).

Gibson, R. and Bathelt, H. (2014) 'Field configuration or field reproduction? The dynamics of global trade fair cycles', *Zeitschrift für Wirtschaftsgeographie*, 58: 216–231.

Golfetto, F. and Rinallo, D. (2014) *Trade Show Events, from Live to Digital: Towards the Development of New Competencies*, SPACES 2014-03, Toronto and Heidelberg. Online. Available HTTP: <http://www.spaces-online.com> (15 April 2014).

Guo, J.-R. (2011) *Blue Book of Convention and Exhibition Economy. Annual Report*

on China's Convention and Exhibition Economy 2011, Beijing: Social Sciences Academic Press (in Chinese).
Guo, J.-R. (2012) *Blue Book of Convention and Exhibition Economy. Annual Report on China's Convention and Exhibition Economy 2012*, Beijing: Social Sciences Academic Press (in Chinese).
Jin, X., Bauer, T. and Weber, K. (2010a) 'China's second-tier cities as exhibition destinations', *International Journal of Contemporary Hospitality Management*, 22: 552–571.
Jin, X. and Weber, K. (2008) 'The China Import and Export (Canton) Fair: Past, present, and future', *Journal of Convention and Event Tourism*, 9: 221–234.
Jin, X., Weber, K. and Bauer, T. (2010b) 'The state of the exhibition industry in China', *Journal of Convention and Event Tourism*, 11: 2–17.
Kay, A. L. K. (2005) 'China's convention and exhibition center boom', *Journal of Convention and Event Tourism*, 7: 5–22.
Lee, P. (2008) 'Opening the door to the Chinese pharmaceutical market', *Chemistry Today*, 26 (5): 76–81.
Li, P.-F. (2014) 'Global temporary networks of clusters: Structures and dynamics of trade fairs in Asian economies', *Journal of Economic Geography*, 14: 995–1021.
Maskell, P. (2014) 'Accessing remote knowledge: The complementary roles of trade fairs, pipelines, crowdsourcing and listening posts', *Journal of Economic Geography*, 14: 883–902.
Maskell, P., Bathelt, H. and Malmberg, A. (2006) 'Building global knowledge pipelines: The role of temporary clusters', *European Planning Studies*, 14: 997–1013.
Metalworking and CNC Machine Tool Show (2011) *Post Show Report*, Shanghai. Online. Available HTTP: <http://www.ciif-expo.com/uploadfile/mwcs/uploadfile/201012/20101217013749332.pdf> (5 January 2012).
Powell, S. (2007) 'Guangzhou, a microcosm of global trade', *Barron's*, 12 March: 57.
Power, D. and Jansson, J. (2008) 'Cyclical clusters in global circuits: Overlapping spaces in furniture trade fairs', *Economic Geography*, 84: 423–448.
Prüser, S. M. (2003) 'Die Messe als Networking-Plattform (Trade fairs as a platform for networking)', in M. Kirchgeorg, W. M. Dornscheidt, W. Giese and N. Stoeck (eds) *Handbuch Messemanagement: Planung, Durchführung und Kontrolle von Messen, Kongressen und Events (Handbook of Trade Fair Management: Planning, Execution and Control of Trade Fairs, Conventions and Events)*, Wiesbaden: Gabler, 1181–1195.
Rinallo, D. and Golfetto, F. (2011) 'Exploring the knowledge strategies of temporary cluster organizers: A longitudinal study of the EU fabric industry trade shows (1986–2006)', *Economic Geography*, 87: 453–476.
Rosson, P. J. and Seringhaus, F. H. R. (1995) 'Visitor and exhibitor interaction at industrial trade fairs', *Journal of Business Research*, 32: 81–90.
Schellkes, W. (2003) 'Entwicklung des Messewesens in der Triade (Development of the trade fair business in the Triad)', in M. Kirchgeorg, W. M. Dornscheidt, W. Giese and N. Stoeck (eds) *Handbuch Messemanagement: Planung, Durchführung und Kontrolle von Messen, Kongressen und Events (Handbook of Trade Fair Management: Planning, Execution and Control of Trade Fairs, Conventions and Events)*, Wiesbaden: Gabler, 685–693.

Sharland, A. and Balogh, P. (1996) 'The value of nonselling activities at international trade shows', *Industrial Marketing Management*, 25: 59–66.
Shi, Y. (2012) 'World's biggest exhibition center set for Shanghai', *China Daily*, 5 March: 13.
Storper, M. and Walker, R. (1989) *The Capitalist Imperative: Territory, Technology, and Industrial Growth*, New York: Blackwell.
UFI – The Global Association of the Exhibition Industry (2011) *The World Map of Exhibitions Venues 2011*, Paris: UFI. Online. Available HTTP: <http://www.ufi.org/> (15 July 2013).
Wang, F.-H. and Guo, J.-R. (2010) *Blue Book of Convention and Exhibition Economy. Annual Report on China's Convention and Exhibition Economy 2012*, Beijing: Social Sciences Academic Press (in Chinese).
Wei, Y. D., Li, W. and Wang, C. (2007) 'Restructuring industrial districts, scaling up regional development: A study of the Wenzhou model, China', *Economic Geography*, 83: 421–444.
Young, R. (2004) 'Plastics in China: Exhibitors mostly tout existing products', *Plastics News*, 16 (24): 14–15.
Zeng, G. (2001) 'Research on the modification of industrial spatial distribution in Shanghai', *Geographical Research*, 20: 330–337 (in Chinese).
Zhang, X. and Zhang, H. (2006) 'Regional economic characteristic of MICE and its development strategy – A case study of Yiwu Fair', *Commercial Research*, 15: 108–111 (in Chinese).

9. Local industry structure and the formation of temporary clusters: the case of the Shanghai International Auto Show (SIAS)

Xiang Kong and Yu-Fei Zhang

INTRODUCTION

Trade fairs are usually regarded as platforms where firms from a specific industry can showcase their latest products or services, study their rivals' activities and acquire the latest market trends. During a trade fair, the suppliers/producers from a specific industry come together in a concentrated space to exhibit their products and services to promote trade (Bertrand 1987; Moeran 2011). At the same time, exhibitors participate in these fairs to maintain and intensify existing customer networks and make new connections (Ramírez-Pasillas 2007). For most exhibitors, trade fairs also provide important opportunities to establish and extend brand influence. In conversations with visitors, they can obtain market information for improving and developing their products and exchange information about technological advances in their fields (see Zeng and Bathelt, *this volume*). In addition, exhibitors have the opportunity to learn about the latest trends of competitors and potential partners, so as to generate new collaborations (Aldebert et al. 2011). As a result, trade fairs are not only platforms for trading, but critical means to expand markets and networks (Herbig et al. 1996) and to keep abreast of technological changes. Given the fact that a trade fair usually lasts only a few days, it can be regarded as a temporary multi-functional platform made up of various types of participants, such as manufacturers, intermediaries, industry analysts, business customers, government agencies, buyers/purchasing groups and media representatives (Browning and Adams 1998).

Exhibitions generally facilitate the growth of related service activities, such as transportation, accommodation, catering, shopping, entertainment and tourism. As studies have shown, the exhibition industry can stimulate the growth effects in related industries through pull and push effects by a factor of nine (Li 2011). For this reason, it is not surprising that many countries promote the development of the exhibition industry, with a special emphasis on international trade fairs.

This is also the case in China, where the exhibition industry has developed rapidly along with general economic growth in the country (see Golfetto and Rinallo, *this volume*; Bathelt and Zeng, *this volume*; Jin and Weber, *this volume*). Shanghai, the economic center of the Yangtze River Delta, is becoming a leading city for international trade fairs. During 2011, 295 international trade fairs were held in Shanghai and the total indoor exhibition space available by the end of 2011 exceeded 420,000 square meters (Guo 2012). The rapid growth of international trade fairs in Shanghai is mainly driven by the local government and industry associations. Although most international trade fairs attract a large number of exhibitors and visitors, valuable knowledge exchange often appears limited, although this can change quickly (Bathelt and Zeng, *this volume*). Exhibitors often obtain very little knowledge on markets and technologies, and the potential value of international trade fairs to stimulate learning processes and industry innovation is limited (Li, *this volume*). This chapter is based on fieldwork conducted at the Shanghai International Auto Show (SIAS), a leading trade show in the automobile industry in Shanghai, which is organized to promote industrial innovation and adaption in the domestic industry.

SIAS was chosen as a case study because the effects of trade fairs in promoting innovation are strongest in technology-intensive industries with high levels of inter-firm interaction. SIAS, which is held once every two years, mainly showcases finished automobiles and is, in the first place, a consumer trade show, rather than an event for industry professionals. It has developed into one of the largest international fairs in China. Since the auto industry in China mainly engages in assembling parts into complete vehicles, an international trade fair that is open to the public provides important market information with respect to the growth of the domestic auto industry. Our chapter studies the mechanisms and pathways by which international business-to-consumer (B2C) fairs encourage industries to innovate and develop further. Although the efficiency of knowledge exchanges in B2C fairs may be lower than that in business-to-business (B2B) fairs, they still play important roles for innovation and industrialization of regional economies.

In the next section, this chapter analyzes the mechanisms by which international trade fairs become temporary clusters that support innovation. Then, the Shanghai auto show's characteristics are investigated in comparison with other leading auto shows in Frankfurt, Detroit and

Geneva. This is followed by an analysis of the specific local characteristics of SIAS and the trajectory of its development. Finally, conclusions are presented and policy implications drawn.

FROM INTERNATIONAL TRADE FAIRS TO TEMPORARY CLUSTERS

(i) International Trade Fairs and Temporary Clusters

International trade fairs and similar recurrent events, such as professional gatherings and scientific conferences, can be viewed as temporary clusters (Maskell et al. 2004; 2006; Bathelt and Schuldt 2008). They form relational spaces for knowledge sharing and market interactions in the globalizing learning economy (Rosson and Seringhaus 1995). More than local/national gatherings, international trade fairs help manufacturers learn about markets and technologies outside the regional context and open channels for transferring external knowledge. This is important as innovation is increasingly a result of collaborative processes involving numerous actors who are endowed with different knowledge bases and competencies (Lundvall 1992). In the related processes, the exchange of tacit knowledge is a key component. Therefore, co-presence and face-to-face contact with other exhibitors/visitors during trade fairs becomes an important feature (Bathelt and Kappes 2009; Bathelt and Turi 2011). On the one hand, attendance and interaction help nurture innovation; on the other hand, external knowledge resources help stimulate learning processes and innovation of local vendors (see Li, *this volume*). As a result, international trade fairs develop into spaces where ideas for innovation are developed and circulated.

They not only provide spaces for communication between vertically- and horizontally-related firms, but also create opportunities for participants from different geographical areas to build trans-local relations. Although an international trade fair lasts only for a short time period, it is a recurrent platform. In this sense, trade fairs are also cyclical clusters. They generate complexes of overlapping spaces that can be reproduced, re-enacted and renewed over time (Power and Jansson 2008). Since international trade fairs have a positive effect on the transfer of tacit knowledge among innovative agents/firms, they can be considered as a knowledge cross-fertilization platform with multiple intended and unintended/accidental outcomes of interaction (Li 2006). Research shows that exhibitors do not only participate in trade shows to stimulate sales but also to acquire important external knowledge and to expand market networks (Belussi and Pilotti 2002). Modern exhibitions are therefore platforms for acquiring knowledge for innovation rather than for just selling goods.

(ii) Formation of a Temporary Cluster

Modern international trade fairs attract manufacturers of the same industry to get together at the same location for a limited time period. This stimulates networking and leads to intentional or unintentional information and knowledge exchanges (Bathelt and Schuldt 2008; Rinallo and Golfetto 2011). All of these are mechanisms by which international exhibitions promote the transfer of ideas and knowledge relevant for industrial innovation. Efficient exchanges of tacit knowledge are likely through the co-presence of technologically leading participants and diversified knowledge platforms, as well as an environment of mutual trust, albeit professional or swift trust likely pre-exists between some of the participants.

The role of international trade fairs in promoting industrial innovation also depends on the respective firms' absorptive capacities (Cohen and Levinthal 1990), which influence the efficiency of knowledge transfers. Thus, for trade fair organizers, attracting innovative suppliers, manufacturers and consumers becomes a crucial task. This is not always easy because, at a global level, international exhibitions in different cities and countries compete with each other, and they are sometimes scheduled almost simultaneously (Power and Jansson 2008). To be successful in this global competition context, international trade fairs need to develop distinctive features to attract the leading manufacturers and professionals.

Nowadays, many international trade fairs have developed lifestyle activities that combine work with fun activities, making it easier for sales people to accept working and living on the road (Amin and Cohendet 2004). At many international trade fairs, exhibition and interaction activities of participants are supported by snacks, drinks, lectures, seminars and presentations creating a relaxed environment for knowledge transfers (Tesar 1988). Diversified channels of communication are key in supporting the exchange of technical and market knowledge among manufacturers, suppliers and consumers, rather than modern information and communication technologies alone. This also includes exchange channels based on local characteristics (Bathelt and Zeng 2012). In essence this means that trade fairs maximize their benefit if they are linked to the local/regional industry structure or, in other words, if trade fair specialization relates to the economic specialization in the local/regional catchment basin (Bathelt et al. 2014; see Zeng and Bathelt, *this volume*), as has been shown to be the case at many European trade fairs.

Studies indicate that a substantial advantage of temporary clusters lies in building trans-local relations through face-to-face exchanges and the expansion of networks (Meyerson et al. 1996). Although there need to be some measures in place to prohibit intellectual property violations and to avoid inappropriate knowledge spillovers (Power and Jansson 2008), it is important to promote common beliefs and strengthen mutual trust. This is because there will be fewer misunderstandings and more efficient knowledge exchanges among professionals with similar technological, as well as cultural beliefs (Bathelt et al. 2010). While international trade fairs provide an environment with infinitely repeated communications that are conducive to the formation of consistent behaviors, they cannot support trust building in the same way as permanent clusters (Torre and Rallet 2005). Yet, the periodic and well-organized face-to-face space still offers unique interaction opportunities for actors from different geographical areas (Gertler 1993; 2001). Over time, through repeated get-togethers in the annual trade fair cycle, a context may be created that gradually strengthens mutual trust at a broader level and promotes global economic connections (Thrift 2000; Allen 2003; Amin and Cohendet 2004).

If organizers are able to develop their local/regional events into international fairs that draw on specific local characteristics, such as a competitive regional industry base, a positive feedback loop may be created between locally embedded economies and international participation. In short, if a trade fair aims to become a temporary cluster to promote the knowledge exchanges and the diffusion of ideas for industrial innovation, it must pay attention to the building of a specific 'brand' that links the event to the regional industry structure (Bathelt et al. 2014).

CHARACTERISTICS OF INTERNATIONAL AUTO SHOWS

Since the debut of the automobile at the Paris EXPO of 1889, the auto show culture has gradually matured and promoted the diffusion of automobiles, related technologies and the way they are used and how they shape our lives on a worldwide scale. The three largest auto shows, held in Frankfurt, Detroit and Geneva, have long histories and played a leading role in the development of the automotive industry, especially in regard to technological innovation. In the following section, we aim to explore the common experiences of these three auto shows in becoming temporary clusters. This is based on a comparison of the Frankfurt Internationale Automobil-Ausstellung (IAA), the North-American International Automobile Show (NAIAS) and the Geneva International Motor Show (GIMS).

(i) Frankfurt Internationale Automobil-Ausstellung (IAA) – Facing Industry Professionals

Frankfurt's IAA, whose predecessor was the Berlin Auto Show launched in 1897, has been held every year in Frankfurt since 1951, displaying passenger vehicles and commercial vehicles in alternating years (Wang 1998). Over time, IAA has become the largest auto show worldwide, reflecting the achievements of the automobile industry and the automobile market in Germany. Germany is the birthplace of the automobile and in 2011 its domestic and overseas car production reached 5.87 million and 4.96 million automobiles respectively (Wu 2012). Germany has strong competitive advantages in the high-end automobile market, including brands such as Mercedes-Benz, BMW, Audi and Porsche, and it is also a major automobile market. Sales of cars in Germany reached 3.17 million in 2011 with nearly two-thirds of domestic consumers choosing German brands, providing supportive conditions for the growth of advanced firms like Volkswagen and Daimler (CAAM 2013).

Relying on a high-end automobile industry and market in the country, IAA attracts a large number of leading-edge exhibitors and professional visitors from Germany and abroad. German domestic firms form a substantial proportion of attendees, showing strong local/national features. Eighty-four percent of the visitors in 2011 were professional visitors, three-fourths of them being representatives from marketing or technical departments (IAA 2012). IAA has become a key event that attracts decision-makers, whose main objective is to obtain the latest information on market demand and technological innovation (IAA 2012). IAA can be regarded as a symbol representing global automobile development, displaying the state of the art in automobile technology and heading future trends in design. Professional visitors pay particular attention to the technology content of new models, the quality of components and even to do-it-yourself maintenance equipment. To support this, the 'Most Innovative' prize is typically awarded to automobile components, which embody this 'professional spirit' of IAA (Zhou 2003).

(ii) North American International Automobile Show (NAIAS) – Facing Advanced Consumption

NAIAS was first held in 1907 as the 'Detroit Auto Show' but changed its name to become a broader platform in 1989. NAIAS is held in Detroit and is, as such, located in the heartland of the headquarters of the three large US automakers: General Motors, Ford and Chrysler. The production of the three automakers reached 13.06 million cars in 2011 (NAIAS

2013). Annual automobile sales in the US account for about one-fifth of the world total (about 13 million cars), as each family in the US has on average 2.7 cars, which is six times above the global average (Zhou 2004). Aside from a very large general automobile market, this also includes a substantial market for luxury vehicles. As a consequence, NAIAS has become the leading platform to showcase luxury vehicles, aimed at high-end consumption (Wang 2012). Exhibitors strive to attract consumer attention by means of creative and consumer novelty displays, which make NAIAS a 'surreal visual feast' (Liu 2007). At the same time, many forums, technology conferences and press meetings are arranged during the event to promote professional communication (NAIAS 2013).

(iii) Geneva International Motor Show (GIMS) – Providing a Neutral Meeting Platform

Geneva is famous for various cultural activities, including conferences and exhibitions. GIMS was first held in 1905 and has been sponsored by a foundation called Org-expo since 1982 (GIMS 2014). Although there is no domestic automobile industry in Switzerland, GIMS is stimulated by the prosperous automobile market in Europe and is simultaneously supported by the automobile manufacturing industries in Italy, France and Germany (Qiao 1999a). It has become a stage for major automakers from different countries to show their new products. As the host country does not have its own auto industry, GIMS is seen as a 'neutral territory' allowing firms from different countries to get engaged at the same time. GIMS is a prominent event for the global automobile industry and has achieved the status as 'the international auto trend benchmark' (Qiao 1999b). As a 'neutral space', GIMS treats automakers from Europe, America and Asia with the same standards. Just as Switzerland is considered to be a neutral country, GIMS is regarded as a particularly 'fair' event for exhibitors from all countries. An important success factor of GIMS is that it is not just about selling cars, but provides an overview of design philosophies by allowing automakers to set up diverse platforms.

To sum up, the three leading auto shows discussed above all successfully cultivate specific characteristics, sometimes with the support of regional/national industry structures. They continually attract particular types of participants to promote the communication of tacit knowledge and establish industry networks. This creates a favorable environment for market-oriented innovation on a global basis. All three fairs pay attention to setting up diverse communication networks to become temporary agglomerations of specific types of professionals in the auto industry. In general, automotive exhibitions tend to focus on the final markets and customer demand and pay particular attention to product display as opposed to the manufacturing process. While they do not tend to stimulate substantial manufacturing or parts-related innovation, they still play a very significant role in the overall direction of auto innovation and display the latest trends.

SHANGHAI INTERNATIONAL AUTO SHOW (SIAS) – ON THE WAY TO A TEMPORARY CLUSTER?

SIAS was founded in 1985 and has been held every two years, alternating with the Beijing International Automotive Exhibition (BIAE). These are the only two shows that are qualified as 'A level motor shows' by the Chinese State Economic and Trade Commission (Baidupedia 2014). The 2011 event occupied 230,000 square meters of exhibition space, which represented an increase of 35 percent over the previous show (SIAS 2013). Two thousand automotive firms from 20 countries gathered at the event in 2011 and attracted more than 700,000 visitors, mostly consumers (SIAS 2013). The consumer event roughly matched the leading international auto shows in terms of size as measured by the number of cars launched, the number of visitors and media presence (see Table 9.1). However, concerning the role of promoting innovation, the influence of SIAS is still relatively minor in comparison with the leading auto shows in Europe and North America.

Based on the rapid development of China's automobile industry and market, this chapter aims to investigate possible development paths for SIAS in becoming a true temporary cluster. The investigation reported

Table 9.1 Basic statistics of leading international auto shows, 2011/12

Name of trade show	Location	Cars released (number)	Visitors (number)	Journalists (number)
NAIAS (2012)	Detroit	42	770,932	5,265
IAA (2011)	Frankfurt	206	850,000	13,261
GIMS (2012)	Geneva	150	702,014	11,680
SIAS (2011)	Shanghai	75	715,718	9,872

Notes: NAIAS = North American International Automobile Show; IAA = Internationale Automobil-Ausstellung; GIMS = Geneva International Motor Show; SIAS = Shanghai International Auto Show.

Sources: BIAE (2014), GIMS (2014), IAA (2012), NAIAS (2013) and SIAS (2013).

Table 9.2 Interviews conducted with executives and managers of automobile firms at Shanghai International Auto Show (SIAS), 2011

Interview indicators		Foreign multinationals (n = 39)	Domestic joint ventures (n = 28)	National firms (n = 35)
A. Number interviewed	Executive	28	13	26
	Marketing manager	9	14	7
	Technical manager	2	1	2
B. Focus of interview	Auto performance/ technology	3	9	11
	Market exploration China	25	12	16
	Development strategy	11	7	8

Sources: SINA (2013), SOHU (2013) and *The Economic Observer and Automobile Weekly* (2011a; 2011b).

in this chapter pays particular attention to the potential role of the local/regional industry structure.

The analysis presented here is based on empirical work by the authors who attended SIAS 2011 in person and obtained information through over 100 interviews with exhibitors and visitors (see Table 9.2). The interviews were conducted during the public days of the event in the exhibition halls. Respondents were selected through random sampling and each interview lasted for about ten minutes. Aside from trade fair reports and our interviews, a special column of *The Economic Observer and Automobile Weekly* (2011a; 2011b) and information from webpages like SINA (2013) and SOHU (2013), which set up thematic websites during SIAS (for instance reporting online interviews), were used to explore the specific position of the Shanghai International Automobile Show.

(i) Rapid Expansion of SIAS

In recent years, the expansion in scale and international impact of SIAS has been closely related to the rapid growth of automobile industry and automobile markets in Shanghai and China (see Table 9.3). From 2008 to 2011, the average annual growth of car production was nearly 30 percent in both China and Shanghai, while the average sales growth was 13.5 percent and 34.6 percent in China and Shanghai, respectively.

Table 9.3 Production and sales data of cars in Mainland China and Shanghai, 2008–11

Year	Production (million vehicles)			Sales (million vehicles)		
	China	Shanghai	Shanghai share	China	Shanghai	Shanghai share
2008	6.74	0.81	12.0%	10.13	0.80	7.9%
2009	10.38	1.25	12.0%	13.68	1.30	9.5%
2010	13.90	1.70	12.2%	14.01	1.69	12.1%
2011	14.49	1.91	13.2%	14.85	1.97	13.3%

Source: CAAM (2014).

Table 9.4 Market structure of the Chinese auto industry, 2012

Market indicator	National origin of automobile brand						Total
	Chinese	German	French	American	Japanese	Korean	
Consumption (thousands)	6,485.0	2,857.4	440.0	1,812.1	2,542.0	1,340.0	15,476.5
Market share	41.9%	18.5%	2.8%	11.7%	16.4%	8.7%	100.0%
Imports of cars (thousands)	–	329.0	24.0	168.7	233.0	87.8	842.5
Import share for non-Chinese cars	–	11.5%	5.5%	9.3%	9.2%	6.6%	9.4%

Source: CAAM (2014).

Meanwhile, a large share of the car sales by multinational and domestic automobile corporations was related to the production capacities in China and Shanghai, and did not result from imports. Overall, the proportion of domestic brands has steadily increased in recent years, while the proportion of finished car imports has dropped (CAAM 2014). In 2012, the market share of domestic passenger vehicles was over 40 percent, and foreign brands were mostly assembled in China through joint ventures (see Table 9.4). Against the background of such patterns of automobile production and consumption, auto shows in China serve to promote the diffusion of a specific 'automobile culture' further in broad consumer markets, support technological innovation of domestic auto corporations and increase opportunities for multinational automobile corporations to enter the Chinese market.

Due to its large market, China increasingly attracts the attention of global automotive firms. In 2011, SIAS occupied 230,000 square meters of exhibition space, including all 13 indoor exhibition halls and some outdoor facilities of the Shanghai New International Expo Center (see, also, Bathelt and Zeng, *this volume*). During this event, automobile parts were shown in two exhibition halls and 22 temporary outdoor pavilions (AutoShanghai 2013). Additionally, 75 new models were launched at the show, including 19 models of foreign manufactures. SIAS also attracted almost 9,900 domestic and foreign journalists. Taking this as an indicator, we can assume that the importance of the event is beginning to more closely reflect the rapid development of China's automobile industry.

(ii) Communication Patterns at SIAS

As a consequence of the rapid development of the trade fair business, Shanghai is now able to organize large exhibitions at an international level with latest technologies (Bathelt and Zeng, *this volume*). This has become clear after the successful organization of the Shanghai Expo in 2010. In 2011, SIAS began providing free handheld terminals to attendees at SIAS who registered online for these technical devices (Zhuang 2011). With the help of radio frequency technology, these handheld terminals provided users with a wealth of information about the cars on display. From the information provided by the devices, visitors can better understand the set-up and organization of the event, and they have access to technical information about each exhibitor while wandering through the fair. It can be assumed that this helps to improve the efficiency of communication and make it more professional. Services carried out by volunteers also aided exhibitors and visitors during the event (Zeng 2011).

Aside from measures to improve the quality of the exhibitors' displays, SIAS also made efforts to improve networking and network-building opportunities between exhibitors and visitors. Many meetings and forums, including the Shanghai International Auto Show Forum and the Shanghai International Automobile Industry Technical Exchange Conference, were established to accommodate more opportunities for knowledge exchange between professionals (SIAS 2013).

However, displays and exhibits are still the center of attention at SIAS, especially those related to high-end car brands, which attracted most attention by visitors and media (Cao 2011). In the 2011 event, the waiting lines for consumers to enter the luxury car exhibition hall were five to six hours long, and the crowded and noisy scene was not conducive to the exchange of knowledge (albeit some interesting communication may have taken place during these waits). Although many exhibitors pay attention to showcasing the unique technological features of their products, consumer-visitors were more interested and curious about design developments and new models.

During our interviews in the exhibition halls, we found that only three of the 11 visitors we interviewed, which had experienced the 'iAuto platform' set out by the Chinese carmaker Chery, had been engaged in thorough communication with staff members. Also in our survey, 70 percent of the visitors suggested that their first goal in participating in the event was to catch a glimpse of new models and foreign luxury automobiles (SIAS 2013). Important component firms, such as YAPP, Clarion and Zhongzi Catalyst, indicated during the interviews that they received many orders during SIAS and also established new collaborations with other firms. In contrast, automobile producers, like Brilliance Zhonghua, Chevrolet or Shanghai Volkswagen, rarely made direct contact with other exhibitors, and there was also little communication across different exhibition halls. These observations suggest that SIAS still lacks effective communication channels to promote in-depth exchanges both among exhibitors and between exhibitors and visitors.

(iii) SIAS' Role in Market Expansion

Despite its recent growth, the automobile industry in China is still in an early development stage, characterized especially by imitation and catching up. While the vehicle assembling capabilities in the country are well developed, the technological level of locally produced key components is still relatively low (Liu 2003). One reason for this is that Chinese consumers tend to pay more attention to the technical characteristics of the finished vehicle rather than to its key components (Chen et al. 2003). Therefore, the primary focus of exhibitors attending SIAS is market expansion rather than technological learning. Visitors who pay attention to the automobiles' performance indicators are in the majority, while professionals who are familiar with automobile technology and the structure of the industry only account for a small proportion of the attendees. However, SIAS provides temporary geographical proximity for interactions between manufacturers and consumers, as well as promotes knowledge exchanges that may lead to the adoption of products according to the specific demand conditions in developing countries.

Unlike IAA, which is known as a venue for the demonstration of technological expertise, SIAS is more like a platform that promotes the local/national diffusion of a specific 'auto culture'. Most of the over-700,000 visitors at SIAS in 2011 were ordinary consumers/hobbyists. With the spreading of an 'auto culture', consumers also get to know more about the technological features of the automobile industry. Therefore, despite being a consumer show, SIAS may be conducive to the development of a stronger technology focus and may attract more technologically sophisticated consumers in the future.

It should also be considered that consumers lacking professional knowledge may still be a valuable source of knowledge as they could express unexpected needs without constraints, thus helping exhibitors to obtain inspirations regarding market-oriented innovation. Unfortunately, there were only a few platforms at SIAS for the attendees to express their ideas in the flood of visually dazzling pavilions. The uneven quality and low number of comments received from attending firms also reduced the potential for innovation. Extensive social media coverage may, however, have helped exhibitors to gain some ideas regarding innovation. SINA, SOHU, NetEase and other media outlets, for instance, provided live coverage of SIAS and carried out online interviews that were portrayed through micro blogs. In contrast to the crowded pavilions that showcased the automobiles themselves, there were relatively few visitors in the exhibitions halls and pavilions for automotive parts, within which professionals from different countries were able to discuss technological issues.

In recent years, the attention given to domestic vehicles during SIAS has significantly improved. During the 2003 edition, for instance, most of the domestic brand exhibits just occupied peripheral areas and corners of the exhibition halls; and several domestic firms could only set up exhibits in the open spaces outside of the exhibition halls (Shen and Chen 2011). During the 2011 edition, in contrast, Chery, Geely, Great Wall and other domestic independent brand producers all made great efforts to exhibit their latest car models and technology centrally during the event. In comparison with leading multinational corporations, the size of the exhibition area occupied by domestic producers was, however, still comparatively small (see Figure 9.1). Yet, of the 75 models launched at SIAS in 2011, domestic cars accounted for 56, indicating that design and construction of new models has significantly improved. Shen and Chen (2011) reported that Martin Winterkorn, chairman of the German Volkswagen Group, personally went to the booth of the Chinese BYD Auto Corporation to inspect the paint and assembling features of BYD's exhibited vehicles, indicating that transnational executives are becoming increasingly interested in Chinese competitors.

Of the 575 auto models that were displayed at SIAS in 2011, 24 percent (138 models) were imports, 33 percent (189 models) domestic Chinese brands and the remainder (43 percent or 248 models) cars from joint venture firms (NetEase 2014). This shows that both foreign and domestic brands use SIAS to introduce their new models to the Chinese market.

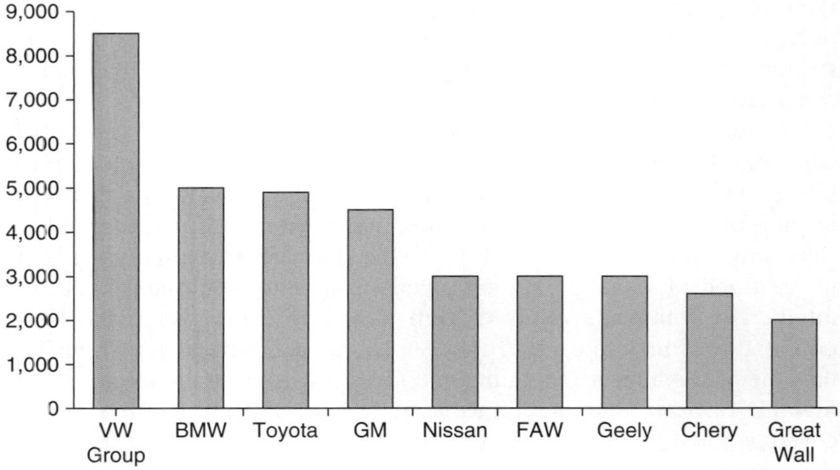

Source: SIAS (2013).

Figure 9.1 Stand space (square meters) of main exhibitors at Shanghai International Auto Show (SIAS), 2011

Small Chinese brands, such as Roewe, Zotye and Youngman – in addition to the large firms Chery and Geely – were also part of SIAS. Leading multinationals, such as General Motors, Volkswagen and Mercedes-Benz, typically had cooperative exhibitions with their joint ventures from China. At the Volkswagen exhibit, for instance, seven of the 23 exhibited models (nearly one-third) were domestically-finished vehicles, and Audi showcased its co-development projects with FAW with respect to new electric automobiles and onboard internet access (Y. Zhang 2011). These examples indicate that exhibits of joint venture firms have become increasingly sophisticated and that such ventures help facilitate important technology spillovers.

The broad participation of leading multinational automobile firms is certainly a success that illustrates the significance of SIAS as an international trade show. In interviews with executives of automobile firms published in special columns by *The Economic Observer and Automobile Weekly* (2011a; 2011b) and on auto show webpages by SINA (2013) and SOHU (2013), market expansion into China was the problem that senior managers were especially concerned about (see Table 9.2). This was especially true for senior managers from established firms, such as Rolls-Royce, Land Rover, Mercedes-Benz, Volkswagen and GM. For example, Klaus Maier, the president and CEO of Mercedes-Benz (China) Sales Co. Ltd, said in an interview that '[n]ew motor types of SLK, CLS and C-Class [referring to different Daimler car model classes] would aim at the personalized demand of Chinese customers, and we shall try to promote the innovation ability and vigorous development in China with the expansion of green products' (L. Zhang 2011). This demonstrates that the Chinese market requires adaptive innovation. In a similar way, Akio Toyoda, Toyota's president, said that '[t]he core and key to realize our vision in China is trying to please Chinese customers' (Wei 2011).

Since automobiles in China are, to some extent, still regarded as a tool to show off wealth (Jia and Gu 2012), multinational automobile firms pay particular attention to optical vehicle appearance and passenger comfort. Exhibitors like Ford, Peugeot and Land Rover showed luxurious internal designs at SIAS, for instance, focusing on adjustable and flexible seats that enhance passenger comfort. China thus not only possesses the largest and most rapidly developing automobile market in the developing world, but may also point at opportunities for multinational auto firms to generate adaptions that better cater to the demands in other developing countries.

It must be pointed out here that many media sources consider SIAS to lack local characteristics in the sense that it lacks a specific connection with the surrounding industry base. Some claim that the event appears like a display of luxury products and that it blindly imitates more established auto shows, but does not develop its own characteristics (Liang 2011). Without specific 'cultural' characteristics, SIAS simply becomes an ordinary event, which may be subject to fierce competition from events in other regions and countries and may not be able to survive (Bathelt et al. 2014). Inevitably, the lack of specific characteristics of SIAS or lack of connections with local/regional industries may be related to the lack of an 'automobile culture' and a low level of local industrial innovation (Tong 2011), but it may also be linked to the unclear orientation of the trade show's organizers. Overall, the goal of SIAS would best be to aim first to link to its regional production basis and domestic market and second to develop unique 'local characteristics'.

CONCLUSION

International trade fairs play important roles in promoting industrial innovation as well as providing ideas for future innovation, mainly because they operate as temporary clusters by gathering geographically dispersed participants of a particular industry in one place. Temporary co-presence stimulates the transfer of tacit knowledge and the construction of networks. This chapter argues that a successful trade fair needs to develop linkages with its domestic markets and regional industry structure while, at the same time, attracting international exhibitors and developing unique 'local characteristics' that can create a competitive advantage for the event.

Relying on the rapid development of Shanghai's and China's automobile industry and market, SIAS has developed substantially since the mid-2000s in terms of size and influence. The event has contributed to the development of the domestic automobile industry and the market expansion of leading multinational automobile corporations. However, to date in terms of temporary cluster formation, SIAS has not convincingly adapted to the regional industry structure and domestic market environment to develop into a unique event. Without doubt, the event has been a success in the recent past and has grown in importance. It has the potential to become a key event that first helps foreign multinationals to learn how to adapt their products to developing countries and second supports Chinese domestic firms to absorb foreign technology and adapt to competition in international markets (see Li, *this volume*). To strengthen and develop these roles would contribute to the sustainable development of SIAS, as well as the automobile industry in China and around the world

REFERENCES

Aldebert, B., Dang, R. J. and Longhi, C. (2011) 'Innovation in the tourism industry: The case of Tourism', *Tourism Management*, 32: 1204–1213.

Allen, J. (2003) *Lost Geographies of Power*, Oxford: Blackwell.

Amin, A. and Cohendet, P. (2004) *Architectures of Knowledge: Firms, Capabilities and Communities*, Oxford: Oxford University Press.

AutoShanghai (2013) *Floorplan*, Shanghai. Online. Available HTTP: <http://www.autoshanghai.org/En/TraderInfo/TheplaneMap.aspx> (30 June 2014).

Baidupedia (2014) *A Level Motor Show*. Online. Available HTTP: <http://www.baike.com/wiki/A%E7%BA%A7%E8%BD%A6%E5%B1%95> (30 June 2014).

Bathelt, H., Golfetto, F. and Rinallo, D. (2014) *Trade Shows in the Globalizing Knowledge Economy*, Oxford: Oxford University Press.

Bathelt, H. and Kappes K. (2009) 'Necessary restructuring or globalization failure? Shifts in regional supplier relations after the merger of the former German Hoechst and French Rhône-Poulenc groups', *Geoforum*, 40: 158–170.

Bathelt, H., Kogler, D. F. and Munro, A. K. (2010) 'A knowledge-based typology of university spin-offs in the context of regional economic development', *Technovation*, 30: 519–532.

Bathelt, H. and Schuldt N. (2008) 'Between luminaires and meat grinders: International trade fairs as temporary clusters', *Regional Studies*, 42: 853–868.

Bathelt, H. and Turi, P. (2011) 'Local, global and virtual buzz: The importance

of face-to-face contact in economic interaction and possibilities to go beyond', *Geoforum*, 42: 520–529.
Bathelt, H. and Zeng, G. (2012) 'Strong growth in weakly-developed networks: Producer–user interaction and knowledge brokers in the Greater Shanghai chemical industry', *Applied Geography*, 32: 158–170.
Belussi, F. and Pilotti, L. (2002) 'Knowledge learning and innovation in Italian industrial districts', *Geografiska Annaler, Series B*, 84: 125–139.
Bertrand, K. (1987) 'Talking turkey on trade shows', *Business Marketing*, 72: 94–103.
BIAE – Beijing International Automotive Exhibition (2014) *Beijing International Automotive Exhibition*, Beijing. Online. Available HTTP: <http://www.chinaautoshow.com/2010bjx/en> (30 June 2014).
Browning, J. M. and Adams, R. J. (1988) 'Trade shows: An effective promotional tool for the small industrial business', *Journal of Small Business Management*, 26 (4): 31–36.
CAAM – China Association of Automobile Manufacturers (2013) *China Association of Automobile Manufacturers – Specific Data*, Beijing. Online. Available HTTP: <http://www.caam.org.cn/zongheshuju/20131114/1505106400.html> (14 November 2013).
CAAM – China Association of Automobile Manufacturers (2014) *China Association of Automobile Manufacturers – Specific Data*, Beijing. Online. Available HTTP: <http://www.caam.org.cn/zhengche/20140121/1305112762.html> (21 January 2014).
Cao, X. (2011) 'Reflection of the Shanghai auto show lack of culture', *The Economic Observer*, 2 May: 26.
Chen, L., Hu, S. and Guo, H. (2003) 'Strategy and analysis on the development of Chinese automobile parts industry', *Beijing Automotive Engineering*, 1: 1–9.
Cohen, W. M. and Levinthal, D. A. (1990) 'Absorptive capacity: A new perspective on learning and innovation', *Administrative Science Quarterly*, 35: 128–152.
The Economic Observer and Automobile Weekly (2011a) 'Autoshow special column – Part I', *The Economic Observer*, 18 April: 35–46.
The Economic Observer and Automobile Weekly (2011b) 'Autoshow special column – Part II', *The Economic Observer*, 25 April: 34–40.
Gertler, M. S (1993) 'Implementing advanced manufacturing technologies in mature industrial regions: Towards a social model of technology production', *Regional Studies*, 27: 665–680.
Gertler, M. S. (2001) 'Best practice? Geography, learning and the institutional limits to strong convergence', *Journal of Economic Geography*, 1: 5–26.
GIMS – Geneva International Motor Show (2014) *Geneva International Motor Show*, Geneva. Online. Available HTTP: <http://www.salon-auto.ch/en> (30 June 2014).
Guo, J. (2012) *Blue Paper of Exhibition Economy: The Development Report of Exhibition Economy in China, 2012*, Beijing: Social Sciences Academic Press.
Herbig, P., Palumbo, F. and O'Hara, B. (1996) 'Differences in trade show behavior between manufactures and service-oriented firms', *Journal of Professional Services Marketing*, 6: 97–109.
IAA – Internationale Automobil-Ausstellung (2012) *Internationale Automobil-Ausstellung*, Frankfurt/Main. Online. Available HTTP: <http://www.iaa.de/en> (30 September 2012).

Jia, G. and Gu, H. (2012) 'Trend of auto culture in China and the strategy of auto companies', *Automobile and Parts*, 53: 29–31.

Li, L.-Y. (2006) 'Relationship learning at trade shows: Its antecedents and consequences', *Industrial Marketing Management*, 35: 166–177.

Li, Z. (2011) 'The driving effects of convention and exhibition industry', *Economic Management Journal*, 6: 125–131.

Liang, C. (2011) 'Inadequacy of auto culture showcased in Shanghai Auto Show', *The Economic Observer*, 2 May: 36.

Liu, J. (2003) 'Finished auto industry encounters bottleneck of key parts: Automobile parts industry needs revolution', *Light Vehicles*, 12: 71–72.

Liu, X. (2007) 'Review of North American international auto show in 2007', *Imp-Exp Executive*, 2: 88.

Lundvall, B.-Å. (ed.) (1992) *National Systems of Innovation: Towards a Theory of Innovation and Interactive Learning*, London: Pinter.

Maskell, P., Bathelt, H., and Malmberg, A. (2004) *Temporary Clusters and Knowledge Creation: The Effects of International Trade Fairs, Conventions and Other Professional Gatherings*, SPACES 2004-04, Toronto, Heidelberg. Online. Available HTTP: <http://www.spaces-online.com> (13 March 2013).

Maskell, P., Bathelt, H. and Malmberg, A. (2006) 'Building global knowledge pipelines: The role of temporary clusters', *European Planning Studies*, 14: 997–1013.

Meyerson, D., Weick, K. E. and Kramer, R. M. (1996) 'Swift trust and temporary groups', in R. M. Kramer and T. R. Tyler (eds) *Trust in Organizations: Frontiers of Theory and Research*, Thousand Oaks, CA: Sage, 166–195.

Moeran, B. (2011) 'The book fair as a tournament of values', in B. Moeran and J. Pederson (eds) *Negotiating Values in the Creative Industries: Fairs, Festivals and Competitive Events*, Cambridge: Cambridge University Press, 119–144.

NAIAS – North American International Auto Show (2013) *North American International Auto Show*, Detroit. Online. Available HTTP: <http://www.naias.com> (30 June 2014).

NetEase (2014) *Special Website of Shanghai Auto Show*. Online. Available HTTP: <http://auto.163.com/special/shanghai-chezhan/> (30 June 2014).

Power, D. and Jansson, J. (2008) 'Cyclical clusters in global circuits: Overlapping spaces in furniture trade fairs', *Economic Geography*, 84: 423–448.

Qiao, Y. (1999a) 'Aftertaste of the Geneva motor show', *Transportation World*, 3: 78–91.

Qiao, Y. (1999b) 'A review of Geneva auto show', *Transportation World*, 3: 185–201.

Ramírez-Pasillas, M. (2007) *International Trade Fairs as Amplifiers of Proximity in Clusters*, Entrepreneurship Profile Working Paper Series No. 2. Växjö: Växjö University.

Rinallo, D. and Golfetto, F. (2011) 'Exploring the knowledge strategies of temporary cluster organizers: A longitudinal study of the EU fabric industry trade shows (1986–2006)', *Economic Geography*, 87: 453–476.

Rosson, P. J. and Seringhaus, F. H. R. (1995) 'Visitor and exhibitor interaction at industrial trade fairs', *Journal of Business Research*, 32: 81–90.

Shen, X. and Chen, W. (2011) 'A review of Shanghai auto show: Prospect and disparity', *Jiefang Daily*, 11 May: 13.

SIAS – Shanghai International Automobile Show (2013) *AutoShanghai*, Shanghai. Online. Available HTTP: <http://www.autoshanghai.org> (30 June 2014).

SINA (2013) *SINA Auto Show Special Website*, Shanghai. Online. Available HTTP: <http://auto.sina.com.cn/shanghaichezhanpre/index.shtml> (30 June 2014).
SOHU (2013) *SOHU Auto Show Special Website*, Shanghai. Online. Available HTTP: <http://auto.sohu.com/shanghaichezhan/2011interview> (30 June 2014).
Tesar, J. (1988) *Trade Shows: Opportunities to Sell a Case Study of Hanover Fair CeBIT*, Hanover: Trade Show Bureau Publication.
Thrift, N. (2000) 'Performing cultures in the new economy', *Annals of the Association of American Geographers*, 90: 674–692.
Tong, N. (2011) 'Shanghai auto show is growing', *Economic Daily*, 19 April: 15.
Torre, A. and Rallet, A. (2005) 'Proximity and localization', *Regional Studies*, 39: 47–59.
Wang, W. (2012) 'A big party in North America auto show', *Era of Automobile*, 4: 119–125.
Wang, X. (1998) 'The 57th IAA Frankfurt motor show', *Global Automobile*, 5: 21–24.
Wei, L. (2011) 'Toyota: Starting to localization', *The Economic Observer*, 25 April: 37.
Wu, W. (2012) 'Germany 2011 motor vehicle sales grows fast', *The Economics Daily*, 17 (1): 21.
Zeng, C. (2011) 'The grand opening of 14th Shanghai auto show', *China Industry News*, 22 April: A1.
Zhang, L. (2011) 'The top seven in Shanghai auto show', *China Economic Times*, 27 April. Online. Available HTTP: <http://finance.sina.com.cn/roll/20110427/08419757906.shtml> (7 May 2014).
Zhang, Y. (2011) 'Architecture of Audi', *The Economic Observer*, 28 April: 36.
Zhou, H. (2003) 'Magic of independent: Internationale Automobil-Ausstellung', *Automobile and Parts Technology*, 38: 16–19.
Zhou, Z. (2004) 'Highlighting the North American auto show', *World Automobile*, 3: 16–27.
Zhuang, J. (2011) '"Guide machine" of originality but with barriers', *Shanghai Evening Post*, 27 April: A2–11.

PART III

Trade fair development in industrialized economies in the Asia-Pacific region

10. Building relationships at local trade fairs in Japan: a case study of the Suwa Area Industrial Messe

Yutaka Yokura

INTRODUCTION

Recent studies on innovation and knowledge creation emphasize the role of temporary geographical proximity (Maskell et al. 2004; 2006; Bathelt and Schuldt 2008; 2010; Wickham and Vecchi 2008; Rallet and Torre 2009). These studies suggest that temporary F2F (Face-to-Face) communication such as business travel, professional gatherings and industry events enable the actors to acquire similar information as in permanent clusters. Trade fairs can be regarded as temporary clusters in that they are economic phenomena where actors concentrate at a specific place for a limited duration and for specific purposes.

The temporary cluster's extraordinary characteristics have an important potential impact on the participants' economic performance. Hansen (2004, pp. 3f.) proposed improvement in employee and customer motivation, in addition to corporate image building and marketing activity, as important purposes of trade fairs. Participants are sensitive to stimulation and they tend to create new ideas through diverse relationships during trade fairs. In addition, Rallet and Torre (2009, p. 17) noted that the participants are removed from daily relations and routines to easily make initial contact with others during the fair.

From the perspective of knowledge-based conceptualization (Asheim et al. 2007), trade fairs can be classified into two categories. The design-intensive type requires symbolic knowledge and artistry or creativity, such as furniture and cultural industries' trade fairs. The technology-intensive type is based on analytical or synthetic knowledge and also attaches special importance to personal meetings because it is difficult to evaluate technical properties from exhibitions (Bathelt and Schuldt 2010, p. 1964).

Focusing on the comic book industry as a design-intensive type, Norcliffe and Rendace (2003, pp. 258f.) argued that networking among creators and publishers at major conventions is rather significant for comic book production. Yoon and Malecki (2010, pp. 255f.) drew attention to global production networks in the animation industry and argued that professional gatherings contribute to knowledge sharing and collaboration among geographically dispersed animation artisans (see Maskell, *this volume*).

Other investigations focused on trade fairs of the Swedish furniture industry (Ramírez-Pasillas 2008; 2010; Power and Jansson 2008). Using social network analysis, it was found that novel knowledge spills over into firms that are not participating at the fairs through their channels of local personal networking and partnerships with exhibitors – although this is based on scanty evidence (Ramírez-Pasillas 2008; 2010). In studies related to technology-intensive fairs, Chen (2009) demonstrated the importance of informal networks in overseas knowledge sourcing. International trade fairs can support those informal networks among exhibitors and visitors to acquire information on markets and technological know-how.

Although these findings suggest several roles of trade fairs, there is a need to better understand the interactions and learning processes in temporary clusters. Little empirical research has thus far explicitly examined how temporary clusters affect actors' activities in industrial agglomerations (or permanent clusters), and vice versa. This study focuses on Japanese local trade fairs held in industrial agglomerations, specifically the Suwa Area Industrial Messe, and investigates the development of various relationships and networks among actors, such as exhibitors and visitors, related to this trade fair. The Suwa Area Industrial Messe, a trade fair of high-precision technology, has expanded its scale substantially and is now recognized as an important event for firms in the Suwa area, Nagano prefecture. Exhibitors are confined to the firms in or near the Suwa area because the fair is intended to promote the local economy. Compared with other local trade fairs, the Suwa Area Industrial Messe has attracted many domestic exhibitors and visitors.

In this research, I conducted one extensive interview with the Executive Committee Chairperson of the Suwa Area Industrial Messe in November 2010 and collected data and lists of exhibitors and visitors from the previous fairs. The data used for this study were derived from the survey questionnaires that were conducted by the executive committee and the Nagano Economic Research Institute in 2004 and 2009. The questionnaires were distributed to all exhibitors of the Suwa Area Industrial Messe and used the same questions about the purposes of exhibitions and the number of business transactions during and after the fairs. Of the 178 questionnaires sent to the exhibitors, 126 were returned in 2004, and 188 of 252 questionnaires were returned in 2009.

The next section shows the development of the Japanese trade fairs, before the context of the Suwa area and its manufacturing industry is discussed on the basis of statistical data. Then, the structure of Japanese trade fairs is described more broadly and the role of the Suwa Area Industrial Messe explained as an example of a local trade fair. Finally, concluding remarks are presented.

DEVELOPMENT OF JAPANESE TRADE FAIRS

Major Japanese trade fairs concentrate in metropolitan areas such as Tokyo, Osaka, Nagoya and Fukuoka. The Tokyo Big Sight has the largest facility for exhibitions and holds the largest number of events in Japan (see Figure 10.1). In addition, the Makuhari Messe and the INTEX Osaka have exhibition areas of over 70,000 square meters. The seven largest exhibition facilities account for more than three quarters of the total number of exhibitions in Japan.

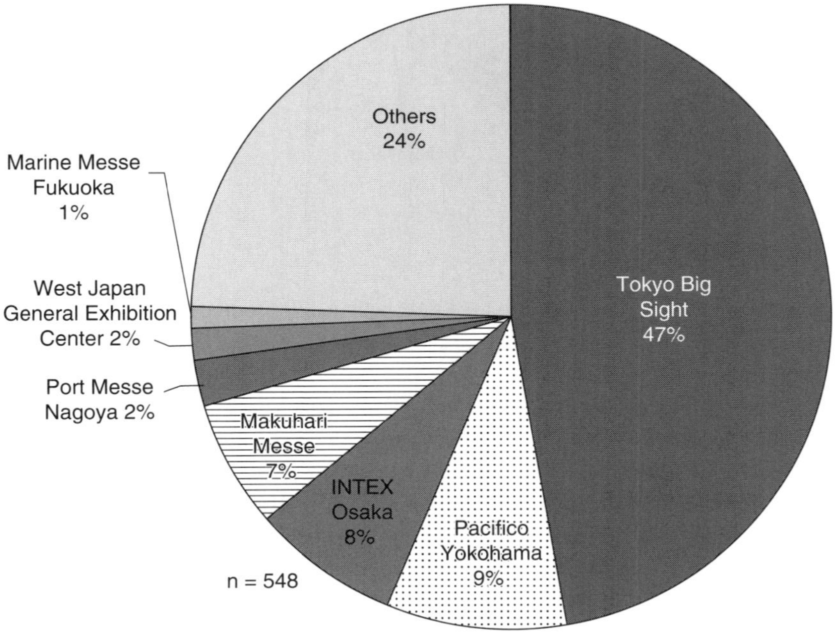

Source: JETRO's online trade fair database and POP Inc. (2010).

Figure 10.1 Exhibition and trade fair facilities in Japan, 2010

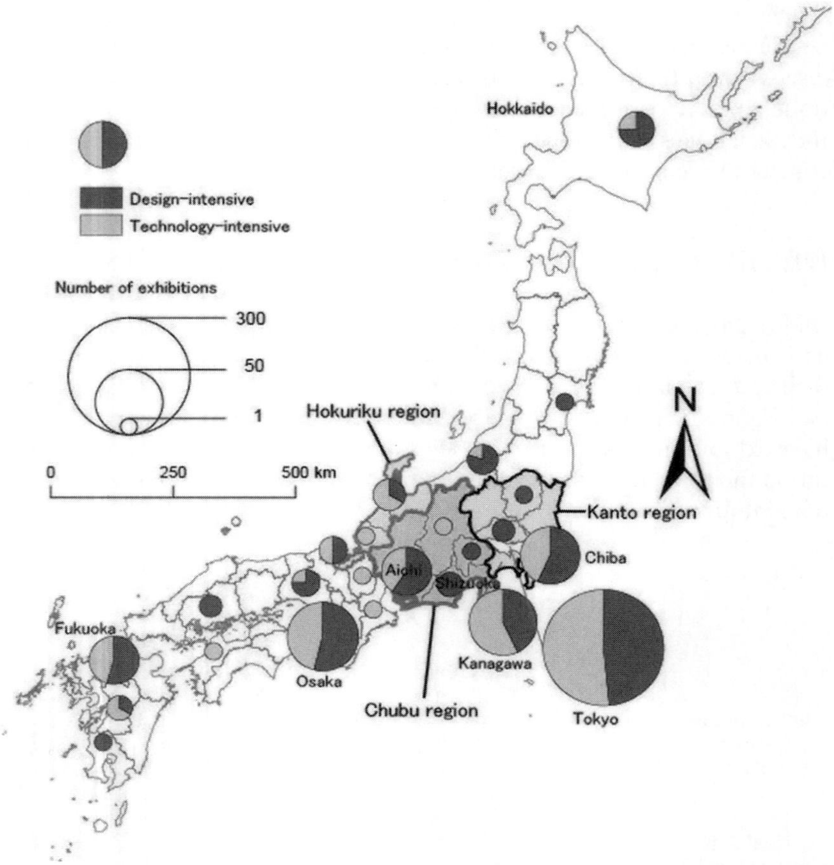

Source: JETRO's online trade fair database and POP Inc. (2010).

Figure 10.2 Geographical distributions of trade fairs by category, 2010

Like other trade fairs, Japanese trade fairs can be classified into two types of exhibition: technology-intensive exhibitions display production goods such as industrial machines, measuring equipment and basic technology; design-intensive exhibitions display consumer goods related to the furniture, advertising, entertainment and cultural industries.

Figure 10.2 shows the distribution of trade fairs in Japan according to the above classification. The numbers of technology-intensive and design-intensive trade fairs are almost equal in Tokyo. However, there are more design-intensive than technology-intensive trade fairs in Osaka, Aichi and Fukuoka. In the Kanto region, design-intensive fairs such as jewelry and housing also feature international firms aside from local firms. In addition, Hokkaido and Shizuoka, famous as major production areas of furniture and wood processing, are leaders in design-intensive fairs. In contrast, technology-intensive fairs are prominent in the Hokuriku region and Nagano prefecture, known for the precision machinery industry.

Table 10.1 shows the major Japanese trade fairs by type of knowledge base (technology- versus design-intensive) and location (metropolitan versus local). From the period of high economic growth in the mid-1950s large-scale exhibitions such as the Tokyo Motor Show have been held in Japanese metropolitan areas for the purpose of industrial development. The main purpose of trade fairs in these days was promotion of the industry rather than business interaction and negotiation. As we can see from the table, the number of foreign visitors is not published at many trade fairs, and the number of foreign exhibitors is also small. In general, highly international fairs are rare, reflecting 'cultural' and other entry barriers for foreign firms. The main purpose of almost all Japanese trade fairs is the cultivation of the domestic market. The situations of Japanese trade fairs are very different from those in other Asian countries such as China, Korea and Singapore, where the states have tried to strategically target overseas markets.

There are several problems with modern Japanese trade fairs. First, they are not based on superior organizing skills as international trade fairs in Japan do not have a long history. Second, since the data used only refers to Japanese trade fairs and was collected locally, we cannot rigorously compare Japanese trade fairs with those in other countries. However, the Japan Tourism Agency, which is under the Ministry of Land, Infrastructure, Transport and Tourism, has focused on international tourism and promotion of Japanese trade fairs in order to develop the overseas markets. The Japan Tourism Agency defined 2010 as 'Japan MICE Year' and tried to increase the number of inbound tourists during meetings, incentive tours, conventions and exhibitions (MICE). In 2012, the Japanese government approved the 'Tourism Nation Promotion Basic Plan' which aims to achieve a further increase in the number of MICE (conventions) held in Japan, striving to become the number one MICE host country in Asia by 2016. Therefore, the number of foreign exhibitors and foreign visitors listed in Table 10.1 will likely increase in the future.

ECONOMIC CONTEXT OF THE SUWA AREA

The Suwa area in Nagano prefecture is located in central Japan. The area is well known as an industrial district of high-precision technology and is

Table 10.1 Major trade fairs in Japan, 2010

Trade fair	Exhibitors (number)	Foreign exhibitors (number)	Visitors (number)	Foreign visitors (number)	Venue	Trade fair type
Cloud Computing Expo Japan	1,241	n.a.	124,056	n.a.	Tokyo Big Site	T/M
Eco-Products	745	4	183,140	n.a.	Tokyo Big Site	T/M
CEATEC JAPAN	616	196	181,417	n.a.	Makuhari Messe	T/M
Tokyo Pack	551	91	170,859	2,516	Tokyo Big Site	T/M
FOOMA JAPAN	406	26	140,576	1,968	Tokyo Big Site	T/M
Shiga Environmental Business Exhibition	313	5	36,580	n.a.	Nagahama Dome	T/L
Suwa Area Industrial Messe	255	n.a.	24,180	n.a.	Lake Suwa Event Hall	T/L
BARI-SHIP IMABARI MARITIME FAIR	179	14	13,985	n.a.	Texport Imabari	T/L
Techno Fair in Hokuriku	163	n.a.	17,621	n.a.	Fukui Industrial Hall	T/L
MEX Kanazawa	103	n.a.	50,068	n.a.	Ishikawa Industrial Exhibition Hall	T/L
Tokyo International Gift Show	2,506	255	201,245	1,354	Tokyo Big Site	D/M
International Jewellery Tokyo	1,257	402	35,763	n.a.	Tokyo Big Site	D/M
Osaka Automesse	251	n.a.	210,118	n.a.	INTEX Osaka	D/M
Tokyo Game Show	194	91	207,647	n.a.	Makuhari Messe	D/M
Tokyo Motor Show	113	14	614,400	21,504	Makuhari Messe	D/M
Shizuoka Hobby Show	79	n.a.	80,000	n.a.	Twin Messe Shizuoka	D/L
Food Service Industry Exhibition in Hokuriku	75	n.a.	28,100	n.a.	Ishikawa Industrial Exhibition Hall	D/L
Kofu Jewelry Fair	73	n.a.	2,223	n.a.	I Messe Yamanashi	D/L
SHIZUOKA KAGU MESSE	67	n.a.	7,500	n.a.	Twin Messe Shizuoka	D/L
Tochigi Housing Fair	53	n.a.	10,000	n.a.	Marronnier Plaza	D/L

Notes: n.a. = not available; T/M = technology-intensive metropolitan trade fair; T/L = technology-intensive local trade fair; D/M = design-intensive metropolitan trade fair; D/L = design-intensive local trade fair.

Source: Based on data from JETRO's online trade fair database and POP Inc. (2010).

called the 'Switzerland of the East' in Japan. The headquarters and branch plants of Seiko Epson Corporation and Nidec Sankyo Corporation are located in the Suwa area and leading Japanese semiconductor and optical device firms such as Kyocera and Olympus have subsidiaries nearby. Many small- and medium-sized enterprises populate the Suwa area industrial agglomeration. The central government of Japan has supported the Suwa area with regional innovation policies, which included 'Industrial Cluster' and 'Knowledge Cluster' programs in the 2000s. Both programs focus on the development of industrial agglomerations by increasing the national competitiveness of innovative products and technologies. The primary goal of Japanese regional innovation policies is to develop R&D networks among industry, academia and the public sector to support start-up processes from collaborative research. Researchers of public institutes, universities and firms perform joint research for each R&D project.

The Suwa area recently experienced severe industrial restructuring after the 1970s. The establishment and enterprise census of Japan reveals that the number of manufacturing employees and firms has decreased since the mid-1980s (see Figure 10.3). The Suwa area has a significantly higher proportion of firms and employees in the mechanical industries such as general machinery, electrical machinery and precision instruments compared to the Japanese economy overall. Additionally, because of shifting production overseas in the latter half of the 1980s, the precision instruments industry was replaced by the electrical machinery and electronic parts and devices industry as the dominant industrial sector.

In such a socio-economic environment of restructuring, several strategies for industrial revival were pursued in the Suwa area which took advantage of historical and institutional thickness in high-precision technology. One such strategy was the local trade fair that was proposed by the Suwa Chamber of Commerce and Industry to create regional brands.

BUILDING RELATIONSHIPS AT THE SUWA AREA INDUSTRIAL MESSE

The Suwa Area Industrial Messe began in 2002 with 174 exhibitors and over 12,000 visitors. Although the Suwa Area Industrial Messe does not (and cannot) attract as many visitors and exhibitors compared to the trade fairs held at the much larger exhibition centers such as the Tokyo Big Sight and Makuhari Messe, it has become famous and compares favorably with other local trade fairs held far away from metropolitan areas. This is because the fair is better at generating various relationships (see Table 10.1). The purpose of Suwa Area Industrial Messe is to place greater

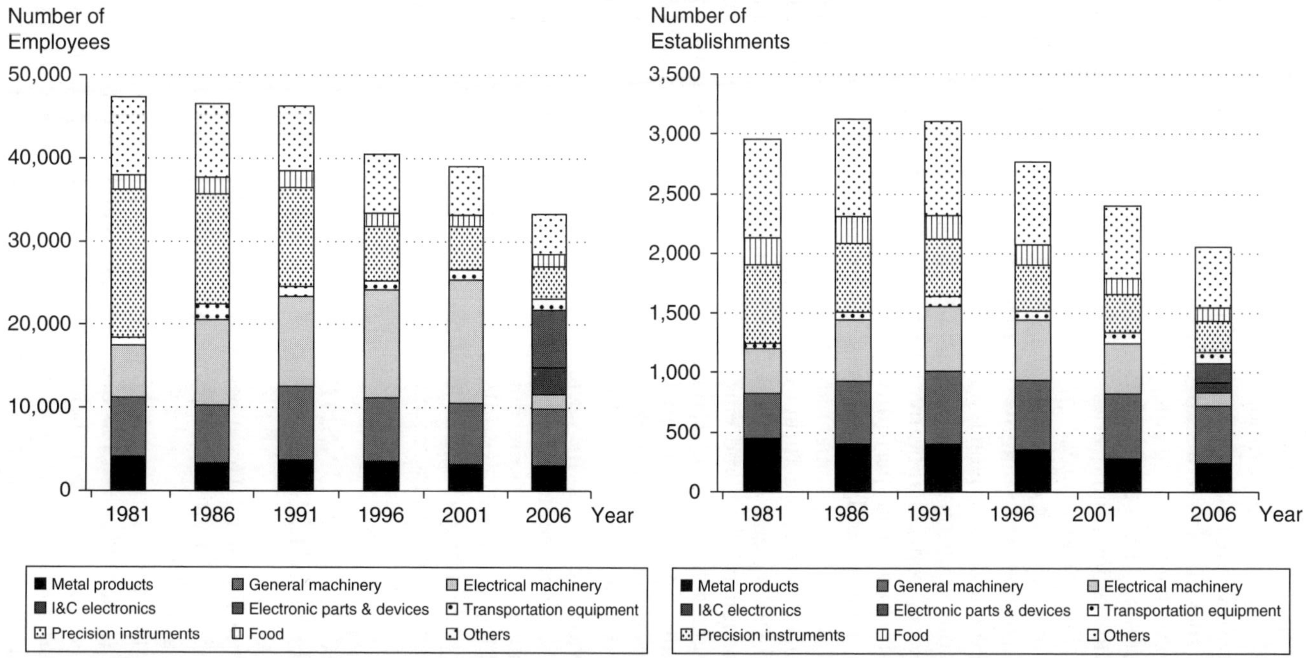

Source: Establishment census of Japan.

Figure 10.3 Number of industrial employees and establishments in the Suwa area, 1981–2006

emphasis on business negotiations and not just on the promotion of the industry. Additionally, the executive committee tries to offer overseas exhibitors in Suwa support from the Japanese government. Through this, the Suwa Area Industrial Messe has different features compared to other large trade fairs in Japan.

The price for hosting the Suwa Area Industrial Messe was approximately ¥40 million (JPY) ($320,000 (USD)) in 2002. Half of the total expense was covered by the subsidies of local governments of the Suwa area, the Nagano prefecture and the central government. The Suwa area Chamber of Commerce and Industry also funded one quarter of the expense. The rest of the expense was covered by the exhibitors through fees for floor space and exhibits.

According to an interview with the Executive Committee Chairperson of the Suwa Area Industrial Messe, the budget for hosting the fair increased to ¥60 million (JPY) ($480,000 (USD)) by 2010. Though the central government abolished subsidies for the Suwa Area Industrial Messe, local governments and the Nagano prefecture continued to support the fair through contributions totaling about ¥20 million (JPY) ($160,000 (USD)). The amount borne by corporate sponsors and exhibitors rose to account for more than half of the total budget thanks to an increase in the number of exhibitors.

The number of visitors also increased rapidly until 2005, after which it gradually increased until the 2009 global recession (see Figure 10.4). The number of exhibitors has remained unchanged since 2004 because the Japanese Fire Service Act prohibits expanding the number of booths within the exhibition hall's space limitations. Therefore, the fair uses a screening system whereby the executive committee enforces qualifications for exhibitors. Priorities for exhibitions are given to actors located in the Suwa area or nearby. Among all applications to exhibit, nearly 20 percent were excluded from the 2010 exhibit.

The executive committee of the Suwa Area Industrial Messe surveyed the characteristics of visitors by collecting visitors' business cards at the entrance starting from the first year in 2002 (the collection rate was over 40 percent in 2002 and was 30 percent in 2009). The survey reported that the proportion of visitors from outside the Suwa area has steadily increased from 48.6 percent in 2002 to 62.7 percent in 2009).

GEOGRAPHICAL DISTRIBUTION OF EXHIBITORS

Spaces for exhibitors' booths are separated into four zones according to the following categories: (1) Processing and Engineering (cutting,

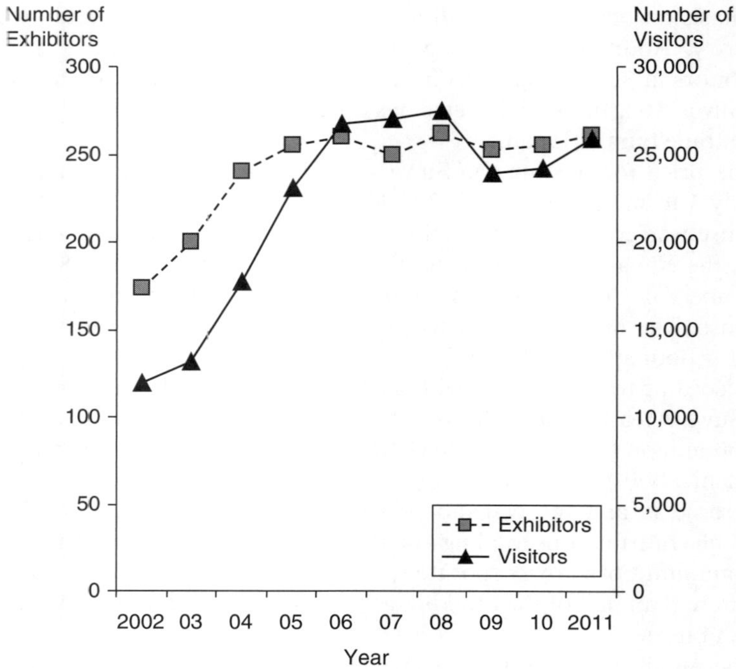

Source: Based on data from the executive committee of the Suwa Area Industrial Messe.

Figure 10.4 Development of the number of exhibitors and visitors of Suwa Area Industrial Messe, 2002–2011

pressing, optics, die casting); (2) Machinery and Finished Products (jigs and tools, molds, machine tools); (3) Industrial–Academic Research (universities, research institutes); and (4) Solutions (software, telecommunications, finance). Figure 10.5 reveals that the proportion of exhibitors from the Suwa area is the largest in all categories in comparison to exhibitors from outside the Suwa area, except Industrial–Academic Research. This result implies that institutional R&D support from outside of Suwa was required because the area had no science-based university until 2002.

Figure 10.6 shows the geographical distribution of exhibitors in the Suwa area. The number of exhibitors totaled 145 in 2002, 74 of which exhibited again in 2009. The share of 'repeat exhibitors' exceeded 50 percent between 2002 and 2009, suggesting that the Suwa Area Industrial Messe satisfied the needs of most exhibitors. The repeater ratio of outside Suwa area is comparatively low: 27 actors outside Suwa area

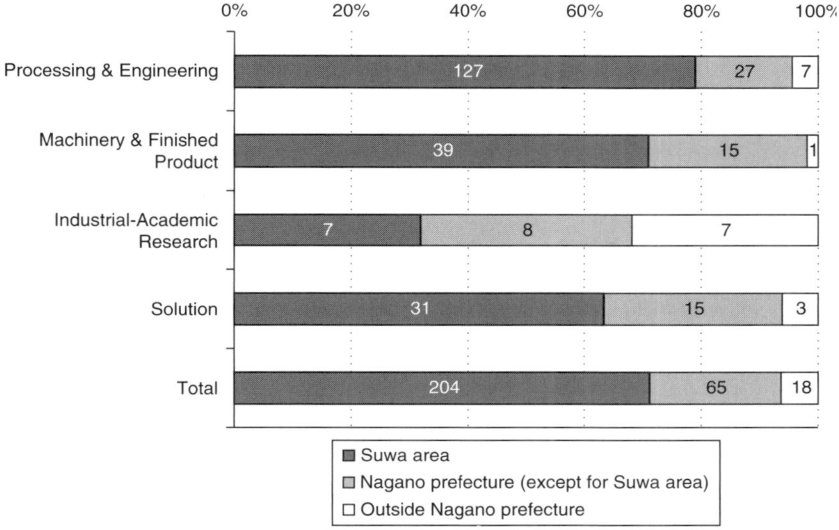

Note: Numbers in the graph refer to the number of exhibitors.

Source: Based on data from the executive committee of the Suwa Area Industrial Messe.

Figure 10.5 Exhibitors by industry group and place of origin at Suwa Area Industrial Messe, 2002

exhibited in 2002, of which only seven exhibitors exhibited again in 2009. In 2002, 44 exhibitors were located in densely inhabited districts (DID). In 2009, in contrast, 84 actors were concentrated in the area north of Lake Suwa, and there was a sharp rise in exhibitors from DID. Large enterprises with more than 300 employees, particularly exhibitors of Machinery and Finished Product, as well as small- and medium-sized firms were located in urban areas (see Figure 10.7). All of this indicates the strong and growing local basis of Suwa Area Industrial Messe.

GOALS OF ATTENDANCE AND STATE SUPPORT

The survey questionnaires used in this study were designed to gather information about the exhibition's purpose and the practices of building relationships with business partners at the fair. The questionnaires were distributed to all exhibitors both in 2004 and 2009. Of the 178 questionnaires sent to exhibitors in 2004, 126 were returned. Similarly, 188 of 252

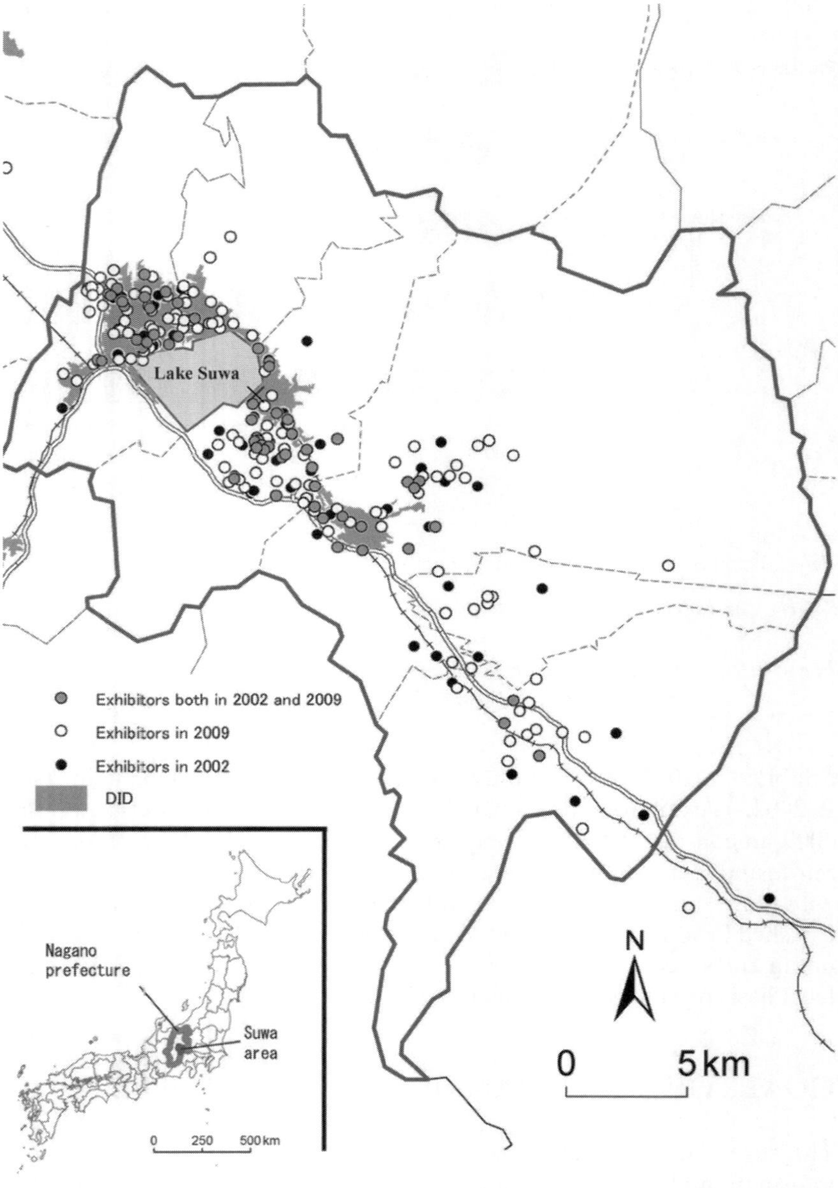

Figure 10.6 *Geographical origin of local exhibitors at Suwa Area Industrial Messe, 2002 and 2009*

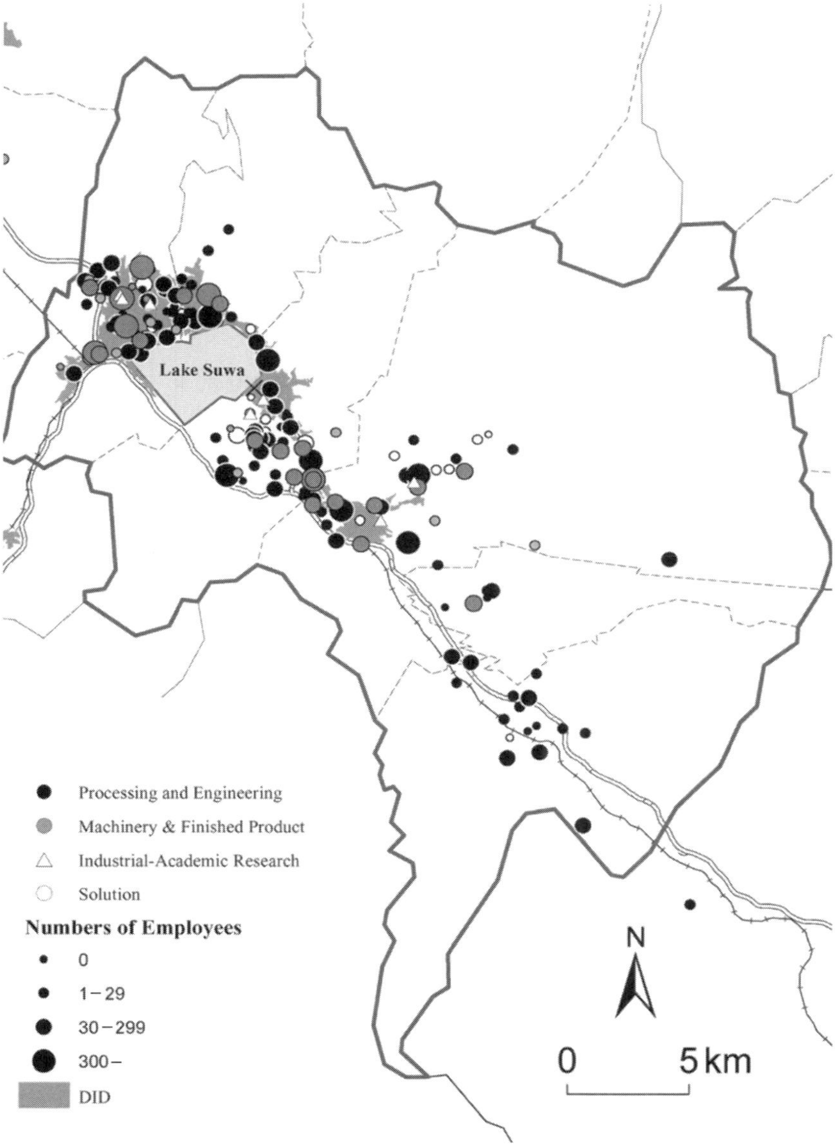

Figure 10.7 *Geographical origin of local exhibitors at Suwa Area Industrial Messe by industrial sector and size, 2009*

were returned in 2009. Focusing on the exhibition's purpose, the 2009 survey revealed that the acquisition of new orders was the most important goal of exhibitors for attending the fair (multiple answers allowed: rated important by 135 (72.2 percent) of 187 exhibitors who answered this question). The achievement of name recognition (49.7 percent) and the exchange of information between exhibitors and visitors (32.6 percent) were also important goals.

Although the average number of business conversations per exhibitor was 6.4, only 15 firms (12.4 percent of the 121 respondents) acquired new orders during the fair. However, a follow-up survey one year after the fair showed that the number of firms acquiring new orders increased (38 firms of 107 respondents).

In an interview, the Executive Committee Chairperson of the Suwa Area Industrial Messe stated that building transactional relationships during the fair was not recommended and explained the reasoning for this as follows: 'Even if exhibitors immediately find new business partners during the fair, it may be too unprofitable or too difficult for exhibitors to follow through on a deal. Those relationships are often not sustainable' (Interview conducted in Japanese on 10 September 2010).

The executive committee of the Suwa Area Industrial Messe stressed that the role of the fair was to offer an opportunity for exposure to potential customers who might be unfamiliar with the exhibitors. The Chairperson considered that the first step of building long-term relationships was the exchange of business cards and broad information during the fair.

There is distinctive institutional support for facilitating interactions between exhibitors and visitors during the Suwa Area Industrial Messe. First, there is an 'on-site business meeting plan' that involves inviting and guiding interested visitors to the exhibitors' factories. In 2009, approximately 20 exhibitors used this plan to build trust by having visitors observe their facilities and equipment. It is virtually impossible to hold on-site business meetings at the metropolitan trade fairs because of the distance between the exhibition halls and the production facilities.

Second, 'private consultation meetings for opening new markets' are held by the Suwa trade fair non-profit organization (NPO). The NPO was established by the Suwa area firms through the Suwa Chamber of Commerce and Industry in 2005 for administrative and clerical support of the Suwa Area Industrial Messe, coordination of the industry–academic collaboration and development of human resources. The NPO collects the firms' registration data and technical information in advance of the fair and supports business matching. In 2009, 30 firms registered for such support and 17 firms acquired new orders.

BUILDING RELATIONSHIPS WITH NON-LOCAL FIRMS

In 2002, the fair obtained full support from Toyota Motor Corporation; for example, the call for visitors to the fair went to related firms and subcontractors, resulting in many visitors from the Chubu region where Toyota is headquartered. Additionally, more visitors from the Kanto region have come to recent fairs. According to the 2009 questionnaires for visitors (577 respondents), approximately 28 percent of the visitors from outside Nagano prefecture were from Tokyo, 36 percent from Kanto (outside Tokyo) and 11 percent from Chubu. Local financial institutions and the local government arrange chartered bus tours and invite non-local firms to the fair.

One of the trade fair's primary purposes is to provide opportunities for local exhibitors to build long-term business relationships and mutual trust with non-local existing customers by inviting them to attend the fair. According to the 2009 questionnaire, more than half of exhibitors advertised the exhibitions in advance and sent out invitations to existing customers. Exhibitors not only guide the firms' factory tours during the fair, but also take visitors sightseeing around Suwa area. They try to build up business contacts with each other through private receptions at restaurants and hotels outside the fair.

The executive committee vigorously creates overseas markets in cooperation with national and local institutions. The JETRO, which is an independent agency of the Japanese government, invites foreign firms interested in marketing and conducts business meetings with them during the fair. In 2009, the JETRO invited automobile parts firms from Switzerland, France, the United States and Canada and covered the visitors' travel expenses such as airfares and accommodation fees. In advance of the fair, the local NPO recommended firms in Suwa as potential partners. In 2009, 50 firms participated in the JETRO's business meetings, and two local firms acquired overseas orders during the fair. In addition, another local support organization invited foreign firms related to the machine tool industry and conducted business meetings.

Analyzing the creation of overseas markets during the fair, this study found that manufacturing wholesalers play a significant role in acquiring information about the needs of non-local markets. The executive committee had rejected manufacturing wholesalers' exhibits since the fair's introduction in 2002, because the purpose of the fair was supposed to be building relationships between local firms and potential customers based on F2F communication during the fair. However, the executive committee reconsidered the role of wholesalers as providers of overseas market information in 2005, and the number of manufacturing wholesaler exhibitors increased to 10 in 2010. The wholesalers' engagement in advertising Suwa firms' high-precision products also supports the building of regional brands.

PROCESSES OF RELATIONSHIP BUILDING AT SUWA AREA INDUSTRIAL MESSE

Having analyzed the specifics of relationship building and inter-firm interaction during the Suwa Area Industrial Messe, we can now try to identify broader patterns of relationship building by distinguishing three stages: the preparatory stage for the trade fair, the stage during the fair and the stage after the fair. Bathelt and Schuldt (2008) propose an initial model to explain processes of trans-local pipeline creation through the effects of international trade fairs. This chapter extends this model by providing an explicit distinction of various stages and clarifying the relationships among exhibitors and visitors.

The Suwa Area Industrial Messe offers not only opportunities for business meetings, but also promotes R&D liaison and matching during the fair. The region is well known for cross-industrial associations/networks that meet regularly through events, such as study meetings and research workshops. These comprise university researchers, firms' engineers and members of research institutions in Suwa for collaborative R&D. These R&D associations have participated in the fair almost every year since the first fair in 2002. To exhibit at the fair, they frequently gather in groups and collaborate in R&D of new technologies and products prior to the fairs. The Suwa Area Industrial Messe thus reinforces and strengthens collaborative R&D relationships as the partners demonstrate the performance of technological capabilities. In addition, it is one of the critical business activities for small- and medium-sized local firms to promote the fairs in advance and send letters of invitation to existing customers (see Figure 10.8).

During the trade fairs, visitors and exhibitors exchange information about industrial trends and observe other exhibitors' levels of technology (see Figure 10.9). The Suwa Area Industrial Messe thus works as the place of acquiring novel information and knowledge. It is very important for local firms to build relationships with non-local potential partners, beginning by exchanging business cards. Some firms try to create and deepen trust and transaction relationships through private receptions at neighboring restaurants and hotels outside the Suwa Area Industrial Messe.

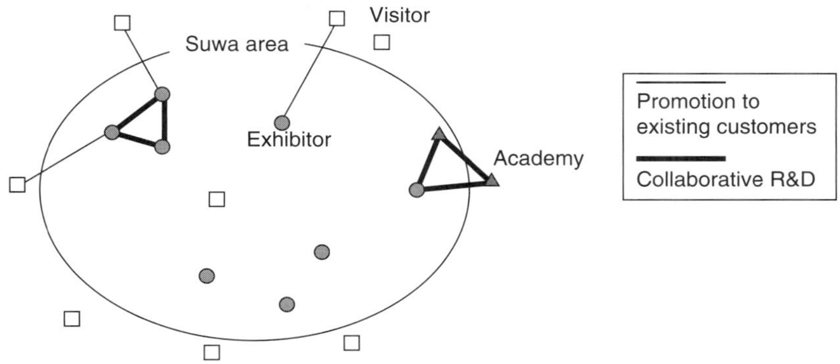

Figure 10.8 Relationship building in preparation for the trade fair

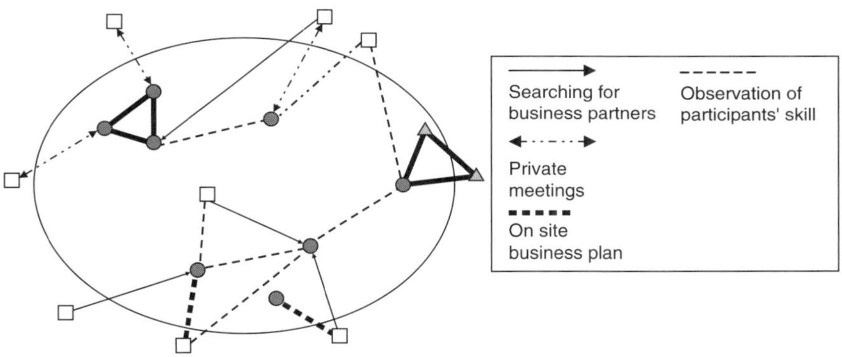

Figure 10.9 Relationship building during the trade fair

Additionally, visitors can observe exhibitors' skills directly through the 'on-site business meeting plan'.

Manufacturing wholesalers and exhibitors that have created overseas markets play an important role in sharing information concerning the needs of non-local markets. The fair strengthens the generally weak marketing capability of small- and medium-sized firms in the Suwa area. Though it is difficult to build up business contacts during the fair, many exhibitors are able to acquire new orders through continued business meetings after the fair (see Figure 10.10).

The fair stimulates not only vertical relationships among exhibitors and visitors, but also reinforces horizontal relationships such as study meetings and research workshops in the industrial agglomeration, which improve

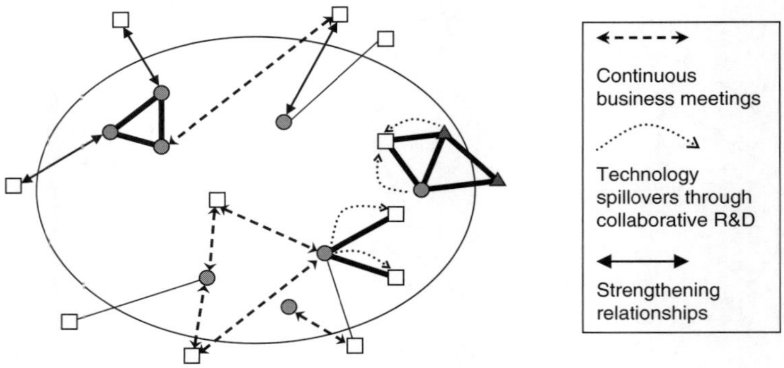

Figure 10.10 Relationship building after the trade fair

exhibitors' technological skills. Through existing horizontal relationships, new information and technology introduced during the fair spills over to non-participating firms. These indirect spillover effects improve the industrial agglomerations and support the building of a regional brand. The establishment of the regional brand for the Suwa region as a Mecca of high-precision technology firms also motivates firms to participate in the fair, creating a self-reinforcing growth cycle.

CONCLUSION

This study investigates the generation of various relationships among actors at local trade fairs held in industrial agglomerations in Japan. The findings of this study offer important implications for methods of upgrading industrial agglomerations through local trade fairs as temporary clusters. Since the first fair in 2002, the Suwa Area Industrial Messe became a trade fair of high-precision technology that has expanded its scale continuously. It is now recognized as an important event for firms in the Suwa area, Nagano prefecture. The purposes of participation at the trade fair are many. First, the observation of other exhibitors' skills and new products is important. Second, business talks with non-local firms who are potential customers and the acquisition of new orders become possible during the fair. In particular, the fair boosts the generally weak marketing power of the small- and medium-sized firms in the Suwa area. Third, the fair offers exhibitors the opportunity to construct long-term business relationships and mutual trust by inviting existing customers to attend.

The manufacturing wholesalers and exhibitors that succeed in export markets play a great role in acquiring information and knowledge about the needs of non-local markets at the fair (see, also, the case of Korea in Kalafsky and Gress, *this volume*). This non-local information and knowledge can spill over to local firms that do not participate at the fairs, via horizontal relationships such as study meetings and research workshops in industrial agglomerations.

At the present time, Japanese trade fairs are at a crucial turning point. Major cities in other Asian countries have been eager to attract international trade fairs and have successfully done so, as the case of China illustrates (see Golfetto and Rinallo, *this volume*; Jin and Weber, *this volume*; Bathelt and Zeng, *this volume*). However, Japan is lagging behind in terms of its trade fair business as compared with other highly developed countries, such as Germany, Italy or France, because there is a shortage of infrastructure, such as large facilities and specialized services for mega events and exhibitions, in Japan. The expansion of institutional support from the Japanese government appears to be key in taking on the contemporary competitive threats.

ACKNOWLEDGMENTS

This work was supported by Grant-in-Aid for Young Scientists (B) (Grant Number 23720399) of the Japan Society for the Promotion of Science.

REFERENCES

Asheim, B., Coenen, L. and Vang, J. (2007) 'Face-to-face, buzz, and knowledge bases: Sociospatial implications for learning, innovation, and innovation policy', *Environment and Planning C: Government and Policy*, 25: 655–670.

Bathelt, H. and Schuldt, N. (2008) 'Between luminaires and meat grinders: International trade fairs as temporary clusters', *Regional Studies*, 42: 853–868.

Bathelt, H. and Schuldt, N. (2010) 'International trade fairs and global buzz, Part I: Ecology of global buzz', *European Planning Studies*, 18: 1957–1974.

Chen, L. C. (2009) 'Learning through informal local and global linkages: The case of Taiwan's machine tool industry', *Research Policy*, 38: 527–535.

Hansen, K. (2004) 'Measuring performance at trade shows: Scale development and validation', *Journal of Business Research*, 57: 1–13.

Maskell, P., Bathelt, H. and Malmberg, A. (2004) *Temporary Clusters and Knowledge Creation: The Effects of International Trade Fairs, Conventions and Other Professional Gatherings*, SPACES 2004-04, Toronto and Heidelberg. Online. Available HTTP: <http://www.spaces-online.com> (10 June 2014).

Maskell, P., Bathelt, H. and Malmberg, A. (2006) 'Building global knowledge

pipelines: The role of temporary clusters', *European Planning Studies*, 14: 997–1013.
Norcliffe, G. and Rendace, O. (2003) 'New geographies of comic book production in North America: The new artisan, distancing, and the periodic social economy', *Economic Geography*, 79: 241–263.
POP Inc. (2010) *Mihonnichi Tenjikai Sougou Handbook 2011 (Handbook of Events and Exhibitions 2011)*, Tokyo: POP Inc.
Power, D. and Jansson, J. (2008) 'Cyclical clusters in global circuits: Overlapping spaces in furniture trade fairs', *Economic Geography*, 84: 423–448.
Rallet, A. and Torre, A. (2009) *Temporary Geographical Proximity for Business and Work Coordination: When, How and Where?*, SPACES 2009-02, Toronto and Heidelberg. Online. Available HTTP: <http://www.spaces-online.com> (10 March 2014).
Ramírez-Pasillas, M. (2008) 'Resituating proximity and knowledge cross-fertilization in clusters by means of international trade fairs', *European Planning Studies*, 16: 643–663.
Ramírez-Pasillas, M. (2010) 'International trade fairs as amplifiers of permanent and temporary proximities in clusters', *Entrepreneurship and Regional Development*, 22: 155–187.
Wickham, J. and Vecchi, A. (2008) 'Local firms and global reach: Business air travel and the Irish software cluster', *European Planning Studies*, 16: 693–710.
Yoon, H. and Malecki, E. J. (2010) 'Cartoon planet: Worlds of production and global production networks in the animation industry', *Industrial and Corporate Change*, 19: 239–271.

11. Trade fairs in peripheral places: towards a political economy of Australian fashion events

Sally A. Weller

INTRODUCTION

This chapter focuses attention on the under-researched characteristics of trade events in peripheral regional locations. The chapter questions whether the learning and innovation effects associated with prominent global events – the events that are the focus of most trade fair research in both economic geography and business studies – are shared by all types of trade fairs; or whether, in fact, processes of interactive learning and knowledge creation are peculiar to events located both physically and discursively at the center of global industry knowledge flows.

The chapter shifts the research focus to the evolution of regional-scale trade events. Here it is possible to examine how the positioning of events conditions their role in a globalizing political economy and how their relation to the evolution of regional production systems, industries and economies shapes their role in economic development. To examine the ways that regional events mediate the relationship between places and industries, the chapter analyzes a group of events held in two regional cities – Sydney and Melbourne in Australia. Poot (2001) describes such cities as being located on the periphery of global interactions, where peripherality is a relational social construct identifying places by their distance in space, separation in time and subordinate relationship to core locations that have allocative power over resources (Giddens 1985). The type of events of interest in this chapter – fashion and clothing industry events – provide an illuminating case study because Australian fashion is spatially and temporally distanced from global fashion hubs and because its rapid restructuring in response to shifts in national and global political economies highlights the coevolution of events and industries.

The analysis will argue that because regional trade fairs aspire to accommodate both local and extra-local interests, their functions and potentials differ from those of global events. In regional contexts, fairs do not simply reproduce the information sharing, networking and temporary clustering effects of global fairs, albeit on a smaller scale. Rather, regional trade fairs mediate among global and local interests, entangling them in the repositioning of national economies and in the reorganization of production systems in response to industrial globalization. In a dynamic industrial context, regional trade fairs crystallize participants' comprehensions of their microeconomic and macroeconomic operating environments and enhance their knowledge of the ways that internationalized production networks touch down in local contexts. As this triggers the search for more competitive network reconfigurations, events become an integral component of the restructuring of industries.

To develop these arguments, the chapter comprises four main sections followed by a brief conclusion. The next section explores the theoretical issues at stake in examining the positioning of regional trade fairs in global industrial development. The third section analyzes the evolution of trade fairs in Melbourne and Sydney in the context of the clothing sector's restructuring as Australia opened its economy to global trade. It describes how different local fashion events articulate with specific segments of this unevenly globalizing industry. The penultimate section then begins the task of specifying a political economy of regional trade fairs. The conclusion stresses that trade fair processes are inextricably bound up with their positioning in places and industries.

LOCATING TRADE FAIRS IN THE ECONOMIES OF PLACES

In economic geography, a now substantial trade fair literature is focused almost exclusively on global fairs that express an industry's core networks of power. Here trade fairs are conceived as one-off occasions – or as sequences of repeated one-off occasions – in which exchanges of information among industry insiders is concentrated in time and space. These fairs bring industry actors from diverse locations together in temporary clusters that stimulate communication, foster interaction and provide access to and exchange of information. This enables firms to identify potential collaborators and forge external linkages, creating new knowledge and triggering innovations that revitalize firm competitiveness (Malmberg and Maskell 2002; Maskell et al. 2006). These processes are also thought to reflect, reproduce and perhaps even reinforce the underlying inter-firm and inter-personal power relations of the event's related industry sector. As well as reducing the search costs and transaction costs of intra-industry trade, events appear to play a crucial role in the 'soft' regulation of economic activities, for example, by establishing the routines and conventions that institutionalize buyer–seller relationships (Skov 2006), by reproducing industry power relations (Entwistle and Rocamora 2006) or by bringing order to annual cycles of industrial activity (Power and Jansson 2008). From this perspective, the intermittently permanent presence of trade events stabilizes production systems, industrial networks and their attendant power relations.

The research focus on premier international events makes it difficult to develop an appreciation of the relationship between events and the configurations of production systems. It is accepted that trade events do not operate in a static industrial landscape. Bathelt and Boggs (2003), for example, demonstrated that trade fairs evolve with the industries they serve, recognizing that their character is shaped by the evolution of their institutional contexts, especially their relationships with industry sectors and governments. Recent work on trade event relocation reveals complex interactions among event practices and representations on the one hand and the strategies of participating industry actors on the other (Rinallo and Golfetto 2011). This suggests that trade events play a role in firms' strategic positioning in underlying competitive contexts. Similarly, awareness of competition among the world's major events, as well as the development of international event hierarchies (Power and Jansson 2008), suggests a strategic component to their staging and evolution. It follows that trade fairs should be viewed as institutions in their own right that influence the evolution of the production systems with which they interact, rather than simply as a microcosm of the power relations of their motivating industries. The need for such a conceptual separation is pronounced in the case of regional trade fairs for four reasons.

First, trade fairs in regional locations have proliferated as regional entrepreneurs or regional governments create them as vehicles to advance regional development. Events are expected to advance multiple, potentially contradictory ends: to elevate the global status of their host cities, to promote the export of locally produced commodities, to stimulate agglomeration processes among local industry actors and networks (with a view to stimulating innovation), to nurture the development of related service industries or to facilitate the integration of local industries into global production structures (Harvey 1989; Lewis et al. 2008; Weller 2008). These additional objectives mean that regional event-based interactions will differ from those of global events and overlap with but not directly mimic the conditions in their associated industries. The nature of the articulation between events and their related industries becomes an empirical question with material consequences.

Second, and in contrast to global events, trade fairs in regional locations have a specific location – or positioning (Sheppard 2002) – in relation to competing trade fairs, to the production networks in their related industries and to the status of their regional location in urban hierarchies and global macroeconomic processes. Regional trade fairs prompt deeper consideration of questions about how the role and evolution of fairs is shaped by their positioning. Although trade events have been shown to generate information and knowledge about the structure of global value chains (Maskell et al. 2006), it is also evident that only a subset of firms are in a position to use that knowledge to extend their inter-firm linkages (Bathelt and Schuldt 2008). Yet the actual nature of these connections remains largely unexplored. Research focused on international trade fairs in central places – fairs that are physically located either at nodes in networks of activity or at high amenity locations (Moeran 2011) – cannot consider how variable distanciations in space and time condition the types of interactions that occur within fairs. Regional fairs, in contrast, negotiate their positioning relative to other events in other places and contribute to the discursive construction of industries and places (Lewis et al. 2008). Research in regional contexts therefore has the potential to reveal how the roles of place, space, timing and positioning shape firms' differential capacities to create and harness event-based knowledge.

Third, because regional fairs accommodate a range of forces that operate at multiple scales, they promise to reveal how indirect associations, such as the effects of shifts in exchange rates, shape event activities and viability. Most trade fair research in economic geography is motivated by a relational understanding focused on the micro-scale of interactions among firms, agents and intermediaries in clustered production networks (see Dicken et al. 2001).This orientation privileges the interactive learning that accompanies event activities, making it possible to explore the competitive challenge of balancing the twin imperatives of internal cohesion and external connection (Bathelt and Taylor 2002). Yet agent-oriented perspectives struggle to incorporate processes that unfold at other scales and that affect production networks indirectly, such as changes in exchange rates or trade policies (Coe et al. 2008).

Fourth, the study of regional trade fairs should shed light on the factors that lead events to prosper in some places, times and sectors but not others (see Power and Jansson 2008). Although the number of regional trade fairs has grown exponentially in recent years, the economics of information exchange suggest that events in sparsely populated or peripheral places will struggle to maintain an audience. To justify its reiteration, an event must attract exhibitors, buyers, sponsors and media interest. However, firms are likely to decide to participate, in any of these capacities, only when the fair's anticipated benefits cannot be accessed more cost-efficiently by other available means (Florio 1994). It follows that firms using trade fairs to expand their markets, extend their networks or refresh their ideas are likely to be attracted to fairs with the greatest density of participants or range of differentiated products. Competition among trade events will therefore tend to culminate in the emergence of multiple specialized monopolies relating to specialist industry segments. These ideas raise fundamental questions about the viability of regional trade fairs.

To understand how trade events in peripheral regional contexts articulate with production systems and firm networks in places requires thinking about regional trade events without assuming that they recreate, at a regional scale, the temporary clustering processes characteristic of international events. It requires a multi-scalar perspective that links the practices and interactions of agents in events with the less immediate processes unfolding at other scales and sites (Swyngedouw 1997). It also requires recognition that trade fairs are economic activities shaped, albeit in contingent and inherently spatialized ways, by both their context and their history (Storper and Walker 1989). The positioning of regional trade fairs, therefore, is likely to both reflect and condition their economic role (Sheppard 2002). The next section adopts such an approach. It describes how a group of trade events in Australia operate as pivots mediating among global and local forces. This, it contends, provides opportunities for industry actors to observe and evaluate the workings of the local production system in the global macroeconomy, creating knowledge and triggering organizational innovations as firms identify competitive strategies that respond to changing microeconomic and macroeconomic contexts.

TRADE FAIRS IN REGIONAL LOCATIONS: FASHION EVENTS IN AUSTRALIA

Australia's open economy is dominated by agricultural and mineral exports, but its urban environments are increasingly oriented to services activities, including the business communications, conventions and events industries. The 13 major exhibition spaces in Australia, as well as numerous smaller spaces, are operated by members of the Exhibition and Event Association of Australasia. In Australia, governments classify trade fairs as a part of the business events industry within the tourism sector where, in parallel with sporting and entertainment events, their success is assessed in terms of their capacity to attract international (business) tourists. Australia-wide trade fairs and exhibitions (known locally as trade shows) are estimated to have

Table 11.1 Trade fair and exhibition attendance in Australia, 2008 and 2011

	Attendees			Estimated expenditures		
	2008 (000s)	2011 (000s)	Change 08–11 (%)	2008 ($ million (AUD))	2011 ($ million (AUD))	Change 08–11 (%)
International visitors	59	53	−10.2	244	220	−9.8
Domestic visitors	473	697	+47.4	434	1,017	+134

Source: TRA (2011).

attracted almost 700,000 domestic and 53,000 international visitors in 2011 (TRA 2011). Trade fairs account for about 6 percent of national business event activity annually. Their value has fallen marginally since the 2007 global financial downturn (see Table 11.1).

Reflecting the composition of the Australian economy, trade fairs in Australia are oriented to services and high technology industry sectors. Importantly, Australia is an English-speaking country so, in contrast to many Asia-Pacific locations, trade fairs have no language mediation role. This section's examination of fashion sector events exemplifies the challenges faced by service-oriented trade fairs in regional locations, distant from the core sites of industrial power. Its content draws on the author's previous research on the Australian clothing sector as well as field observations and impromptu interviews at trade fairs, event press releases, information published on event websites, government evaluations and press reports.

Fashion events include all the marketing, networking and information exchange elements of other trade events. However, they also play a crucial role in the reproduction of the underlying clothing production industry by establishing the value of designs and the status of designers (Entwistle and Rocamora 2006) and by supporting the production of symbolic representations (Rocamora 2001). In addition, fashion events are implicated in the economic development trajectories of their host locations because, *inter alia*, they build the creative credentials of host cities, promote urban tourism and contribute to governmental strategies designed to reposition cities and nations in creativity-led global 'knowledge' economies (Lewis et al. 2008). Fashion change propels the clothing and textiles industries' global production systems. These industries are unusually sensitive to changes in economic and policy contexts because their modest technologies, divisible production activities and minimal immobile 'sunk' costs make them amenable to frequent reorganizations and relocations (Fröbel et al. 1980). Globally, the sector's spatially uneven restructuring over the last 40 years has tended to concentrate knowledge-intensive design functions in particular advanced-economy global cities while dispersing labor-intensive production to low wage countries. The Australian market is small by global standards. Its southern hemisphere location puts it at odds with global fashion rhythms (Weller 2007).

Although the idea of distinctively 'Australian' fashion emerged in the 1950s to challenge the dominance of fashion ideas from Europe, national-scale clothing markets remained under-developed, even into the 1980s (English and Pomazan 2010). This reflected the unique characteristics of the Australian economy: the high costs of linking Australia's dispersed urban centers, the uncoordinated regulatory structures of the Australian federation's member states and a system of industry protection that excluded low value imports and dulled competitive processes among local firms. In 1988 Australia began the process of liberalizing its trade barriers, opening its markets to competition and globalizing its economy. Since then, Australia's clothing and fashion sector has competed directly with better resourced overseas-based producers. While, as a consequence, the local clothing and fashion production sector has declined relentlessly, a small subsector of firms producing fashion attuned to local consumer sentiment has survived (see Webber and Weller 2001). In this new context, the heightened importance of marketing and branding has created an environment suited to the creation of trade fairs and events that engage consumer interest.

The evolution of the clothing industry since 1988 has comprised four identifiable phases. In the first phase, from 1988 to 1996, trade barrier protection was progressively removed. The Australian government's then interventionist industry policies aspired to 'international competitiveness' by promoting the internationalization of local production networks, nurturing the development of national markets and expanding export markets. However, as trade barriers fell, department stores and fashion retail groups developed national markets and import-based supply chains to support them, resulting in the rapid expansion of the import share of the local market. Many local production firms were forced to exit the industry (Webber and Weller 2001; Weller 2006; 2007). After a change of government, the second phase between 1996 and 2000 brought less interventionist policies based on comparative advantage arguments. Most industry assistance was withdrawn. Despite this, local production experienced a brief renaissance as the depreciating value of the Australian dollar put imported fashion products out of the reach of average consumers. After 2000, the third phase saw the production industry decline as an appreciating Australian dollar made imports increasingly more affordable. As Australia's integration into global flows deepened and accelerated, business activity gradually relocated from the southern city of Melbourne, which had been the center of Australia's clothing manufacturing industries, to Sydney, which is Australia's most globally connected city and its importing hub. By the mid-2000s, as the Australian dollar appreciated towards parity with the US dollar, the final phase saw overseas retail chains begin entering the Australian market. Local retailers responded with a renewed emphasis on local design (Demasi 2004). The emerging cosmopolitan generation of fashion design entrepreneurs rejected faux 'Australian' design, instead favoring local interpretations of global moods (Whitfield 2010). Department stores and retail chain stores began commercializing the work of local designers.

As the local clothing industry was exposed to global competition, multiple fashion trade fairs and events – each with different foci and target audiences – emerged (Ford 2002). The evolution and relative importance of trade fairs, exporting fairs, importing fairs and consumer fairs mirrors the changing industry structure. Table 11.2 shows the events held in Melbourne and Sydney in 2012. These are all small events by global standards, each one typically attracting less than 300 participant firms. Most are staged by commercial event production companies, some in conjunction with industry associations.

Buyers' fairs focus on the relationship between wholesalers and retailers. Before the local industry was exposed to global forces, multiple competing buying events were coordinated by different retail buying groups on behalf of their members or customers. In 1998 and 2000, as the local industry was contracting and at the instigation of local suppliers, these fairs merged into a bi-annual clothing, footwear and accessories trade fair called Fashion Exposed, which was organized by Australian Exhibitions and Conferences (AEC). This reorganization aimed primarily to rationalize supplier costs in a declining industry and to focus the industry at a larger venue. The new format brought the once-local event forward to accommodate import timelines (from March to February and September to August). It also created more space for event-based interactions between sellers and established customers, which enabled the event to compensate for cost-cutting rationalizations of the chain of agents servicing regional retailers in more isolated locations (Halliwell 2012). The nature of event transactions changed gradually as purchasing shifted from an indent (made to order) to a direct supply model and as the format was expanded to include industry seminars and other educative components.

Table 11.2 Fashion and clothing events in Sydney and Melbourne

INDEPENDENT BUYER EVENT	Years	Location	Month	Orientation
Frontline advantage	1980–99	Melbourne	April	Independent retailers
ARL Buyers Fair	?–1998	Melbourne		Independent retailers
Fashion Exposed (AEC)*	2000–	Melbourne	March/September	Buyers and Suppliers (local)
Fashion Exposed (AEC)*	2003–	Sydney	March/September	Buyers and Suppliers (local)
Premiere Fashion (AEC)	2011–	Sydney	September	Higher value import agents
Premiere Fashion (AEC)	2012–	Melbourne	September	Higher value import agents
Frontline Aust. Apparel Buying	2013	Melbourne	February	Independent retailers
DESIGNER EVENT				
Australian Fashion Week (IMG)	1996–	Sydney	May	Export/Import replacement
Australian Fashion Week Autumn	2002–07	Melbourne	November/October	Export/Import replacement
Australian Fashion Week Autumn	2008	Sydney	November	Export/Import replacement
IMPORTER EVENT				
TCF International	1995–2001	Melbourne	May	Import
TCF Expo	2001	Sydney	March	Import
Garment Tech and Austex	2002	Sydney	November	Import
China Clothing and Textiles Expo	2003–04	Melbourne	December	Import and components
China Textiles and Clothing Expo	2009–	Sydney	November	Import and components
IMPEX (AES)	1994–2005	Melbourne	June	Import and components
Aust. International Sourcing Fair	2010–	Sydney/Melbourne	November	Importers
CONSUMER EVENT				
Melbourne Fashion Festival	1987–	Melbourne	March	Consumer sales
Melbourne Spring Fashion Festival	1988–	Melbourne	September	Consumer sales
Fashion Festival Sydney	2008–	Sydney	August	Consumer sales
Fashion Weekend Sydney	2012–	Sydney	May	Consumer sales

Note: * = alternating years.

Gradually, the emphasis has shifted from components for use by local makers to finished manufactures for sale by local retailers. Tracking the relocation of clothing industry activity, Fashion Exposed originated in Melbourne, at a time when Melbourne dominated the clothing industry, and expanded to Sydney in 2005.

The designer fashion event, Australian Fashion Week (AFW), was first held in Sydney in 1996 when the Australian dollar was trading at a low value and when policy incentives promoted export market development. The event was instigated by a local firm, Australian Fashion Innovators (AFI), as a commercial venture without industry association links, to promote Australian fashion design and to 'put Australia on the international fashion map' (Phyland 1996). The year 2000 was AFW's most successful year: it was when the Australian dollar was at its lowest (i.e. most internationally competitive) value and when the Olympic Games brought large numbers of overseas visitors to Sydney.

By 2001, the Australian dollar had commenced its upward revaluation and the AFW event began to unravel. First, it had trouble attracting overseas buyers. Given Australia's seasonal positioning relative to global trends, a fashion event located in Australia struggles to accommodate buyers in both local and international fashion markets. Second, there was a capacity problem. Few Australian designer firms were large enough or able to command production resources to fill a large order from an overseas department store, which made AFW's export focus 'a distraction' at best (Meagher 2001, p. 20). Third, there was a familiarity problem. As relationships between fashion designers and national retailers matured, the event's intermediation was no longer required (Huntington 2005). Fourth, there was competition from other events. In 2002, leading Australian designers were opting to show their collections overseas, at larger events attended by more international buyers (McDowell 2002). By 2003 Australian retail buyers were favoring New Zealand Fashion Week, where, as well as being accorded coveted 'international buyer' status, they could access New Zealand manufactures, which were becoming more competitively priced as the Australian dollar appreciated against the New Zealand dollar. There were also tensions over event staging, which led dissenters to establish a concurrent fringe event in the years 2001 to 2003 (Loucas 2002a). In response to these pressures, AFW re-focused in 2003 to feature 'emerging' but under-capitalized designers. The 2004 show featured numerous designers from the Asia-Pacific region, and by 2005 AFW had repositioned to target an Asia-Pacific audience. Soon after, the event was sold to global media firm IMG, which owns a stable of similar fashion events worldwide (Safe 2006). The new format's promise of accommodating both importers' and exporters' interests sat uncomfortably with the competitive realities of clothing production. The fundamental problem remained: the impossibility of synchronizing the temporal rhythms of local and international fashion retail buying calendars. After 2007, when the global financial crisis depressed markets, the event settled back into a domestic market role (Safe 2012).

The AFW reveals the importance of event positioning. An autumn/winter version of AFW was staged in Melbourne from 2002 to 2007, with the support of funding from that city's state government. Its failure to take root reflected its inconvenient timing relative to the rhythms of the global fashion-buying cycle, as well as its lack of local business support in Melbourne (Loucas 2002b). Given that the Sydney AFW event has a poor record in attracting Melbourne-based designers, it seems reasonable to conclude that one event cannot serve both cities. This reflects cost factors as well as the Melbourne–Sydney rivalry. If Melbourne-based designers elect to show away from home, the cost of showing in Sydney is not greatly dissimilar from the cost of showing in more central cities like Hong Kong, New York or London, since airfares are a small part of the total cost. This reality undermines the viability of national and regional trade fairs in peripheral locations.

In 2010, a new import-oriented event 'Premiere Fashion' was created by AEC after its sale to the global information service firm Informa. This event featured high value, mostly imported garments and was held concurrently with AEC's existing Fashion Exposed event, but at a more upmarket venue. The new event was supported by the Apparel Importers Association of Australia, a group of agents representing high value European and US brands, and reflected the increasing market power of these agents as fashion imports became more affordable in the local market. Premiere Fashion originated in Sydney, which had become the center for fashion imports, and expanded to Melbourne in 2012. In this part of the market, the perceived imperatives of customer communication favor the development of separate events in each major city rather than one Australia-wide event. In 2013, Premiere Fashion Sydney was rescheduled to show concurrently with an import-replacement oriented Australian Fashion Week. Separating import and export orientations in concurrent events enables the urban event component of fashion events to accommodate industry schisms.

Increasing import market shares also encouraged the emergence of consumer-based events. Two Melbourne-based and consumer-oriented retail fashion events – the L'Oreal Melbourne Fashion Festival (March) and the Melbourne Spring Fashion Festival (September) – were created in the late 1980s, just as the trade liberalization process increased retailers' capacity to import garments into the local market. At the time of their inception, when local consumers were not familiar with the imported labels that were replacing local manufactures, these urban-scale events assumed an important educative function. By mixing local and imported brands across consumer segments and 'price points', these festivals worked to domesticate imported garments. With garments available immediately for purchase, they also concentrated and expanded sales activity (Weller 2013). Melbourne Spring Fashion Festival, which is sponsored by the City of Melbourne, also had explicit place marketing and urban tourism objectives. The Melbourne consumer events are guided by local steering groups representing retail, cultural, education and tourism interests and include experiential marketing, consumer education activities and business seminars intended to educate the local industry to global fashion trends and business strategies. Both also work with the local fashion college to train fashion students and allocate fashion career opportunities. Two latecomer Sydney events – Fashion Festival Sydney and Fashion Weekend Sydney – imitate the success of these Melbourne consumer festivals.

Finally, another set of trade fairs target the suppliers of production inputs. These orthodox events attract overseas manufacturers hoping to export textiles, equipment, intermediate goods and finished products to local producers and wholesalers. A series of events have appeared then disappeared over the years. In November 2012, the Australian International Sourcing Fair and the China Textiles and Clothing Expo were held concurrently in Melbourne and Sydney. This duplication demonstrates the absence of economies of scale of access in the Australian market and the dominance of China in the production side of the industry.

To summarize: in this regional context, multiple events operate in a fragmented regional economic space. Each relates to a different subsector of the clothing supply chain, articulates with different types of production and import networks, and coordinates to a limited extent with related events. As Australian manufacturing contracted, retail buying fairs first consolidated (into Fashion Exposed), but then fragmented as importers established their own dedicated event (Premiere). The designer fashion event AFW was established to promote exporting, but international buyers could not be attracted to Australia or its out-of-season design cycle. When rising exchange rates made exporting impractical, AFW reoriented to import replacement, becoming an intermediary in the relationship between local department stores and local designers. Consumer events appeared at the start of the internationalization process to introduce imported garments and to facilitate the globalization of clothing markets. They have since evolved as an additional means by which local department stores can harness local fashion trends to maintain their competitive position relative to new retail entrants from overseas. Importers have gradually increased their influence across all event types, albeit in different ways. As the initiatives of local industry associations have been subsumed into a global information services industry, trade fairs have reoriented to now include activities that educate local businesses and consumers about trends at the world's core sites of innovation.

TOWARDS A POLITICAL ECONOMY OF REGIONAL TRADE FAIRS

When viewed from Australia, global flows of people, commodities, ideas and money appear uneven and sporadic, with the depth and exclusivity of transnational linkages continually reordered as exchange rates and trade rules change. This account shows that the globalization of trade fairs is a contingent process. Throughout the 1990s, in the context of a declining exchange rate, Australian firms were optimistic that they could use trade fairs to develop export markets and create global linkages. In 2001, when the Australian dollar reversed its direction, optimism evaporated, and designers with global ambitions acknowledged that to succeed they would have to compete in the northern hemisphere's 'global' fashion events. At the same time, as overseas retailers developed a new (but perhaps temporary) interest in the Australian market, new importer events appeared and existing events took on the role of educating local actors about global trends. These movements are shot through with uneven geographies of power that reinforce local subordination to global trends and stifle – rather than promote – fashion design innovation at the grassroots. The shifting landscape of trade events has both reflected and contributed to reconfigurations of production, supply and distribution networks and shifts in the relative power of different actors within them.

The trajectories of change in both industries and events are partly a product of Australia's dispersed, low density and peripheral industries and markets. In such markets, agglomeration processes are unlikely to develop spontaneously (Poot 2001). This context changes the network potentials of events because here event networking is difficult to translate into new business relationships. Local relationships are for the most part well established, and the market is small enough for most buyers and sellers to be known to each other. In this context, firms are less likely to rely on events to reduce their information search costs (Florio 1994). The development of extra-local relationships, such as links with international firms, are constrained because it has been difficult to attract overseas buyers to Australian venues, even when the organizers pay their costs, and because global actors who do attend seldom encounter offerings that they have not already seen elsewhere. Worse, overseas visitors at Australian trade fairs are likely to be assessing opportunities for independent market entry rather than seeking local collaborators.

For local firms in a shrinking local market, the main role of trade events has been to reduce local transaction costs by providing a venue at which they can maintain face-to-face contact with geographically dispersed customers and suppliers. Because locally based event participants already have information about the previous European season's fashion trends, local events have a limited role in product innovation. The characteristics of this context imply that social networking activities within local events have limited capacity to forge global 'pipelines', expand global connectivity or stimulate product innovation. Because Australians' first language is English, there is no impediment to active participation in larger shows held in central places where there are greater potentials for forging global links.

Despite these limitations, it does appear that trade events have had an important role in organizational innovation, which in itself is an important form of technological change (Webber et al. 1992). For example, local events appear to have played a part in retailers' growing awareness that their competitive advantage depends increasingly on their capacity to cater to local preferences. This has generated new production structures that incorporate local design into the internationalized supply chains of local department stores, chain retailers and buying groups. The interactive knowledge produced in events appears to sharpen awareness of what is – and what is not – possible for local firms, given macroeconomic conditions, national industry conditions, national policies and relationships between nations. These evaluations have the potential to trigger systemic realignments that support, resist or redistribute economic activity, with material consequences for the path-dependent evolution of industries.

CONCLUSION

The literature in geography and in other disciplines too often views trade fairs in isolation from their positioning in relation to industries, production systems, cities and economies. In particular, there has been limited discussion of the ways in which the macroeconomic effects of globalization reshape the relationships between industries and trade fairs. In an effort to expand the scope of analysis and to bring in the national and regional scale, this chapter has developed a political economy perspective to view events as focal points that crystallize multiple influences across scales. It has shown that events evolve in tandem with both production systems and economies, with the intensity of global interactions depending on the host economy's dynamic positioning in a global political economy. Given economies of information, it appears that trade fairs will stabilize at either the global scale or the local urban scale: the evidence in this chapter suggests that without language barriers there are near insuperable barriers to the emergence of regional fairs in global industries. Viable local events tend to be consumer oriented: they do not mimic the innovation-oriented interactions of international fairs and have limited potential to catalyze the integration of local firms into global industry networks. It appears, however, that local trade fairs can function as vehicles to advance the penetration of local markets by global firms when exchange rates are favorable to them. The clear implication is that whether or not the development of the trade fair industry in the Asia-Pacific region (see Golfetto and Rinallo, *this volume*; Li, *this volume*) supports or inhibits national industrial development will depend on the articulation of trade fairs with exporting and importing industries. The central issue is whether – or to what extent – government policy settings, or language and cultural differences, affords producers in other Asia-Pacific locations greater protection from expanding global firms.

These patterns suggest clear spatial variations in the reasons why firms participate in trade events and in the contribution of participation to broader business strategies. Yet to date, the effects of factors operating at scales beyond the immediate interactions in production networks have not been well integrated into research on trade fairs in economic geography. In particular, this chapter raises questions for further research on the relationships between trade fairs and production systems and on the impact of changes in currency values on the configurations of both trade fairs and production networks.

REFERENCES

Bathelt, H. and Boggs, J. (2003) 'Towards a re-conceptualization of regional development paths: Is Leipzig's media cluster a continuation of or a rupture with the past?' *Economic Geography*, 79: 269–293.

Bathelt, H. and Schuldt, N. (2008) 'Between luminaries and meat grinders: International trade fairs as temporary clusters', *Regional Studies*, 42: 853–868.

Bathelt, H. and Taylor, M. (2002) 'Clusters, power and place: Inequality and local growth in time-space', *Geografiska Annaler*, 84B: 93–109.

Coe, N., Dicken, P. and Hess, M. (2008) 'Introduction: Global production networks – Debates and challenges', *Journal of Economic Geography*, 8: 267–269.

Demasi, L. (2004) 'Fighting fit fashion', *Sydney Morning Herald*, 20 January.

Dicken, P., Kelly, P., Olds, K. and Yeung, H. W.-C. (2001) 'Chains and networks, territories and scales: Towards a relational framework for analysing the global economy', *Global Networks*, 1: 89–112.

English, B. and Pomazan, L. (2010) *Australian Fashion Unstitched: The Last 60 Years*, Sydney: Cambridge University Press.

Entwistle, J. and Rocamora, A. (2006) 'The field of fashion materialized: A study of London Fashion Week', *Sociology*, 40: 735–751.

Florio, M. (1994) 'Fair trades by trade fairs: Information providing institutions under monopolistic competition', *Small Business Economics*, 6: 267–281.

Ford, C. (2002) 'Melbourne fashion: Bursting at the seams?', *Ragtrader*, June–July: 8.

Fröbel, F., Heinrichs, J. and Kreye, O. (1980) *The New International Division of Labour*, Cambridge: Cambridge University Press.

Giddens, A. (1985) *The Nation-State and Violence*, Cambridge: Polity.

Halliwell, R. (2012) Personal communication, Frontline Stores, Melbourne, 30 October.

Harvey, D. (1989) 'From managerialism to entrepreneurialism: The transformation of urban governance in late capitalism', *Geografiska Annaler*, 71B: 3–17.

Huntington, P. (2005) 'Wardrobe malfunction as Morrissey exits', *Sydney Morning Herald*, Sydney, 7 April.

Lewis, N., Larner, W. and Le Heron, R. (2008) 'The New Zealand designer fashion industry: Making industries and co-constituting political projects', *Transactions of the Institute of British Geographers*, 33: 42–59.

Loucas, A. (2002a) 'Simon says: Australian Fashion Week', *Sydney Morning Herald*, 24 April.

Loucas, A. (2002b) 'Sydney fashion's big-wigs skirt Melbourne gig', *Sydney Morning Herald*, 11 November.

Malmberg, A. and Maskell, P. (2002) 'The elusive concept of localization economies: Toward a knowledge-based theory of spatial clustering', *Environment and Planning A*, 34: 429–449.

Maskell, P., Bathelt, H. and Malmberg, A. (2006) 'Building global knowledge pipelines: The role of temporary clusters', *European Planning Studies*, 14: 997–1013.

McDowell, C. (2002) 'In search of a style', *The Australian*, 7 June.

Meagher, D. (2001) 'Fashion Weeks: It's all in the figures', *Australian Financial Review*, April: 16–24.

Moeran, B. (2011) 'The book fair as a tournament of values', in B. Moeran and J. Pederson (eds) *Negotiating Values in the Creative Industries: Fairs, Festivals and Competitive Events*, Cambridge: Cambridge University Press, 119–144.

Phyland, J. (1996) 'Fabulous fashion, darlings!', *The Age*, 9 May.

Poot, J. (2001) 'Peripherality in the global economy', in J. Poot (ed.) *On the Edge of the Global Economy*, Cheltenham, UK and Northampton, MA: Edward Elgar Publishing, 3–26.

Power, D. and Jansson, J. (2008) 'Cyclical clusters in global circuits: Overlapping spaces in furniture trade fairs', *Economic Geography*, 84: 423–448.

Rinallo, D. and Golfetto, F. (2011) 'Exploring the knowledge strategies of temporary cluster organizers: A longitudinal study of the EU fabric industry trade shows (1986–2006)', *Economic Geography*, 87: 453–476.

Rocamora, A. (2001) 'High fashion and pop fashion: The symbolic production of fashion in Le Monde and The Guardian', *Fashion Theory*, 5 (2): 123–142.

Safe, G. (2006) 'Designers desert ship as Fashion Week lists', *The Australian*, 27 August.
Safe, G. (2012) 'Between a frock and a hard place', *Sydney Morning Herald*, 28 April.
Sheppard, E. (2002) 'The spaces and times of globalization: Place, scale, networks, and positionality', *Economic Geography*, 78: 307–331.
Skov, L. (2006) 'The role of trade fairs in the global fashion business', *Current Sociology*, 54: 764–783.
Storper, M. and Walker, R. (1989) *The Capitalist Imperative: Territory, Technology and Industrial Growth*, Cambridge, MA: Blackwell.
Swyngedouw, E. (1997) 'Neither global nor local: "Glocalization" and the politics of scale', in K. R. Cox (ed.) *Spaces of Globalization: Reasserting the Power of the Local*, New York: Guilford, 137–166.
TRA (2011) *Business Events Visitors: 2011*, Canberra: Tourism Research Australia.
Webber, M., Sheppard, E. and Rigby, D. (1992) 'Forms of technical change', *Environment and Planning A*, 24: 1679–1709.
Webber, M. and Weller, S. (2001) *Refashioning the Rag Trade: The Internationalisation of the TCF Industries in Australia*, Sydney: University of New South Wales Press.
Weller, S. (2006) 'Networks, commodity chains and crisis: The impact of Fiji's coup on garment production networks', *Environment and Planning A*, 38: 1249–1267.
Weller, S. (2007) 'Fashion as viscous knowledge: Fashion's role in shaping trans-national garment production', *Journal of Economic Geography*, 7: 39–66.
Weller, S. (2008) 'Beyond "global production network" metaphors: Australian Fashion Week's trans-sectoral synergies', *Growth and Change*, 39: 104–122.
Weller, S. (2013) 'Consuming the city: Public fashion festivals and the participatory economies of urban spaces in Melbourne, Australia', *Urban Studies*, 50: 2853–2868.
Whitfield, D. (2010) 'Australia, Paris then New York: Navigating the world's fashion capitals', in B. English and L. Pomazan (eds) *Australian Fashion Unstitched: The Last 60 Years*, Sydney: Cambridge University Press, 191–216.

12. State strategy and industrial socio-economic practices in Taipei's international trade fairs

Jung-Ying Chang, Jinn-Yuh Hsu and Tsu-Lung Chou

INTRODUCTION

The industrialization of conventions and exhibitions is a key state strategy in boosting competitiveness in major cities around the world, especially in Asia. Such state strategy focuses on conventions and exhibitions in three categories. First, the tourism industry builds on tourist attractions, leisure and cultural activities and facilities to promote a city's image as a tourist destination. The second focus is the convention industry viewing convention destinations as places of interactive decision-making and information exchange. Related policy support usually takes place where governmental agencies, non-governmental organizations or corporate headquarters are located. The third policy focus includes industrial trade fairs, with themed activities around the organizing industries. They are often, at least historically, organized in cities known for their particular industrial sectors, with the purpose of promoting learning, marketing and network-building among exhibitors (Chou 2006). Convention and exhibition industries play an important strategic role in stimulating the spatial and industrial development of major cities.

As one of the newly industrialized countries (NICs) in Asia, Taiwan's economic growth is particularly built on the flexibility of small and medium sized enterprises (SMEs) (Chu 1997). Coping with the challenges of leading the country to a transition towards high-end services in a 'post-industrial' period, the government started to promote the trade fair industry in the early 2000s. The government aimed to provide efficient marketing channels, help the transformation of traditional industries and improve the networks between firms. According to statistics from the Executive Yuan, Taiwan's highest administrative government branch, the output of the trade fair industry in Taiwan was valued at approximately

Table 12.1 International trade fairs in Taiwan, 2004–2010

Year	2004	2005	2006	2007	2008	2009	2010
Total floor space (sq.m.)	301,250	341,000	409,750	365,000	458,500	487,250	552,000
Number of events	47	58	60	46	62	63	74
Rank in Asia	7th	6th	7th	8th	7th	7th	6th

Note: sq.m. = square meters (1 square meter = 10.76 square feet).

Source: UFI (2011).

$15,847 billion New Taiwan dollars (NTD) ($530 billion (USD)) in 2008. In terms of exhibition space and facilities, Taiwan's exhibition industry has a capacity of over 6,700 standard exhibition booths; 80 percent of this capacity is concentrated in the Taipei metropolitan area, specifically, in Taipei's World Trade Center and South Harbor Exhibition Center (The Ministry of Economic Affairs 2011b). Statistics from the International Trade Bureau of the Ministry of Economic Affairs indicate that from 2005 to 2009 the numbers of exhibitions held in major exhibition centers in Taiwan increased from 174 to 195 per year (The Ministry of Economic Affairs 2011a). Around 65 percent of all conventions are local trade fairs, in which domestic firms and the general public constitute the bulk of visitors and exhibitors. According to the Global Association of the Exhibition Industry (Union des Foires Internationales – UFI), the number of international trade fairs organized in Taiwan and their net floor space have gradually increased between 2004 and 2010 (see Table 12.1). Exemplars of this growth are COMPUTEX Taipei and TAIPEI CYCLE, which are now among the world's biggest fairs in terms of the number of attendees (UFI 2011).

Trade fairs are increasingly important for regional and urban industries in terms of knowledge exchange and learning about innovation and industrial upgrading in global production networks (GPNs). Contemporary studies characterize international trade fairs as 'temporary spatial clusters' (Maskell et al. 2006). These studies apply concepts used to describe permanent clusters, such as 'local buzz and global pipelines', 'proximity', 'face-to-face' and 'community', to discussions about temporary clusters (Bathelt and Schuldt 2008; Ramírez-Pasillas 2008; 2010; Bathelt and Glückler 2011; Rinallo and Golfetto 2011).

However, while trade fairs can serve as a platform for enhancing swift trust and absorbing knowledge, it remains an open question whether they hold the same significance for Asian 'latecomer economies' as for advanced industrialized countries in orchestrating production networks (see, also, Chen and Chu, *this volume*; Kalafsky and Gress, *this volume*; Bathelt and Zeng, *this volume*). A number of related questions arise from this: As Taiwan is a relatively small country with an export-oriented economy composed of SMEs, what are the specifics of Taiwanese trade fairs compared to other Asian countries? What is the role of state intervention in the development of the trade fair sector? How do industrial restructuring processes of Taiwanese industries affect the trade fair business in Taiwan?

This chapter focuses on the role of policy and the industrial restructuring processes of Taiwanese industries in GPNs. We argue that, rather than a sole focus on learning, one of the key dimensions of state intervention in temporary clusters in Taiwan is to facilitate industrial upgrading and upscaling of place. Combined with state policy, trade fairs thus play a dual role for Taiwan, contributing to both industrial and regional upgrading.

This chapter examines this context empirically by studying TAIPEI CYCLE, the international trade fair for the bicycle industry. This fair has been selected for two reasons. First, the bicycle industry primarily consists of SMEs and was established in the 1950s in Taiwan. With the help of protective government policies, this export-oriented assembling industry gradually flourished and transformed Taiwan into a 'Bicycle Kingdom' (Wong 2011, p. 65) by the mid-1980s. More recently, due to cumulative learning processes, globalization of production and industrial upgrading under government assistance (Chu 1997), Taiwan's bicycle industry has increasingly concentrated on high-end production, research and development (R&D) and brand-building, rather than labor-intensive manufacturing (Ching and Chou 2011). Second, after Japan's suspension of the 'Tokyo Bicycle Exposition' in 1988, the Taiwan External Trade Development Council (TAITRA), entrusted by the central government, decided to launch the annual TAIPEI CYCLE to enhance Taiwan's global visibility. With the improving competitiveness of Taiwan's bicycle industry, TAIPEI CYCLE has gradually grown in scale since then. Compared to 2010, both 2011 and 2012 witnessed a slight increase in the numbers of exhibitors, booths and both domestic and overseas buyers (see Table 12.2).

In terms of attendees, TAIPEI CYCLE has become Asia's largest and the worlds' second largest bicycle exposition (UFI 2011). According to the 'Taipei Cycle 2012 Post Show Report', among the 6,448 overseas buyers, 54 percent were from Asia, 36 percent being from China, Hong Kong, Japan and Korea (see Table 12.3).

After this introduction, this chapter proceeds with a theoretical

Table 12.2 Overview of TAIPEI CYCLE, 2010–2012

Year	Number of exhibitors			Number of booths			Number of overseas buyers	Number of domestic buyers
	Domestic	Overseas	Total	Domestic	Overseas	Total		
2010	216	678	894	719	2,299	3,018	5,160	–
2011	240	708	948	746	2,314	3,060	5,701	16,495
2012	285	807	1,092	801	2,487	3,288	6,448	17,045

Source: TAIPEI CYCLE (2012).

Table 12.3 Percentage of overseas visitors by the top five countries of origin at the 2012 TAIPEI CYCLE

Rank	1	2	3	4	5
Country of origin	China (including Hong Kong)	Japan	USA	Korea	Germany
Share of foreign visitors	16.8%	12.6%	8.8%	7.1%	4.9%

Source: TAIPEI CYCLE (2013).

discussion on temporary clusters in the East Asian context. Subsequently, the evolving dynamics of the specific socio-economic practices of international trade fairs held in Taipei are discussed in the context of strategic state interventions and the industrial restructuring processes of Taiwanese industries in GPNs. Data are mainly collected through field studies of Taiwan's bicycle industry and the related trade fairs held since 2006. The analysis is based on in-depth semi-structured interviews that were conducted between 2006 and 2012 with 15 key informants, including three directors of trade fair organizations, two secretaries of industry associations, three managers of R&D institutions, five SMEs owners and two government officials. The final part of the chapter offers some concluding remarks.

TEMPORARY CLUSTERS IN THE EAST ASIAN CONTEXT

The understanding of the nature and dynamics of regional development in both academic and policy circles has shifted from an earlier focus on endogenous regional assets, such as localized networks of association and trust, to analyzing the complex relationship between economic globalization and regional change. An important concept to analyze this shift is the GPNs perspective (Coe et al. 2004; 2008; Yeung 2005; Harrison 2007; Pike 2007), dubbed 'global value chains' (GVCs) by some scholars (Bair 2005; Gereffi et al. 2005). According to Yeung (2009), the East Asian experience shows that regional development cannot be understood independently from the changing dynamics of GPNs. It is key to study the complex strategic coupling of local and global economic actors, particularly business firms, operating in specific regions with their lead firm counterparts orchestrating trans-regional production networks on a global basis.

(i) GNPs, State Strategy and International Trade Fairs

Processes of strategic coupling explain how key actors in specific regions become part of the imperatives of lead firms in GPNs through dynamic relational processes and mechanisms. As recognized by Yeung (2009), in the East Asian context, three such processes can be identified: (1) changes in industrial organization; (2) initiatives by states and institutions; and (3) the emergence of transnational communities. First, in order to compete more effectively in today's global economy, lead firms in GPNs have to adopt organizational and technological innovations in order to increase their competitiveness. This, in turn, creates new forms of industrial organization that provide a window of opportunity for local and regional actors in Asia to become coupled with GPNs (Saxenian 2002; Lee et al. 2005). Second, the development of organizational-technological capabilities of Asian 'latecomer firms' can be partially explained by the relentless efforts of state institutions, such as industrial policies and fiscal incentives, to pave the way for such strategic coupling to take place. There is no doubt that the rise of Taiwan, Singapore and South Korea as the world's major exporters of information-technology-related producers is an intended outcome of strategic industrial policies actively pursued by the respective governments (Amsden 1989; 2001; Mathews and Cho 1998; Amsden and Chu 2003; Yang et al. 2009). Third, transnational communities have the potential to play an increasingly important role in the evolution of GPNs. These communities encompass the transnational elite of professionals and business persons in East Asia who constantly shuttle around the globe to make business connections (Olds 2001; Coe et al. 2003; Saxenian and Sabel 2008; Yang et al. 2009). Through their constant movements between different regions of the world, these Asian technologists and entrepreneurs have not only provided a direct mechanism for transferring skills and tacit knowledge which has dramatically accelerated industrial upgrading in developing countries, but also contributed to the formal coupling of Asian firms and institutions with lead firms in GPNs (Saxenian 2002; 2006). In this context, trade fairs have become temporary institutions which facilitate firms to realize and grab the value-added created in GPNs or GVCs.

To further elaborate the coupling of firms and institutions in Asian regions with lead firms in GPNs through a variety of organizational arrangements, one needs to understand international trade fairs as a critical coupling mechanism, which constitutes global knowledge pipelines for local firms within the socio-economic spaces of communities of practice. A plurality of activities is carried out during international trade fairs, much more than just doing deals on the trade floor. Thousands of geographically dispersed, socially embedded and culturally diffuse firms gather in convention centers and exhibition halls to engage in product demonstration, price negotiation and social exchange. As such, international trade fairs are a nexus of relational events in which buyers and producers form a kind of GPN by making trade deals and launching innovations. Through these activities, international trade fairs have created alternative windows of opportunity for latecomer Asian firms, setting them on a path of leapfrog development.

(ii) International Trade Fairs as Three-Fold Relational Spaces

Trade fairs constitute a social space where divergent but overlapping relational spaces intertwine and cross-fertilize each other. By and large, three types of relational spaces are theoretically particularly visible.

First, the trade fair is a marketplace where participants engage in and negotiate economic transactions. This is not to argue that the trade fair is a place with pure economic calculation among strangers (Callon 1998), but rather a platform on which long-term business partners perform the rituals of signing deals. In fact, in this age of globalization and sophisticated electronic communication, less trade is being consummated (in the sense of agreeing on contracts) during the show, and more and more deals are concluded either prior to or after the show.

Second, trade fairs are spaces for global learning, as vividly proposed by Maskell et al. (2006). They argue that firms use international trade fairs and conventions to identify knowledge frontiers and select partners that provide access to distant markets and knowledge pools. Relational proximity, rather than spatial proximity, provides opportunities for geographically distant, but temporarily clustered, firms to engage in interactive learning processes. In fact, most of the knowledge gained from the trade fair is pre-processed by being embedded in communities of practice, which are composed of groups of workers informally bound together by shared experiences, expertise and a commitment to a joint enterprise (Bathelt and Schuldt 2008; Ramírez-Pasillas 2010).

Third, the trade fair is a societal space that sustains relationships among buyers, vendors, technicians and engineers which transcends their trade and business concerns (Skov 2006). Being present and generating attention on trade fairs is critical for maintaining trust and a favorable reputation in business circles. Traditional face-to-face communication is believed to enhance trust, which lubricates transactions and renders opportunism ineffective (Williamson 1985). Inter-personal trust is particularly important for those SMEs which lack institutionalized trust to support economic transactions. SMEs rely overwhelmingly on inter-personal trust to ease the efficient coordination and allocation of resources between transacting firms.

These three types of relational spaces are often enmeshed. Participants at trade fairs are in the process of severing old trade relationships, while searching for new opportunities to connect into GPNs. Firms meeting potential partners are induced to exchange ideas and get inspired through socialization (Ramírez-Pasillas 2010). Economic transactions never work in the space of calculation only, but also in encounters taking place in the societal and cultural spaces. Given the complexity and 'messiness' of economic exchange in industrialized societies, firms and other economic actors collaborate and combine to reduce uncertainty and advance their common position, frequently with the aid of the state and other institutional actors. Firms have to combine new sources to develop the ability to monitor changing institutional environments. They have to learn to continually upgrade or shift products and services in new directions. The knowledge spillovers from face-to-face buzz in a community of practice validates the organizational coupling process of firms and economic actors in trade fairs.

In the following sections, we will use international trade fairs in Taipei to demonstrate the state strategic interventions and the overlapping socio-economic spaces in a temporary cluster.

NATIONAL POLICY FOR THE PROMOTION OF TRADE FAIRS IN TAIWAN

Since the early 1960s the relationship between Taiwan and the world economy has been fundamentally established based on Taiwan's economic strategy of combining an export orientation with foreign direct investment (FDI) to stimulate industrialization. In 1965, the national government promulgated the Statue for the Establishment and Management of Export Processing Zones (EPZs) to further integrate Taiwan with the global economy (Gold 1986, pp. 74–81). With Taiwan's entrance into the emerging international division of labor at the bottom end of the product life cycle, a division of labor in the economy among Transnational Corporations (TNCs), local capital and the state formed the dynamic base for Taiwan's economic development, in which each shaped a distinct sphere with numerous vertical and horizontal linkages existing between them (Gold 1986, p. 127). However, faced with an international political identity crisis in the 1970s, forging ties with a broad range of outside actors became imperative for Taiwan. From then on, hosting international trade fairs has been a critical political-economic instrument for the state's legitimation. The policy for the development of trade fairs developed in three distinctive stages.

(i) 1970s: Alternative International Political Identity

After its withdrawal from the United Nations in 1971, Taiwan became gradually isolated from the world economic and political system. In this threatening external environment, the state put strong efforts into promoting Taiwan's industrial integration with the expanding global economy to bolster economic growth and maintain some sort of international identity (Gold 1986, p. 95). International trade fairs were one of the important means by which the state planned to sustain Taiwan's international identity and to increase its ability, both economically and politically, to survive in the 1970s.

Jointly sponsored by the national government, industry associations and several commercial organizations, the Taiwan External Trade Development Council (TAITRA), the foremost non-profit trade promotion organization in Taiwan, was founded in 1970. Its goal was to assist Taiwanese businesses and manufacturers in the process of reinforcing their international competitiveness and coping with the challenges faced in foreign markets (TAITRA 2012). It not only collaborated closely with the Taiwanese government to promote international trade, but also provided business alliance consultancy and worked to connect international firms with local partners in Taiwan. TAITRA has played a critical role in consolidating the coalition among the state, local capital and TNCs since the 1970s. In particular, entrusted by the national government, one of TAITRA's core tasks is to co-organize international trade fairs with various industrial organizations. In 1974, TAITRA hosted the Taiwan Clothing Export Fair in Taipei for the first time, which was tailored to the needs of the then leading textile industry, which produced goods under contract for foreign buyers. Immediately after this event in 1975, the

Taiwan Machine Exporting Fair was initiated in Taipei, which would later become the predecessor to the Taipei International Tool Show (TIMTOS).

In sum, hosting international trade fairs was an alternative approach by which the state attempted to stimulate domestic economic growth and to shore up Taiwan's identity in the precarious global political environment of the 1970s.

(ii) 1980s and 1990s: Para-diplomatic Policy

The breaking off of formal diplomatic relations between the United States and the Republic of China in 1979 left Taiwan nearly devoid of a diplomatic identity. Its overriding mission was survival, which required continuous successful management and intensification of Taiwan's economic interrelations with the world system. However, the 1970s oil crises brought Taiwan's numerous vulnerabilities into sharp focus (Gold 1986, p. 97). These severe external economic and political challenges forced the state to adopt a more flexible foreign policy to entangle the island in as many international networks as possible.

Due to Taiwan's political and diplomatic isolation, the state devised a multifaceted strategy to reduce Taiwan's vulnerability to the instability of the global economy, primarily by vertically integrating Taiwan's SMEs into GVCs. The state encouraged foreign countries to use trade offices as substitute diplomatic representatives (Gold 1986, pp. 100–108). 'Economic complementarity' was the main motivation behind the cultivation of those uninterrupted 'para-diplomatic' relations (Gold 1986, p. 111). Taiwan's economic technocrats adopted a more aggressive stance towards restructuring the economy and inserting Taiwan into a new niche in the international division of labor, in order to promote Taiwan's image as a newly industrialized country. In 1980, the Taipei World Trade Center Co., Ltd was set up and entrusted by the national government as a subsidiary organization of TAITRA to become a member of the World Trade Center Association (TAITRA 2012). Targeting strategic industries key to Taiwan's economic restructuring, such as computers and transportation equipment, TAITRA started to host the annual Taipei International Information Technology Show (i.e. COMPUTEX TAIPEI) in 1982 and the Taipei Cycle Show (i.e. TAIPEI CYCLE) in 1988. Combined with other national policies such as the establishment of Science-based Industrial Parks, the state aimed to nurture Taiwan's own R&D capacity to vertically integrate the electronics industry and create a new global market niche.

As a para-diplomatic polity, hosting international trade fairs throughout the 1980s helped Taiwan to continue commercial relations with nearly

130 countries. Businessmen with interests in Taiwan testified and lobbied on behalf of maintaining a variety of semi-official links with the island (Gold 1986, p. 111). Furthermore, the utilization rate of the Taipei World Trade Center, the main venue for international trade fairs in Taiwan, which opened in 1985, was among the world's highest in the 1990s (Chen 2004). Clearly, the strategy of substituting economic ties for diplomatic relations paid off.

(iii) 2000s: Industrial–Urban Co-upgrading

With the post-industrial economic transformation, hosting international trade fairs has become critical for industrial–urban co-upgrading. Electronics firms, Taiwan's strategic industry, have increasingly concentrated on high-end production, R&D, commercial operations and management while transferring labor-intensive manufacturing to low-cost countries (Amsden and Chu 2003). Service industries, especially producer services, have since the late 1980s grown as propelling sectors for urban economic development. The industrialization of conventions and exhibitions has thus become one of the strategic policy fields for promoting urban restructuring. This strategic transition in urban economic policy is considered particularly vital, as Taiwan's industrial role in the global production network has changed from subcontract manufacturing to industrial trade brand promotion and management. The exhibition industries, and especially industrial trade fairs, have thus become one of the major policy areas.

To develop Taiwan's convention and exhibition industry, the Executive Yuan earmarked $2 billion (NTD) ($67 million (USD)) in a policy spread out over four years in the 'Plan for the Great Leap for the Convention and Exhibition Industry in Taiwan'. This policy is carried out by the International Trade Bureau of the Ministry of Economic Affairs (The Ministry of Economic Affairs 2010). In 2011, the bureau put forward a further plan entitled 'Action Plan for the Convention and Exhibition Industry', which focuses on the establishment of an institutional environment to 'industrialize' trade fairs. In general, the government's policy is directed towards upgrading the urban infrastructure. For instance, through its policies, the government was directly involved in the construction of the Taipei World Trade Center. To build up a complete industry chain, it also actively organized conventions and exhibitions. Hereby, the policy to promote the trade fair industry became an important medium for the restructuring of Taiwan's industrial development.

The industrialization of convention and exhibition activities has become intertwined with the strategic focus of the national policy to construct cultural and creative industries. The trade fair industry is used to facilitate the transformation of Taiwan's industrial structure, which was traditionally based on manufacturing. This strategic goal is particularly visible in the 'Market Trade and Expansion Plan', the 4th sub-plan of the general 'Plan for the Cultural and Creative Industry', which is being carried out by the Culture and Construction Administration. These plans aim to organize important international exhibitions and prize competitions in Taiwan to achieve the three-fold objective of stimulating artistic creation, helping the development of creative industries and creating a dynamic art market. The policy encourages non-governmental organizations to cooperate with the media and hold all kinds of competitions for quality brands, products, elites and new talents related to cultural and creative industries. The objective is to comprehensively promote top-quality cultural and creative products internationally and to create brand names for Taiwan's cultural and creative industries. Moreover, policy seeks to create marketing and exhibition channels for Taiwan's cultural and creative industries by hosting annual conventions and exhibitions relevant to those industries. It also assists creative businesses to establish international cooperation through the Cultural and Creative Industry Network, which is linked to related organizations and associations both in Taiwan and abroad. Furthermore, it encourages creative firms to take part in the China Cultural Exhibition and to explore and enter the art market in Mainland China by cooperating with other ministries and administrations. This policy bears concrete fruits, as the trading volume at Art Taipei 2008 exceeded $750 million (NTD) ($25 million (USD)), a record high. In 2009, Art Taipei expanded its scale by teaming up with the Taiwan Handcraft Exhibition.

LOCAL POLICY ON THE PROMOTION OF INTERNATIONAL TRADE FAIRS

Nearly two thirds of the trade fairs in Taiwan are held in its capital city, Taipei (The Ministry of Economic Affairs 2011a). The municipal government of Taipei has set the development of the convention and exhibition industry as one of its key strategies to stimulate industrial upgrading and transform Taipei into a world city. Besides resorting to the central government's 'Plan for the Cultural and Creative Industry', the municipal government relies on two strategic goals: (1) to build and expand exhibition facilities and to upgrade and develop the surrounding lands; (2) to take advantage of Taiwan's strong industries and to organize international exhibitions to bolster Taipei's manufacturing clout worldwide. With these goals, the city government hopes to shape Taipei's world city image and boost the restructuring of its urban economy.

By using generous support from national policies and its position as the capital city in Taiwan, the Taipei municipal government has developed a broad variety of international exhibitions (see Table 12.4). Recent major exhibitions include the 2010 International Floral Exposition, the 2011 Taipei World Design Exposition and the 2012 Universiade. Through various ceremonial activities, these exhibitions and trade fairs have become a major part of Taipei's world city strategy. This strategy supports the construction of Taipei's convention and exhibition industrial chain and is thereby an impetus for the development of Taipei's cultural and creative industry. More recently, the Taipei city government, with the support of the International Council of Societies of Industrial Design (ICSID), has promoted the 'National Palace Museum Park Project', which utilizes the cultural resources of the National Palace Museum to bid for 'City of World Design 2016'. The primary goal of organizing these types of conventions and exhibitions is to promote the image of Taipei and develop its cultural and creative industries.

In addition to strategic interventions in the development of cultural and creative industries, Taipei hosts many international trade fairs that focus on those manufacturing sectors in which Taiwan's industries have a strong edge in the global market. These international trade fairs are different from the other types of exhibitions discussed above in that they focus on existing industrial strength and actively engage in the construction of global pipelines. They facilitate the upgrading of the functional role of Taiwan's manufacturing industries in the GPNs. Normally, these trade fairs are co-organized by various industrial organizations and the Taiwan External Trade Development Council (TAITRA), which falls under the Bureau of International Trade of the Ministry of Economic Affairs. In 2009, TAITRA hosted 23 international trade shows in Taipei, which attracted 69,368 visitors. Compared to the 67,155 trade fair visitors in 2008, this represents a growth of about 3 percent (TAITRA 2009).

EVOLVING SOCIO-ECONOMIC PRACTICES OF TAIPEI INTERNATIONAL TRADE FAIRS

It becomes clear from the discussion above that trade fairs constitute relational spaces in which complex socio-economic practices take place involving making business, learning and engaging in social contacts. This section investigates the effects of state intervention and the socio-economic practices of trade fairs as temporary clusters using the case

Table 12.4 Economic figures of international professional exhibitions in Taipei, 2010–2011

Name of event	(1) Direct turnover ($10,000 (NTD))	(2) Indirect turnover ($10,000 (NTD))	(3) Turnover of relevant industries ($10,000 (NTD))	(4) Gross turnover ($10,000 (NTD))	(5) = (4)/(1) Turnover/ cost ratio
2010 Taipei Triple International Electronics Exhibition	4,353	6,589	8,122	19,063	4.38
2010 TiGis	1,337	1,413	1,977	4,726	3.54
2010 PV Taiwan	2,856	2,304	4,673	9,833	3.44
2010 Taipei International Floral Exposition	953,000	1,122,922	2,365,700	4,441,622	4.66
2011 TAIPEI CYCLE	6,109	7,803	10,609	24,521	4.01
2011 Yilan Green Expo	6,820	17,385	15,132	39,337	5.77
2011 Taipei AMPA/Auto Tronics	5,840	8,867	11,068	25,774	4.41
2011TaiSPO	3,614	3,113	4,538	11,266	3.12
2011 COMPUTEX Taipei	14,275	49,165	57,119	120,559	8.45
2011 FOOD TAIPEI	3,553	8,497	11,304	23,354	6.57

Note: Direct turnover refers to all sorts of expenditures on products and services by the hosting organization. Indirect turnover denotes all sorts of expenditures on products and services by visitors, including transportation, accommodation, catering, sightseeing, leisure and other consumer needs. Turnover of relevant industries indicates the multiplayer effect produced by direct and indirect turnover. The currency exchange rate between the US dollar and New Taiwan dollar (NTD) was around $30 (NTD) for $1 (USD) during 2010 to 2011.

Source: Ministry of Economic Affairs (2011b, p. xix).

Table 12.5 Evolving socio-economic practices of Taipei international trade fairs, 1970s–2000s

Periods	Objective of state intervention	Trade fairs as a relational space for		
		Business	Learning	Reputation
1970s	Alternative international political identity	Strive for OEM orders	Passive technology follower	Taiwan's political identity
1980s to 1990s	Para-diplomatic policy	Strive for OEM and ODM orders	Active search for R&D partners	Taiwan as a NIC
2000s to present	Industrial–urban co-upgrading	A contingent moment for potential business	R&D and design competitions	Taipei city branding Branding of Taiwan industries and trade fairs

study of TAIPEI CYCLE. The main findings from the aforementioned literature review and in-depth interviews conducted between 2006 and 2012 concerning the evolution of socio-economic practices of Taipei's International Trade Fairs are summarized in Table 12.5. While there are different groups of trade fair participants – those who are part of organized GVCs/GPNs and those who are looking for loose connections with trade partners – the dynamics of the socio-economic practices of trade fairs in Taipei are subject to the specific interventions by the state and the industrial restructuring processes of Taiwanese industries in the context of global networks.

(i) Trade Fairs as Business Space

Taiwan entered the international division of labor in the 1960s at the bottom end of the product life cycle (Gold 1986, p. 81) as an export-oriented economy composed of SMEs. In an increasingly threatening international political environment, nearly devoid of a diplomatic identity, TAITRA not only organized trade fairs for strategic industries, but also actively invited and entertained as many foreign firms as possible. Participating in international trade fairs was a crucial element of this strategy, as they offered critical business moments for Taiwanese SMEs to earn orders from foreign Original Equipment Manufacturers (OEMs) or Original Design Manufacturers (ODMs).

International trade fairs in the present economic environment are seen as important occasions for firms to display their products and technological capacities and to seek business and production partners globally (Maskell et al. 2006). After the relocation of much manufacturing activities to Southeast Asian countries and China in the 1990s, firms that have remained in Taiwan are strongly embedded in specific GPNs and have upgraded to technology-intensive or high value-added production. Interviews with trade fair organizers and the respective industry organizations suggest that international trade fairs offer an effective platform for Taiwanese SMEs to come into contact with both current and potential clients. Whether such relationships formed in temporary clusters transform into actual business relationships is contingent on the ability of the Taiwanese firms to build up social ties and trust with their global counterparts and demonstrate their professional capacity after the trade fair has finished, as one senior secretary of industry association emphasized (Interview 26 March 2012).

(ii) Trade Fairs as Learning Space

Besides their business functions, international trade fairs serve as a platform for interactive learning and a means to become connected to external knowledge communities (Ramírez-Pasillas 2008). This was not the case in the 1970s as Taiwanese SMEs were technology followers at the bottom end of the value chain, passively relying on technology transfers from foreign firms.

However, in the 1980s and 1990s, Taipei's international trade fairs became critical learning moments for Taiwanese SMEs to absorb new technology and search for global R&D partners. Due to the global energy crises and Taiwan's diplomatic isolation, the state shifted its emphasis on industrial restructuring in the 1980s, focusing on the establishment of technology-intensive, non-polluting, energy-efficient industries, rather than continuing to rely on heavy and capital-intensive industries. It hoped to nurture Taiwan's R&D capacity and create a new niche for Taiwan's goods in the global market by providing technical and financial support to small innovative firms headed by dynamic entrepreneurs with experience abroad and links to TNCs (Gold 1986, p. 104). TAITRA started to organize seminars during industrial trade fairs with the purpose of disseminating technology. This helped Taiwanese SMEs to quickly gain the latest technological information about their competitors, suppliers and clients, and set them on a learning curve.

However, since the 2000s international trade fairs have become more of an occasion for Taiwanese SMEs embedded in GPNs 'to see what is beneath the surface' (Interview with the Secretary General of the Taiwan Bicycle Exporters' Association on 9 November 2006) and display their latest technological developments and designs (Interview with bicycle trader on 17 January 2006). In fact, recent studies have pointed out that taking part in an international trade fair sometimes means to 'put on a show' (Andreae et al. 2011). Knowledge flows are just one, not necessarily the most important, of the three functions of international trade fairs. In fact, interviews with the trade fair organizers and industry associations suggest that direct interactive learning and communication is not the most important motivation for firms to participate in trade fairs. From a political economy perspective, to construct a specific reputation and to gain access to potential markets is the crucial intangible benefit from taking part in industrial trade exhibitions. International trade fairs represent an opportunity for firms to showcase themselves on the global stage.

(iii) Trade Fairs as Reputational Space

In terms of reputation, international trade fairs are critical for contemporary Taiwanese companies. In contrast to earlier approaches focused on consolidating Taiwan's international political identity in the 1970s or promoting Taiwan's newly industrialized economy image in the 1980s and 1990s, industrial–urban co-branding is now the ultimate objective for the national state, SMEs and local governments co-organizing international trade fairs.

In general, the government uses trade shows where global media gather to improve the reputation of Taiwan's industries. For instance, at the opening of TAIPEI CYCLE Taiwan's President Ma Ying-jeou declared that 'Cycling is a happiness industry', and introduced the phrase 'MEET TAIWAN' as the common slogan for all international trade fairs hosted in Taiwan (United Daily News 2012). In 2011, the central government further announced its 'Action Plan for the Convention and Exhibition Industry', which focuses on the construction of institutions for the industrialization of trade fairs.

The government uses both formal and informal international connections to strengthen and manifest the global position of the trade fair. Leading firms base their decision to come to TAIPEI CYCLE on the existing formal and informal relations with Taiwanese SMEs, as indicated in the interviews. For instance, 'SHIMANO [the Japanese global leading manufacturer of bicycle gears] is not only our business partner, but also our good friend. Every time we have formal or informal events, they come . . . They sure always show up at TAIPEI CYCLE' (Interview with a bicycle R&D manager on 20 March 2007).

An example of the government's formal approach to using trade fairs to enhance Taiwan's reputation is the slogan 'Think Bicycle, Think Taiwan'. TAITRA entrusted International Forum Design Hannover (iF Design) to organize the 'Taipei Cycle d&i awards' (design and innovation awards) and sponsored the 'Tour de Taiwan 2012' hosted by the International Cycling Union (UCI) during the 2012 TAIPEI CYCLE (Economic Daily News 2012).

Since the government strives to strengthen the international reputation of Taiwan's trade fairs, 'being there' becomes one of the key elements for the participating exhibitors. Being there means an opportunity to gain 'exposure' in the market and a way of 'advertising', so that competitors, clients and potential partners will know that 'the company still exists'. Moreover, for some firms the fact of being present at an international professional trade fair denotes prestige (Interview with the owner of participating small firm on 19 October 2006).

CONCLUSION

In the transformation processes of Asian economies, such as Taiwan, international trade fairs have played an important part by enabling knowledge flows and learning processes related to innovation and the branding of regional and urban industries. However, besides opportunities for learning offered during trade fairs, another key dimension of temporal clusters in Asia is related to the possibilities for industrial upgrading and up-scaling of place fostered by state interventions.

Specific for trade fairs in Taiwan's small export-oriented economy that is dominated by SMEs has been the intervention of the state in organizing industrial exhibitions since the 1970s. Compared to other Asian nations or advanced countries orchestrating production networks, the state is considerably more present in Taiwan due to the dynamics in the international political economy. Whether the state sought to form Taiwan's international political identity during diplomatic isolation in the 1970s, or promote Taiwan's newly industrialized country image in the 1980s and 1990s, international trade fairs now have a dual role as a result of state intervention. Hosting international trade fairs is one of the critical state strategies to stimulate industrial upgrading and city up-scaling. As a result, while international trade fairs offer an ever important opportunity for local traditional industries to upgrade their role in the GPN and to engage in learning and knowledge exchange, reputation construction appears to be the paramount function of international trade fairs in contemporary Taiwan from a political economy perspective.

REFERENCES

Amsden, A. H. (1989) *Asia's Next Giant: South Korea and Late Industrialization*, New York: Oxford University Press.

Amsden, A. H. (2001) *The Rise of 'The Rest': Challenges to the West from Late-Industrializing Economies*, New York: Oxford University Press.

Amsden, A. H. and Chu W.-W. (2003) *Beyond Late Development: Taiwan's Upgrading Policies*, Cambridge, MA: MIT Press.

Andreae, M., Hsu, J.-Y. and Norcliffe, G. (2011) *Performing the Trade Show: The Case of the Taipei International Cycle Show*, unpublished manuscript, Taipei. Available from the authors.

Bair, J. (2005) 'Global capitalism and commodity chains: Looking back, going forward', *Competition and Change*, 9: 153–180.

Bathelt, H. and Glückler, J. (2011) *The Relational Economy: Geographies of Knowing and Learning*, Oxford: Oxford University Press.

Bathelt, H. and Schuldt, N. (2008) 'Between luminaries and meat grinders: International trade fairs as temporary clusters', *Regional Studies*, 42: 853–868.

Callon, M. (1998) 'The embeddedness of economic markets in economics', in M. Callon (ed.) *The Laws of the Market*, Oxford: Blackwell Publishers, 1–57.

Chen, S.-H. (2004) 'The utilization rate of the Taipei World Trade Center is the world's first', *Economic Daily News*, 11 September: C1.

Ching, C.-H. and Chou, T.-L. (2011) 'The cross-strait effects: Differential regional industrial clusters', in R. Y.-W. Kwok (ed.) *The Second Great Transformation: Taiwanese Industrialization in the 1980s–2000s*, Taipei: Chengchi University Press, 123–156.

Chou, T.-L. (2006) *Competition Strategies and Industries in World Cities*, Taipei: Chan's Arch-Publishing.

Chu, W. W. (1997) 'Causes of growth: A study of Taiwan's bicycle industry', *Cambridge Journal of Economics*, 21: 55–72.

Coe, N., Dicken, P. and Hess, M. (2008) 'Global production networks: Realizing the potential', *Journal of Economic Geography*, 8: 271–295.

Coe, N., Hess, M., Yeung, H. W.-C., Dicken, P. and Henderson, J. (2004) '"Globalizing" regional development: A global production networks perspective', *Transactions of the Institute of British Geographers* NS, 29: 468–484.

Coe, N. M., Kelly, P. F. and Olds, K. (2003) 'Globalization, transnationalism, and the Asia-Pacific', in J. Peck and H. W.-C. Yeung (eds) *Remaking the Global Economy: Economic–Geographical Perspectives*, London: Sage, 45–60.

Economic Daily News (2012) '2012 TAIPEI CYCLE, Taiwan bicycle's miracle', *Economic Daily News*, 7 March: D1.

Gereffi, G., Humphrey, J. and Sturgeon, T. (2005) 'The governance of global value chains', *Review of International Political Economy*, 12: 78–104.

Gold, T. B. (1986) *State and Society in the Taiwan Miracle*, New York: M. E. Sharpe.

Harrison, J. (2007) 'From competitive regions to competitive city-regions: A new orthodoxy, but some old mistakes', *Journal of Economic Geography*, 7: 311–332.

Lee, K., Lim, C. and Song, W. (2005) 'Emerging digital technology as a window of opportunity and technological leapfrogging: Catch-up in digital TV by the Korean firms', *International Journal of Technology Management*, 29: 40–63.

Maskell, P., Bathelt, H. and Malmberg, A. (2006) 'Building global knowledge pipelines: The role of temporary clusters', *European Planning Studies*, 14: 997–1013.
Mathews, J. A. and Cho, D. S. (1998) *Tiger Chips: The Creation of a Semiconductor Industry in East Asia, 1975–2000*, Cambridge: Cambridge University Press.
Ministry of Economic Affairs (2010) *Report on 2009 Administration Performance*, Taipei.
Ministry of Economic Affairs (2011a) *Action Plan for Taiwan's Exhibition Industry*, ratified version, 1st time revision, Taipei.
Ministry of Economic Affairs (2011b) *Study on the Promotion of Local Economy by International Events*, Taipei.
Olds, K. (2001) *Globalization and Urban Change: Capital, Culture and Pacific Rim Mega Projects*, New York: Oxford University Press.
Pike, A. (ed.) (2007) 'Wither Regional Studies?', *Regional Studies*, 41 (Special Issue): 1143–1270.
Ramírez-Pasillas, M. (2008) 'Resituating proximity and knowledge cross-fertilization in clusters by means of international trade fairs', *European Planning Studies*, 16: 643–663.
Ramírez-Pasillas, M. (2010) 'International trade fairs as amplifiers of permanent and temporary proximities in clusters', *Entrepreneurship and Regional Development*, 22: 155–187.
Rinallo, D. and Golfetto, F. (2011) 'Exploring the knowledge strategies of temporary cluster organizers: A longitudinal study of the EU fabric industry trade shows (1986–2006)', *Economic Geography*, 87: 453–476.
Saxenian, A.-L. (2002) 'Transnational communities and the evolution of global production networks: The cases of Taiwan, China and India', *Industry and Innovation*, 9: 183–202.
Saxenian, A.-L. (2006) *The New Argonauts: Regional Advantage in a Global Economy*, Cambridge, MA: Harvard University Press.
Saxenian, A.-L. and Sabel, C. (2008) 'Venture capital in the "periphery": The new Argonauts, global search, and local institution building', *Economic Geography*, 84: 379–394.
Skov, L. (2006) 'The role of trade fairs in the global fashion business', *Current Sociology*, 54: 764–783.
TAIPEI CYCLE (2012) *About the Exhibition*, Taipei. Online. Available HTTP: <http://www.taipeicycle.com.tw/> (16 January 2012).
TAIPEI CYCLE (2013) *Taipei Cycle 2012 Post Show Report*, Taipei. Online. Available HTTP: <http://www.taipeicycle.com.tw/> (27 February 2013).
TAITRA (2009) *Proposal to Boost the International Competitiveness of Our Nation's Exhibition Industry*, entrusted with the International Trade Bureau of the Ministry of Economic Affairs, Taipei.
TAITRA (2012) *About TAITRA*, Taipei. Online. Available HTTP: <http://www.taitra.com.tw/about_02.asp> (25 July 2012).
UFI (2011) *The Trade Fair Industry in Asia*, 7th edn, Hong Kong: Business Strategies Group Ltd.
United Daily News (2012) '2012 TAIPEI CYCLE opens. President Ma will make it the 1st in the world', *United Daily News*, 8 March 2012: A4.
Williamson, O. E. (1985) *The Economic Institutions of Capitalism*, New York: Free Press.
Wong, J.-J. (2011) 'Reflections on the structural function of industrial design in

capitalism through development experiences of NICs', in E. N. Shelton (ed.) *Capitalism in Business, Politics and Society*, Hauppauge, NY: Nova Science Publishers, 59–76.

Yang, D. Y.-R., Hsu, J.-Y. and Ching, C.-H. (2009) 'Revisiting the silicon island? The geographically varied "strategic coupling" in the development of high-technology parks in Taiwan', *Regional Studies*, 43: 369–384.

Yeung, H. W.-C. (2005) 'Rethinking relational economic geography', *Transactions of the Institute of British Geographers* NS, 30: 37–51.

Yeung, H. W.-C. (2009) 'Regional development and the competitive dynamics of global production networks: An East Asian perspective', *Regional Studies*, 43: 325–351.

13. Upgrading of latecomer industries in Taiwan and the case of the Taipei International Machine Tool Show

Liang-Chih Chen and Ling-I Chu

INTRODUCTION

Trade shows have long been a key promotional medium for firms in the machine tool industry (Cunningham and White 1974; Patti 1977; USITC 1983; Kotha and Nair 1995). For most machine tool manufacturing countries, holding trade shows has also been critical to not only enhancing marketing but also to reputation-building of their domestic machine tool makers (Cunningham and White 1974; Yang 2011a; Gardner Publications 2013). In the case of Taiwan, to promote its export-oriented machine tool industry, whose export ratio has grown from about 50 percent in the 1960s to 80 percent in the 2000s, state organizations and industrial associations have collaborated to introduce and maintain an international trade show for the industry, the Taipei International Machine Tool Trade Show (TIMTOS). Over time, TIMTOS has emerged as one of the major trade shows in the global machine tool industry. This bi-annual event is also Taiwan's largest trade show and has been adopted by the state to represent the growth and development of Taiwan's convention and exhibition industry (BOFT 2011).

There is already a large body of literature studying the role trade shows play in supporting the marketing activities of firms and industries (Banting and Blenkhorn 1974; Bonoma 1983; Miller 1990; Smith and Smith 2000; Berne and García-Uceda 2008). In addition to this literature, recent studies have further emphasized how trade shows, particularly international events, have become nodes of global knowledge exchange and innovation by providing a platform for inducing interactive learning and pipeline-building among firms around the world (Maskell et al. 2006; Skov 2006; Torre 2008; Bathelt and Glückler 2011; Schuldt and Bathelt 2011). Such events are also considered as key bridging 'institutions' for facilitating linkage-building between industrial clusters and external sources of knowledge, allowing clusters to obtain extra-local competences to break their development inertia (Bathelt et al. 2004; Chen 2009; Ramírez-Pasillas 2010; Rinallo and Golfetto 2011). While many scholars have offered conceptual models and empirical studies to account for the role of trade shows in the current globalized economy, most of these discussions are based on studies of flagship international trade shows and events that take place in advanced industrialized countries. Given these gaps in the existing literature, this chapter investigates the dynamisms found in a trade show hosted in an Asian country that seeks to use such events to enhance its integration into the world economy. More specifically, by using Taiwan's TIMTOS as the empirical case, we investigate how this trade show facilitates learning and relationship-building of the clustered Taiwanese machine tool firms in their attempts to address issues relevant to their business and technological advancement. In so doing, this chapter improves our understanding of the influence of trade shows on upgrading processes of latecomer industries.

The data used in this study is based on three main sources. The first source relates to archival documents, statistics and studies on Taiwan's machine tool industry and TIMTOS. Second, a database was compiled of more than 100 in-depth interviews with decision-makers in Taiwanese machine tool firms and other key industry actors. These interviews were conducted by the first author in 2005–2006 and 2009–2011 as part of an ethnographic research project on Taiwan's machine tool industry. In these interviews, respondents were asked to explain the rationales behind their participation in different domestic and foreign trade shows and to comment on the impact of such events on their firms' technological upgrading process. The third source comprised the first author's field observations of firm activities at TIMTOS in 2011 and 2013.

To present our viewpoints and findings, this chapter begins with a review of literature that discusses the critical functions of trade shows and how these events have been considered as the spaces of learning and networking for firms and clusters. Next, an overview of important trade shows in the global machine tool industry is presented, before TIMTOS and its development is discussed. This leads to an exploration of critical intra-/inter-firm business and technological activities of Taiwanese machine tool firms during or after TIMTOS. Finally, we summarize our main findings and conclude.

INTERNATIONAL TRADE SHOWS AS SPACES OF MARKETING, LEARNING AND NETWORKING

In early marketing research, trade shows have been primarily seen as spaces and events that are designed to facilitate sales and marketing activities of firms and industries. In comparison with other mediums, industrial firms find trade shows to be cost-effective mediums for promoting and selling their products to potential buyers from different places within a short period of time (Bonoma 1983; Miller 1990; Godar and O'Connor 2001; Evers and Knight 2008). At trade shows, exhibiting firms seek to maintain their firms' visibility and promote the perception of their leading or competitive positions in the market place, thus enhancing their reputation (Banting and Blenkhorn 1974; Hansen 2004; Lee and Kim 2008). Furthermore, through interacting or collaborating with other trade show participants (e.g., buyers, visitors, competitors, show organizers or the media), firms are able to use such events to review, as well as influence, industrial and market trends (Power and Jansson 2008; Weller 2008; Ramírez-Pasillas 2010).

In addition to promoting sales and marketing activities, trade shows provide participating firms with other non-selling benefits, such as gathering intelligence on competitors, maintaining and enhancing corporate morale, easier networking with existing and potential collaborators and so on (Bonoma 1983; Sharland and Balogh 1996; Blythe 2002; Hansen 2004; Borghini et al. 2006; Lee and Kim 2008). As 'trade shows are the major industry events that attract attendees who represent a cross-section of authority levels and job functions in an industry, and are positively predisposed toward exhibitors' new product development efforts', Bello and Barczak (1990, p. 48) particularly suggest that such events are appropriate venues for firms to conduct new product research including generating ideas, screening concepts and testing prototypes.

Currently, an emerging theme in the study of trade shows further emphasizes that international trade shows have become essential spaces for knowledge creation and exchange in the globalizing learning economy (Torre 2008; Bathelt and Glückler 2011). Given that these events bring together participants from various regions with different resources and competencies, they are instrumental in establishing knowledge linkages between actors that are spatially and technologically distant (Maskell et al. 2006; Rinallo and Golfetto 2011). Furthermore, trade shows could be considered as temporary clusters, since the improved geographical and organized proximity of show participants enables them to exploit many learning mechanisms similar to those at work in permanent clusters (Maskell et al. 2006, Power and Jansson 2008; Torre 2008).

Studying the functions of trade shows has important implications for the industrial development in the context of catch-up economies. There is consensus that industries and clusters in late-industrializing countries require especially extra-local knowledge to enable further upgrading and the development of higher levels of competitiveness (Bell and Albu 1999;

Guerrieri et al. 2001). International trade shows are widely recognized as essential relationship-building spaces, and it is argued that latecomer firms could use such events to establish linkages with foreign sources of business opportunities and, more importantly, advanced technologies (Bathelt et al. 2004; Wickham and Vecchi 2008; Chen 2009; Ramírez-Pasillas 2010; Bathelt and Glückler 2011; Rinallo and Golfetto 2011). On the one hand, international trade shows provide latecomer firms with low-cost access to extra-local markets that would otherwise be unapproachable. On the other hand, by actively attending foreign international trade shows these firms are able to take advantage of the learning mechanisms at these events to acquire advanced knowledge and to develop and maintain their relationships with extra-local partners.

In the specific case of Taiwan's machine tool industry, foreign international trade shows have been the critical venues where Taiwanese firms obtain the latest product and technological information in their industry. In addition, Taiwanese engineers have been found to use such events to gain exposure to frontier technologies by observing the operations of the products and technologies of leading global firms and, when possible, directly exchanging ideas with those firms' engineers. Furthermore, international trade shows also provide opportunities for Taiwanese machine tool firms to establish and maintain their external linkages with foreign technology suppliers, given that their collaborative relationships with overseas partners in sales, marketing, production or product development are often established during the shows (Chen 2009).

Although much of the literature has enriched our understandings of the critical role of trade shows, most studies are focused on the discussions of international flagship shows and focus on events in advanced industrialized countries. Moreover, while we are witnessing many latecomer economies which have sought to develop their international trade shows for promoting industrial exports and the growth of the convention and exhibition industry, empirical studies of such events in these countries have been relatively rare (Tafesse and Korneliussen 2011). Since trade shows held in advanced and latecomer countries differ in terms of attendee characteristics and motivation (Bello and Barczak 1990; Tafesse and Korneliussen 2011), one might wonder whether the trade show dynamics emphasized in the existing literature are generalizable to latecomer contexts.

This chapter addresses these questions by presenting the results of an empirical study of TIMTOS, a business-to-business international trade show held in Taiwan. We particularly investigate the intra- and inter-firms activities of Taiwanese machine tool firms in relation to their participation at TIMTOS. In addition to discussing how this event has influenced the marketing and technological efforts of Taiwanese machine tool firms, our study points out the key role played by domestically held international trade shows in facilitating relationship-building and learning among local latecomer firms in their pursuit of upgrading. Before presenting our findings, we next introduce the world's major international machine tool trade shows and the development of TIMTOS.

MAJOR INTERNATIONAL MACHINE TOOL TRADE SHOWS

The global machine tool industry is dominated by three major international bi-annual trade shows, namely the Exposition Mondiale de la Machine Outil (EMO) held in Germany (every six years in Italy), the Japan International Machine Tool Fair (JIMTOF) and the International Manufacturing Technology Show (IMTS) in the US. These events are major venues at which actors related to the machine tool industry from around the world exhibit and observe the latest products and technologies. Given that Europe has been the major world region of machine tool production and consumption in the past and that its firms have played a key role in shaping the industry's technology path, EMO is considered as the leading show. EMO is not only the largest show in terms of scale, but also attracts the greatest share of international participants (see Table 13.1). IMTS and JIMTOF are often held in the same year, usually separated by only a few months, and are thus seen as competing shows in the sense that many buyers, particularly those from North America, may skip JIMTOF after attending IMTS (Wang 2012, p. 6).

In addition to these flagship events, the China International Machine Tool Show (CIMT), Seoul International Manufacturing Technology Show (SIMTOS) in Korea and Taiwan's TIMTOS have emerged as other important international machine tool shows in recent years. Despite being latecomers in this industry, China, Korea and Taiwan have become the world's first, fourth and sixth largest machine tool manufacturers, respectively (Gardner Publications 2013), and their trade shows have developed in tandem with the domestic machine tool industries. Given that China and Korea have been major global machine tool importers and consumers, CIMT and SIMTOS have attracted an increasing number of global machine tool makers, and international firms now make up about half the exhibitors at each show (see, also, Bathelt and Zeng, *this volume*; Kalafsky and Gress, *this volume*). While the development of the Chinese and Korean shows is connected to large domestic demand, TIMTOS in Taiwan lacks such a domestic user base. It focuses more on promoting

Table 13.1 Major international machine tool trade shows worldwide

Trade shows	EMO 2013[a]	IMTS 2012[b]	JIMTOF 2012[c]	CIMT 2013[d]	SIMTOS 2012[e]	TIMTOS 2013[f]
Location	Hannover, Germany[g]	Chicago, USA	Tokyo, Japan	Beijing, China	Gyeonggi-do, Korea	Taipei, Taiwan
Year of establishment	1951	1927	1962	1989	1984	1975
Exhibition space (sq.m.)	176,435	115,280	45,828	120,000	100,000	92,116
Exhibitors	2,131	1,909	815	1,406	763	1,009
Foreign exhibitors	60%	50%	29%	46%	62%	25%
Important countries of origin of foreign exhibitors	Italy Taiwan Switzerland China Japan	Japan Germany Italy Taiwan Switzerland	Taiwan Germany Switzerland Korea US	Germany Japan Taiwan Italy Switzerland	Germany Japan Taiwan China US	Japan Germany Switzerland
Visitors	142,804	100,200	128,674	306,000	104,713	46,772
Foreign visitors	41%	n.a.	6%	n.a.	4%	14%

Notes:
sq.m. = square meters (1 square meter = 10.76 square feet); n.a. = not available
a. EMO = Exposition Mondiale de la Machine Outil
b. IMTS = International Manufacturing Technology Show
c. JIMTOF = Japan International Machine Tool Fair
d. CIMTS = China International Machine Tool Show
e. SIMTOS = Seoul International Manufacturing Technology Show
f. TIMTOS = Taipei International Machine Tool Show
g. Milano, Italy hosts EMO every six years.

Sources: Data received from each trade show organizer.

exports and therefore has a lower participation rate of foreign exhibitors (see Table 13.1).

As export-oriented manufacturers, Taiwanese machine tool firms actively attend international trade shows and are major participants in all events mentioned above. In the leading three international shows, Taiwanese machine tool makers not only promote their products, but also learn about the latest technological development and build and maintain relationships with their advanced production partners (Chen 2009). They also have a strong presence at the other two major trade shows held in Korea and China, seeking to penetrate into the domestic markets of these two major competitors. At both SIMTOS in 2012 and CIMT in 2013, Taiwan was the fourth largest exhibitor country, only behind the host economy, Germany and Japan (KOMMA 2012; Wang 2013).

THE EMERGENCE AND DEVELOPMENT OF TIMTOS

In the 1970s, the global oil crisis sparked a serious recession in Taiwan. To stimulate industrial export growth, Taiwan's state sought to hold export exhibitions for specific local export-oriented industries, including the apparel, footwear, furniture and crafts, sporting goods, Christmas lighting and machinery industries. Around the same time, after visiting European international machine tool trade shows, the Taiwan Association of Machinery Industry (TAMI) – the major industrial association of the industry – also acknowledged the need and importance of having similar events in Taiwan to support the Taiwanese machinery connect with foreign markets (Lu 2013). As a result, the first Taiwan Machinery Export Exhibition was organized in 1975 in Taipei by the Taiwan External Trade Development Council (TAITRA) – a government-sponsored trade promotion organization (see, also, Chang et al., *this volume*).

The first exhibition was successful in attracting 101 domestic machinery makers, including 40 machine tool firms, to exhibit their products to about 700 foreign visitors. Many of these visitors had been invited by the government and the industry association (United Daily News 1975). In the following years, the scale of this annual trade show constantly expanded. From 1975 to 1982 the number of exhibitors increased by 134 percent, while the exhibition space grew more than four-fold (Yang 2011a). Recognizing that demand would soon outstrip existing exhibition space, and given the divergent interests and specialization among firms in the machinery industry, the trade show organizers decided to divide the annual machinery show into two bi-annual events, with one specifically designated for machine tool makers, which at that time accounted for two-thirds of the exhibitors. Accordingly, the Taiwan Metal-Working Machinery Exhibition was launched in 1983. Unlike its predecessor, which accommodated only domestic firms, the new show began to also invite foreign exhibitors, attracting 193 machine tool exhibitors (including 31 from overseas) in its first edition. It occupied 873 booth spaces, making it the largest trade show ever held in Taiwan (Yang 2011a).

To accommodate urgent demand for more exhibition space, Taiwan's state built the Taipei World Trade Center exhibition hall with a much larger capacity for 1,300 booth spaces in 1986. In 1987, the machine tool show was relocated from the Songshan Airport Exhibition Hall to this new venue. Furthermore, to reflect the international orientation of the trade show, it was renamed the Taipei International Machine Tool Show (TIMTOS) in 1993. As the state continued to expand exhibition space by building new exhibition halls in 2001, 2005, 2007 and 2009, TIMTOS gradually increased its scale by inviting more local and foreign exhibitors to participate. Along with the development of Taiwan's machine tool industry, which is currently the world's sixth largest producer and fourth largest exporter (Gardner Publications 2013), TIMTOS has grown to become one of world's major international machine tool trade shows, ranking fifth globally and third in Asia in terms of total exhibition space (Table 13.1).

In 2013, for example, TIMTOS had 1,009 exhibitors and 46,772 visitors. Overseas exhibitors, including some leading global machine tool and component makers from countries such as Japan, Germany and Switzerland, accounted for 25 percent of the participants. Besides, the show attracted 6,583 visitors from abroad, two-thirds (67 percent) of whom came from Asian countries, followed by Europe (15 percent) and North America (8 percent). According to survey data, the majority of these foreign visitors were specialized in manufacturing (42 percent) or sales (38 percent), and the main purpose of attending the show was to find Taiwanese suppliers or production partners (TAITRA 2013).

Although being an important international machine tool show, one should note that, compared with other leading events, TIMTOS is more homogeneous as it attracts fewer foreign exhibitors. As discussed above, foreign exhibitors accounted for only about 25 percent of total TIMTOS exhibitors, as opposed to about 50 percent or more at other major shows (with the exception of Japan's JIMTOF). In addition, given the fact that Taiwan is not a major machine tool market, and since TIMTOS has struggled to improve its exposure vis-à-vis other flagship shows, leading global machine tool firms may not see TIMTOS as an arena to exhibit their latest and most advanced products and technologies. As a result, trans-local learning processes that Taiwanese machine tool firms have been enjoying through interaction with foreign exhibitors at international trade shows (Chen 2009) might be limited in the case of TIMTOS.

In order to understand the role of TIMTOS in influencing the dynamism of Taiwan's machine tool industry, the study focuses on investigating the interaction processes among the majority of local firms, as well as their interaction with foreign visitors at the show.

TIMTOS AND UPGRADING PROCESSES IN TAIWAN'S MACHINE TOOL INDUSTRY 1: FACILITATING EXTRA-LOCAL MARKETING AND NETWORKING

As TIMTOS is the event devised to promote Taiwan's machine tool exports, this section first discusses how this event serves its conventional marketing function to help Taiwanese machine tool firms to cultivate and govern their extra-local business relationships. In the next part, we explore the specific role played by TIMTOS in facilitating the intra- and inter-firm activities of the clustered Taiwanese machine tool makers for tackling issues relevant to their technological upgrading.

Although Taiwanese machine tool makers have been major participants in many flagship international machine tool trade shows (see Table 13.1), given the high costs, relatively few local firms are able to participate as exhibitors. However, thanks to TIMTOS, especially the smaller export-oriented Taiwanese machine tool makers with limited resources can take advantage of this event as a cost-effective worldwide marketing instrument. This has resulted in a very high participation rate of Taiwanese machine tool makers in the show. According to the show organizer, about 70 percent of Taiwan's machine tool firms and their major suppliers exhibited at TIMTOS in 2011. This event also attracted more than 5,000 foreign visitors, of whom 86 percent were decision-makers with the main purpose of attending TIMTOS for seeing new products and meeting suppliers (Yang 2011b).

For foreign firms interested in doing business with Taiwanese machine tool makers, either through direct buying/selling or through production collaboration (e.g., original equipment manufacturer/original design manufacturer – OEM/ODM – or subcontracting partnerships), TIMTOS probably provides the only opportunity to meet the majority of capable actors in Taiwan's machine tool industry, from machine tool makers to specialized accessory and component suppliers. In addition to obtaining a quick and direct overview of the industry, foreign visitors at TIMTOS are able to compare the products and capabilities among Taiwanese machine tool firms, allowing them to better evaluate potential suppliers and partners for cooperation.

While most Taiwanese machine tool firms use TIMTOS as a marketing instrument, the event also offers benefits which cannot be simply measured in terms of immediate orders. It has been suggested in the literature that buyers of capital goods, including machine tools, would not make purchasing decisions based solely on their contacts made with the potential suppliers during shows, as several pre-show contacts or studies and post-show meetings and negotiations are often required to finalize business deals (Cunningham and White 1974; Bello 1992; Rosson and Seringhaus 1995; Lee and Kim 2008). In our case, Taiwanese machine tool firms, especially smaller and younger firms, even need to exhibit at TIMTOS several times before attracting foreign buyers. As one machine tool firm founder noted in an interview,

> [u]nlike other industries, we are selling durable products. Typically, our machines will be used by customers more than ten years. No one would dare to source equipment from unfamiliar machine tool makers. In the case of foreign machine tool dealers, for instance, they have to ensure that the Taiwanese suppliers they meet at TIMTOS can survive long-term. Even if they are interested in our firms' products, they would just observe or make brief contact with us. However, after seeing us at the show two or three times, they would have confidence to place an initial order.

Besides serving as a platform for initiating business with foreign firms, TIMTOS is also used by Taiwanese machine tool makers as a venue for maintaining relationships with their overseas dealers. With their limited resources and capacity to build and maintain their own global distribution networks, the majority of Taiwan's machine tool firms rely on foreign dealers (i.e., agents or distributors) to promote their products or perform post-sale services on their behalf in distant and remote markets (Chen 2009). Stable relationships with foreign sales partners are thus of critical importance for Taiwanese machine tool exporters. To conduct face-to-face meetings with their foreign dealers is pointed out by many respondents as one of their primary tasks in attending international trade fairs.

However, the impact of relationship-maintenance efforts is enhanced when such meetings take place in Taiwan, particularly at TIMTOS. For instance, some interviewees stressed that, unlike at overseas trade shows, their firm could organize a larger exhibition at TIMTOS to better demonstrate its products and competencies. This in turn increases the dealers' interests and confidence in sustaining their relationships with Taiwanese partners. In addition, follow-up trips for foreign dealers to visit Taiwanese firms' manufacturing plants during or after TIMTOS can also be easily arranged. Moreover, in acknowledging these advantages for relationship-maintenance, some leading Taiwanese machine tool firms have begun to hold special sessions at TIMTOS, bringing together their dealers from around the world.

TIMTOS AND UPGRADING PROCESSES IN TAIWAN'S MACHINE TOOL INDUSTRY 2: STIMULATING THE INTRA- AND INTER-FIRM DYNAMICS OF CLUSTER FIRMS

After discussing the role of TIMTOS in supporting linkage-building between Taiwanese machine tool makers and foreign partners, this section focuses on the important, but often overlooked potential of such events to influence intra- and inter-firm dynamics of local firms. In Taiwan, most of the machine tool makers are clustered in the central Taiwan region (Chen 2011). Geographical proximity and a specific institutional environment have nurtured intensive networking and collaboration among local actors, and these conditions have been widely cited as a key factor behind the competiveness of Taiwan's machine tool industry (Yeh and Chang 2003; Brookfield 2008; Chen 2009; 2011). However, it is also noted that, due to fierce competition in the market, the clustered machine tool makers have sparse interaction with one another. Moreover, with limited capabilities to tackle issues such as involuntary knowledge spillovers within the cluster and the difficulty of promoting advanced products, Taiwanese machine tool firms are often quite conservative in undertaking intra- or inter-firm investments in the upgrading of technologies and products (Chen 2011). All these factors could be expected to negatively influence the sustained development of the firms and the cluster. Nevertheless, as will be demonstrated below, the unique setting and context of TIMTOS provides opportunities for Taiwanese machine tool firms to address these issues individually or collectively.

(i) Showcasing the Technological Advancements of Firms and the Industry

Despite their latecomer status, Taiwanese machine tool makers are renowned for their competitiveness in terms of production efficiency and flexibility (Liu and Brookfield 2000; Chen 2009; 2011). To catch up with technological frontrunners, they acquired knowledge and competency through exploiting the learning mechanisms embedded in various intra- and extra-cluster linkages (Chen 2009). However, these enhanced or upgraded capabilities of Taiwanese firms, once they were successfully established, needed to be introduced to domestic and foreign customers, competitors and other critical agents through effective mediums including trade shows. Since many of the newly developed machine tool products or technologies were new to Taiwan but not to the rest of the world, they would not be considered suitable for exhibition at the leading international flagship shows. In this context, TIMTOS emerged as an ideal venue providing Taiwanese machine tool firms with valuable opportunities to present their latest advancements. For instance, notable breakthrough products of Taiwan's machine tool industry, such as Taiwan's first computer numerically controlled (CNC) machine tools or first linear motor machine tools, were all initially introduced at TIMTOS, or its predecessors.

Furthermore, domestic firms making incremental improvements to their existing products would also use TIMTOS to debut newly developed products. Taiwanese machine tool makers even organize their R&D plans around TIMTOS so they can regularly present new products at the show (Yang 2011b). In the interviews conducted, some managers of machine tool firms particularly stressed the significance of such presentations that not only provide preliminary customer reactions and feedback, but also help the firms to establish a reputation as serious and innovative machine-builders.

In addition to individual firms, TIMTOS has also become the stage on which actors in Taiwan's machine tool industry can demonstrate their collective technological performance. Since the late 1990s, with state support, a handful of Taiwanese machine tool makers have worked with local firms and public research institutes to develop more sophisticated machine tool technologies and products through research alliances (Yeh and Chang 2003; Chen 2012). In 1997, for instance, TIMTOS featured the launch of products developed through the collaboration of 12 local electric discharge machine (EDM) manufacturers in Taiwan's first state-initiated public–private alliance to develop Taiwan's first PC-based CNC EDM. On the one hand, this event helped the alliance partners to successfully promote the improved endogenous capacity not only of individual Taiwanese machine tool makers, but also of the overall industry, for developing critical machine tool components. This joint effort later paid off and, today, almost all of the CNC EDM units sold worldwide are equipped with Taiwan-made PC-based controllers (MIRL 2007). On the other hand, the demonstration of the alliance's achievements at TIMTOS allowed more domestic firms to learn about the possibilities and benefits of joint action in developing new products and technologies. The successes encouraged additional public–private collaborative research projects in Taiwan's machine tool industry. Moreover, thanks to the active participation of local firms and the assistance of public research institutes, state-sponsored projects have emerged as a crucial 'institution' nurturing inter-firm collaboration within Taiwan's machine tool cluster (Chen 2012), and TIMTOS has continued to be the primary venue for the presentation of such synergies.

(ii) Stimulating Intra-cluster Horizontal Communication and Interaction

Due to cut-throat competition in their markets, the clustered Taiwanese machine tool makers rarely engage in direct interaction with one another. The mutual learning processes of these domestic firms, however, have been found to be very active. Some studies have indicated that local suppliers played an active role in diffusing information and knowledge within the clustered production networks, allowing indirect technological learning among domestic rivals (Liu and Brookfield 2000; Chen 2009). Yet, we will show that TIMTOS also stimulates direct interaction and communication among local machine tool makers.

Direct sources of information about local competition

In the global market, Taiwanese machine tool makers not only compete against foreign firms, but also face fierce competition from their domestic counterparts. Studying the business patterns and technology structures of local rivals is therefore a critical success factor for these firms. One source of such information is publications, such as newspapers or reports published by government agencies or industry associations. Moreover, clustering makes it easy for Taiwanese machine tool firms to access information or insider knowledge related to their local competitors. Through interactions with other cluster actors, especially suppliers (Chen 2009), they know which firms are doing well or badly in selling which products to which markets, and which firms have introduced which kinds of new products or acquired new technologies. While the machine tool cluster is thus an information-rich environment (Bathelt et al. 2004; Dahl and Pedersen 2004), one should note that much information circulated through local-buzz channels is often not very detailed and may have limited credibility. To obtain more complete and accurate intelligence regarding their cluster rivals, machine tool firms need complementary information sources, and such sources can often be found at TIMTOS.

It has been recently stressed in the literature that trade shows provide participating firms with multiple opportunities to observe and compare their products and strategies with those of their competitors (Li 2006;

Skov 2006; Bathelt and Glückler 2011). In the case of TIMTOS, as this show is the venue where Taiwanese machine tool makers would exhibit their most advanced and competitive products, it provides the best channels for these firms to glean further knowledge about their local competitors. In terms of products, for instance, the respondents of our interviews said that the trade show allowed them to get a closer look of their competitors' products and provides an opportunity to acquire more information about machine structures, installed parts and components, and other technical specifications, either through observation or, if possible, through on-site discussions with sales and support staff. Furthermore, marketing strategies and sales conditions of competitors are also investigated. Taiwanese machine tool firms thus obtain first-hand intelligence of their local rivals at TIMTOS that would not be otherwise available through the cluster's regular information networks, enabling them to evaluate their competition and to devise new marketing and technological development strategies in response.

Selection of matching partners for inter-firm collaboration

Based on their own efforts or state support, Taiwanese machine tool firms have aimed to sustain or improve their competitiveness through collaboration. In addition to being the venue for demonstrating the outcomes of cluster firms' collective activities, TIMTOS also serves as a relationship-building space, facilitating the initiation of horizontal collaboration between Taiwanese machine tool firms. Given that TIMTOS is the most important marketing event of Taiwan's machine tool industry, nearly all local machine tool firm owners and key managers show up during the exhibition period, making it the best occasion for executives to socialize with their familiar or unfamiliar counterparts that are located in geographical proximity. Executives can put aside some of their day-to-day administrative work and therefore have more time to either engage in loose discussions or simply hang out with one another (Bello and Barczak 1990; Bathelt and Schuldt 2010). Besides cultivating relationships and enabling knowledge exchange, such informal communication at TIMTOS can lead to new collaborations among Taiwanese machine tool makers. For example, the CEO of one local firm specialized in machining centers explained that he and the owner of a nearby EDM manufacturer have frequently met at TIMTOS over the years: 'We would talk about business ideas and product development . . . Consequently, when the timing was right, we quickly reached an agreement to establish a strategic alliance.' This led the CEO to make a strategic investment in the EDM firm in 2009. Another interviewee also indicated that it was at TIMTOS that his firm had its first informal communication with a local machine tool maker about the former's investment initiative, which ultimately contributed to a successful merger between the two firms much later.

(iii) Supporting Intra-firm Efforts for Pursuing Technological Advancement

To encourage Taiwanese machine tool makers to improve their machine designs and manufacturing capabilities, the organizers of TIMTOS and the Taiwan Machine Tool Foundation have co-hosted the Research and Development of Innovative Products Contest since 2003, inviting Taiwanese machine tool makers to submit their most cutting-edge and innovative products to compete for related awards and prizes. In this contest, submissions are evaluated by a panel of domestic and foreign machine tool specialists recruited from industry and academic institutes based on criteria such as innovativeness, precision and quality, market potential, functionality and applications, and esthetics (TMTF 2012). Through three rounds of reviews with the first round beginning six months in advance of TIMTOS and the final round being staged at the event, the winning products and firms are announced and awarded during the show. For participating firms, recognition derived from this domestic contest have great marketing and reputation-enhancing value since their products and firms gain greater exposure at TIMTOS and in subsequent media reports.

We found that participating machine tool firms might also use such a contest as a means to strengthen intra-firm technological capabilities. From re-examining the design philosophy and the features of their products in the preparation of their submission, and by responding to reviewers' comments, participating firms obtain invaluable experience and knowledge which can be applied to improve existing and future products. Furthermore, some of the firms even use this contest strategically to boost the potential of their staff, as the general manager of one local leading machine tool firm stated: 'Competition creates pressure to pursue innovative excellence which can be difficult to recreate internally within individual firms.' In part because of such impacts, each iteration of the Research and Development of Innovative Products Contest has attracted between 30 to 60 local major machine tool makers to join this contest associated with TIMTOS (Hsu 2013).

CONCLUSION

By using Taiwan's largest international trade show, TIMTOS, as an example, this chapter examines how international trade shows held in latecomer countries influence the ability of local firms to upgrade their products and technologies. We argue that TIMTOS has provided Taiwanese machine tool makers with manifold opportunities to address issues relevant to individual or collective upgrading activities, in addition to supporting global marketing and relationship-building efforts of Taiwan's machine tool industry. First, the trade show has become an effective medium for Taiwanese machine tool firms to display their catch-up achievements resulting from individual or collaborative efforts, allowing them not only to obtain critical feedback for further improvements, but also to establish and enhance their reputation so as to redress marketing disadvantages due to Taiwan's latecomer status in the global machine tool industry. Second, by participating at TIMTOS, Taiwanese firms are able to gain first-hand and complementary intelligence on their local competitors. Such information would not otherwise be accessible via their regular information networks within their industry cluster. Moreover, this event also expedites the matching process between firms, generating a platform to launch profitable collaborations. Third, by staging a trade show associated contest, TIMTOS encourages Taiwanese machine tool makers to engage more aggressively in advancing their products and technologies and, more importantly, creates a mechanism that enables these firms to better manage their intra-firm technological activities.

In addition to illustrating how interaction among local firms is encouraged and becomes easier through participation in a domestically held international trade show, this chapter also points out the overlooked potential of such an event to facilitate 'institution-building processes' among actors in an industrial cluster (Benner 2003). As illustrated, TIMTOS supports clustered Taiwanese machine tool firms in building new or transforming existing institutions by tackling issues relevant to their technological advancement and sustained development. These findings suggest that to understand how local international trade shows contribute to the evolution of latecomer firms or clusters, the specific role such events play in facilitating institution-building processes among firms may be just as important as their well-acknowledged role in marketing, knowledge acquisition and learning.

REFERENCES

Banting, P. M. and Blenkhorn, D. L. (1974) 'The role of industrial trade shows', *Industrial Marketing Management*, 3 (5): 285–295.

Bathelt, H. and Glückler, J. (2011) *The Relational Economy: Geographies of Knowing and Learning*, Oxford: Oxford University Press.

Bathelt, H., Malmberg, A. and Maskell, P. (2004) 'Clusters and knowledge: Local buzz, global pipelines and the process of knowledge creation', *Progress in Human Geography*, 28: 31–56.

Bathelt, H. and Schuldt, N. (2010) 'International trade fairs and global buzz, Part I: Ecology of global buzz', *European Planning Studies*, 18 (12): 1957–1974.

Bell, M. and Albu, M. (1999) 'Knowledge systems and technological dynamism in industrial clusters in developing countries', *World Development*, 27 (9): 1715–1734.

Bello, D. C. (1992) 'Industrial buyer behavior at trade shows: Implications for selling effectiveness', *Journal of Business Research*, 25 (1): 59–80.

Bello, D. C. and Barczak, G. J. (1990) 'Using industrial trade shows to improve new product development', *Journal of Business and Industrial Marketing*, 5 (2): 43–56.

Benner, C. (2003) 'Learning communities in a learning region: The soft infrastructure of cross-firm learning networks in Silicon Valley', *Environment and Planning A*, 35 (10): 1809–1830.

Berne, C. and García-Uceda, M. E. (2008) 'Criteria involved in evaluation of trade shows to visit', *Industrial Marketing Management*, 37 (5): 565–579.

Blythe, J. (2002) 'Using trade fairs in key account management', *Industrial Marketing Management*, 31 (7): 627–635.

BOFT (2011) *An Introduction to the Development of Taiwan's Convention and Exhibition Industry*, Taipei: Bureau of Foreign Trade, Ministry of Economic Affairs (in Chinese).

Bonoma, T. V. (1983) 'Get more out of your trade shows', *Harvard Business Review*, 61 (1): 75–83.

Borghini, S., Golfetto, F. and Rinallo, D. (2006) 'Ongoing search among industrial buyers', *Journal of Business Research*, 59 (10–11): 1151–1159.

Brookfield, J. (2008) 'Firm clustering and specialization: A study of Taiwan's machine tool industry', *Small Business Economics*, 30 (4): 405–422.

Chen, L.-C. (2009) 'Learning through informal local and global linkages: The case of Taiwan's machine tool industry', *Research Policy*, 38 (3): 527–535.

Chen, L.-C. (2011) 'The governance and evolution of local production networks in a cluster: The case of Taiwan's machine tool industry', *GeoJournal*, 76 (6): 605–622.

Chen, L.-C. (2012) 'The evolving roles of the state and public research institutes in the technological upgrading process of industries: The case of Taiwan's machine tool industry', *Journal of Social Sciences and Philosophy*, 24 (1): 19–50 (in Chinese).

Cunningham, M. T. and White, J. G. (1974) 'The role of exhibitions in industrial marketing: An evaluation of the international machine tool exhibition', *Industrial Marketing Management*, 3 (4): 229–241.

Dahl, M. and Pedersen, C. (2004) 'Knowledge flows through informal contacts in industrial clusters: Myth or reality?', *Research Policy*, 33 (10): 1673–1686.

Evers, N. and Knight, J. (2008) 'Role of international trade shows in small firm internationalization: A network perspective', *International Marketing Review*, 25 (5): 544–562.

Gardner Publications (2013) *2013 World Machine Tool Output and Consumption Survey*, Cincinnati. Online. Available HTTP: <http://www.gardnerweb.com/articles/2013-world-machine-tool-output-and-consumption-survey> (15 July 2013).

Godar, S. H. and O'Connor, P. J. (2001) 'Same time next year: Buyer trade show motives', *Industrial Marketing Management*, 30 (1): 77–86.
Guerrieri, P., Iammarino, S. and Pietrobelli, C. (2001) *The Global Challenge to Industrial Districts: Small and Medium-Sized Enterprises in Italy and Taiwan*, Cheltenham, UK and Northampton, MA: Edward Elgar Publishing.
Hansen, K. (2004) 'Measuring performance at trade shows: Scale development and validation', *Journal of Business Research*, 57 (1): 1–13.
Hsu, S.-L. (2013) '2013 Taipei International Machine Tool Show report', *Taiwan Machinery Monthly*, 675: 17–40.
KOMMA (2012) *SIMTOS 2012 in Review: Expansion and Innovation*, Taipei. Online. Available HTTP: <www.simtos.org/file/SIMTOS2012%20In%20 Review.pdf> (10 December 2013).
Kotha, S. and Nair, A. (1995) 'Strategy and environment as determinants of performance: Evidence from the Japanese machine tool industry', *Strategic Management Journal*, 16 (7): 497–518.
Lee, C. H. and Kim, S. Y. (2008) 'Differential effects of determinants on multi-dimensions of trade show performance: By three stages of pre-show, at-show, and post-show activities', *Industrial Marketing Management*, 37 (7): 784–796.
Li, L.-Y. (2006) 'Relationship learning at trade shows: Its antecedents and consequences', *Industrial Marketing Management*, 35 (2): 166–177.
Liu, R.-J. and Brookfield, J. (2000) 'Stars, rings and tiers: Organisational networks and their dynamics in Taiwan's machine tool industry', *Long Range Planning*, 33 (3): 322–348.
Lu, H.-B. (2013) '2013 TIMTOS: Large, new and long-lasting', *Economic Daily News*, 5 March: E.9 (in Chinese).
Maskell, P., Bathelt, H. and Malmberg, A. (2006) 'Building global knowledge pipelines: The role of temporary clusters', *European Planning Studies*, 14 (8): 997–1013.
Miller, S. (1990) *How to Get the Most Out of Trade Shows*, Lincolnwood: NTC Business Books.
MIRL (2007) 'The achievement of the Technology Development Program and the enhancement of machine tool precision processing technology', *Journal of the Mechatronic Industry*, 291: 17–19 (in Chinese).
Patti, C. H. (1977) 'Buyer information sources in the capital equipment industry', *Industrial Marketing Management*, 6 (4): 259–264.
Power, D. and Jansson, J. (2008) 'Cyclical clusters in global circuits: Overlapping spaces in furniture trade fairs', *Economic Geography*, 84 (4): 423–448.
Ramírez-Pasillas, M. (2010) 'International trade fairs as amplifiers of permanent and temporary proximities in clusters', *Entrepreneurship and Regional Development*, 22 (2): 155–187.
Rinallo, D. and Golfetto, F. (2011) 'Exploring the knowledge strategies of temporary cluster organizers: A longitudinal study of the EU fabric industry trade shows (1986–2006)', *Economic Geography*, 87 (4): 453–476.
Rosson, P. J. and Seringhaus, F. H. R. (1995) 'Visitor and exhibitor interaction at industrial trade fairs', *Journal of Business Research*, 32 (1): 81–90.
Schuldt, N. and Bathelt, H. (2011) 'International trade fairs and global buzz, Part II: Practices of global buzz', *European Planning Studies*, 19 (1): 1–22.
Sharland, A. and Balogh, P. (1996) 'The value of nonselling activities at international trade shows', *Industrial Marketing Management*, 25 (1): 59–66.

Skov, L. (2006) 'The role of trade fairs in the global fashion business', *Current Sociology*, 54 (5): 764–783.
Smith, T. and Smith, P. (2000) 'The role of trade shows in business-to-business selling strategies: A method for assessing the effectiveness of marketing communications', *Wood and Fiber Science*, 32 (3): 362–374.
Tafesse, W. and Korneliussen, T. (2011) 'The dimensionality of trade show performance in an emerging market', *International Journal of Emerging Markets*, 6 (1): 38–49.
TAITRA (2013) *The 24th Taipei International Machine Tool Show Review*, Taipei: TAITRA (in Chinese).
TMTF (2012) *Guidelines for Participating in the 2013 Machine Tool 'Research and Development of Innovative Products Contest'*, Taipei: Taiwan Machine Tool Foundation (in Chinese).
Torre, A. (2008) 'On the role played by temporary geographical proximity in knowledge transmission', *Regional Studies*, 42 (6): 869–889.
United Daily News (1975) 'Enhancing the promotion of the machinery export market', *United Daily News*, 9 April: E.8 (in Chinese).
USITC (1983) *Competitive Assessment of the U.S. Metalworking Machine Tool Industry*, United States International Trade Commission Publication #1428, Washington, DC: Government Printing Press.
Wang, J.-C. (2012) 'Introduction to the 2012 Japan International Machine Tool Show', *Taiwan Machinery Monthly*, 670: 5–13 (in Chinese).
Wang, J.-C. (2013) 'Introduction to the 2013 China International Machine Tool Show', *Taiwan Machinery Monthly*, 676: 18–30 (in Chinese).
Weller, S. (2008) 'Beyond "global production networks": Australian Fashion Week's trans-sectoral synergies', *Growth and Change*, 39 (1): 104–122.
Wickham, J. and Vecchi, A. (2008) 'Local firms and global reach: Business air travel and the Irish software cluster', *European Planning Studies*, 16 (5): 693–710.
Yang, K.-L. (2011a) 'The historical retrospect of the Taipei International Machine Tool Show', *Taiwan Machinery Monthly*, 648: 16–21 (in Chinese).
Yang, K.-L. (2011b) *The Key Success Factors of an International Capital Products Trade Show: A Study of the Taipei International Machine Tool Show*, Master's thesis, Taipei, National Taiwan University of Science and Technology (in Chinese).
Yeh, C.-C. and Chang, P.-L. (2003) 'The Taiwan system of innovation in the tool machine industry: A case study', *Journal of Engineering and Technology Management*, 20 (4): 367–380.

14. How and where tigers roam: the role of Korean trade fairs in supporting firms' export activities

Ronald V. Kalafsky and Douglas R. Gress

INTRODUCTION

Over the past three decades, South Korean manufacturers have emerged as acknowledged leaders in several competitive sectors in the global economy. This has been an ongoing process, as in its early stages South Korea practiced a form of import-substituting industrialization with the long-run goal of pursuing sustainable export-oriented industrialization. And while Korea has recently been spearheading successive free trade agreements with countries around the world in the hopes of supporting broad industry bases, export-oriented industrialization beginning in the post-war Park Chung-hee administration was a top-down and interventionist planning exercise, largely favoring targeted sectors, the growing chaebols (South Korean-type traditional business conglomerates), their trading arms and government-owned private enterprises (Song 1997). The success of export-oriented industrialization has been manifested across many globally competitive industries, including information technology, consumer electronics, motor vehicles and shipbuilding, but, by and large, this success has come via a steady and planned transition over the years first from manufacturing and exporting mature products like footwear, then to higher value-added goods such as industrial chemicals and, eventually, semiconductors (Kim 1997). Looking to the future, if the Korean economy aims to remain export-intensive to fuel further growth, thus providing not only employment opportunities for an increasingly well-educated workforce, but also much-needed validation for incumbent political regimes, firms will need to find ways in which to nurture international business relationships and, perhaps of equal importance, to reveal themselves to wider global markets. At the outset, however, entering international markets presents a bevy of obstacles that often differ widely from domestic business practices, especially in terms of information acquisition

(Ellis 2007; Nicita and Olarraega 2007). Distance, whether Euclidean, cultural or institutional (Ghemawat 2001) introduces further costs for potential exporters, in terms of time, effort and finances.

One way to overcome such barriers is through participation in international trade fairs. These venues offer firms the possibilities to expand beyond their local business communities by interacting with various participants in an industry-specific supply chain via temporary clusters (Bathelt and Schuldt 2008; 2010); to assess customer and competitor reactions to their product lines (Maskell et al. 2004); to foster interaction from an international perspective (Ramírez-Pasillas 2010); and, especially for smaller manufacturers, to simultaneously engage in international marketing efforts. Potentially accessing such information is especially critical, particularly within an international business setting, given that firms often have no formal mechanisms for market assessment (Andersen 2012). Trade fairs, thus, can allow global communication and collaboration within a spatially proximate environment (Schuldt and Bathelt 2011).

The present chapter focuses on how South Korean firms can overcome the challenges associated with accessing overseas markets through participation in trade fairs. It will present the case of the machine tool industry, a key sector not only for the Korean economy, but also for most advanced industrial economies. On a related note, it will discuss the policy environment for international trade promotion and for trade shows, along with the functions that these exhibitions serve in Korea, especially regarding export-oriented purposes. Further, this chapter will explore export-related details concerning these Korean manufacturers with regard to a major international machine tool fair, including possible relationships with firm size. Before analyzing the role of global trade fairs for Korean firms, however, it is important to understand the policy-based, export-led context in which these manufacturers operate.

EXPORTS AND THE ROLE OF KOREAN TRADE POLICY

Manufacturing and exporting have long been at the core of South Korea's rise as an economic power. In terms of policy, capital scarcity played a dominant role in the formation of manufacturing firms during Korea's initial economic development. The firms that emerged in the post-colonial era relied almost solely on government support in the form of access to loans (which came from foreign aid), abatements of taxes and the granting of land rights (Kim 1998; Yoo and Lee 1987). Additional government control mechanisms included the use of entry and exit permits for trade, antitrust and fair trade legislation, price and wage controls, labor legislation, taxation, preferential access to government projects and the imposition of 'pseudo-taxes' (Jung 1989). The reliance on government support began to take on a more clearly defined form in 1961. Under the auspices of General-turned-President Park Chung-hee, banks were nationalized and the Economic Planning Board (EPB) was formed. This action signified the beginning of the Korean government's strict control over the private business sector (Fields 1994; Nam 1995).

In the context of export-oriented industrialization, the EPB was important because it deemed both exports (Kim 1991) and machine tools to be key parts of the country's rebuilding and essential elements of the long-term development of the manufacturing sector. In general though, this newly created institution endowed the president and a select number of technocrats with virtually a complete hold of the government's planning and budget mechanisms (Song 1997). By controlling the banks, and by virtue of the foreign aid and capital that came into the country, the government also controlled the burgeoning chaebols (many of which began to manufacture machine tools) that had begun to grow larger under the previous Rhee regime. Systematically, the government began to target and cultivate what it deemed to be growth industries and to implement the first five-year economic plan. The successful execution of this five-year economic plan, as well as the others to follow, was contingent upon the chaebols following the government's growth strategies focused on export-oriented industrialization and specific target industries. The chaebols were expected to follow these strategies supported by preferential low interest bank loans, tax incentives, trade permits and information supplied by the government in return for the financial support of the ruling party (Nam 1995; Steers 1989). Given little other choice, this is exactly what they did, beginning with a period of rapid market domination and expansion into related and non-related industries backed by the government. Indeed, driven by the dominance of chaebols, by the third five-year plan (1972–1976) equity and more balanced regional development had been highlighted as major goals; size and proximity to the government decision-making bodies had already come to matter (Song 1997). In many ways, this long-range strategy, and the eventual role created for a robust, globally competitive machine tool sector, was similar to that of Japan, where the Ministry of International Trade and Industry regarded an export-focused machine tool sector as a vital component of its post-war rebuilding and reindustrialization processes (Sarathy 1989).

In short, Korea, like many other states, used export-oriented industrialization as a policy-led strategy to achieve rapid economic development. Fundamental components of an export-oriented industrialization program include a trade policy focused on exporting commodities and/or manufactured goods; emphasis on promoting export-focused firms; and an industrial policy that is geared toward emerging industries that are export-intensive (e.g. Coe et al. 2007). These components mirror facets of Korea's growth trajectory described above. Especially in consumer electronics, policymakers worked in concert with the chaebols to foster this export-oriented industrialization trajectory. Initial product lines were geared toward price-sensitivity. Later, the plan was to evolve toward higher-end, high-value-added consumer electronics (Kim et al. 2004; Lin and Chang 2009). Of equal importance, the corresponding manufacturers were striving to integrate into global value chains to enable further and geographically broader growth (Yeung 2007). It should also be mentioned that this involved export-driven marketing strategies by the electronics manufacturers as well – strategies that were sensitive to world market demands and transitions (Lee and Griffith 2004). While it appears that Korean firms have indeed taken the abovementioned Japanese development path (see Yokura, *this volume*), we suggest in this chapter that trade fairs play an important role in how firms (especially smaller and medium-sized firms) from different regions and manufacturing sectors reach spatially distant prospective international customers while minimizing risks and costs.

TRADE FAIRS AND INTERNATIONALIZATION IN THE KOREAN CONTEXT

Given the export-intensive environment in which Korean firms operate, they continuously need to expand revenue-creating opportunities. It makes sense, therefore, that they utilize trade fairs as a means to: (i) explore export markets and gather export intelligence; (ii) meet with potential and existing customers; and (iii) become part of larger global networks that include suppliers, service providers, sales agents and customers. Past research on Korean trade fairs has not focused on this aspect. Much of the trade show research has looked at the shows themselves, studying firm-level satisfaction or performance derived from shows. The focus of such research has been to evaluate the quality and success of such events (Kim 2009; Jung 2010; Park et al. 2010). Some recent studies have explored specific firm-level strategies and sales activities at trade fairs and their impacts on performance at individual trade fairs (e.g. Kim and Yeon 2009; Choi and Jeon 2012). Evidence from selected Korean events also suggests that these shows facilitate relationship-building with customers (Li 2006; Kim and Lee 2010), and that firms can benefit from developing networks and trust with various actors (Lee 2011; Park and Yang 2011). Additionally, many Korean shows promote new products, which has long been a primary function of trade fairs worldwide (Yoon and Han 2010). The relationship-building component is especially important in many East Asian business systems, where trust-based relationships are essential for long-term business success (Trompenaars and Hampden-Turner 1997; Choi and Jeon 2012). In line with these findings, increasing evidence from Korea suggests that firms should look at trade show attendance not only in terms of direct sales generating activities, but also in terms of long-term relationship-building activities not necessarily directly related to onsite selling (Jung 2010; Kim 2011).

From a more macro perspective, trade fairs in Korea can be tied to an increasing policy emphasis on balanced regional development on the one hand, and the generation of increased opportunities for small and medium-sized enterprises (SMEs) on the other. As mentioned above, the initial stages of Korea's export-oriented industrialization policies not only created a gap between large chaebols and SMEs in terms of support, market access and export opportunities, but also a hierarchy of places, with Seoul, the capital region, dominating. Beginning in the late 1990s, the Kim Dae-jung administration began to implement balanced regional development policies that would eventually come to support virtually every region in Korea outside of the capital region (Lee 2009). At the same time, the Korean government specifically began to support conventions and trade shows in conjunction with export promotion (Park et al. 2010). Slowly, modern exhibition facilities in Goyang, Busan, Daegu and Cheju Island began to emerge and situate Korea increasingly as a competitor in the trade show business (Yoo 2005; Lee and Lee 2006). In cooperation with the Ministry of Commerce and Industry, the Korea Trader's Association and the Korea Trade Promotion Agency, trade fairs have been actively used to coordinate export efforts for participating firms, with The Korea Society for the Advancement of Machinery Industry specifically assisting machine tool exporters (Cavusgil and Czinkota 1990). These efforts are starting to bear fruit as trade fairs in Korea have recently been shown to have positive local income and employment effects (Kim 2008), as well as a positive impact on exports for participating firms (Hong and Lee 2009).

Taken together then, trade fairs conceivably enable Korean firms to moderate the friction of distance and some of the accompanying difficulties associated with exploring new (and even existing) export markets – that is an acknowledged goal from a Korean policy perspective (Hong and Lee 2009). This last point is essential, given that an export market orientation is crucial to export success (Levy et al. 2007). The unstructured, yet globalized environment cultivated at trade fairs can be especially beneficial to firms that are new to international markets, as it provides myriad ways to learn about customers and global supply chains (Chen 2009).

While the benefits of trade fairs are salient for any firm looking to expand abroad, they become even more relevant for smaller firms with relatively few resources and little international experience. The emerging international presence of the chaebols is well documented and easily seen worldwide. Access to export market intelligence (and markets themselves), however, has been widely acknowledged to be a challenge for SMEs in general (Julien and Ramangalahy 2003). A concern for Korean firms is that they will be left behind in terms of competitiveness if they do not engage in international markets, especially given the fact that they face hurdles with regard to market exposure and access to export intelligence (Seo and Choi 2012). Trade fairs, therefore, provide a venue and means through which smaller firms can explore international markets. Spatial proximity alone can act as a catalyst during these events to forming business relationships, especially in earlier stages of firm growth (Torre 2008). All of this comes at a time when most trade shows are becoming increasingly international in nature (Skov 2006). On balance, then, it appears that the possibilities of securing market information and international experience in a short time period and within a confined setting make it valuable to attend trade fairs, despite concerns about the upfront costs associated with participating (O'Hara et al. 1993).

As the existing literature on Korean trade fairs provides little empirical evidence regarding the dynamics between trade fair participation and export performance (Lee 2008), the next section examines evidence from a survey of exhibitors at a leading advanced manufacturing/machinery trade fair, SIMTOS.

THE CASE OF SIMTOS AND THE KOREAN MACHINE TOOL INDUSTRY

To illustrate the dynamics at work within Korean trade fairs, the following section examines the case of Korean machine tool firms participating at the trade fair SIMTOS in April 2012. This trade fair, held every two years, has transitioned from the 'Seoul International Machine Tool Show' to the 'Seoul International Manufacturing Technology Show', reflecting an emphasis on all forms of advanced manufacturing. A large amount of the show's activities, however, have continued to revolve around machine tools and associated industries such as robotics and tools and dies. In 2012, SIMTOS was attended by an estimated 100,000 visitors and 700 participating firms, with roughly 5,000 visiting from overseas from 35 countries

(SIMTOS 2012). It is one of largest trade shows of this kind among a relatively select number of large trade fairs focused on machine tools, along with others in China, Germany, Japan, Taiwan and the United States (see Chen and Chu, *this volume*). Notably, with the exception of the United States, this is a group of relatively manufacturing-intensive countries. This makes an analysis of firms in this sector especially pertinent as machine tools are generally seen as an indicator of a country's level of innovation and performance in manufacturing (Graham 1993; Kim and Lee 2008). In the Korean context, examining this particular industry provides insights into a key industrial sector, which is part of an overall push for more advanced, higher value-added manufacturing (Ray et al. 2004).

A total of 53 firms were surveyed during SIMTOS in 2012, encompassing only manufacturers of 'complete machines' (e.g. grinding machines, industrial metal presses or machining centers, rather than component producers or service providers). This sample represented approximately one-third of all Korean machine tool producers. These firms were chosen via pre-exhibition website research, an analysis of the SIMTOS program and through explorations undertaken onsite during the first day of the exhibition. The survey incorporated various queries on trade fairs and exporting, including questions on trade show motivations, export intensity and targeted markets. The sample of surveyed firms was representative of the larger machine tool manufacturer population in terms of firm size and machinery offerings.

Focusing on the reasons for participating in SIMTOS, our goal was to investigate whether the event was a possible means by which manufacturers approached potential international customers. On the survey instrument, firms were able to select from eight possible motivations commonly cited within both the trade show literature and trade publications (see Table 14.1). Our results show that export-related motivations placed third, cited by just over half the firms, but two other motivations were notably selected by more respondents: obtaining information on Korean (domestic) customers and meeting with suppliers (either existing or potential). Given that this event was the 'home ground' for Korean machine tool manufacturers, it stood to reason that firms were looking to engage domestic customers. Indeed, many of the machine tool firms are part of wider Korean business networks, including those of the chaebols, and these manufacturers, in turn, sell their products to customers within Korea's still sizeable manufacturing sector. However, there was an additional nuance to this, as five firms revealed in post-survey conversations that, while many sales were domestic, some of this output was later directed overseas by their Korean customers. In essence, some domestically based customers, mostly chaebols or major suppliers to such firms, were taking

Table 14.1 Reasons for trade fair participation at SIMTOS, 2012

Reason for trade fair participation	(1) Percentage of firms	(2) Percentage of (1), also attending because of export motive
Obtain information on Korean customers	62.3	63.6
Meet with existing and potential suppliers	62.3	42.4
Obtain information on export customers	50.9	N/A
Meet with overseas agents and distributors	37.7	60.0
Discover industry trends	32.1	58.8
Benchmark competitors	30.2	68.8
Obtain information useful for innovation	28.3	80.0
Compare competitor price and quality	18.9	70.0

Note: Based on 53 surveyed firms; N/A = not applicable.

Source: Authors' survey.

care of the export process for the machinery seller. The Korea-based purchaser shipped the machine tools overseas along with other machinery to be installed on a factory floor. While amounting to increased sales, these particular sorts of transactions, of course, do not help the machine tool manufacturers gain much-needed international experience and, in fact, can provide additional challenges (Kalafsky and Gress 2013; 2014a). Some representatives at SIMTOS, for example, explained that such 'exporting' arrangements resulted in them not being able to sufficiently service their machines and, therefore, possible client relationships, as they did not maintain service personnel in every country where their products were in operation. All of the firms that mentioned this were smaller firms (under 300 employees), were relatively new to exploring international markets and, at this point, had relatively low export intensities.

Most of the firms participating in the event were suppliers, encompassing functions ranging from tooling to computer numeric controls and to engineering services. The fact that the motivations pertaining to suppliers and to domestic customers were the most frequently selected rationales for SIMTOS participation indicates the importance of relationships formed within Korean business circles (linkages with domestic buyers and sellers) and fostered at Korean trade shows (Lee 2011; Park and Yang 2011). This, in one sense, confirms previous trade show research in other industries and countries regarding the role of fairs as temporary clusters (Bathelt and

Schuldt 2008; 2010). This was especially the case with the smaller surveyed firms, which selected the domestic customer rationale far more often than larger firms. The continued relationships with domestic firms, especially for smaller manufacturers, underline the relative lack of international linkages fostered by smaller firms at many international trade fairs.

Note that none of the remaining five motivations was selected by more than 40 percent of the survey participants. Interestingly, all five of these remaining reasons also tended to be the more complex reasons for attending trade shows (e.g. beyond focusing solely on sales). A different perspective, however, is provided when attendance motivations in combination with the export-related rationale (see Table 14.1) are considered. For instance, three of the motivations selected least garnered the highest percentage of responses from firms that selected the export-led rationale as well. Regarding innovation-related motivations for attending, previous research has demonstrated linkages between innovation and the engagement of markets at progressively wider geographic scales (Kalafsky and MacPherson 2003; Cassiman and Martínez-Ros 2007). Essentially, firms that serve wider markets also tend to have relatively newer product lines and, on average, spend more on research-related activities. In the case of the machine tool firms at SIMTOS, a difference-of-means test confirmed that manufacturers selecting innovation as a motivation were significantly more export-intensive than those that did not. In a way, these innovative linkages can be fostered at a trade show, given that innovation in the industry is driven by constant interaction with buyers, both current and potential (Malerba 2006). Likewise, firms selecting motivations concerning quality, price and benchmarking also tended to be those using SIMTOS as part of their export marketing policy tools. While the current analyses are only preliminary explorations with a relatively small sample size, the results suggest that Korean firms utilizing trade fairs for export-related purposes tend to be those engaging in higher-order, wider ranging practices. These activities parallel conclusions drawn by Blythe (2010) regarding firms' trade show goals and strategies, especially in terms of moving beyond a narrow focus on sales (e.g. Jung 2010; Kim 2011).

Given the aforementioned aim of Korean policymakers to position and support trade shows as export marketing vehicles (Park et al. 2010), another survey question asked firm representatives about the overall importance of exporting to their firms in relation to three key functions that take place at trade fairs: physical inspection of products, new sales and export marketing (see Table 14.2). The results show that the two export-related metrics (its overall importance and the importance of trade shows to export marketing) do not place as high as the new sales and the physical inspection functions, providing an indication of the current roles

Table 14.2 Evaluation of trade fair importance by export focus at SIMTOS, 2012

Importance of trade fairs	Mean score	Mean score, if export importance rated 6 or 7	Mean score, if export importance rated 1 to 5
For physical inspection of products	5.40	6.04	4.73
For new sales	5.11	5.52	4.69
As an export marketing strategy	4.53	5.22	3.81
Overall importance of exports to the firm	4.87	N/A	N/A

Note: Based on 53 surveyed firms; average evaluations based on a seven-point scale from 1 (not important at all) to 7 (extremely important); N/A = not applicable.

Source: Authors' survey.

of trade fairs from the perspective of these firms. First, participation in an exhibition such as SIMTOS is a means of increasing sales. The second reason, physical inspection, is more complex. In order to successfully implement advanced machinery, it is important to have a physical presence to learn the culture of the buyers and for machinery to be seen in a sales setting, preferably functioning in a simulated work environment (Drake and Kalafsky 2011). This is particularly important to foreign visitors, and part of the reason for creating a multifaceted experience for prospective and existing buyers (Rinallo et al. 2010). In this regard, SIMTOS provides an ideal venue for these kinds of displays.

The information in Table 14.2 also emphasizes the export-supporting function of the trade fair. Results presented compare the trade show importance measures differentiated by those firms that evaluated international sales to be important and those that did not. With regard to the magnitude of trade fairs for new sales, firms that place a higher emphasis on exporting also rank this metric significantly higher (difference-of-means t-test; $p = 0.035$) than those with a lower export emphasis. The differences are even more significant when looking at the other metrics in Table 14.2. In the case of export-focused respondents, a similar relationship is somewhat intuitive with respect to the rating of the importance of trade shows for export marketing purposes ($p = 0.004$). This indicates that firms dedicated to exporting clearly recognize the role trade shows play in their internationalization efforts. These relationships continue, as export-focused manufacturers also rated the importance of trade shows for a physical presence of their products significantly higher than other respondents ($p = 0.001$). This finding underlines the importance of trade shows in providing a 'one-stop' place for prospective international customers to not only meet with the representatives of the manufacturers, but to also experience these firms' product lines first hand. When taken together, these findings highlight that firms engaged in exporting take an all-encompassing approach to their trade shows strategies.

The findings in Table 14.2 support our assumption that trade fairs can foster export activities. This leads to a number of questions: what kinds of firms are these exporters and, drawing upon results discussed above, how does firm size play into this? Again, there is concern in Korea that SMEs, despite having the requisite technological capabilities to compete, may be at a comparative disadvantage globally should they be unable to overcome difficulties in export marketing (Seo and Choi 2012). By and large, the survey results suggest that firm size may have some impact on export activities, both overall and in terms of SIMTOS. First, larger firms export significantly more than smaller firms. This difference in export intensities also holds when using the 300-employee demarcation discussed above (22.8 percent as opposed to 53.8 percent for larger firms with over 300 employees). This division is also apparent when applied to the metrics discussed in Table 14.2. The larger machine tool manufacturers rated the importance of exporting much higher, as well as the importance assigned to trade shows as an export marketing strategy.

Table 14.3 presents the evaluation of trade fairs by respondents differentiated by the number of trade show attendances over a two-year window (most major machine tool shows are held on a biannual basis) and in relation to three export-related measures. First, it is worth noting that almost a third of the survey participants attended only SIMTOS. This, in itself, limits the marketing exposure of the respective firms to potential customers. Conversely, it bodes well for Korea's export-oriented economy that over two-thirds of the firms also utilized other trade fairs focused on the machine tool industry. Conversations with the survey participants revealed that many are participating in some of the main industry trade shows (see Chen and Chu, *this volume*). The divide between SIMTOS-only and multi-trade-fair attendees becomes starker as one looks at export-related measures. With regard to the importance of exports to their organizations, an analysis-of-variance (ANOVA) test confirms that firms that attend additional trade shows also place greater importance on exporting ($p = 0.002$). These differences also hold when taking export intensity into consideration; and multi-trade-fair attendees also tend to derive greater sales from exports. Another ANOVA test showed that this comparison was again statistically significant ($p = 0.049$) (Kalafsky and Gress 2014b).

This was further supported when comparing these answers to firms

Table 14.3 Export intensity of firms at SIMTOS by number of trade fair attendees, 2012

Number of trade fairs attended	Percentage of surveyed firms	Importance of exports^	Export intensity#	Percentage of firms expecting high export growth*
Only SIMTOS	30.8	3.63	14.0	21.4
Two to three trade fairs every two years	42.3	5.05	27.2	46.4
Four or more trade fairs every two years	26.9	6.29	36.2	32.1

Notes:
Based on 53 surveyed firms.
^ = average evaluations based on a seven-point scale from 1 (not important at all) to 7 (extremely important)
# = percentage of sales from exports
* = expected export growth over a five-year period exceeding 10 percent.

Source: Authors' survey.

that project high versus low export growth over the next five-year period (asked in a different question). This showed that the manufacturers participating in more trade shows expected greater increases in international revenue (see Table 14.3). Note, however, that more firms attending two to three trade fairs envisaged higher export growth than those attending four or more shows. While the present research did not delve into the matter, this could be a case of more established exporters already having established export programs – a point supported by the relatively higher average export intensity of such firms. There is certainly a size-based element to this as well. One-third of the smaller firms (fewer than 300 employees) attended only SIMTOS, while all of the larger surveyed firms (those with more than 300 employees) also participated in trade shows beyond SIMTOS. Given their higher participation rates, these results would suggest that larger firms are garnering more exposure to a wider (i.e. international) customer base.

In view of the export focus of the present study and the emphasis of Korean policies on global sales promotions and trade shows, we finally examine the targeted markets indicated by the machine tool makers at SIMTOS (see Table 14.4). Once again, a few noteworthy features emerge. Rather than deploying an attendance-based assessment, our next analysis explores firms targeting potential domestic customers versus customers in

Table 14.4 Potential markets at SIMTOS and selected export metrics, 2012

Country of origin of potential customers	Percentage of firms targeting customers from . . .	Importance of exports to firms[1] in . . .	Importance of trade shows for export marketing[1] for firms targeting . . .	Average export intensity[2] for firms targeting . . .
Korea	56.6	4.23	4.30	26.6
China	50.9	6.04	5.04	38.1
Southeast Asia	37.7	5.80	4.75	24.6
East Asia	35.8	6.11	5.11	38.1
North America	32.1	6.29	5.47	41.1
India	32.1	6.24	5.41	40.4
Western Europe	20.8	6.36	5.09	37.5
Brazil	20.8	6.45	5.36	37.7
Turkey	18.9	6.00	5.70	44.5
Eastern Europe	17.0	5.67	5.00	21.3
South Africa	3.8	6.00	6.50	15.0

Notes:
Based on 53 surveyed firms; firms could choose more than one targeted export market.
1. average evaluation of firms targeting that specific market based on a seven-point scale from 1 (not important at all) to 7 (extremely important)
2. percentage of sales from exports for firms selecting that particular targeted market.

Source: Authors' survey.

wider international markets. The fact that only one foreign market, China, was indicated by more than half of the respondents speaks to the nature of a lingering domestic focus of SIMTOS and the firms that take part in this trade show on the one hand, and perhaps a burgeoning regional focus for Korean trade fairs on the other. As with other explorations throughout this chapter, however, an export-oriented approach provides additional insight (see Table 14.4). The most obvious difference concerns the question of assessing the importance placed on exporting. Note that when firms selected other export markets, the average importance placed on exporting increased by a considerable margin, especially when many distant markets, including India and North America, were included.

While the differences are not as great, a similar trend is apparent when location choices are considered vis-à-vis the importance of trade shows as an export marketing strategy. With the exception of Southeast Asia (markets such as Thailand have been long-time destinations for Korean machinery), other targeted markets were rated as being important to very important (5 to 7 on the seven-point scale). The increases in average export intensity for many pursued markets, especially Turkey, North America and India, are also of interest. These analyses point to a group of manufacturers that, while already export-involved, use a 'homegrown' show such as SIMTOS for internationalization purposes. And again, firm size may play a role in this. The larger firms at SIMTOS targeted distant markets, such as North America and Turkey, and relatively tough markets, such as China, at significantly higher rates than their smaller counterparts (Kalafsky and Gress 2014a).

CONCLUDING REMARKS

The evidence from SIMTOS indicates that, in the case of advanced industrial machinery, this Korean trade fair, like many others, serves particularly domestic firms by fostering interaction with their domestic customer base. However, due to the active engagement of the Korean government and impacts from global market forces, this exhibition is rapidly globalizing, a trend mirroring observations made by Skov (2006). The evidence from the study of SIMTOS presents two groups of firms. The group consists of the export-savvy Korean machine tool manufacturers that have already latched onto global trends, as seen by their export performance and, more importantly, their use of a domestically based trade fair for international marketing purposes. The second group is centered on those producers that are still reliant upon sales to Korean firms. Sales to domestic customers (though some of them may then export) do not do much to increase the international experience of these manufacturers. Instead, they act to shield them from the characteristic risks of export markets, thereby prolonging a move toward internationalization and its inherent challenges. This division appears, in some ways, to be linked to firm size. Larger firms tend to place more emphasis on exporting at-large, and they assign more weight to the role that trade shows play in export marketing. Smaller firms, on the other hand, appear to be less export-involved. The important question that is derived from this is whether this second group of manufacturers will (or even can) move toward increased internationalization. On a related note, will the firms have the resources to do so, and will they deploy the necessary staff? These are critical challenges for smaller firms, given limited resources and limited exposure to international markets. It would appear that trade fairs such as SIMTOS can become important means by which such firms can test global waters. Following this logic, the same firms could in a second step expand beyond SIMTOS to other trade shows held abroad.

Another question concerns whether policymakers and trade show coordinators will have the mechanisms in place to nurture an environment that is conducive to export promotion, export marketing and international marketing possibilities. While trade fairs are acknowledged areas of interest in Korean economic circles, should additional emphasis be placed on the role that such exhibitions can play in export promotion to enable the 'tiger to roam further'? Given that South Korea's economic success is strongly linked to exporting, yet with comparatively little SME involvement, this would appear to be a critical avenue to follow. Policies to support this, however, may have to adjust their efforts to facilitate further SME participation in international trade fairs, with a particular focus on the export-related functions of these events. If an industry such as machine tools demands that firms adapt to and explore the international marketplace, then trade fairs such as SIMTOS must transition accordingly.

ACKNOWLEDGMENTS

The authors thank the Association for Asian Studies, Northeast Asian Council for its funding of this study. The analyses presented in this chapter are related to research published in Kalafsky and Gress (2013; 2014a; 2014b).

REFERENCES

Andersen, K. V. (2012) 'The problem of embeddedness revisited: Collaboration and market types', *Research Policy*, 42: 139–148.
Bathelt, H. and Schuldt, N. (2008) 'Between luminaries and meat grinders: International trade fairs as temporary clusters', *Regional Studies*, 42: 853–868.
Bathelt, H. and Schuldt, N. (2010) 'International trade fairs and global buzz, Part I: Ecology of global buzz', *European Planning Studies*, 18: 1957–1974.
Blythe, J. (2010) 'Trade fairs as communication: A new model', *Journal of Business and Industrial Marketing*, 25: 57–62.
Cassiman, B. and Martínez-Ros, E. (2007) *Product Innovation and Exports: Evidence from Spanish Manufacturing*, CEPR Working Paper, London: Centre for Economic Policy and Research.
Cavusgil, S. T. and Czinkota, M. R. (1990) *International Perspectives on Trade Promotion and Assistance*, New York: Quorum Books.
Chen, L.-C. (2009) 'Learning through informal local and global linkages: The case of Taiwan's machine tool industry', *Research Policy*, 38: 527–535.
Choi, J.-J. and Jeon, B.-J. (2012) 'Impact of exhibitors' on-site activities on their

trade show performance: Moderating roles of expertise and empowerment', *Tourism Research*, 36: 297–317.
Coe, N. M., Kelly, P. F. and Yeung, H. W.-C. (2007) *Economic Geography: A Contemporary Introduction*, Oxford: Blackwell Publishing.
Drake, D. M. and Kalafsky, R. V. (2011) 'Entry into China and market intelligence: Machine tool exporters as a case study in economic geography', *Education about Asia*, 16: 17–20.
Ellis, P. D. (2007) 'Distance, dependence and diversity of markets: Effects on market orientation', *Journal of International Business Studies*, 8: 374–386.
Fields, K. J. (1994) 'Developmental capitalism and industrial organization: Chaebol and the state in Korea', in H. Y. Lee and D. J. Chang (eds) *Political Authority and Economic Exchange in Korea*, Seoul: Oruem Publishing, 207–250.
Ghemawat, P. (2001) 'Distance still matters: The hard reality of global expansion', *Harvard Business Review*, 79: 137–147.
Graham, J. (1993) 'Firm and state strategy in a multipolar world: The changing geography of machine tool production and trade', in H. Noponen, J. Graham and A. Markusen (eds) *Trading Industries, Trading Regions*, New York: Guilford Press, 140–174.
Hong, S.-E. and Lee, S.-Y. (2009) 'The effects of Korea's trade show on export', *Journal of Korea Research Society for Customs*, 10: 425–445.
Julien, P.-A. and Ramangalahy, C. (2003) 'Competitive strategy and performance of exporting SMEs: An empirical investigation of the impact of their export information search and competencies', *Entrepreneurship Theory and Practice*, 27: 227–245.
Jung, K. H. (1989) 'Business and government relations in Korea', in K. H. Jung and H. C. Lee (eds) *Korean Managerial Dynamics*, New York: Praeger, 11–26.
Jung, M.-H. (2010) 'Effects of the exhibition services from organizer and objectives of exhibitors on overall satisfaction and performance of exhibitors – The case of World Financial Fair Busan 2010', *Tourism Research*, 26: 547–565.
Kalafsky, R. V. and Gress, D. R. (2013) 'Trade fairs as an export marketing and research strategy: Results from a study of Korean advanced machinery firms', *Geographical Research*, 51: 304–317.
Kalafsky, R. V. and Gress, D. R. (2014a) 'Go big or stay home? Korean machinery firms, trade fair dynamics, and export performance', *Asia Pacific Business Review*, 20: 136–152.
Kalafsky, R. V. and Gress, D. R. (2014b) 'Getting there: Trade fair participation and its importance for Korean machinery exporters', *Professional Geographer*, 66: 621–630.
Kalafsky, R. V. and MacPherson, A. D. (2003) 'Input/output ranges and performance: An examination of US machine tool producers', *Entrepreneurship and Regional Development*, 15: 69–82.
Kim, B.-S. (2008) 'The economic impact of the trade fair industry in Korea', *Hotel Tourism Research*, 10: 30–43.
Kim, H., Hoskisson, R. E., Tihanyi, L. and Hong, J. (2004) 'The evolution and restructuring of diversified business groups in emerging markets: The lessons from chaebols in Korea', *Asia Pacific Journal of Management*, 21: 25–48.
Kim, H.-R. (1998) 'The evolution of the Korean business system', *Sangnam Forum*, 1: 81–110.
Kim, H.-R. (2011) 'A study on the relation of participation purpose, perceived

service quality and satisfaction in an exhibition: A focus on the exhibitor', *Hotel Tourism Research*, 13: 167–178.

Kim, K. S. (1991) *The Korean Miracle (1962–1980) Revisited: Myths and Realities in Strategy and Development*, Working Paper #166, Notre Dame, IN: Kellogg Institute.

Kim, L. (1997) *Imitation to Innovation: The Dynamic of Korea's Technological Learning*, Boston: Harvard Business Press.

Kim, N.-S. (2009) 'Impacts of the exhibitor's trade show performance on satisfaction and intention to visit again', *Tourism and Leisure Research*, 21: 387–406.

Kim, N.-S. and Lee, E.-S. (2010) 'The relationship between the exhibitors' show performance and the service quality of trade shows: As reported by participating exhibitor managers in international trade shows held in Korea', *International Commerce and Information Review*, 12: 3–34.

Kim, S.-Y. and Yeon, Y.-C. (2009) 'An empirical study on causal relationships among pavilion exhibitors' activities, visitors' interest, and exhibitors' performance factors at trade shows', *Journal of Trade Association*, 34: 47–69.

Kim, Y.-Z. and Lee, K. (2008) 'Sectoral innovation system and technological catch-up: The case of the capital goods industry in Korea', *Global Economic Review*, 37: 135–155.

Lee, C. and Griffith, D. A. (2004) 'The marketing strategy–performance relationship in an export-driven developing economy: A Korean illustration', *International Marketing Review*, 21: 321–334.

Lee, C.-H. (2008) 'An exploratory study on the relationships between trade show objectives and performance', *Journal of Trade Association*, 33: 205–224.

Lee, M.-J. and Lee, K.-M. (2006) 'Convention and exhibition center development in Korea', *Journal of Convention and Event Tourism*, 8: 101–120.

Lee, S.-D. (2011) 'The effect of cooperation network of stakeholder on network performance on exhibition and convention', *Tourism and Leisure Research*, 23: 499–514.

Lee, Y.-S. (2009) 'Balanced development in globalizing regional development? Unpacking the new regional policy in South Korea', *Regional Studies*, 43: 353–367.

Levy, O., Beechler, S., Taylor, S. and Boyacigiller, N. A. (2007) 'What we talk about when we talk about "global mindset": Managerial cognition in multinational corporations', *Journal of International Business Studies*, 38: 231–258.

Li, L.-Y. (2006) 'Relationship learning at trade shows: Its antecedents and consequences', *Industrial Marketing Management*, 35: 166–177.

Lin, J. and Chang, H.-J. (2009) 'Should industrial policy in developing countries conform to comparative advantage or defy it? A debate between Justin Lin and Ha-Joon Chang', *Development Policy Review*, 27: 483–502.

Malerba, F. (2006) 'Innovation and the evolution of industries', *Journal of Evolutionary Economics*, 16: 3–23.

Maskell, P., Bathelt, H. and Malmberg, A. (2004) *Temporary Clusters and Knowledge Creation: The Effects of International Trade Fairs, Conventions and Other Professional Gatherings*, SPACES 2004-04, Toronto and Heidelberg. Online. Available HTTP: <http://www.spaces-online.com> (13 March 2013).

Nam, C. H. (1995) 'South Korea's big business clientelism in democratic reform', *Asian Survey*, 35: 357–366.

Nicita, A. and Olarraeaga, M. (2007) 'Information and export performance', *Journal of Industry, Competition and Trade*, 7: 95–111.

O'Hara, B., Palumbo, F. and Herbig, P. (1993) 'Industrial trade shows abroad', *Industrial Marketing Management*, 22: 233–237.

Park, C.-O., Lee, S.-H. and Kang, I.-W. (2010) 'The influence of the pushing and pulling factor on exhibition quality evaluation', *Knowledge Management Research*, 11: 67–77.

Park, W.-J. and Yang, J.-H. (2011) 'The effect of visitors' perceived relational benefits on revisit intention to exhibition', *Journal of Social Science*, 37: 27–48.

Ramírez-Pasillas, M. (2010) 'International trade fairs as amplifiers or permanent and temporary proximity in clusters', *Entrepreneurship and Regional Development*, 22: 155–187.

Ray, P. K., Ida, M., Suh, C.-S. and Rhaman, S. (2004) 'Dynamic capabilities of Japanese and Korean enterprises and the 'flying geese' of international competitiveness', *Asia Pacific Business Review*, 10: 463–484.

Rinallo, D., Borghini, S. and Golfetto, F. (2010) 'Exploring visitor experiences at trade shows', *Journal of Business and Industrial Marketing*, 25: 249–258.

Sarathy, R. (1989) 'The interplay of industrial policy and international strategy: Japan's machine tool industry', *California Management Review*, 31 (3): 132–160.

Schuldt, N. and Bathelt, H. (2011) 'International trade fairs and global buzz, Part II: Practices of global buzz', *European Planning Studies*, 19: 1–22.

Seo, M.-S. and Choi, B.-H. (2012) 'The study on plan of practical application of marketing for securing global competitiveness of small–medium sized enterprises', *Journal of Trade Association*, 37: 257–286.

SIMTOS (2012) *SIMTOS 2012 Overview*, Seoul. Online. Available HTTP: <http://2012.simtos.org/file/SIMTOS2012_Guide%20to%20Exhibit(final).pdf> (27 August 2012).

Skov, L. (2006) 'The role of trade fairs in the global fashion business', *Current Sociology*, 54: 764–783.

Song, B.-N. (1997) *The Rise of the Korean Economy*, Hong Kong: Oxford University Press.

Steers, R. (1989) *The Chaebol: Korea's New Industrial Might*, London: Harper Business.

Torre, A. (2008) 'On the role played by temporary geographical proximity in knowledge transmission', *Regional Studies*, 42: 869–889.

Trompenaars, F. and Hampden-Turner, C. (1997) *Riding the Waves of Culture: Understanding Diversity in Global Business*, New York: McGraw-Hill.

Yeung, H. W.-C. (2007) 'From followers to market leaders: Asian electronics firms in the global economy', *Asia Pacific Viewpoint*, 48: 1–25.

Yoo, J.-J.-E. (2005) 'Development of the convention industry in Korea', *Journal of Convention and Event Tourism*, 6: 81–100.

Yoo, S. J. and Lee, S. M. (1987) 'Management style and practice of Korean chaebols', *California Management Review*, 29: 95–110.

Yoon, S.-H. and Han, J.-Y. (2010) 'Comparison of exhibitors' characteristics between a consumption exhibition and a capital exhibition', *Tourism and Leisure Research*, 22 (1): 311–325.

PART IV

Synthesis and implications

15. Towards temporary knowledge ecologies in the Asia-Pacific region: a synthesis

Harald Bathelt, Peng-Fei Li and Gang Zeng

KEY TOPICS OF THE BOOK

The agenda behind this book is to present an analysis of the rise and development of trade fair ecologies in the Asia-Pacific region by comparing the situation in many of the countries. While we are still far from being able to provide a comprehensive overview of the Asia-Pacific trade fair business, this edited volume substantially advances our understanding of the structures and interrelationships between trade fair activities and economic development in Asia-Pacific economies. When considering the exponential economic growth in many Asian countries since the 1970s, it is surprising how little we still know about trade fairs in the region. In trying to bridge this gap, the contributions of this volume focus on several interrelated research goals: The first goal is to provide an overview of trade fair developments in the Asia-Pacific region and the factors that influence these processes. Although the growth of trade fair activities in this area has been faster than that in other world regions (Golfetto and Rinallo, *this volume*; Jin and Weber, *this volume*), secondly, the individual chapters aim to show that the development of trade fairs in the Asia-Pacific region has been highly uneven, with large differences between industries, city-regions and even countries. The third goal of this book is to synthesize the development of trade fair activities and propose a conceptualization of Asia-Pacific trade fairs in a dynamic perspective.

Since most contributions to the book primarily address the first two goals and investigate trade fair developments in individual Asia-Pacific countries, the final chapter focuses on the third goal, to propose a synthesis of the rise and evolution of trade fairs. Building on the work of Li (2014; *this volume*) and Bathelt et al. (2014), the chapter first summarizes the findings presented in different country cases throughout the book. These findings will then be integrated into an overarching framework that conceptualizes the development of temporary knowledge ecologies in the Asia-Pacific region.

At first glance, the third goal seems at odds with the fundamental diversity of trade fairs between different types of events, industries, city-regions and countries. It is true that large differences of knowledge ecologies can be found between business-to-consumer and business-to-business fairs, between export and import shows, between service and manufacturing events, between local and international trade fairs and so on (Bathelt and Zakrzewski 2007). However, it is also easy to find trade fairs that share remarkable similarities, even across different countries. While we are able to identify a heterogeneous landscape of trade fair activity in every single country case, the agenda of this book is to go beyond this individualistic perspective and draw broader conclusions regarding trends in trade fair developments across the Asia-Pacific economies. To accomplish this, we aggregate data from a micro to a macro perspective. Of course, such generalizations have to be interpreted with caution because they do not necessarily speak to single events in specific contexts. To ease this task, the chapters in this edited volume have focused on business-to-business trade fairs with an international focus, leaving local exchange and consumer events largely out of the picture.

Many of the country cases presented in this book focus on, or speak to, a knowledge-based perspective of trade fairs (Bathelt et al. 2014) by emphasizing the importance of knowledge flows during such events for decision-making processes in marketing, production, innovation and related business strategies. As such, many chapters apply the conceptualizations of temporary markets or temporary clusters, which suggest that structured knowledge flows take place in myriads of short-term intensive observations and interactions between the participants of trade fairs (Zeng and Bathelt, *this volume*). Based on such communications, firms can draw conclusions regarding their industrial field related to collective experiences and sense-making processes during these events. In doing so, many chapters of this book draw from perspectives developed in economic geography, marketing and event management.

Another important level of analysis is linked to a political economy perspective and investigates in which way particular government structures and policies influence trade fair dynamics (Zeng and Bathelt, *this volume*). When studying economic development in East and Southeast Asia, we are faced with a particular state structure that has often been referred to as the 'developmental state' (Johnson 1982; Wade 1990). This concept is used to describe the enhanced capability of states to increase industrial productivity, trigger economic growth and, in many ways, to foster industrialization processes through ongoing systematic support policies. While trade fairs are sometimes viewed as a consequence or by-product of economic development, some chapters in this volume clearly illustrate that trade fair activities are also used as a tool of the developmental state to support specific goals, such as promoting exports by domestic firms, creating reputation for local/national industries, attracting foreign direct investment and connecting local firms with global trade partners (Chang et al., *this volume*; Chen and Chu, *this volume*; Kalafsky and Gress, *this volume*). While such policy initiatives sometimes address national development goals (Weller, *this volume*), at other times they focus on local/regional industrial growth (Yokura, *this volume*). As such, trade fairs in the Asia-Pacific context are both a reflection of and a trigger for economic development (Bathelt et al. 2014). In the context of the literature on field-configuring events (Lampel and Meyer 2008), one can even imagine that trade fairs organized by agencies of the developmental state with the specific goal of shaping regional/national industrial development trajectories will have a significant impact on the formation and structure of the respective 'local (industrial) field'. In this context, the way trade fair organizers in Europe orchestrate the selection of trade fair attendees and impact the nature of knowledge flows (Golfetto and Rinallo, *this volume*; Rinallo and Golfetto 2011; *this volume*) may serve as a role model for state-organized fairs.

In their depth and breadth, the chapters in this volume collectively draw a powerful picture of international trade fairs as relational spaces. Through myriads of communications, interactions and observations, these events generate crucial knowledge ecologies, or global buzz (Maskell et al. 2006; Bathelt and Schuldt 2008; 2010). This has a significant impact on the participating firms by stimulating production, marketing and innovation activities. It also reflects back on the industries in the regional/national catchment basins of the events and thus stimulates economic development in manifold ways (Bathelt and Glückler 2011).

DEVELOPMENT STAGES OF ASIA-PACIFIC TRADE FAIRS

The impacts of trade fairs on economic development and the types of trade fairs in different city-regions, industries and countries in the Asia-Pacific region are quite heterogeneous. For historical reasons, countries in the region have developed different industrial specialization patterns at different times and are therefore in different stages of economic development. As a corollary, this has given rise to different structures of trade fair development in the region. While some countries benefit from the existence of sophisticated knowledge-intensive relationship-building events, others rely on trade fairs primarily to stimulate transactions and generate import or export flows, although the boundaries between the two types of trade fairs overlap in many ways (Bathelt et al. 2014). In the following, we briefly characterize the stage of trade fair development in the main economies of the Asia-Pacific region.

(i) Mainland China

Although the stage of industrialization in Mainland China is not yet as advanced as in Taiwan or South Korea, and much lower than that in Japan and Australia, the country is clearly the hotspot of trade fair activity in Asia (AUMA 2008; Jin and Weber, *this volume*; Zhu and Zeng, *this volume*). Mainland China hosts by far the largest number of events in the Asia-Pacific region, with 517 events certified by the Global Association of the Exhibition Industry (so-called UFI events) in 97 exhibition centers in 2010 (see Table 15.1). While the literature has been skeptical about the

Table 15.1 Trade show activity in Asia-Pacific economies, 2010

Asia-Pacific economies	Exhibition centers (number)	Total gross exhibition space (1,000 sq.m.)	UFI events (number)	Average event size (sq.m.)
China (Mainland)	97	8,517	517	16,475
Japan	12	1,928	329	5,861
Australia	9	528	166	3,181
South Korea	12	802	147	5,461
India	13	763	127	6,014
Hong Kong	3	870	98	8,878
Singapore	4	250	80	3,125
Taiwan	4	552	74	7,459
Thailand	8	432	71	6,092
Vietnam	4	141	50	2,830
Malaysia	4	265	49	5,408
Indonesia	3	167	43	3,901
Philippines	3	128	38	3,375
Pakistan	2	66	27	2,472
Macau	2	125	17	7,353
Total	180	15,534	1,833	8,477

Note: sq.m. = square meters (1 square meter = 10.76 square feet).

Source: BSG (2011).

sustainability of this development and the quality of events overall (Kay 2005; Jin et al. 2010), the country has meanwhile developed advanced trade fair ecologies, especially in coastal cities, that are professionally organized (Bathelt and Zeng 2014). A differentiated trade fair business is developing that is characterized by a functional differentiation between leading events. Whereas some events already have the character of knowledge-intensive trade fairs that focus on information exchange, producer–user interaction and knowledge generation in similar ways as top events in Europe and North America (Bathelt and Zeng, *this volume*), other fairs are in the process of developing into similar temporary clusters (Kong and Zhang, *this volume*). And further trade fairs have developed into advanced events that focus on relationship-building and networking, while, at the same time, other modern venues exist that specialize in large-scale transaction and sales events to accommodate the need for efficient temporary markets (Bathelt and Zeng, *this volume*), in a situation that is still characterized by high market uncertainties overall (e.g. Maskell, *this volume*). All of this illustrates that Mainland China is not only the most dynamic trade fair market in the Asia-Pacific region and worldwide, but that it has also developed a highly differentiated trade fair landscape.

(ii) Japan

Japan is the most highly developed economy in the region. With 12 exhibition centers in 2010 and 329 UFI events (see Table 15.1), Japan is also an important location of trade fair activity in Asia – albeit with signs of stagnation in recent years (AUMA 2011). Yet, compared to its global importance as a producer and exporter in many medium- and high-technology industries, the trade fair business in Japan is relatively small and generally not as highly internationalized as in Europe. In particular, trade fairs in Japan are not as large as their leading European counterparts, with relatively few international exhibitors and visitors. International reference events are rare and many of the larger industrial fairs have primarily local/national importance. In Japan, trade fairs are not primarily viewed as events where products are sold or contracts negotiated, but as places for the development and maintenance of new and existing relations with partners. As such, events are sometimes used as policy tools to stimulate local/regional industries to develop trans-local, sometimes nation-wide, networks (Yokura, *this volume*).

(iii) Australia

As a highly developed economy neighboring East and Southeast Asia, Australia benefits in many ways from increasing trade with the countries in the region. Similar to Japan, the development of trade fair activity in Australia does not fully represent the advanced level of economic development. In 2010, there were 166 UFI events that took place in nine exhibition centers (see Table 15.1). The relatively low level of trade fair activity is related to the small size of the economy and its peripheral location with respect to other world markets. While the Australian national government tried to actively stimulate the development of international trade fairs in the past and used financial incentives to attract foreign participants to events like Australia Fashion week, such support policies have not been successful in establishing global reference events and stimulating economic growth for Australian industries (Weller 2008; *this volume*). It seems that Australia, while benefiting from its relative proximity to Asia, is also left in the shade by Asian industrial growth. Weller (*this volume*) suggests that the success of government policies depends on location and macroeconomic conditions, and that in remote, less industrialized areas, such policies are potentially more successful if they support events that focus on strengthening regional industries, rather than aiming to stimulate global trade fairs.

(iv) South Korea

Compared to Taiwan, South Korea has developed a substantially larger trade fair business with 147 UFI events in 12 exhibition centers in 2010 (see Table 15.1). Whereas international participation at these events is limited, and while the large Korean industrial groups depend less on these national events, trade fairs are particularly valuable for small and medium-sized Korean firms. These firms use the events to strengthen their export competencies and develop linkages with participating firms from overseas (Kalafsky and Gress 2014; *this volume*). While national economic policy puts less emphasis on trade fairs compared to Taiwan, these events are increasingly viewed as instruments to improve the market competencies of small and medium-sized firms.

(v) India

India, the second largest Asian economy, lags behind China's economic development in many ways. While the country hosted 127 UFI events in 13 exhibition centers in 2010 (see Table 15.1), the number of trade fairs is still relatively small compared to other Asian economies. At this point, India's trade fair development is not nearly as advanced and events are less sophisticated as compared to China. This may change, however, with continued economic growth and active government initiatives, related to the immense growth potential of the country over the medium term (AUMA 2005). The development of knowledge ecologies can especially be expected in industries and events with a substantial regional catchment basin, such as the software industry in Bangalore.

(vi) Hong Kong

Related to the British influence and its relative independence, Hong Kong developed early on into a strategic place for trade fairs and a gateway to Mainland China, as well as to other parts of Asia. It hosted 98 UFI events in its three exhibition centers in 2010, many of which were of a substantial size with large international participation and Asia-wide importance (see Table 15.1). Although Hong Kong is no longer independent and has been outpaced by the rapid growth of trade fair activities in Mainland China, it has been able to remain an important trade fair location for numerous events (Rinallo and Golfetto, *this volume*). Supported by the economic development of the dynamic Pearl River Delta region, trade fairs in Hong Kong, such as Hong Kong Fashion Week (Skov 2006; Weller, *this volume*), have become knowledge spaces that increasingly showcase new designs of products. The present building boom of new exhibition centers in Mainland China (Kay 2005; Jin et al. 2010; Bathelt et al. 2014) and other Southeast Asian countries, however, may not leave much growth potential for Hong Kong trade fairs in the future (AUMA 2007).

(vii) Singapore

Although Singapore is, like Hong Kong in the past, a relatively small city-state in Southeast Asia, and despite the lack of strong domestic industries, it has become an important hub for trade fairs in Southeast Asia (AUMA 2007). Many trade fairs in Singapore are quite international in terms of visitors and exhibitors, although closer examination reveals that events primarily attract participants from Southeast Asian neighboring countries. In 2010, Singapore hosted 80 UFI events in its four exhibition centers (see Table 15.1). The future development of Singapore as a regional (sub-continental) hub seems uncertain though, since countries such as Thailand have significantly invested in new exhibition centers and are now competing with Singapore for events (AUMA 2007).

(viii) Taiwan

Along with Taiwan's successful transition into an industrialized economy during the post-World War II period, trade fairs have developed rather well compared to other Asian economies. In 2010, 74 UFI events were held in four exhibition centers (see Table 15.1). Although being organized in only a few venues, some trade fairs have achieved international importance and have become reference events in their industries for Asia (Chen 2009; Chen and Chu, *this volume*). Due to strong political pressure in Taiwan to integrate into the world economy in order to avoid political isolation, the country utilized trade fairs as instruments of industrial policy to link regional/national firms to global production chains and to foster economic transition processes (Chang et al., *this volume*; Chen and Chu, *this volume*).

(ix) Thailand

Since the 1990s, Thailand has also experienced high economic growth, although at a much lower level compared to Taiwan and Mainland China (Walker 2011). The country's economic success has been accompanied by the rapid development of trade fairs. As of today, trade fair activity in Thailand is more developed than that in other Southeast Asian economies, except for Singapore. In 2010, the country hosted 71 UFI events in eight exhibition centers (see Table 15.1). An important driver for trade fair development in the country has been the specific role of the developmental state. The country has perhaps the most state support for trade fair development in Southeast Asia in terms of venue construction, financial support and industrial policies. Because of this, Bangkok has begun to compete with Singapore for trade fairs of international importance in Southeast Asia (AUMA 2007).

(x) Vietnam

Consistent with a newly developing economy, trade fairs in Vietnam are less developed than those in Mainland China and other more developed Asian economies. In 2010, only 50 UFI events took place in four exhibition centers (see Table 15.1). Not only were there fewer events than in many other countries, these events were also on average smaller. A feature of trade fairs in Vietnam is that they are characterized by larger international participation compared to events in other less developed economies in East and Southeast Asia. However, this should not be interpreted as an indication of rising knowledge ecologies. Without a strong industrial base, trade fairs in Vietnam are much more trade-oriented due to the country's integration into the world economy through resource exports. Similar to events in Malaysia, Indonesia, the Philippines or Pakistan, trade fair activity in Vietnam is still in an embryonic stage (AUMA 2007).

TOWARD A MODEL OF DYNAMIC TRADE FAIR ECOLOGIES IN THE ASIA-PACIFIC REGION

A dynamic model of trade fair ecologies in the Asia-Pacific region emerges if we examine the development of trade fairs in a comparative perspective across the country cases discussed above, abstracting from individual specificities. Figure 15.1 shows the structure of trade fair activities using the percentage of international exhibitors and visitors in an attempt to represent each country's trade fair business by a single data point (Rinallo and Golfetto 2011; Golfetto and Rinallo, *this volume*; Li, *this volume*). Numerous conclusions can be drawn from this figure when combining

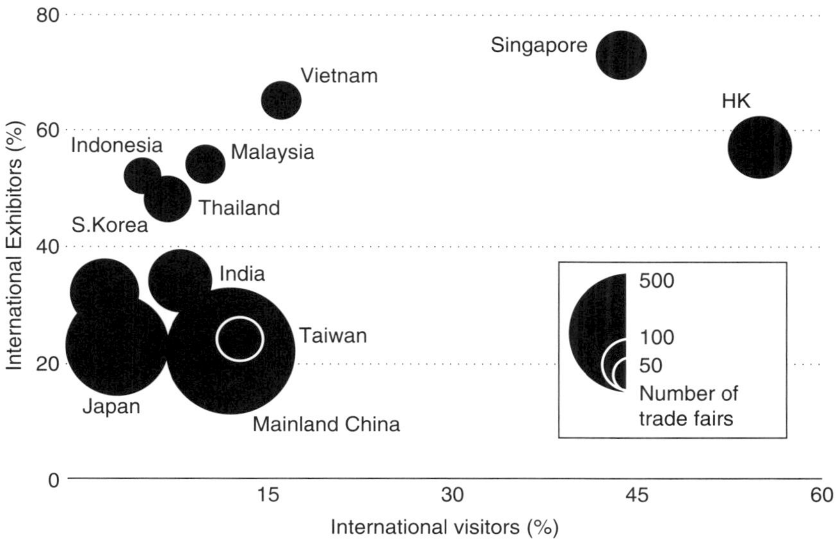

Note: Due to data limitations, Australia is not included.

Source: Own compilations based on Li (2014).

Figure 15.1 Structure of Asian trade fairs according to exhibitor/visitor origin, 2010

the internationalization degree of trade fairs with the stage of economic development.

At a first glance, it appears that dynamic Asian economies start internationalization processes at different levels and are involved in these processes to varying degrees. As small city-states and gateways to Asia, Singapore and Hong Kong have the most internationalized trade fairs in the region. Although many trade fair participants in these two economies originate from nearby countries in East and Southeast Asia, local firms are often involved to a lesser degree, especially in Singapore where the regional catchment basin of industries is generally not very strong. The trade shows resemble hub events, which are primarily composed of foreign exhibitors and foreign visitors and few local/domestic attendees. Since foreign participants originate from different national contexts, they have grown under different circumstances and developed dissimilar technical capabilities and understandings of market trends compared to local firms. To the degree that the foreign population of firms is characterized by different, yet overlapping, knowledge bases, such hub events establish an excellent platform for knowledge circulation and learning. Many international hub fairs develop unique knowledge ecologies, which are beneficial to the participating firms and important for global knowledge flows in the industrial field. This is consistent with observations of trade fairs in Hong Kong and Singapore (Lew and Chang 1999; Skov 2006). Because of the minimal engagement of local firms in such events, however, learning effects are strongest for international participants, while the knowledge exchanges may have a limited impact on regional industrial development and technological upgrading – or it may simply take a long time until broad regional upgrading processes can be expected.

This implies that developmental states in small economies may find it hard to cultivate innovation activities of local industries based on experiences gathered at international trade fairs (Maskell, *this volume*; Weller, *this volume*). At the same time, trade fairs that are based on a weak regional catchment basin likely experience strong competition from similar events in other countries. This situation illustrates the context of some trade fairs in Singapore, which is challenged by rising exhibition activities in Thailand and other South Asian economies. It is at this point that experiences drawn from the evolution of European trade fairs become highly relevant as events do not compete with each other in an isolated manner, but in conjunction with their underlying regional/national economies (Golfetto and Rinallo, *this volume*; Rinallo and Golfetto, *this volume*).

Aside from Hong Kong and Singapore, most other Asian economies in Figure 15.1 host trade fairs with a lower degree of international participation, although the numbers vary. In terms of the overall structure of trade fairs, no country is positioned in the extreme upper-left or lower-right corners of the figure. The upper-left corner illustrates pure import fairs that are characterized by predominantly foreign exhibitors and mostly local/national visitors. In a country with a weak manufacturing base, a closer integration into the global economy usually depends on substantial imports of foreign products. Such a context provides favorable conditions for the development of import fairs. In the Asia-Pacific region, stereotypical import shows are likely associated with regional/national economies that are at the beginning of industrialization. Figure 15.1 presents evidence to support this point. It shows that Vietnam and Indonesia, which are both in initial stages of economic development, are closest to the upper-left corner of the graph. Knowledge ecologies therefore likely play a minor role at trade fairs in these contexts.

The lower-right corner in Figure 15.1 characterizes a pure export fair with mostly local/national exhibitors and foreign visitors. It is clear that such events can only be organized if a well-established local/national industry base already exists. Although not visible in the average trade fair patterns in Figure 15.1, several important export-intensive events can be found in Asia, such as the famous former Canton Fair in Mainland China (Bathelt and Zeng, *this volume*). Such export shows are often supported by local/national governments or business associations that help organize and finance these events to stimulate export activities of industries in the catchment basin. In this sense, export shows become important policy instruments in the tool kits of developmental states. They can be instrumental for small and medium-sized firms to extend their business internationally and get access to foreign market information that rests outside their capabilities (Chang et al., *this volume*; Kalafsky and Gress, *this volume*; Chen and Chu, *this volume*; Yokura, *this volume*).

Although development strategies for local industries building on export fairs have worked for some Asian economies in the past, it is hard to pursue such export-oriented strategies today for three reasons (Chang 2002; Wade 2003): First, countries whose economic development relies heavily on exports, leading to unbalanced trade surpluses, are facing increasing pressure from other countries. The trade battle between Japan and the US during the 1980s clearly shows that it is no longer acceptable to only export products to other countries while, at the same time, keeping domestic markets closed. In terms of average national patterns, no country in East and Southeast Asia is characterized mainly by export events in the lower-right corner of Figure 15.1. The second reason for difficulties in organizing export shows at the national level is that business organizations have changed substantially over the past decades with the deepening globalization process. The widespread use of new information and communication technologies in commerce and the rise of global outsourcing strategies have led to a situation in which many buyers no longer rely on trade fairs to find their best suppliers. Large manufacturing firms in developing economies especially benefit from the globalization process and develop global organizational networks of their own, reducing the need for pure export events. The third and perhaps most fundamental reason for the unpopularity of export events is that knowledge ecologies for regional/national innovation and upgrading processes, which are important for the success of temporary gatherings in the knowledge economy (Bathelt et al. 2014), are harder to develop in trade-oriented events, although some important market information can be accessed through transaction relations (Rinallo and Golfetto, *this volume*).

In Figure 15.1, most of the dynamic Asian economies are situated in areas characterized by a mixed configuration of local/national and international participants, although the share of international exhibitors is typically much larger than the share of international visitors. The country cases analyzed are not located in extreme corners where trade fairs are overwhelmingly dominated by either foreign or national exhibitors, and vice versa for visitors. Since both local and global firms are present at these events in larger numbers, industrial knowledge bases related to advanced production technologies, which are crucial for the upgrading processes in developing economies, are more likely to be circulated and transferred through interactions and observations between the participating professionals. It is in such types of temporary gatherings that local knowledge pools and global innovation networks can most intensively be connected and that windows of opportunity for trans-local learning processes can be wide-open. These events are extremely important for the long-term prosperity of regions and nations in creating innovation-based economies. It is not surprising that trade fairs in the most dynamic Asian economies in Figure 15.1 are closest to such local–global clustering and learning events (Li 2014; *this volume*). India and Mainland China, the two largest developing economies, for instance, host trade shows with an average share of 20 to 35 percent foreign exhibitors and 10 to 15 percent foreign visitors. Comparing both economies, Mainland China has a more central position in the figure as a consequence of stronger industrialization processes with a quickly growing number of national exhibitors. Although many trade fairs in Mainland China are still in a developing stage, others have already formed knowledge ecologies, similar to those in developed contexts (Bathelt and Zeng 2014; *this volume*; Kong and Zhang, *this volume*).

Compared to the two largest economies, Thailand and Malaysia attract a relatively small number of domestic exhibitors and are therefore characterized by a higher share of international exhibitors. While similar in size,

Taiwan's economy is more developed than that of Thailand or Malaysia, with a strong industrial base and a large share of innovative small and medium-sized firms. Therefore, trade fairs in Taiwan are characterized by a strong involvement of domestic exhibitors as well as a large participation of global buyers. In terms of the mix of foreign and domestic participants, Taiwan is represented in a more central position in Figure 15.1, suggesting that many trade fairs have created learning spaces with plenty of opportunities for local small and medium-sized firms to acquire global know-how, learn from worldwide competitors and upgrade within their value chains (Chang et al., *this volume*). These processes have even triggered further regional/cluster-based learning and institution-building processes (Chen and Chu, *this volume*). Because of this success, other developing economies in the Asia-Pacific region can possibly learn important lessons from the case of Taiwan, related to both (i) the co-evolution of trade fairs and local industries and (ii) the active role of state policies in this development.

When extending our analysis further to include Japan and South Korea, their locations in Figure 15.1 seems at odds with our prior theoretical synthesis of trade fairs in the context of Asian economic development. In this synthesis, we have argued and illustrated that along with the development of economies to an advanced stage, trade fairs tend to have a more mixed configuration of domestic and foreign participants consistent with the development of significant technological learning spaces that benefit regional/national economic development. However, in both developed economies, international participation at trade fairs – especially on the visitor side – is lower than expected. To understand the reasons behind this, we need to view trade fairs from a broader cultural perspective. Several reasons may help to explain this: First, it could be that trade fair organizers have developed strategies to focus on specific participant groups for their events, thus shifting the overall mix of exhibitors/visitors by origin (Golfetto and Rinallo, *this volume*; Rinallo and Golfetto, *this volume*). While this may lead to the development of rich learning spaces for individual events, it is less likely that it will impact the trade fair business of the entire economy.

Second, both Japan and South Korea differ from other Asian countries in their economic structure, in that large industrial groups play a dominant role in economic development (Johnson 1982; Amsden 1992). These large corporations have often developed transnational structures and take part in the global trade fair cycle. The pressure to participate in domestic trade fairs is very low for these corporations. As pinpointed by Maskell (*this volume*), trade fairs are one, but not the only, form of accommodating trans-local learning. Depending on the type of knowledge required and where it resides, best practices for the acquisition of external knowledge can be quite different, and trade fairs as temporary clusters may only play a minor role. For large corporations, for instance, a crucial way to learn about global markets and technologies may particularly involve intra- and inter-organizational networks over distances, which provide durable and targeted knowledge pipelines to specific partners.

Third, the two countries, especially Japan, have traditionally been relatively closed and difficult to access for foreign firms. The earlier trade conflict between the US and Japan that centered around the lack of openness for foreign products, as well as existing language and other barriers for market entry, are indications of this. This is reflected in a low degree of international participation at many of the trade fairs – a situation that policies in South Korea are now beginning to tackle (Kalafsky and Gress, *this volume*).

The cases of Japan and South Korea also illustrate in different ways the importance of regional catchment basins for trade fair development and suggest that what matters to establish dynamic temporary knowledge ecologies is not just the size and status of the respective economies, but also their particular organizational capabilities in mobilizing local/domestic actors to accept an open society/economy. From a policy perspective, this suggests that governments should not take a standardized approach in developing trade fairs for regional industrial upgrading. An effective policy for establishing wider knowledge ecologies and knowledge pipelines has to be consistent with the capabilities of local industrial communities. Such an approach may, in fact, require extending our understanding of developmental states in Asia, which are credited for successful industrial policies in favor of large corporations. It may require developing contextual approaches that take into consideration the needs of specific local/regional industrial communities. Clearly, the situations in Japan and South Korea demonstrate that there is a strong interest from small and medium-sized firms for learning at trade fairs (Yokura, *this volume*; Kalafsky and Gress, *this volume*).

CONCLUSION: CONTEXTUALIZING TRADE FAIRS IN THE KNOWLEDGE ECONOMY

The goal of this chapter has been to integrate the individual country cases of trade fair development in this edited volume by providing a synthetic framework of the rise and evolution of trade fair ecologies in the Asia-Pacific region. Although consistent with the highly diverse economic landscapes in the region, trade fairs also develop structurally unevenly across the different national economies. A hidden pattern that has been revealed in all chapters is that trade fairs evolve from transaction-oriented places to knowledge-based and relational spaces, linked to the structural transformations in their regional/national economies. The co-evolution of trade fairs and regional/national economies establishes a two-way interdependent dynamic process (Bathelt et al. 2014) in that the development of knowledge ecologies during temporary events shape, and at the same time are shaped by, industrial upgrading processes in the regional/national catchment basins.

The rise of the knowledge economy fundamentally changes many of our ideas and understandings of economic development. As intangible knowledge pools become key for economic growth, the national endowments and low-cost advantages in production, which have been at the core of conventional studies of regional/national economies, become less significant. In this context, a common challenge for almost all regions and nations is related to the question as to how to support the rise and development of knowledge-creating firms and industries, as access of remote knowledge has become easier thanks to advances in communication and transportation technologies. It has been widely recognized that broad access to a combination of both local/internal and non-local/external knowledge pools is indispensable for generating innovation in the age of globalization. However, the answers that we are able to provide to these challenges, thus far, are still preliminary. Yet, within this context, temporary get-togethers of industrial communities at trade fairs have experienced a renaissance in the social science literature as crucial places that support knowledge sharing and circulation, sense-making, learning, relationship-building and the reproduction of institutional arrangements (Bathelt et al. 2014). This book contributes to the contextualization of trade fairs in the knowledge economy, especially from the perspective of developing countries.

An important observation of the chapters in this volume is that trade fairs, despite being neglected in past research, have been quite important for the rise of economies in the Asia-Pacific region. The significance of trade fairs for urban and regional economies goes far beyond generating regional multiplier effects associated with the trade fair service economy, as new knowledge ecologies are being created within these economies that are crucial inputs for innovation. Dynamic fast-growing Asian economies host an increasing number of knowledge-intensive trade fairs that attract both local and global participants, while such knowledge ecologies are not yet well developed in low-performing countries. Although a more precise understanding of the co-evolution of trade fairs and Asian economies requires further research, it appears clear that we need to view trade fairs in the context of long-term economic development processes in these countries, rather than focus on short-term pecuniary benefits from these events. We hope that the analysis presented in this book will motivate others to develop this research agenda further and engage with the gaps that still exist in our understanding of temporary knowledge ecologies and the trade fair business in the Asia-Pacific region.

REFERENCES

Amsden, A. H. (1992) *Asia's Next Giant: South Korea and Late Industrialization*, Oxford: Oxford University Press.

AUMA – Ausstellungs- und Messeausschuss der deutschen Wirtschaft (2005) *Messemarkt Indien (Trade Fair Market India)*, Berlin: AUMA. Online. Available HTTP: <http://www.auma.de/_pages/d/04_MessemaerkteAusland/0402_Laenderprofile/040212_Indien/download/Messemarkt%20Indien.pdf> (10 June 2012).

AUMA (2007) *Messemarkt Südostasien (Trade Fair Market Southeast Asia)*, Berlin: AUMA. Online. Available HTTP: <http://www.auma.de/_pages/d/04_MessemaerkteAusland/0402_Laenderprofile/040224_Suedostasien/download/Suedostasien.pdf> (10 June 2012).

AUMA (2008) *Messemarkt China (Trade Fair Market China)*, Berlin: AUMA. Online. Available HTTP: <http://www.auma.de/_pages/d/04_MessemaerkteAusland/0402_Laenderprofile/040208_China/download/Messemarkt_China.pdf> (10 June 2012).

AUMA (2011) *Messemarkt Japan (Trade Fair Market Japan)*, Berlin: AUMA. Online. Available HTTP: <http://www.auma.de/_pages/d/04_MessemaerkteAusland/0402_Laenderprofile/040214_Japan/download/Messemarkt_Japan.pdf> (10 June 2012).

Bathelt, H. and Glückler, J. (2011) *The Relational Economy: Geographies of Knowing and Learning*, Oxford: Oxford University Press.

Bathelt, H., Golfetto, F. and Rinallo, D. (2014) *Trade Shows in the Globalizing Knowledge Economy*, Oxford: Oxford University Press.

Bathelt, H. and Schuldt, N. (2008) 'Between luminaries and meat grinders: International trade fairs as temporary clusters', *Regional Studies*, 42: 853–868.

Bathelt, H. and Schuldt, N. (2010) 'International trade fairs and global buzz, Part I: Ecology of global buzz', *European Planning Studies*, 18: 1957–1974.

Bathelt, H. and Zakrzewski, G. (2007) 'Messeveranstaltungen als fokale Schnittstellen der globalen Ökonomie (Trade fairs as focal intersections in the global economy)', *Zeitschrift für Wirtschaftsgeographie*, 51: 14–30.

Bathelt, H. and Zeng, G. (2014) 'The development of trade fair ecologies in China: Case studies from Chengdu and Shanghai', *Environment and Planning A*, 46: 511–530.

BSG – Business Strategies Group (2011) *The Trade Fair Industry in Asia: An UFI Report*, Paris: UFI.

Chang, H.-J. (2002) *Kicking Away the Ladder: Development Strategy in Historical Perspective*, London: Anthem Press.

Chen, L.-C. (2009) 'Learning through informal local and global linkages: The case of Taiwan's machine tool industry', *Research Policy*, 38: 527–535.

Jin, X., Weber, K. and Bauer, T. (2010) 'The state of the exhibition industry in China', *Journal of Convention and Event Tourism*, 11: 2–17.

Johnson, C. (1982) *MITI and the Japanese Miracle: The Growth of Industrial Policy: 1925–1975*, Stanford, CA: Stanford University Press.

Kalafsky, R. V. and Gress, D. R. (2014) 'Go big or stay home? Korean machinery firms, trade fair dynamics, and export performance', *Asia Pacific Business Review*, 20: 136–152.

Kay, A. L. K. (2005) 'China's convention and exhibition center boom', *Journal of Convention and Event Tourism*, 7: 5–22.

Lampel, J. and Meyer, A. D. (2008) 'Field-configuring events as structuring mechanisms: How conferences, ceremonies, and trade shows constitute new technologies, industries, and markets', *Journal of Management Studies*, 45: 1025–1035.

Lew, A. A. and Chang, T. C. (1999) 'Where the world meets: Regionalism and globalization in Singapore's convention industry', *Journal of Convention and Exhibition Management*, 1: 17–36.

Li, P.-F. (2014) 'Global temporary networks of clusters: Structures and dynamics of trade fairs in Asian economies', *Journal of Economic Geography*, 14: 995–1021.

Maskell, P., Bathelt, H. and Malmberg, A. (2006) 'Building global knowledge pipelines: The role of temporary clusters', *European Planning Studies*, 14: 997–1013.

Rinallo, D. and Golfetto, F. (2011) 'Exploring the knowledge strategies of temporary cluster organizers: A longitudinal study of the EU fabric industry trade shows (1986–2006)', *Economic Geography*, 87: 453–476.

Skov, L. (2006) 'The role of trade fairs in the global fashion business', *Current Sociology*, 54: 764–782.

Wade, R. (1990) *Governing the Market*, Princeton, NJ: Princeton University Press.

Wade, R. (2003) 'What strategies are viable for developing countries today? The World Trade Organization and the shrinking of "development space"', *Review of International Political Economy*, 10: 621–644.

Walker, A. (2011) *Thailand's Economic Success*, Canberra: New Mandala, Australian National University. Online. Available HTTP: <http://asiapacific.anu.edu.au/newmandala/2011/08/21/thailands-economic-success/> (18 September 2014).

Weller, S. (2008) 'Beyond "global production networks": Australian Fashion Week's trans-sectoral synergies', *Growth and Change*, 39: 104–122.

Index